SHAPERS

—— OF THE ——

GREAT DEBATE

—— ON ——

CONSERVATION

SHAPERS
—— OF THE ——
GREAT DEBATE
—— ON ——
CONSERVATION

A BIOGRAPHICAL DICTIONARY

Rachel White Scheuering

Shapers of the Great American Debates, Number 4
Peter B. Levy, Series Editor

GREENWOOD PRESS
Westport, Connecticut • London

Library of Congress Cataloging-in-Publication Data

Scheuering, Rachel White.
    Shapers of the great debate on conservation : a biographical dictionary /
    Rachel White Scheuering.
        p.   cm.—(Shapers of the great American debates, ISSN 1099–2693, no. 4)
    Includes bibliographical references (p.).
    ISBN 0–313–32826–9 (alk. paper)
    1. Conservationists—United States—Biography—Dictionaries.   2.
    Environmentalists—United States—Biography—Dictionaries.   I. Title.   II. Series.
    S926.A2S36   2004
    333.72'092'273—dc22   2004053046

British Library Cataloguing in Publication Data is available.

Library of Congress Catalog Card Number: 2004053046
ISBN: 0–313–32826–9
ISSN: 1099–2693

First published in 2004

Greenwood Press, 88 Post Road West, Westport, CT 06881
An imprint of Greenwood Publishing Group, Inc.
www.greenwood.com

Printed in the United States of America

The paper used in this book complies with the
Permanent Paper Standard issued by the National
Information Standards Organization (Z39.48–1984).

10 9 8 7 6 5 4 3 2 1

Dedicated to those with the courage of their convictions.

CONTENTS

SERIES FOREWORD

American history has been shaped by numerous debates over issues far ranging in content and time. Debates over the right, or lack thereof, to take the land of the Native Americans, and the proper place and role of women, sparked by Roger Williams and Anne Hutchinson, respectively, marked the earliest years of the Massachusetts Bay Colony. Debates over slavery, the nature and size of the federal government, the emergence of big business, the rights of labor and immigrants, were central to the Republic in the nineteenth century and, in some cases, remain alive today. World War I, World War II, and the Vietnam War sparked debates that tore at the body politic. Even the Revolution involved a debate over whether America should be America or remain part of Great Britain. And the Civil War, considered by many the central event in American history, was the outgrowth of a long debate that found no peaceful resolution.

This series, *Shapers of the Great American Debates*, will examine many of these debates—from those between Native Americans and European settlers to those between "natives" and "newcomers." Each volume will focus on a particular issue, concentrating on those men and women who *shaped* the debates. The authors will pay special attention to fleshing out the life histories of the shapers, considering the relationship between biography or personal history and policy or philosophy. Each volume will begin with an introductory overview, include approximately twenty biographies of ten to fifteen pages, an appendix that briefly describes other key figures, a bibliographical essay, and a subject index. Unlike works that emphasize end results, the books in this series will devote equal attention to both sides, to the "winners" and the "losers." This will lead to a more complete understanding of the richness and complexity of America's past than is afforded by works that examine only the victors.

Taken together, the books in this series remind us of the many ways that class, race, ethnicity, gender, and region have divided rather than united the inhabitants of the United States of America. Each study reminds us of the frequency and variety of debates in America, a reflection of the diversity of the nation and its democratic credo. One even wonders if a similar series could be developed for many other nations or if the diversity of America and its tradition of free expression have given rise to more debates than elsewhere.

Although many Americans have sought to crush the expression of opposing views by invoking the imperative of patriotism, more often than not Americans have respected the rights of others to voice their opinions. Every four years, Americans have voted for president and peacefully respected the results, demonstrating their faith in the process that institutionalizes political debate. More recently, candidates for the presidency have faced off in televised debates that often mark the climax of their campaigns. Americans not only look forward to these debates, but they would probably punish anyone who sought to avoid them. Put another way, debates are central to America's political culture, especially those that deal with key issues and involve the most prominent members of society.

Each volume in the series is written by an expert. While I offered my share of editorial suggestions, overall I relied on the author's expertise when it came to determining the most sensible way to organize and present each work. As a result, some of the volumes follow a chronological structure; others clump their material thematically; still others are separated into two sections, one pro and one con. All of the works are written with the needs of college and advanced high school students in mind. They should prove valuable both as sources for research papers and as supplemental texts in both general and specialized courses. The general public should also find the works an attractive means of learning more about many of the most important figures and equally as many seminal issues in American history.

Peter B. Levy
Associate Professor
Department of History
York College

ACKNOWLEDGMENTS

I owe a debt of thanks to many people and institutions for assistance in getting this book finished. Much of my research was conducted at the Multnomah County Library in Portland, Oregon—I extend a most grateful thank you to the staff there, especially those working the microfilm desk. Thank you also to Kristen Stone and Sue Kopp at the Otto F. Linn Library at Warner Pacific College in Portland; Janene Ford at the Holt-Atherton Special Collections at University of the Pacific in Stockton, California; the staff at the CU Environmental Center at the University of Colorado in Boulder; Greg deBruler from Columbia Riverkeepers in Portland for reference information; and Dr. Adrienne Anderson at the Environmental Studies Program at the University of Colorado in Boulder. Also thanks to those who helped me gain interviews or get contact information: Anita Furu at Denmark's Environmental Assessment Institute in Copenhagen; and Rachel Sykes and Jen Barkan at the International Society for Ecology and Culture in Berkeley, California, and Dartington, Devon.

Support, encouragement, and inspiration have come from many quarters. I owe a lifetime of thanks to my amazing parents for just about everything, but especially for allowing me the space and time to work on this project—thank goodness for Easy-Bake ovens and seemingly endless grandparental energy. I also want to thank Anne Becher for recommending my work and for being such an excellent editor and long-distance mentor; Anna Marshall for pointing me toward the writing path in the first place after setting such a shining example herself; Eric Scheuering, without whose affection and enormous sacrifices of time this book would have taken at least five more years; Libbey White for careful reviewing of chapters and valuable suggestions; Sylvia Salazar, Terri Caldwell, and Emily Laughlin for moral support; and Greg Kinzer—for reviewing chapters with wry humor and intelligence, for excellent writing advice and constant encouragement, for all manner of technical assistance, and most of all, for just being there. Thanks also to Professor Peter Levy of York College in Pennsylvania, Series Editor; Sarah Colwell, Editorial Assistant at Greenwood Publishing Group; and Arlene Belzer, Copyeditor. Finally, thanks to Miles Scheuering for being patient and for making sure I took breaks once in awhile.

I am also especially grateful to those who agreed to interviews or otherwise provided me with information about their lives: Dr. J. Michael Fay, Christopher Swain, Ross Gelbspan, S. Fred Singer, Bjørn Lomborg, Helena Norberg-Hodge, and Helen Chenoweth-Hage. Christopher Swain, Ross Gelbspan, and Helena Norberg-Hodge also kindly reviewed their chapters, which I greatly appreciated.

INTRODUCTION: THE HISTORY OF THE AMERICAN CONSERVATION MOVEMENT

[Americans'] one primary and predominant object is to cultivate and set-
tle these prairies, forests, and vast waste lands. The striking and peculiar
characteristic of American society is, that it is not so much a democracy
as a huge commercial company for the discovery, cultivation, and capitalization of its enormous territory. . . . The United States is primarily a
commercial society . . . and only secondarily a nation.
                    —Emile Boutmy (1891), French political scientist
                (*Studies in Constitutional Law* [London: Macmillan, 1891])

The haste with which the first European settlers began transforming North
America's luxurious forests into a prospering civilization can hardly be surprising. Having come from a crowded land with scarce trees, wild game, or
opportunities, they were suddenly confronted with an idyllic abundance of
natural resources: The woods were filled with deer, the skies were constantly
punctuated by flocks of wild geese and ducks, the rivers teemed with fish.
The endless sea of trees provided timber enough to build all manner of
houses and barns and fuel enough to banish the long New England winters.
They had found a land of plenty—a land that held the raw materials for the
building of a nation and the materialization of an ideal. The fact that they
had to alter its landscape radically and dispossess the native people of the

continent in order to establish themselves did not dim their vision nor diminish their industriousness.

In trying to imagine those magnificent forests from the perspective of the twenty-first century—crowded, hectic, with forests thinned into second and third growth; wild native species such as the grizzly confined to tinier and tinier pockets of wilderness; and valuable land squabbled over by environmentalists and developers—it is easy to idealize the appeal of their immense, pine-scented purity. But while the earliest colonists did appreciate the unspoiled abundance of the forests, they were simultaneously beset by an overwhelming cultural desire to whittle and carve them into orderly settlements, farms, and roads. The woods, not yet shaped by human hands, loomed like a specter. Appraising his strange new home from the deck of the *Mayflower* in September 1620, William Bradford pronounced it "a hideous and desolate wilderness full of wilde beasts and wilde men."[1] Even when the trees were not needed for building houses or for heat, settlers cut them down, believing they needed to let redemptive air and light into the musty gloom.

As they imprinted their will upon an immense canvas of political and geographical freedom, the first Americans forged a national identity out of these conflicting perceptions of wilderness. The seemingly unlimited bounty of natural wealth contributed an almost utopian sheen to the New World, and yet the Puritan colonists felt the untamed wilderness needed to be redeemed. Paradoxically, their greatest asset and their most dismal adversary were the same.[2] These views, combined with the lust for development—for legitimacy—consumed Americans from the start, and little if any thought was given to the duration of the "endless" natural wealth in question.

As the once-vast eastern forests inevitably began to shrink and become more and more populated, eyes began turning westward. Before the Lewis and Clark expedition returned from the Pacific Coast in 1806, describing "scenes of visionary enchantment," the enormous continental interior had been a conceptual blank to the six million Americans living along the eastern seaboard. But Lewis and Clark had examined the landscape—possible trade routes, suitable farmland, river systems, climate, mountain ranges, and valleys—and filled in the details. Opened up to the nation's imagination—its commercial value analyzed and identified—the land west of the Mississippi aroused a new passion that came to be known as Manifest Destiny—the idea that Americans were preordained to control the entire temperate zone of the continent. As the 1800s progressed, the eastern forests that had so stunned the pilgrims became nearly logged out; land became extensively cultivated; and the forces of industry and technology began their ascent toward dominance. The westward migration was thus urged along by a desire to gain possession of further sources of natural wealth.

To possess this land and its resources meant to conquer its wildness. Expansive tracts of land—untouched by American colonists but occupied by established and diverse communities of Native Americans—were seen as un-controlled and useless. What remains of these wildlands is now coveted by environmentalists, developers, and extractive industries alike; but at the time, these areas presented a managerial burden to the federal government, which saw them as redeemable only through settlement, cultivation, and profit. Hoping to encourage this empire-building "redemption" of the land, the U.S. government gave it away through the Homestead Act, land grants to railroads, and deeds to states. Disposal of the public domain became the primary focus of governmental land policy, eventually leading to the ceding of well over a billion acres of the nation's entire 2.3 billion-acre territory to private, corporate, and state hands. These property transfers were overseen by the General Land Office, which was mandated to smooth the privatization of public land.

The Homestead Act was a particularly potent distillation of policies directed at increasing private landownership in the west. Passed in 1862, it deeded 160 acres of the public domain to any citizen who paid a filing fee and agreed to work the land for five years. The West was expected to conform to the rest of established America: settled and agrarian. Since most Americans equated land with prosperity and landownership with freedom, a stream of settlers began to rush to the frontier and grew to a flood after the Civil War. And as more and more pioneers acquired title to American soil and began to make their mark on it through farming, logging, and homesteading, the sense of foreboding from the uncivilized wilderness began slowly to relent. Native American populations were driven onto reservations, unprepared to defend themselves and their land against the onrushing wagons and plows.

The inroads civilization was making into wild territories accelerated with the completion of the transcontinental railroad, which joined the coasts in 1869. With breathtaking rapidity, the frontier retreated and retreated; by 1890 it had disappeared. That year the U.S. Census Bureau announced that settlement had succeeded in amassing a density of no less than two people per square mile from coast to coast. Historian Frederick Jackson Turner ascribed important psychological and geopolitical meaning to the closure of the frontier. For one thing, there was no longer a "safety valve" for absorbing expanding populations: civilization now enclosed the nation like bookends. This also brought forward the understanding that the nation's resources—land, fertile soil, minerals, water, coal—were finite. To add a further layer of apprehension, the feverish Industrial Revolution was devouring raw materials at an unprecedented pace, fueled by the new accessibility afforded by rail transportation, which had opened channels for the outflow of the rich natural resources of the American West. Post–Civil War expansion added to the explosive growth of urban centers, complete with steel mills, smelters, factories, and shipyards. The exploitation of resources is what fed these factories and plants—add to that the unchecked pollution that was a byproduct of the American industrial machine, and it is easy to see how the nation's rapid industrial transformation led to a huge legacy of environmental problems.

Along with the rapid changes taking place on the American landscape lurked a sense of loss, though it was not often given voice. Hints that Americans had begun to view wilderness as a treasure to be protected could be glimpsed, such as in the preservation of the 2 million acres of stunningly beautiful and geothermically unique land of Yellowstone National Park in 1872 (although even this act may have been due less to foresight and wilderness appreciation and more to pressure from the railroad industry as a gimmick for luring passengers west). Other voices were less equivocal in fighting the reduction of the natural world. In 1864 George Perkins Marsh published *Man and Nature; or, Physical Geography as Modified by Human Action* a revolutionary study of farming, logging, and resource use that concluded that humans were having a very destructive impact on much of the world.

Meanwhile, Henry David Thoreau and Ralph Waldo Emerson were making preeminent literary contributions to a national environmental ethic through their perspicacious attention to their natural surroundings and their understanding that human perception of nature profoundly influences other experiences: reading, learning, thinking, living. Both saw nature as something other than a source of material wealth to be exploited. Emerson challenged the systematic capitalization of the land with his transcendentalist vision of the natural world as the source and salvation of the human spirit; Thoreau famously proclaimed, "In wilderness is the preservation of the world." Their prophetic articulation of the importance of the relationship between the human and natural worlds carved channels through the bedrock of American thought through which large outpourings of future environmental perceptions would flow.

THE FIRST WAVE

Though Thoreau and Emerson praised nature, they were not advocating a particular course of action regarding conservation policy. It would not be until sometime around the turn of the twentieth century that the conservation movement became an active force for change. In the interim, wilderness enthusiast John Muir, prompted by a love for wild places and wild things, wrote rhapsodic accounts of his wanderings through the Sierra Nevada for several decades, hoping to impart to a general audience his appreciation of the mountains, trees, and wildflowers that so enchanted him. "I care to live," he wrote in 1874, "only to entice people to look at Nature's loveliness."[3] In the last decade of the 1800s he branched out and took a more activist role in wilderness preservation when he embarked on a vigorous campaign to have Yosemite declared a national park, which was accomplished in 1890.

As the nineteenth century drew to a close, Muir's preservationist impulses were offset by the more utilitarian ideas of Gifford Pinchot. America's first trained forester, Pinchot subscribed to the idea of conservation rather than preservation: That is, natural resources (such as trees) should be managed in such a way that provides a source of wealth and national prosperity. Destructive, unsustainable practices such as clear-cutting were anathema to Pinchot—yet he also opposed the thought of setting aside parcels of forestland or wilderness to be entirely protected from human hands. With his practical approach and emphasis on the self-interest of the economy and business, Pinchot—the materialist—had the ears of the nation's industrialists. But it was Muir—the sentimentalist—who won over the larger constituency. Pinchot's articulation of "forestry management" and "sustainable yields" seemed irrelevant to the masses, whereas Muir's glorification of the natural world appealed to their Romantic hearts. But while Muir represented public opinion, Pinchot represented political opinion—and in the end, politics is what creates the policy that determines the fate of the land.

When Theodore Roosevelt stepped up as president after William McKinley's assassination in 1901, Pinchot's brand of conservation suddenly found itself to be the centerpiece of the national political agenda. Roosevelt himself was alarmed at the prospect of disappearing wildlife, forests, and wilderness, and used his executive powers to integrate natural resource stewardship into a basic platform of policies that helped formulate a national ethos. This marked the beginning of the First Wave of the conservation movement. In 1907, President Roosevelt said, "In utilizing and conserving the natural resources of the Nation, the one characteristic more essential than any other is foresight. . . . The conservation of our natural resources and their proper use constitute the fundamental problem which underlies almost every other problem of our national life."[4] Roosevelt put this idea into practice by creating 230 million acres of protected areas in the form of 18 national monuments, 5 national parks, 51 national wildlife refuges, and 150 national forests during his presidency.

At this stage, conservation tended to be an elitist passion—something only those with money and time to spare could be concerned about. Even when the national parks system was created, it remained out of reach for those without means for travel and lodging. As Bjørn Lomborg and Jason Cowley have pointed out, "Ecological movements are, on the whole, the inspiration of the wealthy and educated in the western world. The beauty of a butterfly, it seems can best be appreciated on a full stomach."[5] Roosevelt and Pinchot (who both came from privileged backgrounds) tried to put a democratic spin on conservation by promoting the idea that saving natural resources put them to the best possible use for the general welfare of the nation, whereas private plundering resulted in concentration of wealth in the hands of the few. Still there were those who criticized the fact that those in power could advocate for wilderness and wildlife while neglecting the needs of working-class private citizens.

Another undercurrent of resistance to conservation came from the fact that it must rely on bureaucratic systems of law and regulation to achieve its goal. In a nation that prided itself on independence and freedom from centralized power, conservation's inception created a beehive of complex impulses. When Roosevelt was succeeded by the less conservation-friendly William Howard Taft, conflict stirred almost immediately. Taft's secretary of the Interior Department, Richard Ballinger (former head of the General Land Office), cornered himself in a furious controversy by attempting to further the nineteenth-century policy of turning government lands into private property. Pinchot resolutely fought Ballinger's policies; and the ideological clash between them helped define conservation as a struggle between individual rights and the greater good of a larger community—exemplifying the tension between regulatory authority and local primacy that has made the conservation movement such a defining and uniquely American conflict. Because of this tension, conservation decisions caused debate from the very beginning—and still do. But the fact that it is a debate that has been a part of almost every land-use decision made in this country in the past 100 years is a testament to the powerful legacy of leadership and advocacy left by the First Wave of conservation.

THE SECOND WAVE

After Theodore Roosevelt's presidency, policymakers and land managers continued to attempt a socially responsible balance between resource use and conservation. But the movement generally remained in an elitist realm above the economic needs of the public. Then, under the New Deal policies in the 1930s, Theodore Roosevelt's fifth cousin Franklin Delano Roosevelt gave conservation another push of momentum when he used conservation programs as a way to create jobs. The Civilian Conservation Corps (CCC) served both land and people, providing work such as tree planting, preventing erosion, cutting trails, and clearing brush for nearly three million jobless Americans. In addition to providing employment, the CCC promoted a practical vision of conservation and instilled an appreciation for the outdoors that many of its employees had never had the opportunity to develop.

But World War II sent conservation issues to the shadows. Distracted by the urgencies and deprivations of war, the nation had no time for a conservation agenda. By the war's end in 1945, conservation had largely returned to its elitist roots, ensconced in hiking clubs like the Wilderness Society and the Sierra Club. Subsequently, in a dramatic postwar boom, the nation began undergoing a major transformation toward economic, social, and geographic expansion. Quality of life improved across the board, and industry began pushing forth a torrent of new consumer goods—plastics, labor-saving appliances, processed foods, bigger cars—with television advertising spurring the frenzy of consumption. Americans had new amounts of time and money, and began showing more appreciation for the natural world as a source of recreation and also as a source of fresh air and clean water—especially as rapid industrial growth began spewing out more and more pollution. The conservation movement reacted to these changes, evolving from the turn-of-the-century emphasis on utilitarian resource-use policies into an emphasis on quality-of-life issues. Environmental historian Samuel P. Hays noted, "We can observe a marked transition from the pre–World War II conservation themes of efficient management of physical resources, to the post–World War II environmental themes of environmental amenities, environmental protection, and human scale technology. Something new was happening in American society, arising out of the social changes and transformation in human values in the post-war years."[6] And while postwar prosperity wrought external changes to the movement, new blood was also making changes within. When David Brower took over the Sierra Club after the war, he began turning it from a passive social club into a forceful protector of wilderness. Lobbying tirelessly to block dams and create new national parks, Brower helped the conservation movement organize itself enough to begin influencing electoral politics again.

The course of conservation was changed forever in 1962 with the publication of Rachel Carson's *Silent Spring*. A talented scientist and a beguiling writer, Carson jolted the entire nation into an awareness of what the clumsy use of pesticides was doing to the planet. Public nervousness over environmental hazards like dichloro-diphenyl-trichloroethane (DDT), radiation from nuclear power plants, and air pollution began redefining the conservation movement, and by the end of the 1960s, "environmentalism" was becoming a household word. Conservation had focused on judicious use of finite resources; environmentalism began to focus on an emerging ecological awareness that perceived humans as part of the larger community of the natural world. This perception entailed the recognition that human activities were putting heavy burdens on the fragile systems that support life. Environmentalism, as it became a coherent concept, also became a potent force for change. Public allegiance to the idea became more and more vocal amidst the general social ferment of the 1960s, and by the end of the decade, the Second Wave of environmentalism had arrived.

Thanks to the efforts of David Brower and Wilderness Society director Howard Zahniser, 1964 saw the signing of the Wilderness Act, a radical admission by the federal government that land had value even when left undisturbed. This marked the beginning of a spate of federal legislation reflecting the nation's increasing environmental concerns. The Federal Water Quality Act (the Clean Water Act) was passed in 1965, the Clean Air Act in 1967, and the Wild and Scenic Rivers Act in 1968. When the groundbreaking National Environmental Policy Act (NEPA) was signed in 1969, requiring the federal government to analyze and report on the environmental effects of its activities through environmental impact statements, it showed that even the Republican Nixon administration felt compelled to respond to the public desire for environmental legislation.

By April 22, 1970, the first Earth Day, environmentalism had arrived. In December 1970, Nixon created the Environmental Protection Agency (EPA), setting a new standard for federal responsibility over environmental issues. The EPA became a tool for a powerful bipartisan movement that was managing to establish an environmental agenda through the intricate relationships it was building with new administrative bureaucracies. The Second Wave of environmentalism was defined by these close ties with political power and by the environmental legislation it was able to enact during the late 1960s and 1970s.

Of course, as the movement gained power, it mobilized its detractors. There have always been critics of environmentalism who believe its policies foster an anti-development, anti-capitalism, and anti-business ethic that hampers progress. Dixy Lee Ray, for example, who became director of the Atomic Energy Commission in 1973 and who pushed aside public concern over the ecological hazards of nuclear energy, felt this way. So did James Gaius Watt, who by the end of the 1970s was helping to incite an anti-environmental uprising in the west through his work for the conservative, pro-development Mountain States Legal Foundation (MSLF)—founded by right-wing corporate millionaire Joseph Coors. Watt, Coors, and a coalition of leaders from resource extraction industries were lashing out at the environmental legislation of the 1960s and 1970s, which had prompted greater scrutiny of grazing, mining, and logging activities in western states, which led to increased restrictions. In a manifestation of their belief in individual rights and state sovereignty, this uprising—which came to be known as the Sagebrush Rebellion—demanded reducing or eliminating federal regulation and transferring ownership of federal land to the states. When President Ronald Reagan came to power in 1981, he announced that he too was a Sagebrush Rebel, and his presidency marked the end of the environmental movement's Second Wave and its fledgling relationship with political power.

THE THIRD WAVE

Reagan's administration, which included James Watt as secretary of the Interior and anti-environmentalist Anne Gorsuch (who later became Anne Gorsuch Burford) as head of the Environmental Protection Agency, saw environmentalism as an obstruction to the continued ascendancy of American industry. Its thirst for deregulation threatened the gelling of the environmental agenda of the 1970s: Watt attempted to sell off huge amounts of public land to the private sector and pushed for unlimited development of natural resources, while Gorsuch loosened Clean Air Act restrictions and significantly weakened the EPA's power structure.

In the end though, the administration failed to grasp the extent to which the nation had already embraced environmental values. Public concern over population growth, overconsumption of non-renewable resources, and pollution grew during the 1980s. The friction between the Reagan vision of unrestricted resource use and the environmental movement's uneasy sense that the planet eventually would run out of those resources was encapsulated in a famous bet between free-market economist Julian Simon and conservation biologist Paul Ehrlich. In 1980, Simon challenged Ehrlich's warnings about the consequences of overconsumption of natural resources by wagering that by 1990 prices of certain raw materials such as grain, oil, or metals would have dropped—which he claimed would indicate that they were not getting scarcer. The bet was widely publicized, though for the most part the public was unconvinced that the market trends of five metals could be an accurate indicator of the state of the plant's environmental health.

The public in fact was getting fed up with cutbacks in environmental enforcement during the 1980s; in its collision with the mechanisms of deregulation espoused by Watt and Gorsuch, the environmental movement underwent changes that led to the emergence of the Third Wave. The ten major environmental organizations, which came to be known as the "Group of Ten," experienced huge membership growth and increased donations. Watt and Gorsuch, it seemed, haplessly had become effective "recruiters" for the environmental movement through the brazenness of their policies. Invigorated by financial gains and energized by its mission to save the environmental agenda of the 1960s and 1970s, the Group of Ten began to focus efforts on Washington, D.C., as lobbyists and litigators. The Third Wave is defined by the new face of these national environmental groups. They projected a new professionalism and willingness to work within existing political and economic systems to achieve their goals. Additionally, the anti-environmental backlash of the 1980s had convinced them of the importance of the powers of persuasion, and marketing became just as important to environmental groups as it was to the retail industry. Direct mail, canvassing, media relations, and publicity campaigns all came to define the new tactics of the Third-Wave environmental movement.

As the movement grew more professional, it also became more bureaucratic. Some would say this has made it more realistic, while some argue that environmental groups are now unfortunately too quick to compromise with the industrial capitalist system that so threatens it. Still, neither environmentalism nor human enterprise can exist alone; both must somehow seek a sustainable balance. For example, J. Michael Fay, the conservation biologist who walked 2,000 miles through the heart of the central African jungle to document wildlife and draw attention to the desperate need for conservation there, promotes the idea of ecotourism—a solution that aims to incorporate human prosperity with wilderness preservation.

There have been several results of the Third Wave's emphasis on publicity. One is the emergence of "ecocelebrities," such as Julia Butterfly Hill and

Christopher Swain, who call attention to environmental causes by their own extreme feats of physical endurance, and therefore rely completely on mass media to get their message out. Still, although regular coverage of environmental issues is necessary to keep the public informed and concerned about the state of the planet, pessimistic and daunting news of overwhelming problems such as global warming can also lead to numbness and a sense of hopelessness. Some have argued that the popularity of "contrarian" books like Bjørn Lomborg's *The Skeptical Environmentalist*—which insists that the environmental movement has gone too far with its anxious hype—is due to the public's need for some "good" news for a change.

Relying on the media to keep the public informed on environmental issues can have other drawbacks. Ross Gelbspan, a retired journalist and global warming activist, has expressed frustration with the media's misuse of the journalistic standard of balanced coverage. This practice requires reporters to present more than one side of an issue in order to avoid journalistic bias. This has an unfortunate impact on coverage of global warming since it allows for the views of a small handful of "greenhouse skeptics" like S. Fred Singer (who receives funding from oil and coal interests) equal footing with the vast international consensus of climate scientists who agree that global warming is already happening and gravely needs to be addressed.

In recent years, the environmental movement has had to expand its scope to recognize global problems such as climate change and the impacts of free trade (see, for example, the chapter on Helena Norberg-Hodge). At the same time, it has been struggling to become more socially inclusive. The imposed morality of the environmental movement in presuming to know what is best for the rest of the world has been challenged by such social activists as ecofeminist Vandana Shiva and environmental justice advocate Dana Alston. Shiva sees a connection between the degradation of the environment and the oppression and devaluation of women, and pushes the environmental movement to address the same inherent inequalities that have allowed men to dominate women and humans to dominate the earth. Alston's work promoted the recognition that people of color are disproportionately at risk to environmental hazards such as toxic waste, pesticides, and nuclear testing. The environmental justice movement that Alston helped create envisions an environmental agenda that integrates social, racial, and economic justice by honoring the fact that the protection of the earth demands the protection of the people who live there. Through the efforts of people like Shiva and Alston, the movement is slowly being broadened and redefined, and changes that have been a longtime coming are surfacing. The current environmental movement strives to embody a diversity of issues and goals and to embrace a diversity of people and viewpoints, but it is united by one thing: not the fear of the deep dark woods that haunted European settlers, but a profound apprehension of the human capacity to permanently alter our world.

SCOPE OF THE PRESENT WORK

Aiming to breathe life into the debate over conservation, I selected twenty people to write about. This selection process presented a challenge. These twenty biographies had to be further (roughly) divided between opposing camps, leaving about ten slots available for each side of the debate. I wanted to include a range of historical eras within both camps, and for both to have as equal a distribution of men and women as possible. Also, I wanted to include some of the most famous and revered figures in the environmental movement in recognition of their paramount place in shaping the ways in which the human impact on the natural world is perceived. But the more canonical the figure, the more published material already exists. It is easy to find information on Theodore Roosevelt or Henry David Thoreau for example; so, rather than add to the accumulation of literature, I also included some influential people who have not yet been placed on the shelf of history.

Contemporary environmentalism has become highly diverse. To reflect this, I have tried to include a variety of perspectives. These biographies include scientists, policymakers, activists, a writer, an economist, a corporate millionaire, and an athlete. Their work involves a range of environmental issues: population control, property rights, global climate change, habitat conservation, ecofeminism, defining the government's role in land-use regulation, globalization, environmental justice, pesticide use, and the perceived limits of natural resources. To fill in some of the inevitable gaps, an appendix provides abbreviated biographical sketches of other figures who have contributed to the debate. (Throughout the text, names of subjects are cross-referenced by appearing in **boldface** when they are mentioned in sections other than their own biographies.) However, this book is not meant to be comprehensive, but to furnish an introduction to a complex issue and to provide perspectives on opposing views of conservation issues so that readers can make their own informed foray into the current debate.

The biographies are grouped in chronological order rather than in separate pro- and anti-conservation sections. This is partly to avoid presenting the debate as completely polarized, which would give a somewhat inaccurate appearance of fragmented extremes. In reality, interpretations of environmentalism are not always this easily reduced, but expand along a continuum of beliefs, definitions, and viewpoints. Certainly no one would argue that David Brower or John Muir or Rachel Carson were anything but pro-environment. Similarly, James Watt or Helen Chenoweth-Hage or Dixy Lee Ray, their human complexities aside, never promoted themselves as friends of the natural world. But other figures project a little more ambiguity. Gifford Pinchot, for example, walked a line: He fought destructive turn-of-the-century logging practices but also held that resources should be utilized to meet the needs of society. He even advocated damming Muir's cherished Hetch Hetchy Valley, believing it would better serve the people of San Francisco as a water receptacle. Bjørn Lomborg similarly eludes being pinned down. A former Greenpeace member who doesn't believe in owning a car, he considers himself an environmentalist (though a "skeptical" one). Yet the views he presented in his book, *The Skeptical Environmentalist*, have outraged environmentalists and conservation biologists and instigated a tense debate. Conversely, Christopher Swain, who swam the entire 1,243-mile length of the Columbia River to raise awareness of how egregiously polluted it has become, rears at being called an environmentalist, believing it alienates other outdoor-oriented groups, such as hunters. The term anti-environmentalist, with its negative connotation, presents similar quandries. In the current political climate, being labeled an anti-environmentalist can have a detrimental effect on a public figure's popularity, so that even those who oppose environmental protections sometimes distance themselves from the term, preferring to call themselves "pro-business" or "pro-jobs" instead. However, for the most part, the people selected for the "anti-" side of the debate for this volume have tended to be rather outspoken in their denouncement of environmentalism and have therefore accepted or even celebrated being labeled an anti-environmentalist. Still, it is human nature to resist being relegated to pre-defined roles or sides of an argument. To paraphrase Tennyson: labels half reveal, half conceal the truth within.

With that said, however, there are several examples in this book of directly antagonistic debates between opposing parties: the Pinchot-Ballinger controversy, the bet between Paul Ehrlich and Julian Simon, and the opposing interpretations of global climate change of Ross Gelbspan and S. Fred Singer. Debate of this kind bears fruit in several ways: It forces the protagonists to define and defend their views fully, it opens the controversy up to outside inspection, and its quarreling drama can draw even the most apathetic into the fray of public discourse. As writer Jeff Walker has noticed, "There can be something peculiarly magnetic about someone who seems completely unconflicted."[7]

Because of the natural magnetism exuded by passionate people, biography can be a compelling conceptual device for examining issues like the debate over the proper role of humans in their environment. Rather than disembodied explications of the history of the environmental movement based solely on theory, analysis, dates, and facts, it may be through the companionship of another person's life history that we can best apprehend our own understanding of the dynamics of nature and culture. There are many layers of influence and personal development that sculpt a person's environmental beliefs: personal events, family life, and other interpersonal relationships. For example, Rachel Carson was encouraged in her early career by a beloved mentor, while Vandana Shiva's enduring environmental ethic was born on the numerous extended camping trips her parents took her on in the foothills of the Himalayas. Others, such as the Ehrlichs and Julian Simon, have been influenced by books—or in the case of Bjørn Lomborg, by a single magazine article.

Cultural trends and historical conditions—as well as underlying issues of race, gender, ethnicity, privilege, and oppression—also melt into a broad context of influence on a person's appreciation of the natural world. For example, the roots of Dana Alston's leadership in the environmental movement came out of her concern for racial and social justice issues. Meanwhile, Ayn Rand's promotion of capitalism and distaste for environmentalism was surely a product of her upbringing in Soviet Russia during the revolution. In the end, as Muir biographer Steven Holmes stated, our task is to "look for the psychological and spiritual dynamics of self-construction and of meaning-making, for the spark that is struck when cultural symbols, environmental realities, and historical circumstances scrape against a living, breathing, growing human being."[8] As any biography reveals, each person is simultaneously shaped by their unique entanglement of circumstances and possesses the power to shape them. The twenty people featured in this book deftly exemplify the courage it takes to wield that power and to change the shape of the debate over the environment.

NOTES

1. Quoted in Leo Marx, *The Machine in the Garden* (New York: Oxford University Press, 1964), p. 41.

2. See Roderick Nash, *Wilderness and the American Mind*, 4th ed. (New Haven: Yale University Press, 2001) for further exploration of early relationships with the American wilderness.

3. William Frederic Badè, *The Life and Letters of John Muir* Vol. 2 (Boston: Houghton Mifflin, 1924), p. 29.

4. Theodore Roosevelt, Address to the National Editorial Association, Jamestown, Virginia, June 10, 1907.

5. Bjørn Lomborg and Jason Cowley, "The Rich Man and the Butterfly," *New Statesman* Vol. 131 (July 29, 2002), pp. 34–36.

6. Samuel P. Hays, "From Conservation to Environment: Environmental Politics in the United States since World War II," *Environmental Review* Vol. 6 (Fall 1982), p. 19.

7. Jeff Walker, *The Ayn Rand Cult* (Chicago: Open Court Publishing Company, 1999), p. 14.

8. Steven J. Holmes, *The Young John Muir: An Environmental Biography* (Madison: The University of Wisconsin Press, 1999), p. 10.

BIBLIOGRAPHY

Regarding the history of the conservation (and environmental) movement in the United States, see Philip Shabecoff, *A Fierce Green Fire: The American Environmental Movement* (New York: Farrar, Straus and Giroux, 1993); and *Earth Rising: American Environmentalism in the 21st Century* (Covelo, CA: Island Press, 2000). Also see Leo Marx, *The Machine in the Garden* (New York: Oxford University Press,

1964); Samuel P. Hays, "From Conservation to Environment: Environmental Politics in the United States since World War II," *Environmental Review* Vol. 6 (Fall 1982), pp. 14–29; Kirkpatrick Sale, *The Green Revolution: The American Environmental Movement, 1962–1992* (New York: Hill and Wang, 1993); Mark Dowie, *Losing Ground: American Environmentalism at the Close of the Twentieth Century* (Cambridge, MA: The MIT Press, 1995); J. R. McNeill, *Something New Under the Sun: An Environmental History of the Twentieth-Century World* (New York: W.W. Norton and Company, 2000); Hal K. Rothman, *Saving the Planet: The American Response to the Environment in the Twentieth Century* (Chicago: Ivan R. Dee, 2000); and Roderick Nash, *Wilderness and the American Mind*, 4th ed. (New Haven: Yale University Press, 2001).

JOHN MUIR
(1838–1914)

Thousands of tired, nerve-shaken, over-civilized people are beginning to
find out that going to the mountains is going home; that wilderness is a
necessity; and that mountain parks and reservations are useful not only
as fountains of timber and irrigating rivers, but as fountains of life.

—John Muir

John Muir once said all he needed to flee the strictures of the daily grind was
to "throw some tea and bread in an old sack and jump over the back fence."
Famous for hiking, exploring, and mountain-climbing his way to a love of
the land, Muir embodied the American tradition of freedom, and because of
that he became a cultural hero. To him, to enter the wilderness of mountain
meadows, waterfalls, and sequoia forests was to engage in reverential worship of nature and of life. A self-styled "poetico-trampo-geologist-bot. and
ornith-natural, etc!-!-!," he believed that all people should explore and enjoy
wild lands, that in fact the experience would leave them richer and happier,
as it did him. He related his wilderness experiences through writing, making
legendary and colorful contributions to the blossoming American literary
scene; he also followed his ethical compulsion to preach the message of preservation, to inspire political debate and activism. Muir argued that the land
should be protected in its own right—preserved for its beauty and spiritual
value, not managed for efficient resource use, as some of his opponents

believed. In the purity of his preservation ideals he articulated an American folk wisdom, an understanding that America's greatness lies in its natural treasures, and he has since been called by many the "father of American environmentalism." A study of Muir's position within the nascent conservation movement provides a miniperspective of early twentieth-century American attitudes toward nature. But his legacy stretches far beyond his lifetime: Overall, Muir has achieved an almost mythic importance in American environmental rhetoric and consciousness.

John Muir was born on April 21, 1838, in the coastal town of Dunbar, Scotland, the third child and oldest son in a family of eight children. His parents, Daniel Muir and Anne Gilrye Muir, both descended from Scottish Highlanders, made their home in a three-story building out of which Daniel also ran a prosperous grocery business. Daniel Muir adhered fanatically to a strict form of evangelical Presbyterianism, and his family was forced to bear the burden of his spiritual convictions. John Muir said later that in his early childhood he learned "about three fourths of the Old Testament and all of the New by heart and sore flesh."[1] His mother, Anne, had a much more compassionate nature and gained what comfort she could out of her life with a tyrannical husband by devoting herself to her children and shielding them from his authoritarian rigidity.

John Muir could and did make temporary escapes from his father's religious zeal by venturing off to the seashore or the countryside. The first sentence of the autobiography he wrote of his childhood reads: "When I was a boy in Scotland I was fond of everything that was wild, and all my life I've been growing fonder and fonder of wild places and wild creatures."[2] His maternal grandfather, who lived across the street, took him on exploratory walks, beginning when John was only 3 years old. Before he turned 4, John was sent to school. Although the school provided a somewhat narrow curriculum of religious and classical subjects, it was here that he first was exposed (albeit fleetingly) to natural history through ornithologists John James Audubon and Alexander Wilson's written descriptions of American fauna. Schoolhouse discipline ran along the theory that education must be instilled by regular whippings, meaning that "salutary" violence followed Scottish children from home to school and back home again, often with a schoolyard fight on the playground in between. Later in life Muir detested any unnecessary violence or cruelty of any sort, but at this time, he and his schoolmates offered their own expressions of violence by tormenting any helpless creature they could find. They would roam the landscape as a gang, stealing apples, throwing stones at cats, provoking dogfights, and robbing birds' nests—sometimes doing their damage by sneaking out at night after they were supposed to be in bed. After these rampaging forays, Muir would face a methodical thrashing by his father, which, he stated with pride, never once deterred him from going out again. In this way, much of John's childhood was shaped by his uncompromising rebellion against his father.

In John's grammar school books, the few pieces of literature that described the natural world were set in America, a land still mostly wild, where forests went on for miles and birds flocked in dancing swarms. John Muir was already starry-eyed about the "wonder-filled" land of America when talk of gold discoveries started circulating in 1849. Emigration-fever ran wild, and Daniel Muir got caught up in the prevailing desire for the "newness" promised by the American social and physical landscape. It wasn't gold he was after, but a chance to find fertile ground for his religious austerity. He had given up the established Presbyterian Church and found a sect that fit his ideology; called the Disciples of Christ, it was characterized by emphatic demonstrations of Christian belief, a radical anti-institutionalism, and a return to the primitive ways of the apostles. The sect had its stronghold in the wilderness of America, with its unencumbered "innocence," and Daniel was drawn to the promise of freedom from the established religions in Scotland. He bought a farm in Wisconsin, near Madison, and uprooted the family early in 1849. The only remorse or misgivings 11-year-old John had were for leaving behind his beloved grandfather, who would be deserted in his old age. But John was a beehive of excitement at the thought of the strange new wildlife and landscapes he would soon be able to explore. When his grandfather expressed his insight and foreboding—telling the Muir children that they were in fact in for a life of hardship—young John gave the warning not a second thought.

Grandfather's warning of course turned out to be true. The American frontier was being transformed from wilderness to farmland, and, in breaking in the land, the pioneering farmers and their children endured an unending succession of back-breaking work. Daniel Muir had purchased 80 acres of virgin woodland, four miles from the nearest neighbor and bordered by a small glacial lake, which he named Fountain Lake but which the neighbors called Muir Lake. John rejoiced in the wild land—the lake, the spring flowers in the meadows—and in the marvelous new species of birds, and he especially revered the learning experiences they offered. He described the Wisconsin wilderness as "Nature streaming into us, wooingly teaching her wonderful glowing lessons, so unlike the dismal grammar ashes and cinders so long thrashed into us. Here without knowing it we were still at school."[3] This would not be the last time he would express his approval of gaining knowledge from the vast and intricate natural world.

With the exception of Sundays, which were dedicated to Bible lessons and church services, John Muir's days—cold or warm, rain or shine—were filled with grueling farmwork. There was no time for reading anything but the Bible or working on any of the usual hobbies that fill childhood with unmeasured hours of play and self-absorption. As he got older and his hunger for worldly knowledge and critical thinking grew, he began trying to steal a few hours after meals to read borrowed books and teach himself geometry and trigonometry, which, for a few minutes at a time, took his mind away from the relentless heavy chores. After eight years of work on the Fountain Lake farm—with the outbuildings all built and the fields in perfect order—Daniel Muir purchased half-section of wild land to the east of the farm, and the groundbreaking hard work started anew. The second farm, called Hickory Hill, lay high and dry with no surface water, and a well of ninety feet had to be dug through solid sandstone. The task fell to John. For months he chipped through stone with a mason's chisel, day after day, and as it got deeper, he had to be lowered into it by a wooden bucket. One morning when he was lowered into the 80-foot hole he began to pass out from an accumulation of poison carbonic acid gas that had settled at the bottom during the night. By sheer force of will he managed to climb feebly back into the bucket so that his alarmed father could haul him up. He was lucky to be alive, but was given only two days to recover before being sent back to the well to finish the job. The closest he came to expressing his anger at his father's treatment were these lines in his autobiography: "Constant dropping wears away stone. So does constant chipping, while at the same time wearing away at the chipper. Father never spent an hour in that well. He trusted me to sink it straight and plumb, and I did."[4]

John Muir's busy mind never wearied, and he constantly sought free time to devote to his intellect. His father, angry that he repeatedly had to order John to leave his reading and go to bed, once told him that he had permission to get up early in the morning if he wanted to read. From then on—despite the strong call of sleep after working on the farm all day—every night, John arose at 1:00 A.M., after only five hours of sleep, to work on his inventions. A mechanical genius, John whittled, filed, and tapped out astounding contraptions: waterwheels, curious door locks, thermometers, hygrometers, pyrometers, clocks, barometers, an automatic contrivance for feeding a horse at any required hour, an automatic fire lighter, and, poignantly, a machine he called an "early-rising machine"—a bed that could be set to tilt on end at any hour, tossing its sleeper to the floor.

His machines provided a mental escape from the routine of drudgery and religious strictures, and they eventually provided him a real escape from the farm. Encouraged by a friendly neighbor, he took some of his inventions to the state fair in Madison, leaving home for the first time. He was 22 years old. Both Muir, with all his rural earnestness, and his striking creations were looked on as wonders at the fair, and made a great hit. Suddenly free to find his own way in the world, he was offered a job on a steam-powered iceboat on the Mississippi River; he took it, but quit after three months, finding the work oppressive. When he returned to Madison, his dearest wish was to enroll at the University of Wisconsin to continue his education, which had all but stopped when he came to America at age 11. Though he was afraid he couldn't afford the tuition, and was burdened with shyness and a painful awareness of his ignorance, he approached the acting university president, who quickly welcomed him into the freshman class.

During the two and a half years he studied at the university, beginning in 1861, he took a variety of classes—including botany and geology—and made an impression on Ezra Slocom Carr, a science professor. Professor Carr and his wife, Jeanne Carr, who both remembered Muir from the fair exhibit, took a deep interest in him and became his close friends and mentors. Jeanne shared an interest in botany with Muir and in later years nurtured his literary talents, becoming a crucial influence on the gift he would give the world through his writing.

Muir's time in Madison was a wonderful mind-expanding experience. But while he was there, exuberantly pursuing knowledge and celebrating his sense of independence, the Civil War was casting a sobering pall over the nation. He finished his spring term in 1863 with the intention of transferring to medical school in the fall, but he feared conscription and, during the winter of 1863–1864, lived with his sister and her family while deciding what to do. He felt no call to fight in this war, partly because he didn't consider himself to be an American, and partly because of his unwavering pacifism. When President Lincoln signed an order for a draft that spring, he left for Canada. He put a positive spin on the circumstances of his leaving college after two and a half years when he proclaimed that he was only leaving one university for another, the University of Wisconsin for "the University of the Wilderness."

Heading north, he followed the wildest routes and disappeared into the Canadian forests. For months he lived a solitary, wandering life, collecting plants and rejoicing in his freedom. Though there is little record from the two years he spent in Canada, he documented one day in great detail in his journal. He was making his way through a dense swamp when he found a cluster of the rare orchid *Calypso borealis* on a stream bank. Their unassuming beauty, so unexpected amidst the mess of the swamp, seemed to be a benediction; he wept with joy and emotional release. The natural world always had been a solace to him, and now that he was friendless and homeless, nature again provided comfort. "They were alone," he wrote in his journal. "I never before saw a plant so full of life; so perfectly spiritual, it seemed pure enough for the throne of its Creator. I felt as if I were in the presence of superior beings who loved me and beckoned me to come."

That winter he found a job at a woodworking factory in Meaford, Ontario, where he stayed to work even after the war ended a few months later. His mechanical aptitude was given elbow room here, and he succeeded in doubling the factory's production with his various inventions and improvements. In March 1866, a fire destroyed the factory and most of Muir's possessions, including his botanical notebooks; but instead of staying to help rebuild, he returned to the United States, where he continued wandering, studying plants, and looking for work. In Indianapolis, Muir quickly found a position in a steam-powered factory building wagon parts, but, though his skills with machinery led to promotion after promotion, he was beginning to feel that he was doomed to live "among machines" and that no line of work would channel his passionate interest in wild nature.

One night in the spring of 1867 he stayed late to work on a new belting system, tugging at the heavy lacings. When they suddenly sprang loose, his hand glanced upward and the sharp file he was holding pierced his right eye. To his horror, his sight in his right eye went dark, and by the next day, his left eye, in sympathetic nervous shock, had gone dark too. Agonizing in his bed, he feared he would never again see the gloriousness of the natural world, which so sustained his spirit. He so despaired at the thought of all the days he had "wasted" working in factories that, when he did regain his sight—completely in his left eye and partially in his right—he was determined "to store my mind with the Lord's beauty." This crisis and its happy outcome were a turning point for Muir, as he felt he had been given a new chance and didn't want to waste it. Impelled into the wilderness, he made plans to walk a thousand miles to Florida and then take a boat to South America. He would never again call Wisconsin home.

At 29 years of age, Muir left on a ramble that would be an exploration as much of himself as of the natural universe. He traveled light but always had his plant press with him and a few books: the New Testament, the poetry of Robert Burns, and *Paradise Lost*. Shedding the traps of civilization as he walked through Kentucky, Tennessee, the tip of North Carolina, Georgia, and Florida, Muir also began to shed some of the more oppressive artifacts of his childhood. The beliefs that were instilled in him from his father's harsh religious gloom—that the world was a fearful, sinful place, and that salvation can be found only through strict Christianity—seemed out of place in the sunlit world where Muir found nothing but beauty and delight for every sense. Where was the evil? The joy he felt banished even the fear of death, and the living dynamics of nature showed him that death is all a part of the ongoing harmony in the natural world. These realizations were a powerful assertion of his own beliefs, and as he came to reject the religion he inherited from his father, he deepened his spiritual connection with nature.

At the same time, the rest of the nation was undergoing its own transition as it reconstructed itself after the Civil War. Life was becoming more fast-paced and less rural due to rapid increases in industrialization and westward expansion, which had the reactionary effect of making many Americans yearn for the simpler, quieter days of their youth. For a broad segment of Americans it also marked the dawning of a new concern about the impacts of growth and a desire to see some kind of control over the exploitation of land that had become standard practice as settlers moved west. This was the first stirring of a conservationist ethos, and its presence fostered among Americans a yearning receptiveness to the message that Muir would be sending out in the next few decades. As he arrived in Florida, the last leg of his land journey, Muir was simmering with his own formulation of an environmental ethos—one that recognized the natural world as a place of beauty, wonder, and spiritual sustenance. He was beginning to see the arrogance of the entrenched mindset that held humans to be the sole purpose of all of creation. "The world, we are told, was made especially for man, a presumption not supported by the facts," he wrote in his travel journal.[5] The universe would not be complete without humans, Muir saw, but likewise it would not be complete without the smallest gnat or blade of grass. Muir's recognition of the inherent worth of all interrelated creatures and plants, as well as of the mountains and meadows where they live, was actually quite radical for that time. It was also an embryonic expression of some of the basic concepts of ecology, which eventually would expand to become one of the founding doctrines of the American environmental movement.

Meanwhile, Muir arrived in Florida in October 1867, and spent a few days at Cedar Keys on the Gulf of Mexico, enjoying the lushness and new plants. He wanted to book passage on a ship to begin his journey to South America, but found that the next one out wouldn't be leaving for two weeks, so he found a job at a local lumber mill while he waited. But an ominous lethargy came over him, and within a few days he was near death with a vicious malarial fever. For three weary months he fought malaria, gaining strength with excruciating slowness. By January, though still very frail, he felt ready to book passage to Cuba, though once he got there he was disappointed that he had no stamina for climbing any of the mountains around him. So he got on a ship for New York, where he found another ship to take him by way of the Isthmus of Panama to California and the fabled Yosemite Valley, which he had been hearing about and with which he one day would come to be inextricably and eternally identified.

The California landscape was more magnificent than Muir had imagined. After disembarking at San Francisco on March 28, 1868, he spent six weeks hiking across the state to the Yosemite Valley in the Sierra Nevada, filling his journal with reveries all the way. On his first visit, he spent eight days in the valley, where he encountered the sequoias of the Mariposa Grove, the thrilling 3,000-feet-high valley walls, and the waterfalls—all of which only left him hungry for more. He found work as a sheepherder in the nearby Central Valley, a job that allowed him to remain in the area and earn enough money to buy food through the next winter. He returned to the Sierra Nevada in the summer of 1869, this time on a sheepherding crew, helping to move the flocks of sheep higher and higher as the snows melted in the mountains. Though the job suited Muir—providing him a source of income while allowing him a flexible schedule and plenty of opportunities for sketching, plant collecting, and simply rejoicing in the mountains—he did have some misgivings about bringing these "hoofed locusts" into the pristine meadows. In later years he fought to have sheep banned from the area, and from all of Yosemite National Park.

Muir had found his spiritual home in the mountains of Yosemite, and his journal from that summer provides a narrative of his discoveries and ecstatic responses.[6] On July 9 he described waking up: "Exhilarated with the mountain air, I feel like shouting this morning with excess of wild animal joy." With his love of the land came the realization that not all humans felt the way he did, which incited in him a desire to protect it. Later in the same journal entry he wrote, "[S]o extravagant is Nature with her choicest treasures, spending plant beauty as she spends sunshine, pouring it forth into land and sea, garden and desert. And so the beauty of lilies falls on angels and men, bears and squirrels, wolves and sheep, birds and bees, but as far as I have seen, man alone, and the animals he tames, destroy these gardens." As he led the trampling sheep into the mountains, Muir was seeing the beginning of the need for preservation and protection from the destructive aspects of human industry and "progress."

Muir returned to the valley that fall and found work with a local hotel-keeper and mill owner. He spent the winter building a sawmill, renovating the hotel, and tending to livestock—occasionally skipping sleep so that he could steal some time to continue his explorations of the Sierras. He built himself a little cabin on the sunny side of the valley, a simple structure with a wild fern growing inside and a brook running through it. At this point he was an unknown, working manual-labor jobs while becoming a highly expert mountaineer in his spare time. But within five years, thanks to the publication of some of his written work, he was a naturalist of standing in American literary and scientific circles, and was on his way toward a reputation as a magnificent writer. His entrance into the public arena first came through his contributions to science: His endurance, boldness, and inventive mountain-climbing techniques had granted Muir unique views of the Sierras, and he had a unique theory on the geological origin of the Yosemite Valley.

One of the leading geologists of the day, Josiah D. Whitney, held to the theory that the valley had been created by a stupendous cataclysmic collapse of its floor. Muir devoutly disbelieved this theory, insisting that he had seen a different story written on the rocks themselves: No "catastrophe" had formed this land; it was the effect of glaciers, the slow scraping out of the lakes and valleys that Muir had seen in the "strange, raw, wiped" appearance of the cliffs and the deposition patterns of boulders. His dear friend Jeanne Carr, with whom he had kept in touch since his days in Wisconsin, ardently supported his literary talents and convinced him to write up his theory for publication. He put together an article, "Yosemite Glaciers," and on December 5, 1871, the *New York Tribune* printed it, sending the startled Muir $200. The next year he began publishing a series of articles for the *Overland Monthly* called "Studies in the Sierra," which became very popular and allowed him to shift toward a more general audience. He was beginning to realize he might make a living as a writer despite the fact that writing was a painstaking chore for him, mostly because of his conviction that nature is more magnificent than any words ever can convey. However, writing provided a way to get his message out—something that would become vital in his activist days—and an escape from manual labor.

With his career decision, as with many aspects of his life, Muir had to negotiate a precarious search for balance. Nature provided nearly everything he needed, and his truest happiness came from the time he spent wandering in the mountains. Nature was his religion, nature was his school. But one thing it couldn't provide was human contact. When he was in the company of other people, he famously talked in a rushing stream, perhaps making up for the hours when there was no one to listen. Within his personality were two conflicting needs: the need for the solitary freedom of the mountains and the need for the connectedness of civilization with its promise of intellectual cultivation and a community of friends. His loneliness, at least intellectually, was felt most acutely in the spring of 1871, when a select party of Boston literati, including the great philosopher **Ralph Waldo Emerson**, visited Yosemite. Emerson had reached the end of his career and was traveling to see some of the splendors of the West that he had read about. Muir, buzzing with excitement at meeting someone he regarded as a role model and an inspiration, felt too shy to approach Emerson in person, but handed him a letter inviting him to his little cabin. Every day for the rest of his visit, Emerson came back to see Muir, and the two enjoyed rich conversations and companionship. When Emerson and his party left the valley, Muir felt more acutely lonely than he ever had in the mountains. On his return home, Emerson sent Muir two volumes of his collected essays, which Muir carried with him, read closely, and made numerous notes in during the following years.

In 1874 Muir accepted the loss of his individual freedom and moved from the mountains to the city of Oakland, where he composed his Sierra studies for the *Overland Monthly*. Though he begrudged the time he spent writing, he remained determined to get his message out in the hopes that he might convert readers to an appreciation of the Sierra landscape. He also begrudged city life, feeling that the grid lines of cluttered streets, the entrapping buildings, and the daily toils of commerce sapped his vitality. Though he had come to see the importance of doing something in the way of public service—of fulfilling his duties as a part of a larger society—he never fully resolved the issue and certainly never felt at peace in the city. For the next six years he moved between the city and the wilds, leaving his base in the valley for long exploratory treks and then returning to write about his experiences.

In 1878 Muir turned 40. As conclusive insurance against the loneliness that seemed always lurking in his life, he began a courtship with the daughter of some close friends, 31-year-old Louie Wanda Strentzel. Relatively little is known about Louie except that she was an accomplished pianist and that she wrote poetry that hinted at an affinity to the natural world, something that no doubt warmed Muir's heart. Their courtship followed their own unconventional terms, terms that allowed ample freedom for Muir to continue his rambling lifestyle: In fact, shortly after their engagement in June 1879, he departed on a six-month voyage to Alaska. While Louie stayed behind and waited for him, Muir went mountain climbing, studied plants, explored glaciers, and took an 800-mile canoe trip around Glacier Bay.

On April 14, 1880, a few months after Muir's return from Alaska, he and Louie Strentzel were married, and for the first time since leaving his family's Wisconsin farm, he was again part of a family. He and Louie moved into the house formerly occupied by her parents, and Muir began a new career as a fruit farmer in Martinez, California. For the next decade Muir bent himself into the shape of careful provider, attentive husband, and doting father. His orchards flourished under his practical, hardworking methods, and his fields of tokay grapes, cherries, and Bartlett pears soon began yielding his family large profits. His daughters, Wanda (born 1881) and Helen (born 1886) delighted him to no end, and he frequently took them on nature walks and told them stories of his adventures.

The decade Muir spent fulfilling his responsibilities as a family man and fruit grower began to take its toll on him. Louie, recognizing that a vital element was missing from his life, began urging him to take time away from the ranch, which he finally did. Besides his own need to reconnect with the land, a growing sense of urgency compelled his attention toward the wilderness at that time because of the changes being wrought throughout post–Gold Rush California. The abundance of rich natural resources and fertile land in California was rapidly being plundered and concentrated in the hands of a relative few. A small portion of Yosemite had been made a state park in 1864 by President Lincoln, but, as a rule, setting land aside as protected went against the grain of the century-old American drive to populate the wild unknown and find a way to turn a profit from it. Because he recognized this, Muir initially felt that the fate of the wilderness he loved was a lost cause and was skeptical that the public could be convinced to preserve American wild places. However, he was heartened by the attitude of an optimistic New York editor named Robert Underwood Johnson, who came out to meet Muir and recruit him to write some articles for his *Century Magazine*, a popular journal. Muir took Johnson camping in Yosemite to discuss the proposed articles and to design a campaign for extending the boundaries of the protected area in Yosemite and making it into a national park. Muir rose to the challenge and agreed to write two articles, one describing the splendors of Yosemite and detailing the threats to its natural features, and one explaining the need to designate it all as a national park. Thus, at the age of 51, he began the final stage of his career, that of a political activist.

For most of his adult life Muir's reputation was based on his eccentric ramblings, his hair-raising stories, and his rapturous descriptions of trees, storms, glaciers, and wildflowers; now he channeled his years of personal experiences in the wild into a fight for the preservation of some of California's most unique and beautiful natural areas. "Unless reserved or protected, the whole region will soon or late be devastated by lumbermen and sheepmen, and so of course made unfit for use as a pleasure ground," he wrote in one of the *Century* articles. Muir's contention was that the wilderness should persist because of its inherent grandeur and because of the pleasure and aesthetic fulfillment it gives, not because of its usefulness for grazing or timber harvesting. He believed it was of the profoundest arrogance to presume that humans existed separately from nature and that nature was simply there to be used up. The land should be set aside and cherished in its own right: This was the extent of Muir's definition of resource use, and it was far narrower than the definition with which many politicians felt comfortable. Muir's impact suddenly became much sharper now that he had turned to activism, because, as he formulated his ideas into a political philosophy, he provided a counterpoise to the strong tide of American utilitarianism and lust for progress in the late nineteenth century, a culture that had invented itself through industrialization that fed directly off the land and its resources.

The efforts of Johnson and Muir resulted in Yosemite being declared a national park in September 1890. In some sense this marked a significant victory, and because of Muir's passionate fight, he would come to be regarded as the founder of the national park movement that spread through the nation and eventually through the world. Yet the battle for Yosemite's future was far from over. Though it had attained national park status, it remained under the jurisdiction of a state commission that continued to allow livestock grazing in the park and that generally promoted development. The struggle between special interests and preservationists continued for years before California receded Yosemite to the federal government under orders from a bill signed by President **Theodore Roosevelt** in 1905.

In 1892, Muir, who had been catapulted into the public eye during the battle for the fate of Yosemite, joined a local network of influential naturelovers in organizing a preservationist group modeled after the Audubon Society and the wilderness advocacy clubs in the East. They officially convened in May of that year, unanimously electing Muir president, and the Sierra Club was born. Its mission statement expressed its promise to "enlist the support and co-operation of the people and the government in preserving the forests and other features of the Sierra Nevada Mountains." In Muir's day the fledgling club had many challenges, not the least of which was political infighting and ideological disputes among founding members. But today, after a distinguished history, the Sierra Club boasts of being the nation's oldest and largest grassroots environmental organization, with 700,000 members. Debate over the direction the Sierra Club has taken still raises sparks, yet the principles it was founded on have had a wide-ranging influence: encouraging public responsibility for the land and its resources, encouraging people to reconnect with the land through recreation, and encouraging political involvement in conservation issues.

During Muir's time, the fight to preserve nature was becoming more professional and more mainstream, thanks in part to his unceasing efforts. He found his final battle in his fight to save the Hetch Hetchy Valley, a beautiful region of grassy meadows similar in topography and vegetation to Yosemite. At Muir's urging, the valley had been included in the national park designation of 1890, but a few years later the city of San Francisco began hinting at a plan to dam the southern end of the valley to create a reservoir that could supply a cheap source of municipal water. Though Muir and the Sierra Club succeeded in rebutting the plan for years, it kept resurfacing throughout the 1890s and into the early 1900s. Fighting for Hetch Hetchy put Muir into a truly adversarial position against a man with whom he was once friendly and who seemed to share his motives of forest protection: **Gifford Pinchot.** But by the time Pinchot became the first head of the U.S. Forest Service in 1905, a vast gulf had developed between the former friends. Muir was a true preservationist—he wanted the land protected for its own sake—whereas Pinchot was a conservationist, a utilitarian, believing the land should be managed for its most highly efficient use so that less waste is involved. Pinchot pushed for the dam at Hetch Hetchy and represented the political opinion that national park resources should be tapped for the benefit of society. The fight became embroiled in political tensions and turned into a source of prolonged anguish for Muir. For him, the battle had deeply troubling implications. It seemed that a precedent would be set that would allow other national parks to be developed as utilitarians saw fit. Worse, Hetch Hetchy had such intensely personal meaning to Muir, since he had spent some of his best, most inspiring days there. "That anyone would try to destroy such a place seems incredible," he wrote, "but sad experience shows that there are people good enough and bad enough for anything. The proponents of the dam scheme bring forward a lot of bad arguments to prove that the only righteous thing to do with the people's parks is to destroy them bit by bit as they are able."

On December 1913, the decision to dam Hetch Hetchy was made. Muir lived alone by then—Louie having died in 1905—and was working on a book about his Alaska days. His life and work already had become strong influences on many Americans who believed in the struggle to preserve the integrity of wildlands. Even though the Hetch Hetchy battle had been lost (and many admit today that the dam turned out to be a conclusive mistake), a tradition of amateur resistance, fueled entirely by conviction and idealism, had been started by John Muir, who had turned his life into a powerful and enduring social movement. On December 23, 1914, one year after the crushing defeat of Hetch Hetchy, Muir caught pneumonia and died shortly thereafter.

NOTES

1. John Muir, *The Story of My Boyhood and Youth* (Madison: University of Wisconsin Press, 1965), p. 27. Originally published in Boston and New York by Houghton Mifflin, 1913.

2. Ibid., p. 3.

3. Ibid., pp. 52–53.

4. Ibid., p. 186.

5. Muir's travel journal from this walk was published posthumously as *A Thousand Mile Walk to the Gulf* (Boston and New York: Houghton Mifflin, 1916), p. 136.

6. Muir's *My First Summer in the Sierra* (Boston and New York: Houghton Mifflin, 1911) reproduces his journal from that summer and includes his own illustrations.

BIBLIOGRAPHY

Muir's papers are held in the Holt-Atherton Special Collections at the University of the Pacific library in Stockton, Calif. Ronald H. Limbaugh and Kirsten E. Lewis have compiled a microform catalogue called *The Guide and Index to the Microform Edition of the John Muir Papers, 1858–1957* (Alexandria, VA: Chadwyck-Healey, 1986). Muir wrote *The Story of My Boyhood and Youth* (Boston and New York: Houghton Mifflin, 1913) as a moral tale for children, but it has become an environmental classic for adults. Other writings by Muir include *The Mountains of California* (New York: Century, 1894); *Our National Parks* (Boston and New York: Houghton Mifflin, 1901); *My First Summer in the Sierra* (Boston and New York: Houghton Mifflin, 1911); *The Yosemite* (New York: Century, 1912); *Travels in Alaska* (Boston and New York: Houghton Mifflin, 1915); and *A Thousand Mile Walk to the Gulf* (Boston and New York: Houghton Mifflin, 1916). There are many excellent studies of Muir, including William Frederic Badè, *The Life and Letters of John Muir*, 2 volumes (Boston: Houghton Mifflin, 1924); Stephen Fox, *John Muir and His Legacy: The American Conservation Movement* (Boston and Toronto: Little, Brown and Company, 1981); Michael P. Cohen, *The Pathless Way: John Muir and American Wilderness* (Madison: University of Wisconsin Press, 1984); and Frederick Turner, *Rediscovering America: John Muir in His Time and Ours* (New York: Viking Penguin, 1985). Badè was Muir's literary executor and a colleague at the Sierra Club. Linnie Marsh Wolfe was a family friend of the Muirs and wrote what some consider to be the standard biography of him: *Son of the Wilderness: The Life of John Muir* (New York: Knopf, 1945). It was awarded the 1946 Pulitzer Prize for biography.

RICHARD BALLINGER
(1858–1922)

You chaps who are in favor of this conservation program are all wrong. You are hindering the development of the West. In my opinion, the proper course to take with regard to this [public lands] is to divide it up among the big corporations and the people who know how to make money out of it and let the people at large get the benefits of the circulation of the money.

—Richard Ballinger

"They showered you with suspicion, and by the most pettifogging methods exploited to the public matters which . . . paraded before a hysterical body of headline readers, served to blacken your character and to obscure the proper issue of your honesty and effectiveness as a public servant,"[1] wrote President William Howard Taft to Richard Ballinger in March 1911. Ballinger had just resigned from his post as secretary of the Interior, unable to escape the lingering consequences of his role in one of the major controversies in the history of the conservation movement. While serving as Interior secretary, Ballinger had been accused of misconduct involving claims on valuable coal lands in Alaska. At stake was not just the fate of these specific plots in Alaska, but also the role of government in controlling the nation's lands, and the continued supremacy of the conservation platform built up by **Theodore Roosevelt**, Taft's predecessor. With decisive and strong moral leadership, Roosevelt had drawn the public's attention to its dwindling natural resources. This presidential advocacy—combined with the publicity magic of his friend and head of the U.S. Forest Service, **Gifford Pinchot**—had created a vibrant and expanding conservation movement. But by the time Taft and Ballinger took office in 1909, the movement had grown so broad that, without the dynamic leadership of Roosevelt, it became difficult to control. Taft and Ballinger had fundamentally different views of conservation than Roosevelt and Pinchot, and their rise to power threatened to fragment the already splintering conservation movement. Pinchot, still serving as chief forester, wrestled through several power struggles with Ballinger in his fight to keep the Roosevelt policies alive. When rumors of misconduct involving coal land claims began to circulate around Ballinger, Pinchot used them to try and agitate the conservation movement back into one cohesive force. And though it was never conclusively proven that Ballinger had committed any wrongdoing, he was vilified for favoring private business interests at the expense of public resources. Ballinger never lived down the public criticism following the controversy and it also tainted Taft's political future, costing him the re-election in 1912.

Richard Achilles Ballinger was born on July 9, 1858, in Boonesboro (now Boone), Iowa, to Richard H. and Mary E. (Norton) Ballinger. His father, an abolitionist, studied law in the office of Abraham Lincoln and fought in the Civil War. When young Richard was only 6 years old, he spent several months with his father in a soldier's camp at Milliken's Bend, near Vicksburg, Mississippi. The soldiers kept him amused by fashioning a drum for him out of an old box, which he sometimes employed to "accompany" the musicians at the head of the regiment. At an early age he earned a reputation as a fighter prone to boisterous outbreaks. On one occasion he saw a soldier "bucked and gagged" for chasing his officer with an axe. This was a particularly harsh form of military disciplinary action in which a soldier was made to sit on the ground with a rifle passed under his knees with his elbows crooked under each end of the rifle. With his hands and ankles securely tied and mouth gagged, the soldier might be kept in that position for six to twelve hours—the circulation all but stopping in his limbs—and would often be unable to walk when cut loose. After witnessing this punishment, which sometimes left a soldier sobbing uncontrollably, the 6-year-old Ballinger repeated the treatment on a young black boy.[2]

After the war, the Ballinger family moved to Nilwood, Illinois, where Richard's father went into the sheep business. Richard, accompanied by a sheep dog, spent long dusty days herding the sheep over the central Illinois prairies. Later his father was appointed postmaster of the nearby town of Virden, Illinois. Richard attended school only sporadically. His school experiences brought out more examples of his characteristic bursts of irrepressible energy: He once thrashed a boy for mistreating his dog, and was then punished in kind by the teacher. When he wasn't in school, he earned money by running a news-stand in the corner of his father's post office; in the evenings he sold newspapers on the street. Richard, Sr. eventually bought a small weekly newspaper and put his son to work setting type and working the handpress.

Richard, Sr. moved on to cattle raising, compelling the family to move to Larned, Kansas, when Richard was 15. He proudly called himself a cowboy after three years riding herd from the saddle. Once, out on the range near Rattlesnake Creek, as he prepared to spread his blanket for a nap, he first had to dispatch several rattlesnakes. This encapsulated his pugnacious personality so well that it became part of his reputation: When he entered political life some years later, he would refer to the trampling of his political enemies as "killing snakes." Throughout his youth, his education was spotty, but in Larned he was able to cobble together some knowledge of Greek and Latin—studying Latin with a local hospital steward and Greek with a cler-gyman. He also used his time herding cows to commit to memory some of the poetry of Robert Burns. Taking an opportunity to earn some money for college, Richard worked for two years as deputy clerk in the office of the county clerk and treasurer of Larned. This money bought him three years of study divided between the University of Kansas at Lawrence and Washburn College in Topeka. From there he worked his way through Williams College in Williamstown, Massachusetts, graduating in 1884 at the age of 26. Two years later, on August 26, 1886, he married Julia A. Bradley, a woman from a prominent family of Lee, Massachusetts and the sister of one of his class-mates at Williams College. They eventually had two sons, Edward B. and Richard T. Ballinger. That same year, Ballinger was admitted to the bar at Springfield, Illinois. In 1888 he began practicing law as the city attorney of Kankakee, Illinois, where his father ran a newspaper.

After a year in Kankakee, Richard and Julia and Richard's father moved to Decatur, Alabama, a boomtown nestled on the banks of the Tennessee River. Having been selected as the eastern terminus of the first railroad line west of the Appalachian Mountains, Decatur was growing rapidly and had become a center of economic opportunity. This suited the young upstart Ballinger per-fectly. Describing what he had going for himself at that early stage in his life, he said, "I had nothing but nerve and energy and an optimistic view of the fu-ture."[3] He set up a general law practice and also went into business with his father opening a nail factory called the Southern Horse Nail Company. Since his wife's family was highly respected back in Lee, Massachusetts, Ballinger often went there to sell stock in his company and to persuade families to move to Decatur and work for him. But the nail factory was not prosperous. Ballinger had bought second-rate machinery to outfit the factory, and when mechanical problems arose, failure soon closed in. Gathering his family, Ballinger cut his losses and moved west to Port Townsend, Washington, leav-ing behind unpaid debts accrued to his bankrupt factory.

Starting over on the West Coast, Ballinger again began practicing law, going in with a relative and creating the law firm Ballinger & Ballinger, which
dealt almost entirely with mercantile collections. Though rumors would
later circulate about some of Ballinger's shady dealings, he was also ascend-
ing, rung by rung, a career ladder that would one day boost him into the
president's cabinet. From 1890 to 1892 he served as a U.S. court commissioner, during which time he tried several Chinese exclusion cases.[4] In 1892,
while serving as chairman of the Port Townsend bar association, charges of
corruption were brought against a local superior court judge. Impeachment
proceedings failed in the legislature, but the judge was not re-elected, and in
November 1892, Ballinger was elected to replace him. He served as judge of
the superior court in Port Townsend from January 1893 until January 1897.

In 1898, Ballinger moved into the nearly riotous hubbub of Seattle. Standing as a portal into and out of Alaska during the fervor of the Gold Rush,
Seattle was then experiencing a constant flood of people. Ballinger continued
to practice law, which brought him into contact with many influential people in the region. Though ambitious and determined, he never sought out political stature for himself, and in fact throughout his life would only hold
public office with some reluctance. He nurtured an inherent suspicion of
power, a predisposition that would one day make it hard for him to accept
President Roosevelt's heavy-handed interference in public land policy. Instead, he felt more comfortable upholding the law through his private practice and attempting to secure retribution for the wrongdoings of others.
Impatient with the corruptions of society, such as gambling or prostitution,
he sought to punish and reform the individual, not the broader societal
causes for corruption that a politician or policymaker might attempt to
address.

Seattle at that time provided ample opportunities for chastisement of the
immoral. Enlarged by a transient population of gold seekers and prospectors
whose luck had turned against them, the city saw a growing redlight district
and increased gambling. Civic leaders professed concern. Ballinger, propelled by his sense of righteousness, stepped into the fray and in 1904 he was
elected mayor of Seattle on the Republican ticket. He served only one two-
year term, and by many accounts his efforts turned the city back around.
"After two years of vigorous effort, organized vice was driven underground,
the more obvious bribery and corruption in government were eliminated,
and the affairs of the city were organized along 'sound business principles,'"[5] wrote James Penick, Jr., in *Progressive Politics and Conservation:
The Ballinger-Pinchot Affair*. One term was enough, and in 1906 Ballinger
returned to private practice. However, the success of his leadership had drawn
interested glances from around the country and had even prompted an old
college classmate from Williams, James R. Garfield, to begin a sporadic
correspondence with him. At the time of Ballinger's mayorship, Garfield was
President Roosevelt's commissioner of corporations, but he soon thereafter

moved up to the post of secretary of the Interior Department. As such, Garfield had a considerable influence in guiding and implementing Roosevelt's conservation goals, which had become the cornerstone of his domestic policy.

Roosevelt was unabashed in exerting his executive powers to help shape the role of government concerning federal lands at a time when public perception of these lands was evolving. In the first few decades after the Civil War, when economic expansion and development were widespread, a sense of disillusionment had begun to creep across the country. It was beginning to dawn on many Americans that the land and resources of the nation were passing into the hands of wealthy corporations. American society and government had to begin grappling with issues of industrial capitalism and governmental control—a struggle that defined the foundation of the Progressive Era. Roosevelt aroused the electorate with his guiding principle that federal lands in the public domain should be protected for the general welfare of the nation, not for private interests. In helping to carry out Roosevelt's vision, Interior Secretary Garfield wanted to recruit strong leaders to governmental offices. Impressed with Ballinger's record in Seattle, Garfield tried to convince Ballinger to come to Washington, D.C., to head the General Land Office (part of the Interior Department). The position had already been offered to two other candidates who had both declined. Ballinger at first declined too. Roosevelt knew almost nothing of Ballinger, except that Garfield recommended him and that he was a westerner—something of an unspoken requirement for the position. Also, Ballinger had several attractive assets: He ran an established, lucrative law firm; he had the respect of the bar as the author of two widely known law books (*Ballinger on Community Property* and *Ballinger's Codes and Statutes of Washington*); and he had become expert in handling legal questions regarding mining, landownership, transportation, and use of natural resources—issues that the Land Office dealt with closely. One account holds that Roosevelt was won over by Ballinger's reputation for killing snakes: the first time literally, out on the range of Kansas, and the second time figuratively, during the reform of Seattle.[6] When Garfield and Roosevelt both personally beseeched Ballinger to take the job, he gave in and moved to the nation's capital.

The General Land Office was badly in need of reform. Ballinger's eventual political foe, Gifford Pinchot, who headed the Forest Service and was one of government's most vocal proponents of conservation, often complained loudly that the Land Office was inefficient and archaic. In its history of supervising the sale and disposition of public lands, it had indeed accumulated a few disreputable incidents. When Ballinger inherited the office in 1907, it was his job to eliminate lingering corruption and inefficiencies as he had done with the city of Seattle; he was to integrate the office into a new and improved system of government. At that time, the Land Office still dealt with homestead law settlements (which held that anyone could apply to receive

160 acres of public domain in exchange for working the land for five years), though the spasm of mass subscriptions for settlement land was waning. But whatever its current project, the Land Office—with its mandate to dole out the public domain—worked at odds with the overall tone of the Progressive Era (1900–1917), as well as the Roosevelt administration and its record on the legal interpretations of resource policy often didn't match well with the Pinchot-Roosevelt view of conservation.

In his new post, Ballinger immediately began reinvigorating the dusty political machine that the Land Office had become. He dismissed almost all of the field division chiefs (who oversaw claims investigations) and hired fresh blood. One new chief was 23-year-old Louis Russell Glavis, who was put in charge of the division in Portland, Oregon, which investigated and processed land claims from the Pacific Northwest region. This part of the country presented Ballinger's General Land Office with its most complicated bureaucratic and political snarls. Infamous land fraud problems in Oregon were part of the reason the Land Office had fallen into such ill repute. But for the time being, the office was preoccupied with coal land claims from Alaska. As the frenzy of gold speculation subsided in Alaska, interested fortune seekers had turned toward other mineral treasures, such as coal. At that time, public land laws were still very lax: At the turn of the century, any individual could obtain title to 160 acres of coal lands as long as they followed the correct filing procedure. But this law had several flaws. For one, once the government gave up the title, it no longer had any regulatory authority over the development of that land. Furthermore, since 160 acres was considered too small for a profitable coal-mining enterprise, the law encouraged fraudulent claims.

Concerned with the conservation implications of this law, Roosevelt officially proclaimed on November 12, 1906, that coal lands would be completely withdrawn from further entry, but that claims already filed would still be considered in due course. Four months later, when Ballinger became commissioner of the Land Office, there were 900 such coal-land claims pending. Only thirty-three of them had been "carried to entry," that is, the required fees had been paid and the claims had been filed with proof of complicity with the law. Of all the 900 claims, only these few had any chance of gaining final title, and it appeared as if only the glacial movements of governmental approval processes stood in the way of their success. It was now under Ballinger's guidance that these governmental processes moved forward. Partly due to mistakes in the way he wielded this responsibility and partly due to the political climate of the day, these thirty-three claims—lumped together as "the Cunningham claims"—would haunt Ballinger for the rest of his life.

Clarence Cunningham had been surveying coal fields in Alaska for several years to locate these thirty-three claims comprising 5,280 acres. The other claimants filing with Cunningham were businessmen from around the Northwest—Washington, Oregon, and Idaho—and many already were involved in mining enterprises or sawmills. In order for Ballinger's General Land Office to clear the claims, it had to ascertain whether the Cunningham claimants had entered into any agreement prior to the location of the claims to consolidate their holdings, which would have violated public land laws. Once the claims had been carried to entry, planning to combine claims was no longer illegal. When Ballinger took over in 1907, as part of his crackdown on the Land Office he hired his own special agent to assist the agent already investigating the Alaskan claims. This complicated matters, for it turned out that the two special agents despised each other, which infested their joint effort with thorns.

Meanwhile, the claimants, who by this point had already cleared the required process of claims entry, began to forge a lucrative agreement with the most powerful financial interest (other than the U.S. government) in the region: the Morgan-Guggenheim syndicate. J. P. Morgan, a financier, together with the heirs to the Guggenheim fortune, had joined forces to create a financial empire, one that already dominated the mining industry and transportation facilities in Alaska. Since one of their Alaskan ventures—a railroad they were constructing to tap their principle copper mine—was hampered by a lack of a domestic coal supply, a collusion with the Cunningham claimants was practically inevitable. In July 1907, representatives of the Morgan-Guggenheim syndicate and members of the Cunningham group entered into an agreement to create a corporation in which the syndicate would provide the money and means to develop the coal fields in exchange for an unlimited supply of coal for their own venture. The agreement was finalized in December 1907, at which time a representative of the Cunningham group, who was also an old acquaintance of Ballinger's, paid a visit to Ballinger in his office to ask about the status of the Cunningham claims. There is no doubt that Ballinger was under some pressure from these claimants—some of whom were his political allies—to follow through with the necessary procedures in a timely fashion so that they might gain title as soon as possible. Ballinger went over the reports from the special agents investigating the claims and decided to proceed with the final steps toward clearlisting the claims.

Louis Glavis, who had been promoted to head the Portland field division of the Land Office as part of Ballinger's reinvigoration campaign, raised a protest when he heard that the claims were on their way to being cleared. One of the field reports from the dueling special investigators was unreliable, argued Glavis, and the other report alluded to a connection between the Cunningham claimants and the Guggenheim companies and recommended further strenuous investigation. On Glavis's request, Ballinger halted the clearlisting of the claims and instructed Glavis to investigate the issue thoroughly. A few months later, in March 1908, after leading the General Land Office for only twelve months, Ballinger resigned from his post and returned to private practice.

Having pulled the Land Office into a high state of efficiency, he left with both Roosevelt and Garfield commending his efforts. But by this time, Ballinger had already antagonized Chief Forester Pinchot, who was throwing all his weight behind perpetuating Roosevelt's conservation policies. For instance, Ballinger had recommended in his annual report that all remaining timber on public domain lands (except in the national forests) be chopped down and sold to the highest bidder so that the clear-cut land could then be disposed of under homestead laws. Pinchot, who stridently believed in a scientific process of sustainable timber harvest, was infuriated by the idea. It is no small irony that Ballinger, as head of the General Land Office, had done exactly what Pinchot had been demanding for years: That is, he gave the office a boost of effectiveness. In the end, this new effectiveness served to create more friction with Pinchot, as it only brought the Land Office more power to encroach on Forest Service jurisdiction.

Ballinger came into the Land Office in vague agreement with current administrative ideas about land management, and in fact regularly professed to being a follower of Roosevelt. This might seem preposterous considering the role Ballinger eventually would occupy as an enemy of Roosevelt's conservation program. But polarizing the two men and their positions on conservation obscures the more subtle reality of their beliefs. During the coal-land controversy, Ballinger was branded as a champion of big business against public interest—though in reality he was more of a champion of the small entrepreneur against big business. His experiences as a small business owner and the perspective he gained from seeing the economic development of Seattle gave him a sympathy for independent interests and a distrust of any entity achieving economic or political dominance. This explains his aversion to the type of broad governmental control of resources favored by Pinchot and Roosevelt; and yet he also did not approve of unchecked exploitation of those resources, nor of monopolistic accumulations of power and wealth by giant corporations, as he was eventually accused. The longer he stayed in public office, the sturdier his beliefs became—their foundation resting on a moderate pro-industry vision infused with a distrust of power. "His own recommendations for conservation called for classification of natural resources to eliminate fraud in their acquisition, legislation to speed up the determination of claims for legitimate claimants, and protection against monopoly. In essence his was a position which favored retaining the broadest possible opportunities for economic development by private capital, with provision for certain reforms to remove unnecessary administrative obstacles to investment,"[7] wrote Penick, Jr.

Ballinger had stayed in the General Land Office for long enough to create tension with Pinchot and others in the administration over these beliefs, and it was likely with some relief that he re-entered the world of private law in 1908. But strands of the entangled web of conflicting interests that made up the issue of the coal-land claims followed him even after he left the Land Office. Given his insider's knowledge of the Land Office—and as a member of a law firm that specialized in land matters—he was quickly sought out by Cunningham claimants and even Cunningham himself. Ballinger gave them legal advice on matters regarding their case and wrote a letter to his successor in the Land Office, recommending that the entries be cleared as speedily as possible. Meanwhile, Glavis had dug up an interesting piece of evidence: Cunningham's journal. Perhaps unaware there was anything damning in it, Cunningham had handed it over to Glavis willingly. Glavis found, in the entry for February 1, 1903 (before the location of the now notorious claims), a description of an agreement existing among each of the claimants "to deed his interest to a company to be formed for the purpose of developing and marketing said coal." This appeared to prove conclusively that the claimants had colluded illegally before the claims had been located. In April 1908, Glavis submitted to the Land Office a copy of the journal, but though his supervisors were now convinced of the fraudulence of the claims, further action on the matter was halted, for various reasons, for almost a year.

In March 1909, Taft succeeded Roosevelt as president. Ballinger had campaigned actively for Taft in the Northwest, and because of his generally congenial relationship with the Roosevelt administration (excepting Pinchot), he was still associated at that time with their conservation goals and policies, which, because of their popularity with the general public, had become a political requisite. It didn't come as a surprise, therefore, when Taft selected Ballinger to be the next secretary of the Interior, replacing James Garfield. Expressing some reluctance to take a public office again, Ballinger nonetheless accepted and took the office in March 1909. Though firmer than ever in his opposition to big government and federal regulation of natural resources, he was still loathe to portray himself as anti-conservation. After taking office, Ballinger trotted out his familiar reassurance: "I pride myself on being a follower of Theodore Roosevelt in the matter of conservation of the public utilities in all parts of the country where the government can regularly and legally interfere," he insisted to the editor of the *Outlook* in May 1909.

But actions speak louder than words, and Ballinger showed his true intentions by almost immediately overthrowing many of the conservation accomplishments of the previous administration. When he was head of the General Land Office, he ranked just high enough to contribute to the dialogue over conservation issues; but as head of the Interior Department he actually could overthrow policy on conservation issues, and that's exactly what he did. In an outright assertion of his own initiative, he officially refused to deal directly with Pinchot, insisting that he would only work with Pinchot's boss, the secretary of the Department of Agriculture. This threw a stick into the gears of what had been a fairly smoothly running machine of interdepartmental communication that had imbued the conservation movement with unification and strength. Ballinger also tried to overturn Garfield's last-minute closure of over 3 million acres of land bordering rivers and streams in the West—a measure that gave Pinchot's U.S. Forest Service regulation of the land in order to prevent private interests from gaining title to waterpower sites. Ballinger believed the withdrawal of lands to be illegal and ordered the land restored to the public domain, making them available again for private entry. After some deliberation in various governmental departments, a large proportion of the withdrawn land was then returned to its previous status of availability to private interests. Objecting fiercely, Pinchot took the matter straight to Taft. At this early stage of his presidency, Taft was still laboring under the powerful shadow of Roosevelt, and though he was more inclined to agree with Ballinger on the matter, he was not yet ready to repudiate openly the policies of his predecessor. A few days after Pinchot met with Taft, Ballinger was forced into the awkward position of having to order the re-withdrawal of the lands.

Ballinger's new and powerful station in the federal government once again brought the Alaska coal-land issue back into his lap. Almost as soon as he was appointed secretary of the Interior, he was visited by a Cunningham claimant and a representative from the American Mining Congress, both of whom pressed him for quick action. Since he had given legal advice to the Cunningham group as a private attorney, Ballinger disqualified himself and passed responsibility for the coal-land issue on to his assistant secretary.

In the meantime, slowly and meticulously, Glavis had been working on his investigation, gathering evidence and preparing to submit a report on his findings. Urged by his superiors to hurry, he felt increasing pressure to complete his report, and when he protested that he didn't have enough time, he was removed from the case in July, 1909. Although he was relieved of his duties, Glavis refused to abandon his cause. Feeling that much was at stake, he took drastic action: He decided to appeal to the Forest Service for help. Considering the enmity between the Forest Service and the Department of the Interior, this was tantamount to treachery. But believing in his cause as he did, Glavis felt he had few other options. On August 5, 1909, he sought out Pinchot, who was attending a conservation congress in Spokane. Glavis offered Pinchot his argument that high-ranking officials in the Interior Department were guilty of misconduct, and presented his accumulated evidence. Perhaps not surprisingly, considering the difficulties Ballinger had created for him, Pinchot almost fell over himself in his haste to turn Glavis's charges into a political weapon to be used against Ballinger. The first step, he decided, was to bring the matter to the attention of the president. He wrote Glavis a letter of introduction to give to President Taft, in which he vouched for Glavis's credibility, saying in his eagerness that he had known Glavis for years (which wasn't true).

Glavis met with Taft and brought forth the following case: Ballinger had been and was using a public office to further the interests of private businessmen, many of whom were personal friends of Ballinger's from his

Seattle days. As commissioner of the General Land Office he had tried to clearlist the claims in spite of their doubtful legality. Glavis also felt that Secretary of the Interior Ballinger still had his hand in the matter and was working behind the scenes to help the claimants. But the most flagrant impropriety was the fact that Ballinger had served as attorney for the Cunningham interests in the interim between holding public offices. Glavis honestly felt the coal claims had not been given enough investigation and was resentful that he had been taken off the case. Because of this, Glavis had come to see the issue very narrowly, and his interpretation of the evidence was as condemning as he could make it, even if it meant highlighting selected facts and ignoring others.

Taft reserved judgement at first, and passed the report on to Ballinger, asking for his side of the story. Ballinger was irate. Rumors about the "scandal" in the Interior Department started flying, and upon returning from a business trip in order to deal with the charges, Ballinger stepped off a train in Washington, D.C., and hissed to the throng of reporters, "I intend to kill some snakes." Taft stood by his Interior secretary. In a letter dated September 13, 1909, Taft exonerated Ballinger of all the allegations in Glavis's report, describing Glavis as clinging to "shreds of suspicion without any substantial evidence to sustain his attack." Three days later Glavis was dismissed from government service for insubordination.

Though the next two months were quiet, they proved to be the eye of the storm. Glavis was not one to let the matter rest, and with an article in the November 13 issue of *Collier's Weekly*, an influential popular magazine, he went public with his accusations. The cover read, "Are the Guggenheims in Charge of the Department of the Interior?" and the article detailed his charges in their entirety. The hurricane had arrived, and Ballinger was lambasted in magazines and newspapers across the country, although even this furor might have abated eventually if only Pinchot had felt satisfied. But he was not one to let the matter rest either, and, in a highly premeditated move, he wrote a long, detailed letter praising Glavis for acting bravely to defend the interests of the people and broadly implying that Taft had made a mistake in exonerating Ballinger. He dispatched the letter to a senator, who then read it aloud on the Senate floor. The underhandedness of the act left Taft no choice but to fire Pinchot. This was exactly what Pinchot had planned. He was a popular and well-known figure, a link to the Roosevelt days, and he knew that his dismissal would fan the flames of the controversy rather than let it die out.

Three weeks later, a congressional investigation started, and it lasted from January 26 to May 20, 1910. Thanks in part to Pinchot's bid for attention, the hearing was watched closely by the press and the general public. The composition of the twelve-person committee favored Ballinger: seven Republicans, four Democrats, and one insurgent Republican. On almost all matters requiring a vote, the committee voted 5 to 7 along these party lines in favor of the Taft-Ballinger side. Glavis was represented by Louis Brandeis, a Boston lawyer with a nearly surreal memory for detail and an enormous capacity for understanding the technicalities of public land law. After absorbing the numbing array of facts and information surrounding the issue, Brandeis presented Glavis's case as that of a devoted public servant watching out for the national interest—managing in the process to incriminate Ballinger as an enemy of conservation.

This was the accusation that would stick, and that eventually would cost Ballinger his reputation. The actual charges against Ballinger—the charges that the congressional committee had to rule on—were never entirely clear and in fact involved considerations of policy that were highly technical in some aspects, and in others, open to interpretation. Some of the questions regarding who was finally "right" or "wrong" regarding the coal land claims are rendered irrelevant because of this ambiguity. The bottom line was that Ballinger wasn't accused by Glavis or Pinchot of corruption, just of being ill-suited for the office he held. The office of Interior secretary put him in charge of all the nation's natural resources and land, ironically (considering his distrust of power) giving him more power over the material interests of the nation than any other cabinet member. In his closing argument, Brandeis summed up the charges that had propelled the issue to such a feverish controversy: "Is Mr. Ballinger a man single-minded, able, enlightened, and courageous, so zealously devoted to the interests of the common people, so vigilant and resolute in resisting the insidious aggressions of the special interests, that to him may be safely entrusted the carrying forward of the broad policy of conservation of our national resources?" Glavis and Pinchot clearly thought not. But the congressional committee as a whole was neither persuaded of any overt wrongdoing on Ballinger's part nor convinced of the need to champion the cause of conservation. Several of the members felt it was merely an elaborate and self-serving scheme on Pinchot's part. Voting along their usual party lines, the majority of the committee cleared Ballinger of the charges and recommended that the Alaska coal land be leased.[8]

But the damage had been done. The result of the highly specific and pointed questions of Brandeis was that Ballinger was forced to take a stand, and his position on conservation finally was brought into stark relief. In the midst of the congressional hearings in the early spring of 1910, Ballinger gave a speech before the State Conservation Convention in St. Paul, Minnesota, in which he attempted to formulate his set of beliefs on conservation and his doubts about the power of the federal government to control the public domain:

> It seems to me that we should not try to impose the whole burden of
> conservation on the general government, but leave it to the states and to
> the municipalities to work out, except insofar as national interference

is necessary to protect national interests; and I want to be understood as opposed to the theory that because the state has not exercised to the full its powers in the matter of reforms, ipso facto the national government must exercise them.[9]

The controversy reached ideological significance when the position of Ballinger clashed with the ideas of Pinchot, who favored a strong national authority in the implementation, regulation, and enforcement of the conservation of natural resources. This clash brought definition to the issue and made it palpable to the general public. The nation had followed the process with baited breath through a popular press that maligned Ballinger at every turn, and had come to its own conclusion that he was an unfit public servant.

With his Interior secretary on the stand, Taft also was forced to step away from the smokescreen of bureaucratic reassurances and define his conservation policies to the nation. Previous to the congressional hearings, Taft had been trying to negotiate the difficult terrain created by the popularity of Roosevelt and had been fighting to maintain unity of action within his administration. The position he and Ballinger took in trying to defend themselves from accusations that they were anti-Roosevelt, and therefore anti-conservation, was in opposition to the policy changes they wrought (which insinuated direct criticism of the former administration). Their position was made more awkward by the growing political momentum of the conservation movement; during the congressional hearings, that tension was broken wide open. The consequences were disastrous to both Taft and Ballinger. Unable to defend his actions in standing behind Ballinger, and with his authority crumbling under the weight of controversy and public scrutiny, Taft failed to win re-election in 1912. Ballinger stayed in his post as Interior secretary for less than a year before resigning in March 1911, due to ill health. He resumed his private law practice in Seattle, but never recovered fully from the strain. On June 6, 1922, he died at his home in Seattle.

Ballinger's place in history rests somewhat on happenstance rather than on the force of his personality or on any unusually momentous actions he took or convictions he held. The comments of a popular news magazine of the day, the *Outlook*, provide a useful explanation of Ballinger's predicament: "The verdict of history will be that he did not understand either the spirit and purposes of the people of his time or the duties and functions of his great office." Or perhaps he understood the spirit and purposes of *some* of the people of his time, but wasn't politically savvy enough to placate the others. In any event, through a series of events both under his control and far beyond his influence, Ballinger unwittingly ended up in the middle of a culminating political and ideological struggle to define the proper approach to natural resource use and to determine the best method for establishing a unified power structure to carry it out. In the end, despite his established reputation as a killer of snakes and an irrepressible fighter, Ballinger was crushed under the weight of public opinion, and will be forever remembered, justly or not, as an enemy of conservation.

NOTES

1. Taft to Richard Ballinger, March 7, 1911, reprinted in "Mr. Ballinger Resigns," *Outlook* Vol. 97 (March 18, 1911), p. 567.
2. Willard French, "Richard A. Ballinger: Secretary of the Interior," *Independent* Vol. 67 (October 28, 1909), p. 964.
3. Ibid.
4. In 1882, a law was passed that prohibited any further immigration of Chinese people. The motivation for the law was the belief that Chinese laborers endangered the American job market, even though Chinese people made up only .002 percent of the nation's population at the time. The Chinese Exclusion Act also became an infamous example of concerns over maintaining white "racial purity," and was finally repealed in 1943.
5. James Penick, Jr., *Progressive Politics and Conservation: The Ballinger-Pinchot Affair* (Chicago: The University of Chicago Press, 1968), p. 21.
6. French, "Richard A. Ballinger," p. 965.
7. Penick, Jr., *Progressive Politics and Conservation*, p. 38.
8. Before resigning, Ballinger introduced a bill advocating that the fate of the Cunningham claims be turned over to a court of law rather than letting the General Land Office proceed. A few months after Ballinger resigned, the commissioner of the General Land Office unequivocally cancelled the Cunningham claims.
9. "Pinchot-Ballinger Hearing," *Outlook* Vol. 94 (March 26, 1910), p. 644.

BIBLIOGRAPHY

A flattering bio-sketch of Ballinger, written just after Taft exonerated him with the September 13, 1909 letter is: Willard French, "Richard A. Ballinger: Secretary of the Interior," *Independent* Vol. 67 (October 28, 1909), pp. 963–965. Ballinger's early business enterprises are discussed in "Some Lighter Aspects of Ballinger," *Collier's Weekly* Vol. 44 (March 5, 1910), pp. 22–23; and C. P. Connolly, "Ballinger, Shyster," *Collier's Weekly* Vol. 45 (April 9, 1910), pp. 16–17. Glavis's account of Ballinger's misconduct during the coal-land claims investigations is in L. R. Glavis, "The Whitewashing of Ballinger," *Collier's Weekly* Vol. 44 (November 13, 1909), pp. 15–17. Another look at the Ballinger-Pinchot controversy, one that exonerates Ballinger of wrongdoing, is H.L.C. Ickes, "Richard A. Ballinger, an American Dreyfus," *Saturday Evening Post* Vol. 212 (May 25, 1940), pp. 9–11+. Also see "Conservation in Dispute," *Review of Reviews* Vol. 40 (October 1909), pp. 398–400; "Secretary Ballinger and Our National Resources," *Outlook* Vol. 93 (November 13, 1909), pp. 617–618; "Can This Be Whitewashed Also? (New Quagmires for Ballinger)," *Collier's Weekly* Vol. 44 (December 18, 1909), pp. 8–9; "Pinchot-Ballinger Hearing," *Outlook* Vol. 94 (March 26, 1910), pp. 641–644; and "Mr. Ballinger Resigns," *Outlook* Vol. 97 (March 18, 1911), p. 567. For an overview of the controversy, albeit one that favors the Pinchot viewpoint, see Alpheus Thomas

Mason, *Bureaucracy Convicts Itself: The Ballinger-Pinchot Controversy of 1910* (New York: The Viking Press, 1941). A more balanced and nuanced perspective can be gained from the excellently written work of James Penick, Jr., *Progressive Politics and Conservation: The Ballinger-Pinchot Affair* (Chicago: The University of Chicago Press, 1968).

GIFFORD PINCHOT
(1865–1946)

Conservation is the application of common-sense to the common problems for the common good, and I believe it stands nearer to the desires, aspirations, and purposes of the average man than any other policy now before the American people.

—Gifford Pinchot

Not many people get the opportunity to create an entirely new profession and then watch that profession achieve powerful national status during their lifetime. Gifford Pinchot, a true crusader, devoted his life to the science and politics of forestry, a field totally new to the United States in his time. And as he ushered in a brand-new concept—the management of the nation's forests—he also helped usher in a brand-new movement: conservation. Pinchot did not believe that in order to protect the natural world humans must be excluded. He knew that for humans to prosper, even just to survive, they must successfully make use of the natural environment—and in this way he differed from preservationists who wanted forests and wilderness to be completely sealed off from human industry. As he wrote in his book *The Fight for Conservation*, "Conservation demands the welfare of this generation first, and afterward the welfare of the generations to follow."[1] In other words, the land and the people must be treated equitably. Conservation, to the pragmatic Pinchot, meant the greatest good for the greatest number of people.

Gifford Pinchot was born at his family's summer home in Simsbury, Connecticut, on August 11, 1865. His parents, James Wallace Pinchot and Mary Jane (Eno) Pinchot both came from wealth, and added to it through James's business selling fine interior furnishings. He sold mainly to hotels, and his business grew so successfully that he would later confess to being embarrassed by how far out of proportion his profits were from his original investment. James and Mary had four children, Gifford (the eldest), Antoinette (Nettie), Amos, and a fourth child—a daughter—who died of scarlet fever at the age of 2. The first home Gifford knew was a red-brick house at stylish Gramercy Park in New York City.

Gifford's parents ran in exclusive circles, continually sought out social activity, and counted among their friends some of the most celebrated people in the country. Civil War hero General William Tecumseh Sherman was their close friend and traveling companion in Europe, as was the famous Hudson River School painter Sanford Gifford, after whom the Pinchots named their first son. The Pinchot children grew up surrounded by the privileges of a wealthy upbringing: a French governess; extended holidays at family homes in Pennsylvania, New York, and Connecticut; and frequent travels in Europe. The Pinchots had special family ties to France in particular: Gifford's paternal grandfather, Cyrille Constantine Désiré Pinchot, was a captain in the army of Napoleon before immigrating to Pennsylvania in 1816. The Pinchots spent three years in France—from Gifford's sixth year to his ninth—and what he lost in terms of consistent schooling during this time he gained in cultural breadth through his immersion in French life. He and his younger siblings studied art, dance, and literature, and became fluent in French. For the next five or so years, the family traveled between Europe and their homes in the United States, all the while cultivating in their children an appreciation for pastoral landscapes and the beauty of the rural frame of reference.

At that time in post–Civil War society, the roar of industrialization was getting louder, and cities grittier. Pinchot's parents, like others in genteel society, often escaped to the countryside to assuage their discomfort with the burgeoning of commerce and the resulting denser, more polluted cities. In 1879, when Pinchot was 13, they went into the Adirondacks for a two-week vacation, staying in lodges in the woods. He and his father made a side trip without the women, hiking and camping their way into a wilder landscape. James Pinchot had given Gifford a fly rod just before the trip, and Gifford was as elated by his first experiences with fishing as he was by their journey into this place of intense natural presence. He gained many impressions on that trip, and through them began forging a relationship with the wilderness.

Upon returning to the United States from another trip abroad in 1881, Gifford's parents decided to stiffen his educational regimen and enrolled him at Phillips Exeter Academy in Andover, Massachusetts, a private college preparatory school. Once there, he developed a fascination with the sciences, a course of study he hadn't been given much exposure to up to that point.

His parents always had been heavy-handed in shaping the contours of Gifford's life, and his mother particularly sought to steer him in a suitably Christian direction. On discovering his growing interest in science, she entreated an acquaintance to write Gifford and counsel him about the proper approach to scientific study. The family friend advised Gifford not to fall victim to a common mistake made by many in the sciences—that of failing to "see God in nature." In years to come, especially when compared to the lyrical naturalist **John Muir**, who wrote of the rich spiritual meaning inherent in the natural world, Pinchot would be accused of being a materialist who viewed the natural world in a completely logistical way. However, in many of his writings, it is clear that he felt a deep affinity to the world's wild places, an affinity born of a complex appreciation.

Though the young Pinchot was thriving at Exeter—involved in lacrosse, football, tennis, and several clubs and student activities—his parents continued to fuss over him. In the winter of 1883–1884 they withdrew him from school citing health concerns: Gifford had been having trouble with weakness in his eyes. The course of treatment they espoused involved sending him into the wilderness of the Adirondack Mountains for several months, accompanied by a tutor, his sister Nettie, and her governess. Despite the bitter cold, Gifford spent most of his time during his "wilderness cure" outdoors: hiking, snowshoeing, and learning to shoot and to find his way in the woods. The cure worked and he regained his strength, though he ended up staying out of school for an entire year. But despite the gaps in his education, he passed the entrance exam for Yale University—though with five "conditions," or extra academic requirements he needed to fulfill before he could be admitted. He successfully completed these by the fall of 1885, and began taking classes.

Sometime during the summer before Gifford began his college career, his father, with one pointed query, set Gifford on a path that eventually would have national consequences. "How would you like to be a forester?" James asked his son, a question outside of the realm of any existing possibilities at the time. Gifford took immediately to the prospect. That the science of forestry was unheard of in the United States did not deter him from wholeheartedly agreeing to pursue it as a profession. For two generations, the Pinchot family had been interested in forested lands, beginning with Gifford's grandfather, Cyrille Pinchot, who had made large profits from clear-cutting wooded areas and processing the lumber in his own sawmills. James, Gifford's father, took a broader and less mercenary interest in forestry, and was especially intrigued by the practice of it in Europe, where it had developed into a respectable discipline. The United States, with its birthright of vast timberlands, had less incentive to study scientific management practices, and therefore had a vast ignorance of trees and their ecology. But time was rapidly running out for these timberlands, especially in the East. In fact, by the last half of the nineteenth century, the great eastern forests were nearly logged out, and some people began to raise concerns. In 1875, the American Forestry Association (AFA) was founded by a group of horticulturalists and laypersons to address the future of forested land in the United States. James Pinchot was actively involved in bringing forestry to the attention of Americans, publishing various articles on the topic and serving for a while as vice president of the new AFA. James conveyed to Gifford a belief that America was in need of a basic understanding of the principles of stewardship, care, and forest management. When encouraging his son to take up forestry as a profession, he was asking him to plunge into a field that was relatively unknown in the United States, and therefore potentially impractical for making a living—but he was also sharing his own passion. For his own part, Gifford relished the chance to break new ground, perhaps because he would have a chance to be of service, perhaps because it afforded him the opportunity to make a name for himself and gain national attention. "I shall have not only no competitors, but even a science to found," he wrote to his parents from Yale. "This surely is as good an opening as a man could have."

Pinchot's resolve was bolstered by the writings of **George Perkins Marsh**, a scholar and proponent of resource conservation. On Pinchot's twenty-first birthday, in August 1886, his parents bought him an 1882 edition of Marsh's *The Earth as Modified by Human Action* (originally published in 1864 as *Man and Nature; or Physical Geography as Modified by Human Action*). This book was written after Marsh had spent years overseas studying how human activity had inflicted destructive alterations on the land, sometimes even to the point of causing the collapse of certain civilizations. Showing an incredibly advanced understanding of forest ecology, Marsh outlined the consequences of deforestation: erosion, desertification, siltation of streams, reduced soil fertility, and damaged watersheds. He warned of the dangers of careless land-use practices and emphasized the fact that environmental problems can escalate to the point where resource-based economic systems may self-destruct. While his book was met with acclaim in the United States, most Americans were complacent about their wealth of natural resources—trees included—and were not fully ready to heed the warning about conservation. Marsh still had hope for the nation, however, and mixed into his book a healthy dose of optimism, arguing that the lessons of past cultures need not be repeated and that through careful forestry practices America had the opportunity to become "a well-ordered and stable commonwealth, and, not less conspicuously, a people of progress." These ideas framed the goals of the Pinchot family, and buoyed Gifford along in his aspirations.

He was enjoying his time at Yale, quickly making friends and reveling in the pranks and rambunctiousness of an active social life. He also had joined Bible study classes and was heavily involved in the local Young Men's Christian Association (YMCA)—to such as extent that he even began to consider switching his career path away from forestry toward devoting his life to being a missionary. His father, who had come to assume Gifford would be traveling to Europe after college to study scientific forestry thoroughly, felt a bit shaken by Gifford's hesitance, especially when Gifford was offered the position of general secretary at the Yale YMCA and gave it serious thought. But in the end, Gifford reaffirmed his earlier adventurous attitude toward founding a new science. At his commencement in 1889, having won the Townsend Prize for debate, he was invited to speak at his graduation. Instead of speaking from the script he had written, he impulsively conveyed his belief in the importance of forestry, for the first time publicly declaring his intention to make it his lifework.

This meant he would have to leave the United States for a while to gain what knowledge he could in Europe. In October 1889, he boarded a ship to England with $600 and the intention of finding some books on forestry and perhaps even meeting some of their authors. He had no previous connections with anyone in the profession in Europe and was setting an unprecedented course—a revelation that occasionally gave him moments of doubt. Generally self-confident, he managed to ignore these occasional doubts and seek out trained foresters in England and France. He also eventually made his way to Bonn, Germany, where he met Dietrich Brandis, a retired forester who was widely recognized as a leader in the field. Brandis took Pinchot under his wing and would in time become an influential mentor through Pinchot's early career. Brandis recommended that Pinchot attend L'Ecole Nationale Forestière in Nancy, France—a school established in 1824 to train students to manage forests for the benefit of the nation. Pinchot enrolled right away. And though he chafed at many of his classes and held most of his fellow students in contempt for what he perceived to be a lack of respect for the profession, he did gain a new understanding of forestry as a type of agriculture. Trees could be managed like a crop, he realized, using a rotational system of cutting and planting that could be supervised in such a way to guarantee a steady supply of lumber.

After thirteen months of study in Nancy, Pinchot felt he had gained all the knowledge he could and returned to the United States at the end of 1890, eager to find out where he stood and what he could begin to accomplish. Things were different in America: Not only were the forests in a much younger stage ecologically, but, in their haste to conquer the wilderness, Americans had not stopped to consider the idea that forests could be cut without being completely destroyed. Pinchot was unsure of how easily his European ideas and methods would translate, but soon realized what a challenge awaited him in America, where policy changes had to move through the sluggish channels of public opinion. Despite the common sense of his basic approach—that proper scientific management of a forest could make timber harvesting both profitable and sustainable—he faced years of hard work before he would begin to win the country over to his conservationist principles.

And where to start? During his last year at Yale, he had submitted a proposal to the chief of the Forestry Division in the U.S. Department of Agriculture (USDA), offering to work there free of charge so he could learn the ins and outs of the office and scope out any future prospects it might hold for him. Though his studies in Europe postponed this plan, he renewed the possibility once he was home again, and this time he was offered the post of assistant forester, a good shoe-in for the position of chief.

The groundwork for the creation of the Forestry Division had been laid in 1876, when Congress authorized the USDA to conduct a study of the status of the nation's forests. The result was three highly detailed and meticulous reports on America's forests and the forest-product industry, and the founding of the tiny unit within the USDA that officially became the Division of Forestry in 1881. After consulting with Brandis and his mother, Pinchot accepted the job with the division, but with the request that he not start for six months. In the meantime, he knew he must rectify what had become something of an embarrassment to him: Despite all his foreign travel, he had never been west of the Alleghenies in his own country. In order to gain national distinction as a forester, he needed to acquaint himself with the nation's forests. Taking a winding train route, he set off on a three-month tour through the South and Southwest and into California, stopping for longer explorations of the Grand Canyon and Yosemite, then along the Pacific coast and back to New York through parts of Canada. But upon his return, instead of jumping feetfirst into his new position at the Division of Forestry, he stalled. He had received counsel from influential family friends and from his father advising him against taking the job after all: The Division of Forestry had no standing as of yet, and would perhaps taint Pinchot by association.

While stalling, he received a titillating invitation. George W. Vanderbilt, heir to one of the biggest fortunes in the country, offered Pinchot the job of managing 5 thousand acres of his forestland on his Biltmore estate near Asheville, North Carolina; Pinchot quickly accepted, bowing out of his previous commitment to the Division of Forestry. He began work in January 1892. Vanderbilt had already hired **Frederick Law Olmsted** as a landscape architect to work out an aesthetically pleasing vision for Biltmore's forest. Olmsted was well known for designing New York City's Central Park, Brooklyn's Prospect Park, and parks in Chicago, Boston, and Washington, D.C. His progressive designs sought to harmonize urban spaces by introducing natural areas and greenery into cities that were suffering from the increasingly dirty and crowded effects of the Industrial Revolution. Olmsted believed that nature and culture were intertwined, and that humans are attracted to a certain perception of nature: wild and untamed, yet also aesthetically pleasing and not *too* wild. In other words, he sought to strike a balance between the wild and the civilized, a balance that would humanize nature at the same time that it naturalized human-constructed landscapes.

Pinchot's job was to implement the vision, to do the groundwork necessary to make the plan unfold. His own vision of landscape management was well matched to Olmsted's, at least in terms of aesthetic purpose. Because his parents indoctrinated in him at an early age the idea that a pleasing landscape is one that combines scenic nature and a careful human hand, he saw forestry as a way not only to raise a profitable crop of trees, but also to beautify the land for human pleasure. In this respect, he was the perfect candidate for working closely with Olmsted. However, Pinchot's lack of experience became evident during this experiment in land-use planning. Olmsted had hoped that the outcome of his and Pinchot's work at Biltmore would serve as a prototype for management of landscape across the nation, but the capacity of the Biltmore forests to turn a profit under Pinchot's management was not immediately evident. For the Chicago World's Fair in 1893, Pinchot published a seemingly positive report titled *Biltmore Forest*, in which he claimed that his forestry practices had produced income. But his bookkeeping methods were suspect, and others in the profession knew better than to believe his claims.

That Pinchot still had learning to do was further evidenced in 1895, when he helped a German forester named Carl Schenck cut lumber at Biltmore using scientific forestry techniques. Pinchot already had expressed the desire to resign his post at Biltmore in order to start up an office as a consulting forester in New York City, and Schenck had been hired to replace him. During the transition, Pinchot and Schenck worked together to plan the logging of a new tract of land that Vanderbilt had purchased in the Pisgah Forest. Pinchot decided to float the logs down Big Creek to Mills River, and then to French Broad River, which would take the logs to Asheville for processing. But he underestimated the force of the water's release, especially when spring rains augmented the normal streamflow. The logs rushed down Big Creek and rammed into the opposite bank of Mills River, causing heavy damage and unleashing a torrent of lawsuits. The ecosystem of Big Creek was devastated, prompting Schenck to despair over the direction American forestry might be headed. Pinchot, on the other hand, qualified the damage done to the landscape by emphasizing the inexperience of the men on the logging crew, and audaciously summed up the operation as a "good job."

Pinchot seemed untroubled by insecurities and doubts, even during these early phases of his career. He was also sustained by the strength of his belief in forestry as a science and his belief that the forests were there to serve a useful purpose to humans. He didn't subscribe to the idea that a perfect forest is an untouched forest. In fact, he wrote in his autobiography, *Breaking New Ground*, that the "friends of the forest" who want to save every tree have it all wrong: "Their eyes were closed to the economic motive behind true Forestry. They hated to see a tree cut down. So do I, and chances are that you do too. But you cannot practice forestry without it."[2]

On this point, Pinchot represented a significantly different viewpoint than John Muir, the naturalist who fought for the creation of Yosemite National

Park and for the preservation of forests and wildlands. Much has been made of the adversarial nature of their relationship and how their ideological and political opposition helped define the interpretive framework of the pliant early twentieth-century conservation movement. When these two men first met, however, they esteemed each other highly, and were good friends and hiking companions. Their first meeting came in 1892 in the Adirondacks in Hamilton County, New York, where they were exploring a large tract of forestland owned by Vanderbilt's brother-in-law. After spending several days hiking through the woods together, Muir had made such a positive impression that when Pinchot returned to Biltmore, he sent Muir a large hunting knife as a token of his admiration.

But it was in the summer and fall of 1896, as they traveled through the American West as part of the National Forestry Commission, that Muir and Pinchot had a better chance to get acquainted. Created by President Cleveland's administration, the commission's purpose was to evaluate western forests and to explore the possibility of setting aside some of these lands to protect them from logging and grazing. Pinchot served as the commission's secretary, and Muir came along in an ex officio capacity. For three months the commission toured through Montana, Oregon, California, Arizona, New Mexico, and finally Colorado, before returning home to write their final report. During that time Muir and Pinchot had plenty of opportunity for male-bonding and schoolboy-type stunts. In the Grand Canyon, for example, they snuck off from the rest of the commission for a day of exploration together, reveling in the canyon's beauty and experimenting with different visual perspectives by doing handstands. They stayed out all night, alternately talking and sleeping under the cedars and pines at the canyon's edge. As dawn broke at 4:30 A.M., they crept back to their hotel rooms like truants. Muir had become not only a friend, but a mentor of sorts to Pinchot, and their subsequent letters reveal a well of mutual respect and affection. While serving on the commission, they not only developed a personal bond, but also seemed to be political allies, as both men were eager to protect forests from unregulated private exploitation.

But this close affinity between the two men began to fray when it came time for the commission to write its final report. Muir's main concern was that the forests be preserved—protected by the government as sanctuaries where nature would be allowed to run its course free from any human intervention. Like Muir, Pinchot wanted the government to protect the forests from runaway private development, but he also wanted them to be managed— in other words, available (with appropriate supervision) to commercial interests. In the formulation of these differing viewpoints, the separation between preservation and conservation was born. Pinchot desired the creation of a civilian service, a trained force of foresters, to administer and regulate the use and protection of these federal forest lands. Out of this concept the U.S. Forest Service eventually would emerge, but in 1896 the idea was too new.

Most of the commission, along with Muir, argued against this type of system, advocating instead for the inviolable closure of forest reserves, which would be defended and policed by the U.S. Army. The recommendations from Muir's side formed the gist of the final report, though several compromises were made to try to accommodate Pinchot's ideas. Nevertheless, the final report infuriated Pinchot to the point that he nearly wrote a dissenting minority opinion.

Following the recommendations of the report, President Cleveland announced in 1897 the creation of new forest reserves totaling more than 21 million acres throughout the West. This appeared to be a victory for the Muir camp, but in reality the decision created a furor of political clashing and also started the permanent unraveling of good relations between Muir and Pinchot. The fact that they genuinely liked each other probably allowed them to disagree amicably during the negotiations over the final report, but this personal affinity became more and more strained as their political views diverged more and more starkly.

The creation of forest reserves in the West set off a brushfire of rage and resentment among ranchers, miners, and the lumber industry. Throughout the relatively short history of white settlement of the American West, the majority of land was in the public domain, development was encouraged, and the West was viewed as a land of economic opportunity. Timber grabbing and forest devastation were an entrenched and accepted way of life. One of the first attempts to put an end to this way of life came in 1891 when the Fifty-first Congress passed the General Revision Act with a vague amendment (the Forest Reserve Act) giving the president the authority to set aside forest reserves out of the public domain. The passage of the Forest Reserve Act got little public reaction, and a similar apathy had greeted President Harrison's decisions during 1892–1893 to lock up fifteen forest reserves totaling 13 million acres. The implications of the Forest Reserve Act on national policy took a while to register among western business interests. But these implications had become much clearer five years later when the National Forestry Commission's report resulted in further setting aside of forest lands; and this time the action was met with instant defiance that could not be ignored. A result of the fury was that the presidential order was suspended until March 1, 1898, pending congressional hearings. In the meantime, to prepare for the administration of these reserves once the suspension ended, Congress enacted legislation giving broad control over the forest reserves to the secretary of the Interior. Soon after this, Pinchot was hired by the government to act as a "confidential forest agent" to tour the newly appointed reserves, recommend modifications of their boundaries, and plumb the depths of western opposition to their designation. He was also to conceive of a practical plan for establishing a forest service, a task that must have brought him at least a small sense of vindication after losing this battle with the Forestry Commission.

In this capacity, Pinchot ventured west in July 1897. Exploring one reserve in the Rocky Mountains of northwestern Montana, Pinchot reported back to the secretary of the Interior that "public sentiment in the regions I have visited is far more ready to support the reservations than I had ventured to hope."[3] While it was probably a relief for Pinchot to find some support for Cleveland's action, there was no denying the complexity of the issue, and, if nothing else, the stridency of reactions to the setting aside of forest reserves proved the need for some kind of cohesive forest policy. A few weeks after Pinchot submitted his report to the secretary of the Interior, the chief of the Division of Forestry (for whom Pinchot had almost worked after returning from his studies in Europe) resigned, leaving his post vacant. Pinchot was tapped for the position. He still harbored misgivings that the division was ineffectual and unpopular, but eventually was persuaded to take the job. He took office in 1898—inheriting a staff of sixty—and single-mindedly and systematically began turning the department into a highly organized office of 500 workers. Though the Division of Forestry did not have control over the forest reserves, since they fell under the jurisdiction of the Department of the Interior, it did influence the management of private and state-owned forests. And it was not long before officials in the Interior Department were coming to Pinchot's office to ask for advice on how to manage the reserves. Pinchot felt sure that he would successfully obtain the transfer of forest reserves to his department, a goal to which he clung dearly. But it would not happen without a prolonged fight, since many business interests in the West fought the transfer tooth and claw, realizing that forest reserves under Pinchot's governance would be much less vulnerable to plunder.

Recognizing the need for more trained professionals in forestry, Pinchot persuaded his family to donate $150,000 to Yale to start a forestry school. In the fall of 1900, the Yale Forestry School opened and Pinchot was appointed a member of its governing board. At this point he was on the verge of the most glorious and influential period of his career. He had quickly and thoroughly learned the skills of administration and was becoming more and more skilled at the political manipulation of public opinion through the media. His common-sense approach and persuasive style won over many a legislator. Nevertheless, much of the time he needed every ounce of that skill to forge ahead with any of his ideas, since he constantly fought against the heavy weight of status quo public land policy.

At the turn of the century Pinchot received a strong reinforcement in his battle for the cause of progressive conservationism—and from a surprising direction. In 1900, Republican William McKinley was elected president, with **Theodore Roosevelt** as his vice president. Six months after the inauguration, McKinley was assassinated by a deranged anarchist at the Pan-American Exposition in Buffalo, New York; and Roosevelt became president. Pinchot and Roosevelt already held each other in high regard and were mutual admirers of each other's outdoorsmanship, backgrounds, and conservation philosophies. Thus it was no surprise that Pinchot achieved his highest national status during Roosevelt's presidency. The conservation-minded Roosevelt strongly supported (and was easily influenced by) Pinchot's plans for implementing a pro-conservation policy toward natural resources. President Roosevelt and Pinchot were so closely united in these beliefs that Pinchot often wrote Roosevelt's conservation speeches for him, and was always consulted on policy matters regarding the nation's natural resources. The particular brand of conservation espoused by the Pinchot-Roosevelt team came to be regarded in some corners as a compelling example of democracy at work. Unregulated and profligate exploitation of the nation's natural wealth tends to concentrate wealth in the hands of the few; while conservation of these resources as a public trust yields benefits to the general populace. Just as democracy relies on equality of opportunity, conservation (in theory) means making available the nation's riches for all people. This notion was difficult for some to swallow however, since it meant the loss to a centralized authority of local control and, to some extent, the individual primacy so treasured by many Americans. Amidst this tension between self and society, the Roosevelt-Pinchot team forged the nation's first political agenda for conservation. Ever since their efforts, land-use decisions in this country have involved debate and discussion over the proper course to take to balance the goals of conservation and industry.

Roosevelt proceeded to make his decisions based on his belief that the federal government should serve the interests of the citizenry at large, and, with these principles in mind, he established the first national wildlife refuge at Pelican Island in Florida in 1903. He would eventually add over fifty more refuges to the federal system—plus eighteen national monuments and five national parks. In addition, in 1905, with Roosevelt's help, Pinchot finally got his wish: the transfer of the federal forest reserves to the U.S. Department of Agriculture. This entailed the creation of the U.S. Forest Service, a huge political victory for Pinchot, who immediately became its first chief forester. By 1907, the U.S. Forest Service had accumulated 150 million acres in its reserves and was on its way to becoming one of the most powerful bureaus in the federal government.

During these years of glory and power, Pinchot made decisions and political moves that cemented his philosophy of pragmatism and efficiency in resource management. One decision in particular set him forever apart from John Muir's brand of preservationism: his approval of a dam in the Hetch Hetchy valley in Yosemite National Park. Vested interests in San Francisco had been eyeing the Hetch Hetchy as a reservoir for the city's drinking water, but all attempts to build a dam had met vociferous opposition from Muir and the Sierra Club. In 1907, Pinchot wrote a report conceding the natural beauty of Hetch Hetchy, but arguing that its practical use for the people of San Francisco overrode aesthetic considerations. The fight over the fate of the valley burned for several years, until in 1913, the final decision was made and the dam was built, forever flooding the valley that Muir had once compared to a holy cathedral.

In 1907, the Inland Waterways Commission was formed and became a pivotal force in the conservation movement. Pinchot served on the commission with a group of other leaders within the natural resource agencies of the federal government. These men worked closely together, and eventually turned the Inland Waterways Commission into a powerful cadre that promoted ideas of conservation to the Roosevelt administration, and also to the nation. It was the Inland Waterways Commission that came up with a proposal to stage a huge national conference on conservation and to make sure the conference be presented before the eyes of the nation as a highly visible declaration of conservation's importance. The Conference on the Conservation of Natural Resources—held at the White House in May 1908—brought together the governors from all fifty states and some of the most important government officials and scientists in the nation. The conference was a success, both in terms of alerting the states that their resources were vanishing and in dramatically gaining the public's attention.

Pinchot's career entered a new phase when Roosevelt was succeeded in office by William Howard Taft in 1909. Taft differed in many ways from Roosevelt and sought legislation that was antithetical to many of Roosevelt's programs. With Taft, Pinchot no longer had full presidential support regarding aggressive implementation of conservation policy. Taft's appointment of **Richard A. Ballinger,** a former director of the General Land Office, as secretary of the Department of the Interior presented even more challenges for Pinchot since he and Ballinger already had clashed over conservation issues. It eventually became clear that Ballinger and Taft were set on dismantling many of the conservation policies set forth by Pinchot and Roosevelt. Attempting to counteract Ballinger's plans, Pinchot founded the National Conservation Association in 1909, which pressed for implementation of his policies. The following year, Pinchot published *The Fight for Conservation*, a summary of his beliefs about the importance of a careful, governmentally regulated program of conservation for insuring the nation's continued prosperity. He wrote:

> The first great fact about conservation is that it stands for development. There has been a fundamental misconception that conservation means nothing but the husbanding of resources for future generations. There could be no more serious mistake. Conservation does mean provision for the future, but it means also and first of all recognition of the right of the present generation to the fullest necessary use of all the resources with which this country is so abundantly blessed.[4]

Pinchot's final, most decisive conflict with the new administration arose when an official named Louis Glavis from the General Land Office approached him with evidence that the Land Office under Ballinger's supervision had allowed monied interests to file fraudulent claims for coal land in Alaska. Pinchot used his influence to make the claims public, rouse conservationists around the country, and demand a congressional investigation. Taft immediately dismissed Glavis for insubordination, and when Pinchot continued to create a fuss, he too was fired from his post as chief forester. From January 26, 1910, to May 20, 1910, congressional hearings were held, and though in the end the committee exonerated Ballinger, his anti-conservationism was made abundantly clear during the investigation. The controversy, which was followed by the breathless public, cast the Taft administration in a bad light, and ended up splitting the Republican Party and costing Taft re-election. (For complete details on the Pinchot-Ballinger controversy and its consequences for the conservation movement, see the chapter on Richard A. Ballinger.)

Pinchot quickly re-immersed himself into an active civic life after the Ballinger controversy ended. His personal life took on a burst of happy activity as well: In August 1914, at the age of 49, Pinchot married Cornelia Bryce, a politically savvy women's rights activist. They had one son, Gifford Bryce Pinchot, born in December 1915. Cornelia was very active in Pinchot's political career, acting as a strong supporter and adviser to him. During the 1920s and 1930s, Pinchot served two terms as governor of Pennsylvania (1922–1926 and 1930–1934). Throughout the 1920s he also pushed for federal regulation of private forests, but never succeeded. Four times he sought a seat in the U.S. Senate, but failed each time. His commitment to conservation never wavered, nor did his interest in forestry. From its founding in 1900 until 1936, he lectured at the Yale Forestry School. He continued to lead the National Conservation Association until 1923, and participated in many forestry organizations, some of which he had founded.

Pinchot failed to incite the passions and longing for the wilderness that Muir, the dramatic writer and free spirit, did. When the National Wildlife Federation created a Conservation Hall of Fame in the 1960s, Pinchot's name was eighth on the list, well behind John Muir's. But Pinchot opened a new vision of conservation, widening its scope by unapologetically placing humans within the landscape. It was this ability to accept human activities and to fight for the continued ascendancy of American commerce that allowed him to be a successful politician, one who unarguably won many a conservation victory.

After struggling with leukemia, Pinchot died in Milford, Pennsylvania on October 4, 1946. In 1949, the state of Washington renamed the Columbia National Forest the Gifford Pinchot National Forest. But perhaps a more poignant tribute came from the Sierra Club (which was founded by Pinchot's one-time friend and eventual political foe, John Muir). In the Muir Woods, a beautiful grove of redwoods north of San Francisco, the Sierra Club selected the best possible tree and dedicated it to Pinchot with the following plaque:

This tree is dedicated to
Gifford Pinchot
Friend of the Forest
Conserver of the Common-wealth.

NOTES

1. Gifford Pinchot, *The Fight for Conservation* (Seattle and London: University of Washington Press, 1910), p. 42.

2. Gifford Pinchot, *Breaking New Ground* (New York: Harcourt Brace Jovanovich, 1947), p. 28.

3. Ibid., p. 129.

4. Pinchot, *The Fight for Conservation*, p. 42.

BIBLIOGRAPHY

Pinchot's personal papers are archived at the Library of Congress. His zealous estimation of his own stature in the conservation movement led him to save every scrap of correspondence—diaries, journals, etc.—and his collection of papers is awesome in size. His writings include an autobiography, which is also a highly political argument for his views: *Breaking New Ground* (New York: Harcourt Brace Jovanovich, 1947). It was republished in a commemorative edition by Island Press in 1998. He also wrote *Biltmore Forest* (Chicago: R.R. Donnelley & Sons, 1893); *The Fight for Conservation* (Seattle and London: University of Washington Press, 1910); *To the South Seas* (Philadelphia: Winston, 1930); and *Just Fishing Talk* (Harrisburg: The Telegraph Press, 1936). For a biographical study of Pinchot's work and influence on environmental thought, see Char Miller, *Gifford Pinchot and the Making of Modern Environmentalism* (Covelo, CA: Island Press, 2001). Also see the earlier M. Nelson McGeary, *Gifford Pinchot: Forester Politician* (Princeton, NJ: Princeton University Press, 1960). For a further look at the Pinchot-Ballinger conflict, see Alpheus Thomas Mason, *Bureaucracy Convicts Itself: The Ballinger-Pinchot Controversy of 1910* (New York: The Viking Press, 1941); and James Penick, Jr., *Progressive Politics and Conservation: The Ballinger-Pinchot Affair* (Chicago: The University of Chicago Press, 1968). Other examinations of Pinchot's impact on public policy and environmentalism are Michael Williams, "The End of Modern History?" *The Geographical Review* Vol. 88 (April 1998), pp. 275–300; and Sally Fairfax, Lynn Huntsinger, and Carmel Adelburg, "Lessons from the Past," *Forum for Applied Research and Public Policy* Vol. 14 (Summer 1999), pp. 84–88.

AYN RAND
(1905–1982)

Ecology as a social principle . . . condemns cities, culture, industry, technology, the intellect, and advocates men's return to "nature," to the state of grunting subanimals digging in the soil with their bare hands.

—Ayn Rand

Tears in her eyes, 21-year-old Ayn Rand walked off the oceanliner onto a snowy pier on the Hudson River and beheld New York City's skyscrapers for the first time. She had come from Soviet Russia to start a new life in America, having lived through the blood-soaked Russian Revolution of the early 1900s and endured the poverty and sacrifices of a Communist dictatorship. From early in her life she was in love with the tangible evidence of the power of the human mind—such as technology, cities, and industry—while fiercely resisting anything that stood in the way of individual freedom, including the notion of conservation (or as she called it, "ecology"). She disparaged collectivist values and altruism, with their implied sacrifice of individualism, and she forged a writing career by rhapsodizing super-achievers who strive for wealth and success in an industrial world. Calling herself a "radical for capitalism," her promotion of self-interested money-making coincided with the pre-*Silent Spring* period of industry and prosperity following World War II. Although corporate CEOs could appreciate her sentiments, her ideas were antithetical to the communal impulses and

restraints to development inherent in the quietly stirring conservation movement, and therefore made a lasting mark on the environmental debate.

She wrote two mammoth novels, *The Fountainhead* and *Atlas Shrugged*,
and as reviewer Claudia Roth Pierpont pointed out, "[F]ew American novel-
ists since Mrs. [Harriet Beecher] Stowe have had the force or the desire to
turn readers into disciples, to shape political or religious or moral convictions."[1] Rand in fact demanded such loyalty to her ideas that some came to
regard her followers as a type of cult. Her books became known in the publishing world as classic cult novels, receiving little critical acclaim but climbing the best-seller charts and selling steadily by word of mouth. A 1991 joint
survey by the Library of Congress and *Reader's Digest* listed *Atlas Shrugged*
as the second most influential book for Americans today, with the Bible
listed first.

Ayn Rand was born on February 2, 1905, in St. Petersburg, Russia, as
Alissa Zinovievna Rosenbaum. She grew up with two younger sisters in a
spacious apartment overlooking one of the city's great squares. She was
raised Jewish, though in a perfunctory way, and she never fully identified
herself as a Jewish person. Her father, Fronz Rosenbaum, took pride in his
heroic struggle against the poverty of his youth: After working his way
through college, he achieved wealth and success as a chemist. Though Alissa
admired his firm convictions and strong sense of individualism, and though
she would later develop a close relationship with him based on shared political ideas, throughout most of her childhood her father maintained a chilling
emotional distance from his daughters. Their mother, Anna Rosenbaum,
was also distant and disapproving—going so far as to tell her daughters that
she had never wanted to have children and cared for them only out of a sense
of duty. The coldness of her parents undoubtedly had a painful impact on
Alissa's early years: She eventually learned to wrap herself in a protective
cloak of intellectualism and emotional repression. She quickly grasped
the fact that displays of intellectual brightness earned adult attention, and
these displays became her only way to experience any admiration from her
parents. Early in her life she came to equate intelligence with moral worth, a
connection that her future writings would asseverate explicitly. Every bit as
determined as her self-made father, Alissa wasted no time in establishing herself as precociously smart, and by the age of 6 she had taught herself to read
and write.

Reading became a beloved escape. When she was 9 she encountered a
story in a boys' adventure magazine called "The Mysterious Valley," which
held her rapt and riveted. She implicitly recognized that the leading character, Cyrus, totally encapsulated her ideal of the perfect human. Even decades
later she could recall the story down to its smallest details, so impressed had
she been. Cyrus was a strong, dashing British officer who fearlessly fought
an evil rajah in India and avenged his friends. Describing the essence of

Cyrus and her reaction to him, she later said, "There's nothing that I can add in quality to any important love later on that wasn't contained in that. Except that being the first, the intensity was almost unbearable. I was a woman in love in a serious sense. The whole reality around me lost all meaning. If, before, I felt that I was imprisoned among dull people, now it was: they don't know, but I do—this is what's possible."[2] Inventing stories that created similar heroes became a new and abiding passion. She found she could conjure precise and ideal worlds that were filled with important people and were happier and nobler than her own life. Through fiction she could invent and make concrete a reality that fit her values: This goal stayed with her throughout her life and framed her entire adult career as a fiction writer.

The Rosenbaum family spent a six-week vacation in Switzerland the summer after Alissa turned 9. Roaming the majestic mountains there was the first form of physical activity Alissa had ever enjoyed. That summer was idyllic and spiced with just enough adventure to keep the voraciously imaginative Alissa occupied and amused. She later used a similar Swiss setting for the childhood homes of her protagonists, Francisco d'Anconia and Dagny Taggart, in her epic *Atlas Shrugged*. But, as her own family traveled to Paris on their way home, World War I broke out, ending their sun-filled vacation and encasing them in fear as they tried to make their way back to Russia. Through the early months of the war, Alissa and her sisters were sheltered by their parents from its brutal details—and Alissa was usually so deeply engrossed in her writing notebook that she took little notice of what was happening in the world. But eventually the war's atmosphere and its consequences for Russia seeped into her consciousness. Bread lines, shortages of fuel for heating homes in the bitter winters, and increasing outbreaks of violence formed an oppressively bleak backdrop to Alissa's life and came to represent in her mind the natural outcome of a collectivist ideology.

Soon after the Bolshevik Revolution, Fronz Rosenbaum's chemist store was stormed and confiscated in the name of the state. Seeing her father's outraged indignation, Alissa unequivocally determined that Communism was unjust and brutal, and she couldn't fathom why more people weren't as vehemently opposed to it as she was. She was quickly developing a highly romanticized and very black-and-white concept of good and evil, and in fact would later say that "grey areas" were of no interest to her. Out of the hardships of these years was born her opposition to any kind of self-sacrifice or any political system wherein control is imposed upon anyone—and it was a position she never wavered from for the rest of her life. In the fall of 1918, her family picked up the few belongings they had and moved to the Crimean city of Odessa, where they lived for several years in dire poverty, subsisting mostly on millet (though Anna Rosenbaum insisted on finding ways to obtain onions to feed to her family, having read that they could prevent scurvy). Alissa attended high school, where she took classes in American history and discovered that the American system of government was based on principles such as freedom and individualism, which fueled her devout love affair with American culture.

After three years in Odessa, the Rosenbaums returned to St. Petersburg—now named Petrograd. Alissa enrolled at University of Petrograd, which was free to all students. Every day she walked three miles each way to her classes, barely sustained by miserable rations. During her college years she developed a fierce appreciation of Aristotelian logic, deeply scorned the works of Plato and Shakespeare, and discovered the pure escapist pleasure of going to the theater. In the spring of 1924, she graduated with the highest honors and a degree in history. Then, through her mother's connections, she was hired as a tour guide in a local historical museum, a job that meant nothing to her but food and clothing. Depressed by the grimness of life in Soviet Russia, simmering with incandescent intelligence, and fervently devoted to a personal philosophy centered on the virtue of self-interest—which had crystallized for her at the age of 18 and which she would never deviate from for the rest of her life—her existence at the time was defined by the feeling that her real life was being kept at bay by the strictures of those in power.

The following year something happened that provided Alissa with a way out and changed her life forever: A letter arrived for the Rosenbaums from the United States. Relatives who had left Russia a few decades earlier were now writing out of the blue to Alissa's family, inquiring after their welfare and describing an enviable life in Chicago. Nothing could divert Alissa's attention from the new hope that this family connection could lead to starting her life over in America. Over the next twelve months, the two families made arrangements very slowly through the mail, for Alissa's move, while she prepared herself to make use of this tiny window of opportunity. She had recently become enamored of American films, which always depicted glamorous heroes brimming with initiative, and romantic stories of success and prosperity. She formed a plan to make her living as a screenwriter once in the United States.

Finally, in January 1926, Alissa left behind her family, her country, and her life of Russian poverty, never to return. When she disembarked in New York, she had even decided on a new name: Ayn Rosenbaum, after a Finnish writer she had heard about. The few days she spent in New York City were filled with a blazing reverence for the skyscrapers, which she saw as symbols of achievement, and for the purposeful activity all around her. But her relatives lived in Chicago, so for the time being she had to leave New York behind. For the next few months, she stayed in the homes of various relatives, being shunted from one house to another when her strange routines and thoughtless habits became too difficult to live with. She would stay up late into the night typing loudly, oblivious to the noise and disruption she created in the small apartment where the rest of the family tried to sleep. Her obsession with germs led to endlessly long baths and cleansing rituals, which she also conducted at night, again keeping the family awake. Though she wasn't being intentionally rude, her intense self-absorption and her compulsion to succeed as a writer made it impossible for her to intuit the needs of anyone around her.

During this period in Chicago she wrote four movie outlines and formulated a plan to move to Hollywood. She changed her last name as well, partly due to fear that her outspoken anti-Communist message would endanger her family back in Russia once she became famous—something she never for a moment doubted would happen. Sitting at her Remington-Rand typewriter, she latched onto the name "Rand," and Ayn Rand she stayed. Her Chicago relatives made the necessary arrangements to have her visitor's visa renewed, gave her $100 that they could barely afford, and saw her off on her journey to Los Angeles. Rand found a place to live and—through a combination of luck, perseverance, and coincidence—wound up finding work as an extra, for which she earned a stupendous $7.50 a day. Though the screen originals she had written were disparaged as unrealistic and too romanticized, she was not discouraged from continuing her writing, which she felt certain would eventually bring her fame.

One day while at the film studio, she saw an arrestingly handsome man, also an extra, who seemed the perfect embodiment of Cyrus, the British officer in the children's story she had fallen in love with as a 9-year-old. Again she fell in love, this time with a real person, though she didn't even know his name and had few social skills at her disposal for attracting his attention. They met once on the set of a movie, but he could barely understand what she said under her thick Russian accent. Then, months later, they ran across each other in a library and struck up a friendship. Two years later, on April 15, 1929, Ayn Rand and Frank O'Connor were married. Some of their friends suspected an ulterior motive behind the marriage: Rand's visa was about to expire. Rand herself would later joke about it: "Ours was a shotgun wedding—with Uncle Sam holding the shotgun."[3] Soon thereafter she applied for, and received, American citizenship, a status she cherished for the rest of her life.

For three years Rand held down a creatively uninspiring job as the head of the wardrobe department at RKO Studios; and with Frank also working steadily, they entered the Depression in financial security. But Rand longed for an avenue of self-expression and for the recognition she felt was her due, so she began working on a novel called *We the Living*. Set in the Soviet Union in the early 1920s, it featured an aristocratic heroine named Kira (the Russian feminine form of Cyrus) who is single-mindedly devoted to two entities: her work as an engineer and the man she loves. Rand carefully outlined it as both a glaring condemnation of the forced sacrifices of Communism and a glowing paean to the sanctity and value of individual lives. The writing came excruciatingly slowly for Rand, and, in her impatience, she took some time off to write another screenplay, which she thought might bring her enough financial compensation to quit her job at RKO Studios so she could write full time. The result was *The Red Pawn*, an extravagantly romantic tale of a brave wife who saves her husband from a Soviet labor camp. To Rand's delight, Universal Studios bought it for $1,500 early in 1932, though for various reasons it never saw production. But Rand felt the first flush of success with her writing and immediately quit her day job to devote herself to her novel.

In 1933, one more small project interrupted her novel's progress: a play she wrote called *Penthouse Legend*, which she defined as a work of romantic symbolism. A courtroom drama, the play followed the trial of a woman accused of killing her lover and used the gimmick of drawing an actual "jury" from the audience—based on the jury's verdict, there were two possible endings. It premiered in Hollywood in 1934 under the title *Woman on Trial*. That same year a Broadway producer made an offer on the play and she agreed to the contract, which called for immediate production. This necessitated a move to New York City, and in the late fall of 1934, Rand and O'Connor left Hollywood for the big city, a move that thrilled Rand.

Shortly after completing the play, Rand finished *We the Living*, though it would not be published until 1936, after three years of rejection from various publishing houses. It received little praise and never sold well until it was reprinted after she had achieved fame with other novels. But *We The Living* was really just a kind of practice exercise for Rand since it did not yet capture the shining image at the core of her ideology—that of the "ideal man." She knew that, in order to be true to her beliefs, she must attempt a portrayal of the ideal man. Tall, strong, sexually potent, and audacious in his individuality, he must embody her aesthetic, which she defined as "the concept of man as a heroic being, with his own happiness as the moral purpose of his life, with productive achievement as his noblest activity, and reason as his only absolute."[4] In her early notes for the book that would become *The Fountainhead* she wrote that her main purpose in the novel would be a "defense of egoism." This idea, that each person should have ultimate freedom to fulfill their every requirement for comfort and success, left no room for any restraints imposed by broader social concerns such as conservation. Rand didn't explicitly address issues like conservation during these years—partly because the conservation movement was still somewhat submerged—but when it eventually became a more potent force during the 1960s, she uncorked the full venom of her arguments against it.

Howard Roark was the name she chose for the protagonist whom she hoped would bring her artistic aspirations to life in *The Fountainhead*. An ambitious architect of strict artistic integrity, he opts to dynamite the housing project he has designed rather than alter it according to the demands of unthinking bureaucrats. Since Rand had always seen the skyscraper as a symbol of human greatness, architecture provided an obvious and natural framework for the plot of her story. And being in New York City allowed

Rand both the intellectual inspiration of the Manhattan skyline and the opportunity to research the architectural details of her book by working as a filing clerk for the famous New York architect Ely Jacques Kahn—which she did without pay for six months. Peter Keating is another leading character in the book, and is also a striving architect, though nowhere near as self-directed as Roark. Rand used the two men as a study in contrast to further illuminate her standard of the perfect man. Keating's ambition is based on secondhand values and he is easily molded by others, whereas Roark is entirely motivated by internal convictions. In a speech in which he defends his actions in blowing up the low-income housing project rather than let someone alter his design, Roark says:

> I came here to say that I do not recognize anyone's right to one minute of my life. Nor to any part of my energy. Nor to any achievement of mine. No matter who makes the claim, how large their number or how great their need. I wished to come here and say that I am a man who does not exist for others. It had to be said. The world is perishing from an orgy of self-sacrifice.[5]

A huge and taxing project, *The Fountainhead* ended up being over seven hundred pages, and Rand struggled with each page. Her perfectionism and her need to present painstakingly every angle of her argument for individualism slowed the process considerably. As further discouragement, each time she submitted samples of the book to publishers it was rejected as being commercially unviable. Money was running out, and O'Connor didn't have a stable job, so tensions ran high at home. Rand fell prone to sudden fits of rage, not just toward O'Connor, but also toward people who had been her friends—and especially anyone who didn't agree with her philosophy.

Twelve publishers eventually turned *The Fountainhead* down as improbable, controversial, or too coldly intellectual before, finally, Bobbs-Merrill accepted it and gave her a year to complete it. The deadline was January 1, 1943. That year Rand worked grueling hours at her typewriter in a race to complete her book on time. She also worked on weekends as a reader for the story editor at Paramount Pictures to bring in some much-needed money. When her energy flagged, she tried to bolster herself with rich cheeses and chocolates, but often at the end of a long day of work she would collapse in a pile on her bed. In addition, her adopted nation was fighting desperately in World War II, which deflated the joy she felt as she neared completion of her novel. But her efforts bore results, and on December 31, 1942, she carried the finished manuscript to the publishers, filled with the quiet knowledge that it had been written precisely as she wanted it. In fact, she insisted that she be the only one to make any necessary edits, and, amazingly, her publishers agreed.

In May 1943, the book came out and the negative reviews came in. Many reviewers were uncomfortable with the arrogance of the leading character and with his tantrum-like behavior when he didn't get control over his building design—especially given the fact that it was a housing project for the poor. Rand's central idea that "the world is perishing from an orgy of self-sacrifice" went against the superficial American reverence for generosity, philanthropy, and kindness, and was a difficult notion for many to swallow. Sales were very slow at first, which Rand attributed to poor marketing by the publishing company.

The fall after it was first published, Rand's agent informed her that Warner Brothers was inquiring after the movie rights to *The Fountainhead* and wanted to know her price. Insisting she knew the value of her book, she demanded $50,000, a fantastic amount at the time. Ten days later word came back: Warner Brothers had accepted, sending Rand and her husband from penny-scrounging financial worries to luxurious affluence in one day. The contract required Rand to move to Hollywood to write the script, so, in December 1943, they left by train for Los Angeles. They bought a 13-acre ranch in the San Fernando Valley, where Frank's interest in gardening and rural living could thrive, and where he would enjoy the happiest years of his life. Rand in the meantime faced the disappointment of five years' worth of delays to the production of the movie version of *The Fountainhead*, in part because of wartime cutbacks. During those years of waiting in California, she traveled to Washington, D.C., to testify before the House Un-American Activities Committee. Violently opposed to Communism, Rand spoke out against the pro-Soviet movie *The Song of Russia* and the people who made it. Over the years she continued to gain notoriety for her willingness to argue against anything she saw as morally bankrupt Communist propaganda.

When production for the movie version of *The Fountainhead* finally began, Rand was elated with the casting of Gary Cooper in the leading role of Howard Roark. He represented Rand's vision of an American hero, especially in physical appearance. Her positive view of the movie-making process ended there, however, and the months that followed filled Rand with frustration and disillusionment. The actors were not capturing the essence of her characters, the director didn't understand her vision, and she had to fight to keep those in charge from making any changes to her script. The movie premiered in July 1949, and Rand watched it, numb with disappointment, until the climactic scene where Roark makes his speech defending his actions. Rand realized in a flash that the line, "I wished to come here and say that I am a man who does not exist for others" had been cut. She was infuriated and, despite the fact that the movie gained her book a wider audience and increased its sales, she forever resented the movie and the experience of making it.

Even before the movie came out, an underground swell of interest in *The Fountainhead* had begun to spread, largely by word of mouth, and during its first two years in print, sales shot upward. In 1945 alone *The Fountainhead* sold 100,000 copies, and its reign of popularity was only beginning. During the next decade, as Rand's book became more and more well known, post-war America experienced rapid economic growth fueled by military spending, and abundance and affluence began to seem possible to almost everyone. Technology introduced entirely new markets of consumer goods, and a whole new consumer culture was being formed. Rand's urge to champion the cause of unmitigated self-interest was finding a highly receptive audience in this new era of abundance and consumption—an era against which the fermenting environmental movement eventually would rebel.

A new project soon took over Rand's life. It was another novel, and she had begun working on it almost as soon and she and O'Connor had left New York City. Her guiding theme for the new book was "the mind on strike." It explored what would happen if the nation's creative minds withheld their talents and refused to work. These brilliant minds included a distinguished philosopher, a famous composer, and several leading industrialists and powerful businessmen, and all were led to strike by the hero of the novel and Rand's ultimate and exalted tribute to the "ideal man": John Galt. Serene, rational, and contemptuous, Galt convinces these leaders to abandon the work they love so that the world would no longer take them for granted.

Rand set these individuals up as examples of achievement and steely self-esteem, alone in a nation that is decaying intellectually, morally, and economically under an evil system of altruistic values. Altruism was an anathema to Rand: She saw it as a concept that turned people into self-sacrificing martyrs. She left nothing open to interpretation in *Atlas Shrugged*. As reviewer Granville Hicks remarked after the book came out, "[I]t has only two moods, the melodramatic and the didactic, and in both it knows no bounds."[6] She spelled her ideas out through a series of earnest speeches, all justifying her argument for the unhindered pursuit of individual fulfillment and the permanent stamping out of altruism. Galt's speech, her crown jewel, takes up sixty pages and took her two years to write. At 1,168 pages, *Atlas Shrugged* was an epic—in fact, its sheer size and heft seemed symbolic to some of Rand's intention to crush anyone opposed to her message.

Early in 1950, as she worked on writing *Atlas Shrugged*, Rand received a fan letter from a young man who would have an enormous and eventually devastating effect on her life. Nathaniel Branden's letter was filled with insightful and intriguing questions about Rand's previous work. Feeling he deserved a meaningful response, she made an exception to her usual habit of sending fans a form letter, and she wrote him back personally, even inviting him to send her his phone number. This he did, and though she was somewhat ambivalent about it, she called him and invited him to her home. Dashing, articulate, and handsome, Branden charmed Rand with brilliant conversation and was quickly invited back. The next time, he brought his girlfriend Barbara Weidman, and before long the young blond couple was a fixture at Rand and O'Connor's house. They all enjoyed philosophical discussions, and, since both young fans adhered faithfully to Rand's ideas, she accepted them and doted on them. Eventually Rand and the couple became quite close, and when Branden and Weidman moved to New York City in 1951 so that Branden could attend graduate school, Rand and O'Connor followed soon thereafter, citing the desire to maintain a close proximity to their young friends. When Branden and Weidman got married in 1953, Rand and O'Connor were matron of honor and best man.

Realizing by then that *The Fountainhead* had become a sleeper hit and that she actually was developing a devoted following, Rand began feeling the first thrills of triumph. Her close professional and personal relationship with Branden was becoming similarly heady. In 1954, when the Brandens, Rand, and O'Connor took a road trip to Toronto, Branden and Rand realized with a sudden urgency that they had fallen in love. He was 24 and she was 49. They embarked on an affair, but only after calling a meeting with their spouses to announce their intentions. Arguing that they must act according to rational thought, Rand explained that the affair was based on logic and reason and was therefore inevitable. Faced with her calculated arguments and the force of her will, both Frank and Barbara acquiesced. The affair lasted fourteen years.

Atlas Shrugged, Rand's climactic and highly dramatized defense of capitalism, was finally published in 1957. Again critics had very few positive comments and treated it as a romantic drama rather than a work of serious literature. One reason perhaps is that in her obsessive argument for her philosophy she allowed no room for dialogue and instead sneered at anyone (including the scholars who might review her book) who held a different viewpoint than her own. Granville Hicks of the *New York Times* wrote, "Perhaps most of us have moments when we feel that it might be a good idea if the whole human race, except for us and the few nice people we know, were wiped out; but one wonders about a person who sustains such a mood through the writing of 1,168 pages and some fourteen years of work."[7]

After the publication of *Atlas Shrugged*, Rand experienced a bit of a letdown. She was burned out from the long, exhausting years of intensive writing and was discouraged by the thought that she had completed her life work and had no further ambition. But Branden restored her sense of purpose with a new venture: an organization that would present and promote Rand's philosophy (which she had named "Objectivism") through a lecture series. He called it the Nathaniel Branden Institute, and began preparing a course of twenty lectures called "The Basic Principles of Objectivism." Rand fashioned a guiding definition for Objectivism for the growing movement: "Objectivism holds that reality exists as an objective absolute; that reason is man's means of perceiving it, that morality is a rational science, with man's life as its standard, self-interest as its motor, individual happiness as its goal, and a free society as its consequence."

The course drew hundreds of people in New York, and soon study groups sprang up around the country using taped recordings of Branden's lectures.

Rand made herself available during the question-answer period that followed Branden's lectures, and even began to accept public speaking invitations at colleges around the country. The institute became highly profitable, and through the years it claimed over 25,000 "graduates." She and Branden also began a monthly publication called the *Objectivist Newsletter*, which included original essays by Rand, Branden, and like-minded friends, and applied Objectivist analyses of current events, which were beginning to involve environmental ideas. One of the regular contributors was Alan Greenspan, a Rand follower who eventually became chairman of the Federal Reserve Board.

The lecture series brought Rand into frequent contact with admiring minions, and she gloried in the attention. But Rand was a thorny person. Famous for her reluctance to suffer fools, she would fix a person with a level stare, as an egret gazes at a fish. And though her philosophy dictated that people think for themselves, she had a contradictory deep emotional need for unquestioning loyalty to her ideas. For this reason she offended many, and by the end of her life she had few friends left. Her disillusionment spread beyond her social circle, as well, for during the 1960s she felt she was witnessing the moral collapse of a nation that had been built on progress, economic development, and industry. In reaction, she began to call herself a "radical for capitalism." She disparaged hippies for having no thought, no purpose, and for "the inarticulate extolling of emotions above reason, of 'spirituality' above matter, of 'nature' above technology."[8] The arousal of interest in the environment during this era was further cause for scorn, and she redoubled her efforts to defend capitalism against this new threat by writing essays and excoriating environmental activists as "anti-rational." She began writing polemics against what she called "ecology"—her term for the environmental movement. "Now observe that in all the propaganda of the ecologists—amidst all their appeals to nature and pleas for 'harmony with nature'—there is no discussion of man's needs and the requirements of his survival. Man is treated as if he were an unnatural phenomenon. Man cannot survive in the kind of state of nature that the ecologists envision—i.e., on the level of sea urchins or polar bears."[9] Through the Branden Institute, through newsletters and essays like this one, and (indirectly) through her fiction, Rand's ideas were being projected into mainstream American consciousness at a time when environmental questions were becoming more and more part of a national debate.

In 1968, a tortured Branden finally told Rand that he had fallen in love with a much younger woman and that he wanted to end their sexual liaison. Enraged, Rand severed all ties with both Brandens, socially and professionally, and ordered her followers to do likewise. The Brandens eventually moved back to California to escape from the confusion, accusations, and bitterness Rand had unleashed. The infighting also led to a schism in the Objectivist movement, and the Nathaniel Branden Institute was closed. Rand tried to pick up the pieces of the splintering movement and continued to print the *Objectivist Newsletter* for a few years, though after a drop-off in subscribers, she eventually redesigned it and renamed it the *Ayn Rand Letter*. She also published in book form a few collections comprising essays taken from the newsletter and philosophical excerpts from her fiction.

Rand has been criticized for her polemical arguments and for gaps in her philosophical training. She never had any schooling after attending the crumbling University of Petrograd and was notorious for resisting new ideas. Also, her rejection of "grey areas," rather than bolstering the force of her convictions, served to deprive her arguments of subtlety. But though her philosophy was regularly dismissed by the academic establishment, her influence as the environmental movement picked up steam in the 1960s was substantial. As Jeff Walker wrote in *The Ayn Rand Cult*, "[T]hough Rand's works appear to non-Objectivists as neither first-rate literature nor first-rate philosophy, they surely constitute effective propaganda on behalf of capitalism during an era of considerable anti-capitalist rhetoric and policy-making."[10] The main emphases of the new environmental movement included reduced consumption, careful use of natural resources, and increased governmental protections—all "anti-capitalistic" restraints that Rand deplored. In her writings and in speeches she denounced the effects of government intervention (including any environmental regulation), and celebrated the privatization of commerce and industry—both of which are ingredients of classic anti-environmental thought that would be used in arguments against environmental protections for years to come. Appearing at public speaking events and on television wearing a gold pin in the shape of a dollar sign, she proudly symbolized the glorification of material gains. Rand's influence—her celebration of industry, selfishness, and a total separation between the human world and the natural world—helped shape the views of middle-class America, especially during the resurgence of capitalism in the 1980s with its emphasis on deregulation and the accumulation of material possessions. And conservative politicians have admitted to being influenced by Rand's ideology: Former Idaho congresswoman **Helen Chenoweth-Hage,** for example, read her novels and tacitly agreed with their premises.

Rand's opposition to the ideals of the environmental movement could be quite overt, as seen in her essay titled "The Anti-Industrial Revolution,"[11] in which she projects the consequences of allowing environmental concerns to dictate public policy. "A current trend proclaims that technology is man's enemy and should be restricted or abolished. Let us project what this idea would mean in practice." She then paints a pathos-dripping picture of a young family struggling to find any enjoyment in a life filled with restrictive archaic laws. Electrical appliances are banned because "they consume electric power, which contributes to the load of power stations, which contributes to air pollution." The poor working father burns his toast in the oven, and, since cars are outlawed, it takes him two and a half hours to commute to work by public transportation. "The mining of metal has been severely curtailed," so there are no metal lunchboxes or thermoses, and the man must eat a stale lunch and drink cold coffee. The company he works for manufactures paper containers and is stagnating financially because "business expansion has been arrested," and "paper consumes trees, and trees are essential for the preservation of life on earth, and forests must not be sacrificed for the sake of self-indulgent luxuries"—therefore his job and livelihood are in grave jeopardy.

Meanwhile, the man's wife is mired in drudgery at home, with no refrigerator, no disposable diapers, no vacuum cleaners, and no shopping centers because "they despoil the beauty of the countryside." Rand continues to paint it on thickly: "Since there are no canned foods and no frozen foods, she starts cooking dinner three hours in advance, peeling and slicing by hand every slimy, recalcitrant bit of the vegetables." Advances in medicine have been halted, leading to epidemics of diphtheria and the early death of the wife's mother due to a heart ailment, which could have been cured by a pacemaker if environmentalists hadn't insisted upon such a state of technological regression. In Rand's argument, the environmental movement posed a dire threat to humankind. She perceived its goal to be the demolition of industrial civilization, and disseminated the idea that environmentalists wanted to do away with technology, culture, cities, and human intellect, when in fact some of those very things provide environmentalists with their greatest tools. Rand condemned concern over the impact of industry on the nation's air and water as an attempt to undermine the economy. Her philosophy included a total severing of the human and the non-human, relegating nature to the status of raw materials to be used in factories and ignoring any broader ecological dependency.

Rand has influenced the environmental movement in a less direct way as well—through the widespread popularity of her fiction. Fast-paced, drama-soaked, and filled with heated romances, her novels draw readers in with their hyped-up storylines while allowing her ideological message to seep in slowly. Her novels have sold more than twenty million copies, a figure that continues to grow by about a quarter of a million copies a year. Her writings have been very popular with young people, though often younger readers "outgrow" her as they expand their perspectives through further reading and thinking.[12] But she appeals to adults as well: Her assuaging of all guilt over selfish desires for wealth and success and her lone-individual-against-the-world ethos can come across as a self-help panacea.

In 1975, Rand was diagnosed with lung cancer, no doubt an outgrowth of her decades-long habit of smoking two packs of cigarettes a day. Though surgery removed any immediate danger to her life, her weakened state forced her to discontinue work on her newsletter. In 1979, Frank O'Connor died after several years of struggle with alcoholism and accelerating senility, leaving Rand truly bereft. A few years later, on March 6, 1982, Rand died of lung cancer in her New York apartment, with only a nurse present. At her memorial service, her casket sat next to a six-foot-tall dollar sign sent by one of her fans.

After her death, the executor of Rand's literary estate, a man named Leonard Peikoff, founded The Ayn Rand Institute, an educational organization seeking to perpetuate her teachings. Through public speaking events and online commentaries, the institute openly vilifies the environmentalist cause. A recent online editorial on the institute's website was entitled "Earth Day Celebrates Hatred of Man" with the subtitle "If Environmentalists Succeed, They Will Make Human Life Impossible." Other commentaries offer arguments against energy conservation and urge the drilling of oil in the Arctic National Wildlife Refuge. The same kind of black-and-white thinking that propelled Rand's rage is prevalent. One of the former executive directors of the Ayn Rand Institute thought in much the same way: "To save mankind requires the wholesale rejection of environmentalism as hatred of science, technology, progress, and human life," he wrote. "To save mankind requires the return to a philosophy of reason and individualism, a philosophy which makes life on earth possible."

NOTES

1. Claudia Roth Pierpont, "Twilight of the Goddess," *New Yorker* (July 24, 1995), pp. 70–81.

2. Barbara Branden, *The Passion of Ayn Rand* (New York: Doubleday and Company, Inc., 1986), p. 12.

3. Ibid., p. 93.

4. Ibid., p. 52.

5. Ayn Rand, *The Fountainhead*, 50th Anniversary Edition (New York: Penguin Books, 1994), p. 686.

6. Granville Hicks, "A Parable of Buried Talents," *New York Times Book Review* (October 13, 1957), pp. 4–5.

7. Ibid.

8. Ayn Rand, *The New Left: The Anti-Industrial Revolution* (New York: New American Library, 1971), p. 235.

9. Ibid., p. 136.

10. Jeff Walker, *The Ayn Rand Cult* (Chicago: Open Court Publishing Company, 1999), p. 331.

11. Rand, *The New Left*, pp. 127–129.

12. Walker, *The Ayn Rand Cult*, p. 328.

BIBLIOGRAPHY

Barbara Branden's biography, *The Passion of Ayn Rand* (New York: Doubleday and Company, Inc., 1986), provides a thorough detailing of Rand's personal history, but is also highly subjective and includes large sections dealing mainly with Branden's own experiences. Nathaniel Branden's *Judgment Day: My Years With Ayn Rand* (Boston: Houghton Mifflin, 1989) is almost entirely autobiographical, with sparse useful information about Rand and her ideas. Before their split with Rand, Barbara and Nathaniel Branden co-wrote the highly adulatory *Who is Ayn Rand?* (New York: Random House, 1962). Chris Sciabarra attempts to locate Rand's philosophical roots in her Russian upbringing in *Ayn Rand: The Russian Radical* (University Park: Pennsylvania State University Press, 1995), while Jeff Walker's *The Ayn Rand Cult* (Chicago: Open Court Publishing Company, 1999) explores her impact on American cultural thought and her cult-like following. Informative articles from the popular press include Granville Hicks's review of *Atlas Shrugged*, "A Parable of Buried Talents," *New York Times Book Review* (October 13, 1957), pp. 4–5, and Claudia Roth Pierpont's profile of Rand, "Twilight of the Goddess," *New Yorker Magazine* (July 24, 1995), pp. 70–81. Rand's own works include *The Fountainhead* (Indianapolis: Bobbs-Merrill, 1943); *Atlas Shrugged* (New York: Random House, 1957); *Anthem* (New York: Signet, 1961); *The Virtue of Selfishness: A New Concept of Egoism* (New York: New American Library, 1966); *Capitalism: The Unknown Ideal* (New York: New American Library, 1966); and *The New Left: The Anti-Industrial Revolution* (New York: New American Library, 1971).

RACHEL CARSON
(1907–1964)

The more clearly we can focus our attention on the wonders and realities of the universe about us, the less taste we shall have for destruction.
—Rachel Carson

Rachel Carson, whose name has become one of the most famous and revered in conservation, was not a crusader by nature. Quiet and introspective, she grew up loving nothing more than solitarily meandering through the wooded hills near her home and teaching herself about the natural world. Yet underneath her reserved demeanor lay a personal belief in the beauty and mystery of life on earth, a belief so powerful that it would one day propel her from the woodland shade into the public spotlight. Both a gifted writer and a meticulous biologist, she first gained recognition for her books about the sea—unique combinations of radiant prose and accurate, up-to-date scientific information. Her subsequent fame required her to adopt a public persona as an unofficial "spokesperson of the sea." But it was her final book, *Silent Spring*, a critique of the proliferation and rash use of chemical pesticides, that sent shock waves throughout the world and sparked a new awareness of the potential humans have for ecological destruction. When she started her writing career, the general public had never heard the word "ecology," and conservation issues had no political influence. The publication of *Silent Spring*, and the public uproar that followed, helped shape the beginnings of a revolutionary social movement that would impact the course of American history. By the time of her death in 1964, she had testified at a Senate hearing, appeared on television programs, and given numerous speeches devoted to breaking the knowledge barriers around the dangers of pesticides and around the impact humans and technology have on the environment. In the decades following her death, she has been acclaimed as one of the most influential thinkers of the twentieth century and has been given credit for the birth of ecological consciousness in America.

Rachel Louise Carson was born on May 27, 1907, in Springdale, Pennsylvania, an Allegheny River town of about 1,200 people. Her family owned a 64-acre tract of land where they kept an orchard, a large garden, and an assortment of farm animals. Rachel's parents, Robert Carson and Maria McLean Carson, had met fourteen years earlier in a nearby town at a choral festival, at which Robert performed in a quartet and Maria was featured as an alto soloist in a women's quintet. Maria was gaining recognition for her musical ability, but when she married Robert she had to abandon her musical career. Robert worked various jobs—as a clerk, as a self-employed insurance salesman, and later as an electrician—but often had trouble meeting the family's expenses. Rachel was the third child born to Maria and Robert: Marian Frazier was 10 and Robert McLean was 8 when she was born. With the two older children at school, Rachel's mother had all day to devote to her new baby daughter, and spent many hours outside with her in the woods and hillsides surrounding their rural homestead. Possessing an enduring love of natural history, Maria sought to instill in her children an appreciation of the natural world and nurtured young Rachel's love of the outdoors.

Having siblings who were quite a bit older and living in a rural setting several miles from the heart of town conspired to keep Rachel quite alone, and she spent hours in the woods. In addition to her lone explorations, she relished another solitary pursuit: reading. From an early age she read eagerly, and was especially drawn to authors who wrote stories about the ocean, such as Joseph Conrad, Herman Melville, and Robert Louis Stevenson. Immersing herself in literature led to an interest in writing, which she would eventually turn into a career that would enable her to shape the way future generations would think about nature and technology. "I can remember no time, even in earliest childhood, when I didn't assume I was going to be a writer,"[1] she later said.

Inspired by the children's literary magazine St. Nicholas, to which her mother had subscribed for years, Carson began her writing career early. Aimed at children aged 5–18, St. Nicholas featured a variety of poems and stories, both fiction and nonfiction, with high-quality illustrations. Probably the most beloved feature was the "St. Nicholas League," which children could join by contributing their own writing or artwork. When she was 10 years old, Rachel sent off her first entry to the magazine: a story about World War I titled "A Battle in the Clouds." She won a silver badge for excellence in prose and was delighted to see it published, saying later that no royalty check ever compared to the joy she felt on receiving that award. Over the next few years she sent in several more stories and essays, joining the ranks of other writers such as E. B. White, William Faulkner, F. Scott Fitzgerald, and Eudora Welty. The last one she entered was in 1922 in the category of "My Favorite Recreation," and it recounted roaming the woods with her dog in search of birds.

Carson excelled at school, though she maintained her reserve when it came to interactions with her peers. Her social isolation increased as her father struggled, often unsuccessfully, to keep steady work and pay the bills. By the time she was in high school, her family's situation was attracting comment in town and had become a source of shame. While this may have had an effect on her social life, it did not lower the high standards she set for herself, nor did it dim her passionate pursuit of knowledge. When she graduated from high school in 1925, the school's yearbook editors summed up her intellect and precision in this poem which accompanied her photo:

> *Rachel's like the mid-day sun*
> *Always very bright*
> *Never stops her studying*
> *'Til she gets it right.*[2]

For Carson, there was never any doubt that she would go on to college and further her studies. She applied to Pennsylvania College for Women (which became Chatham College), a private institution in nearby Pittsburgh with a prestigious academic reputation. As a self-disciplined, intellectually self-confident, ambitious, and socially reserved young woman, Carson entered college and planned to focus on her writing. She retained her deep love of the natural world and her fresh delight in new discoveries: Her first composition for a freshman English class described her fondness for wild creatures and the out-of-doors. But while she thrived in her English classes, it was a biology class taken for a science requirement that changed the course of her life. Taught by a dynamic and fiercely intelligent woman named Mary Scott Skinker, this class sparked an emotional and intellectual fire in Carson, one that brought meaning and structure to her love of nature and reinforced her belief in the beauty and mystery of life. She eventually changed her major from English to biology, and would stay on that path through years of graduate studies and a biology career. In 1929, when Carson graduated with honors from Pennsylvania College for Women, she had already applied and been accepted, complete with a scholarship, for a master's program in zoology at Johns Hopkins University in Baltimore. During the summer before graduate school, she took the advice of Mary Scott Skinker and participated in a research program at the Marine Biology Laboratory in Woods Hole, Massachusetts. There Carson finally encountered the sea, which had so fascinated her since childhood. During her eight weeks of field studies there,

Carson honed her analytical skills and became even more captivated by the ocean and its variety of life.

Her graduate work coincided with the rise of the Great Depression, which heightened the financial straits that had plagued Carson throughout her college years. Always having gotten by with scholarships and loans, she was already in debt and received little support from her cash-poor family, who had moved in with her in Baltimore. Partway through her graduate studies, Carson took on part-time work, first as a research assistant in a Johns Hopkins laboratory, and later as a biology teacher at the University of Maryland. In 1932, after completing her master's degree, with a thesis entitled "The Development of the Pronephros during the Embryonic and Early Larval Life of the Catfish (*Ictalurus punctatus*)," she began work toward her doctorate at Johns Hopkins, taking classes in zoology and conducting experiments on the salt tolerance of eels. But, as the Depression continued working its miseries, her family's situation faltered further. Her parents now supported their oldest daughter Marian and her two children, with little help from their unreliable son Robert. As the most highly educated family member, and with the best prospects for full-time employment, it fell to Rachel to help out with the support of her family, leaving her little choice but to abandon her doctoral studies in search of employment in addition to her part-time teaching job. For a while, Carson turned to her writings as a potential source of income. She polished some of her college poems and stories and sent them to various magazines, but was rejected each time.

Her situation took a more desperate turn in July 1935, when her father died, breaking the final thin strands of the financial security net the family had. Again taking the advice of Mary Scott Skinker, who had become a close friend and mentor, Carson took the federal civil service exam to become eligible for a government job. Skinker then urged Carson to visit Elmer Higgins, the Biology Division chief at the U.S. Bureau of Fisheries (which later became part of the U.S. Fish and Wildlife Service). Higgins had no full-time openings, but was impressed by Carson's credentials and had another idea. The bureau recently had undertaken a series of educational radio broadcasts about the sea called "Romance under the Waters," and Higgins had been struggling to find writers for the scripts of these short pieces, which office staff had nicknamed "seven-minute fish tales." In what came to be a turning point in Carson's career, he asked if she would like to try writing them, for a part-time wage. Combined with her part-time teaching job, this would alleviate the financial worries of her family.

The attainment of this fortuitous part-time job allowed Carson to glimpse a future that could combine her two passions—biology and writing. Armed with a lifelong enthusiasm for the sea, impeccable writing skills, and a penchant for meticulous research, Carson took immediately to the task, and her radio scripts got an enthusiastic reception. When the series ended, Higgins had a new assignment for her: to write a government brochure introducing marine life to the general public. Meanwhile, her radio script research had stimulated ideas for other articles, and she began submitting feature articles to the *Baltimore Sun*, many of which were published. Her articles often focused on respect for life and all its intricacies and on her concern about human exploitation of the natural world: themes that would resurface throughout her later writings. When she finished her "government brochure," she turned it in to Higgins and sat quietly watching while he read it at his desk. She later remembered how he "handed it back with a twinkle in his eye. 'I don't think it will do,' he said. 'Better try again. But send this one to the *Atlantic*.'"[3] The *Atlantic Monthly* was considered the top literary magazine of the day, and Carson recognized her chief's suggestion as high praise. Still, it was over a year before she would submit the article, due to various preoccupations. She applied for a full-time junior aquatic biologist position and was accepted, making her one of only two women in professional positions in the Bureau of Fisheries at the time. Her writing was going well; she was advancing the ranks of government work and was succeeding in keeping her family afloat. Yet misfortune found her in early 1937, when her older sister lost a battle with pneumonia and passed away, leaving two daughters, 11 and 12 years old, to be brought up by Carson and her mother. In order to be closer to Washington, D.C., where she often had to travel for her new job, and perhaps to get a sense of making a new start, Carson moved her mother and nieces into a modest two-story rental house in Silver Spring, Maryland.

She eventually did submit the article entitled "Undersea"—and when the *Atlantic Monthly* published it in 1937, it verified her as a writer of distinction and gave the nation its first real sample of her unique voice. In clear lyrical prose, she drew on her detailed knowledge of biology and marine life, rendering it understandable and beguiling to the general public:

> Thus we see the parts of the plan fall into place: the water receiving from earth and air the simple materials, storing them up until the gathering energy of the spring sun wakens the sleeping plants to a burst of dynamic activity, hungry swarms of planktonic animals growing and multiplying upon the abundant plants, and themselves falling prey to the shoals of fish; all, in the end, to be redissolved into their component substances when the inexorable laws of the sea demand it. . . . Against this cosmic background the life span of a particular plant or animal appears, not as a drama complete in itself, but only as a brief interlude in a panorama of endless change.[4]

The response to her article was intoxicatingly positive. Carson received letters from some of the biggest names in the publishing world encouraging her to write a book. She began to realize how rich a source of subject matter her knowledge of biology was for her writing. This article, and the book that followed, helped Carson formulate her powerful blend of creative writing, scientific fact, and her personal philosophy about the importance of respecting the eternal rhythms of nature.

For the next few years she continued writing newspaper feature articles, some of which touched on her conservation ethic by describing the impact of humans on the landscape—the draining of marshes, the cutting of timber, and the destruction of wildlife. She also continued with her increasingly demanding job at the Bureau of Fisheries, doing research, analyzing field reports, and writing public brochures. And though her free time was dominated by the normal household chaos of living with her two nieces and elderly mother, she began carving out some quiet time in the evenings and on weekends so that she could start working on her first book, basically an expansion of the *Atlantic* article. Her mother helped with the running of the household to allow her time to write, and also typed up her revisions and manuscripts. On New Year's Eve, 1940, Carson sent the manuscript for her first book, entitled *Under the Sea-Wind*, off to Simon and Schuster, who published it on November 1, 1941, selling it for $3.00 a copy. Though the critics responded immediately with praise, world events overwhelmed any chance of commercial success for the book: A month after publication, Japanese war planes bombed Pearl Harbor, and the United States began to prepare for war.

In later years, Carson admitted a special fondness for *Under the Sea-Wind*, realizing that no writer ever quite recaptures the freshness of her first book. But the fact that it sold less than 1500 copies in its first year disappointed her, and years later in describing its publication, Carson remarked that "the world received the event with supreme indifference."[5] At the time, though, she soon became distracted, because, as with all government agencies, her office was mobilizing for the war effort. To relieve the new shortage of office space in Washington, D.C., Carson's office was temporarily relocated to Chicago, and she and her mother made the move, leaving her two nieces, who had graduated from high school, back in Silver Spring. Carson's contribution to the war effort included writing booklets urging Americans to make use of seafood as a protein source in order to reduce reliance on rationed meats. By April 1943, they were back in Maryland, where Carson received a promotion. Having risen steadily in rank, she had proven herself a success with her government work; but as she gained recognition and responsibilities, she had less time to devote to creative writing, though she continued to publish an occasional magazine article and constantly came up with ideas she wanted to write about. She had started becoming alarmed at early test results of dichloro-diphenyl-trichloroethane (DDT), a new synthetic pesticide that had been hailed as a miracle for its impact on malaria-causing mosquitoes during the war. In July 1945, Carson sent a proposal to *Reader's Digest* for an article on DDT's effect on wildlife, but was rejected. For the time being, she moved on to other topics.

By 1946, Carson had been promoted to information specialist and found herself in an increasingly effective position to improve the quality of bureaucratic publications, though she often wished she could have a wider impact on public education. The perfect opportunity for that arrived with the "Conservation in Action" series of booklets, illustrated guides to the national wildlife refuges, of which there were approximately 300 in existence in the late 1940s. Carson was responsible for their publication, and wrote some of them herself. To her delight, in order to write them she had to travel across the country on field trips to various wildlife refuges to gather background material and take photographs. These trips became one of the highlights of her government career. In stating the purpose of the project, she voiced the importance of conservation amidst human's generally detrimental impact on the natural world, and introduced ecological principles of interdependence that were practically unheard-of at the time:

> The Western Hemisphere has a relatively short history of the exploitation of its natural resources by man. This history, though short, contains many chapters of reckless waste and appalling destruction. . . . All the people of a country have a direct interest in conservation. . . . Wildlife, water, forests, grasslands—all are parts of [our] essential environment; the conservation and effective use of one is impossible except as the others also are conserved. . . . Like the resource it seeks to protect, wildlife conservation must be dynamic, changing as conditions change, seeking always to become more effective. We have much to accomplish before we can feel assured of passing on to future generations a land as richly endowed in natural wealth as the one we live in.[6]

By the summer of 1949, Carson had risen to the position of biologist and chief editor of all U.S. Fish and Wildlife Service publications. At the pinnacle of her government service career, she also finally hired a literary agent, Marie Rodell, and began to get serious about writing a second book. Even though she often returned home exhausted from her ever-expanding duties at the office, she still managed to begin writing, slowly and painstakingly, her next book, which would also be about the sea. Curious and ever eager to expand her experience of the marine world, she arranged to go out on the U.S. Fish and Wildlife Service's research vessel, the *Albatross III*, a converted fishing trawler used to explore the Georges Bank—the deeply submerged sandbank and famous fishing ground 200 miles east of Boston. One obstacle to her plan was that government officials were reluctant to send a woman out alone with the crew of fifty men. Carson satisfied their misgivings by inviting Rodell to accompany her as a "chaperon." They spent ten days at sea, enduring occasionally adverse conditions; but Carson came away with some vivid impressions, such as seeing the nets come up with huge loads of fish, sponges, starfish, crabs, and strange bottom-dwellers. Being out on the open sea at night thrilled her, and the sensation of being surrounded by water gave her a new appreciation of the ocean and its immensity.

   Carson completed work on her second book, *The Sea around Us*, and sent it off to Oxford University Press, but before it was published she was hospitalized for the surgical removal of a tumor in her left breast, which her doctors told her was not malignant. She then applied for and won a Guggenheim fellowship, which allowed her to take a year's leave of absence from her job to devote to writing. *The Sea around Us*, published in July 1951, created a tidal wave of critical and popular enthusiasm, and turned Carson into an immediate literary sensation. She began receiving bushels of fan mail, much of which made clear a widespread thirst for knowledge about the natural world. Her book stayed on the best-seller list for eighty-six weeks, and was eventually translated into thirty-two languages. Oxford University Press had a difficult time keeping enough books in print to meet the demand—by the end of 1952 over 250,000 copies had sold. *The Sea around Us* was named the Outstanding Book of 1951 by the *New York Times*, won the National Book Award for nonfiction, and the John Burroughs Medal for nature writing (the award she most coveted). Carson also began accumulating honorary doctorates from various institutes of higher learning. Furthermore, in a rare publishing phenomenon, Oxford University Press reissued *Under the Sea-Wind*, which promptly appeared on the best-seller list alongside *The Sea around Us*, giving Carson a sense of vindication.

   While being recognized for her work was thrilling, it also required of her a new boldness. But she overcame her fear of public speaking and eventually even stepped into the role of social commentator, promoting her belief that scientific knowledge should belong to the public and not just to an elite group. In one speech, she asserted, "The materials of science are the materials of life itself. . . . [T]he aim of science is to discover and illuminate truth. And that, I take it, is the aim of literature, whether biography or history or fiction. It seems to me, then, there can be no separate literature of science."[7] Through the success of her writing, Carson shattered the myths that only scientists were intelligent enough to grasp scientific concepts and that the general public wanted only oversimplified, "popularized" science.

   Spurred by success, Carson began writing her next book, an intensively researched ecological exploration of the Atlantic seacoast. Her royalties from *The Sea around Us* gave her enough financial security that she finally could resign from her position with the U.S. Fish and Wildlife Service, which came as a deep relief. She also now had the means to acquire a small piece of land on Southport Island in Maine, where she would have a summer cottage built. This wooded spot along the shore of the estuary of the Sheepscot River would become a sanctuary of peace and joy for the rest of her life.

   When her next book, *The Edge of the Sea*, was published in 1955, it brought Carson more honors: the Achievement Award of the American Association of University Women and, from the National Council of Women of the United States, the book's designation as "the outstanding book of the year." It brought further credibility to Carson as an established literary figure and again left her in constant demand for public appearances and various short-term writing projects. She worked on a variety of literary endeavors for the next few years, reaching new audiences and enjoying her acclaim. But in February 1957, her life changed drastically: Her niece Marjorie died of pneumonia, leaving her 5-year-old son Roger. Carson, just short of 50 years old, then adopted Roger and began the difficult task of learning to raise a child.

These were the circumstances facing Carson as she began her next project, one that would take four and a half years to complete and would catalyze an extraordinary scientific, philosophical, and political furor. The genesis for *Silent Spring* came from an inquiry written by a friend, Olga Owens Huckins, a former writer for the *Boston Post*. The Huckins property, which included a large bird sanctuary, had been sprayed repeatedly with DDT for mosquito control in the summer of 1957, and songbirds had died in numbers. Huckins wrote a letter to the *Boston Herald* (sending a copy to Carson) and demanded that spraying poisons from the air be stopped until evidence of its effects on wildlife could be gathered. Carson had been interested in the role of toxic pesticides in the environment for years and had grave misgivings about their use, especially since comprehensive studies had never been done. She began looking into the situation, and the more she learned, the more horrified she became about the abandon with which the chemicals were used.

DDT was first used as an insecticide in 1939. It was cheap and easy to make, and just a few grains of the white powder could wipe out whole colonies of mosquito larvae. Its widespread use in the Pacific during World War II gave it a favorable reputation. After the war it helped to eradicate malaria in the developed world almost completely, and drastically reduce it elsewhere, saving millions of lives. Then, despite the fact that definitive tests of the chemical's toxicity had never been conducted, the Department of Agriculture approved the release of DDT to the civilian market in 1945. By the late 1950s, DDT production had nearly quintupled from World War II levels, and municipal authorities began using it on American suburbs. It became apparent to some that DDT killed indiscriminately, wiping out beneficial insects, birds, and other species as well as pests—and that it could cause serious environmental consequences, though most information on the topic was tucked away in academic publications. Carson, who had other projects she wanted to accomplish, tried to interest various people in writing a book about the ecological implications of pesticides. No one took the bait, and, realizing that pesticides posed a threat to everything she stood for as an ecologist, she decided she must write the book herself.

She began researching, thoroughly and carefully, everything she could find about DDT and other organochlorine pesticides and their use. Her mind still whirring with the possibilities of other books she wanted to write, she hoped that she could finish this project quickly and move on. But once again, events in her personal life overwhelmed her determination. On November 30, 1958, her mother, from whom she had never been separated for more than nine months at a time, died of a stroke. Carson spent the next year struggling with parental responsibilities and becoming increasingly involved in intensive research for her book. By early 1960, she had drafted several chapters and was beginning to see an end in sight for her book. But in March she found more lumps in her breast, and this time doctors recommended a radical mastectomy, implying that it was merely a precautionary measure. Recovery from surgery took months, and Carson eventually discovered that her doctors had been dishonest about the results of the pathology reports: She actually had breast cancer and it had metastasized. Subsequent treatments left her weakened and sick and seriously diminished her capacity to write. Eventually, despite illness and despair, she began making progress again, and early in 1962 she finally completed the book. That summer, before it was published, the *New Yorker* magazine ran a three-part series of excerpts from it, creating an immediate sensation. The *New Yorker* began receiving more mail than ever before, with many readers writing to express shock and anger at the excessive use of dangerous chemicals. Others criticized the article and Carson herself as hysterical and alarmist. After the third installment appeared, the Velsicol Corporation, a pesticide manufacturer, threatened to sue the *New Yorker* for libel. The magazine's legal counsel, insisting that all of Carson's statements were accurate, told the company to proceed with legal action. They never did, but this was only the beginning of bitter attacks on the book and its message.

Finally, with word already spreading throughout the press, *Silent Spring* was published on September 27, 1962, and immediately flew to the top of the *New York Times* best-seller list. It also was selected for the Book-of-the Month Club, and by December more than 100,000 copies had sold. A beautifully written book full of awareness of the living world, it also sounded a horrifying wake-up call to a nation that had become more and more complacent about the use of toxic pesticides. The accessibility of Carson's writing helped her introduce to a wide audience a sound scientific understanding of the natural processes, especially in regard to the abstract ideas involving ecology: In order to show how these poisonous chemicals upset the balance of nature, she first had to describe clearly the interwoven fabric of life.

Silent Spring opens with a sketch of a hypothetical small town stricken by a mysterious blight: "There was a strange stillness. The birds, for example— where had they gone? . . . On the mornings that had once throbbed with the dawn chorus of robins, catbirds, doves, jays, wrens, and scores of other bird voices there was now no sound; only silence lay over the fields and woods and marsh."[8] In the chapters that followed, Carson provided a "Who's Who" of toxic chemicals, introduced ecological concepts such as biomagnification, and explained the effects of pesticides in the tissues of living creatures. A chapter on cancer documents some of the known carcinogens in various pesticides and chronicles a rise in diseases related to the use of these toxic agents. Along with the steady barrage of facts and examples, Carson took a broader view and explored the relationship between humans and the earth. Before the dawn of this type of ecological consciousness, the environment to most people had been a distant, disconnected concept, valuable only as an economic resource. But Carson reminded readers that humans are the first species ever able to exert an influence over its environment, and that some of these influences can have detrimental and sometimes unpredictable consequences:

> The balance of nature is not the same today as in Pleistocene times, but it is still there: a complex, precise, and highly integrated system of relationships between living things which cannot safely be ignored any more than the law of gravity can be defied with impunity by a man perched on the edge of a cliff. The balance of nature is not a *status quo*; it is fluid, ever shifting, in a constant state of adjustment. Man, too, is part of this balance. Sometimes the balance is in his favor; sometimes—and all too often through his own activities—it is shifted to his disadvantage.[9]

Her carefully researched book provided proof that this was already happening: Certain chemical pesticides, such as DDT, were creating ecological catastrophes and causing irreversible damage in humans. After establishing these dangers, Carson took her argument further, explaining that the impacts from pesticides had not been tested thoroughly, especially when separate chemicals were combined in the environment. She also showed that many pest insects become resistant to the sprays, and when beneficial insects that normally prey on these pests are themselves wiped out by the sprays, it can actually lead to a population explosion of pests. Yet Carson did not simply criticize these tactics and leave it at that. She also suggested strategies for pest control, such as introducing predator species, integrated pest management, and the use of safer sprays. She also made it clear that she was not advocating the complete abandonment of chemical control. Her criticism was not that pesticides control harmful insects, but that they control insects poorly and inefficiently, and that the harmful side effects had not been studied carefully.

However eloquent and levelheaded her arguments though, the chemical industries reacted as if bitten. They immediately tried to dismiss her findings, using any excuse possible—including the fact that Carson was a woman, and thus too "emotional." They spent a quarter of a million dollars trying to reassure a panicking public, printing a stream of literature in defense of pesticides, parodies of *Silent Spring*, attacks on Carson, and attacks on her science. The reason Carson's arguments against pesticides scared them was not so much a concern over their expected profit margins, but that she questioned the whole attitude of the industrialized society toward control of the natural world and caused people to examine their relationship to the environment. This was what the chemical companies couldn't tolerate, and this was what made her a hero of generations of conservationists.

In spite of failing health, Carson continued to make heroic efforts to publicize her cause. In addition to numerous speeches, she made a calm and dignified appearance on a television program called *CBS Reports*, in which she answered interview questions and read passages from *Silent Spring*. In June 1963, Carson testified before the U.S. Senate Subcommittee on Reorganization and International Organization in a hearing on environmental hazards. Her testimony focused on evidence of pesticide pollution and called for new policies to protect human health and the environment. Her cause already had attracted the attention of the president, John F. Kennedy, who immediately had set up the President's Science Advisory Committee to investigate the effects of pesticides. Its report largely vindicated Carson's findings and concluded that use of persistent pesticides must be reduced. It also recommended educating the public on the issue, noting that "until the publication of *Silent Spring*, people were generally unaware of the toxicity of pesticides."[10]

By the end of 1963, Carson's cancer had spread through her bones and she endured constant pain. She also suffered from angina, her heart weakened by the harsh radiation treatments and metastasizing cancer. She knew she was nearing the end of her life, and was distressed at the thought of the writing she would never be able to do. But by this time she could take comfort in the fact that her work was exerting enormous influence in the world. A glittering and impressive collection of awards and honors acknowledged her contributions to science, conservation, and literature. She received the Audubon Medal, and, in what she said was the most satisfying honor bestowed upon her, she was elected to the American Academy of Arts and Letters—one of only three women in the fifty-member club. She also was awarded the Conservationist of the Year Award from the National Wildlife Federation in 1963. But time soon ran out for Rachel Carson, and on April 14, 1964, she suffered a fatal heart attack at her home in Silver Spring, Maryland.

The public debate touched off by *Silent Spring* helped spawn a new environmental consciousness that gradually would evolve and develop into a movement. When the Environmental Protection Agency was established in 1970, it was given authority to regulate the use of pesticides and quickly decided on the total phasing out of DDT in the United States by 1972. Carson's book also led to much higher public awareness and concern over the general use of pesticides, though the debate over the use of chemicals has yet to be resolved. Pesticides are still widely used, and many insist that they remain a significant threat to human and environmental health. *Silent Spring* reported that over 637 million pounds of pesticides were produced in 1960. In 1999 the EPA reported that 1.6 billion pounds of pesticides were being produced annually in the United States, and that approximately 5 billion pounds were used in the United States,[11] although most pesticides used today are less toxic and less lasting. According to the Carson tradition, solutions to pest control problems—and any interaction that threatens environmental health—call for gathering all available information, searching for alternatives to damaging methods, and for considering the future. "It is human nature to shrug off what may seem to us a vague threat of future disaster,"[12] said Carson, and these words—besides explaining how the use of toxic pesticides came about in the first place and illustrating her sensitivity to the different attitudes people have toward the natural world—summarize the complications and challenges inherent in any argument for conservation.

NOTES

1. Rachel Carson, "The Real World around Us," speech delivered to Theta Sigma Phi, Columbus, Ohio, April 21, 1954. Reprinted in Linda Lear, ed., *Lost Woods: The Discovered Writing of Rachel Carson* (Boston: Beacon Press, 1998), p. 148.

2. *Parnassus High School Yearbook*, 1925. Reprinted in Linda Lear, *Rachel Carson: Witness for Nature* (New York: Henry Holt and Company, 1997), p. 24.

3. Carson, "The Real World around Us," speech. Reprinted in Lear, *Lost Woods*, p. 150.

4. Rachel Carson, "Undersea," *Atlantic Monthly* Vol. 160 (September 1937), pp. 322–325.

5. Carson, "The Real World around Us," speech. Reprinted in Lear, *Lost Woods*, p. 150.

6. Rachel Carson, *Guarding Our Wildlife Refuges, Conservation in Action*, # 5 (Washington, DC: U.S. Fish and Wildlife Service, Government Printing Office, 1948). Reprinted in Paul Brooks, *The House of Life: Rachel Carson at Work* (Boston: Houghton Mifflin, 1972), pp. 100–101.

7. Rachel Carson, speech, National Book Award, January 29, 1952. Reprinted in Lear, *Rachel Carson: Witness for Nature*, p. 219.

8. Rachel Carson, *Silent Spring* (Boston: Houghton Mifflin, 1962), p. 2.

9. Ibid., p. 146.

10. "The Uses of Pesticides: A Report of the President's Science Advisory Committee" (Washington, DC: U.S. Government Printing Office, May 15, 1963). Reprinted in Lear, *Rachel Carson*, p. 451.

11. David Donaldson, Timothy Kiely, and Arthur Grube, *Pesticides Industry Sales and Usage: 1998 and 1999 Market Estimates*, Report No. EPA–733–R–02–001 (Washington, DC: U.S. Environmental Protection Agency, 2002), pp. 9, 10.

12. Carson, *Silent Spring*, p. 189.

BIBLIOGRAPHY

Linda Lear's *Rachel Carson: Witness for Nature* (New York: Henry Holt and Company, 1997) is the definitive biography. Before it was published, the main source of information on Carson's life was a book written by her editor, Paul Brooks, *The House of Life: Rachel Carson at Work* (Boston: Houghton Mifflin, 1972), which has been reprinted as *Rachel Carson: The Writer at Work* (San Francisco: Sierra Club Books, 1998). Lear also edited an anthology of Carson's unpublished writings, *Lost Woods: The Discovered Writing of Rachel Carson* (Boston: Beacon Press, 1998). For a record of a decade-long correspondence between Carson and her close friend Dorothy Freeman, which provides the only real autobiographical writing Carson ever did, see *Always, Rachel: The Letters of Rachel Carson and Dorothy Freeman, 1952–1964*, edited by Martha Freeman (Boston: Beacon Press, 1995). Carson's own work includes "Undersea," *Atlantic Monthly* Vol. 160 (September 1937), pp. 322–325; *Under the Sea-Wind: A Naturalist's Picture of Ocean Life* (New York: Simon and Schuster, 1941); *The Sea around Us* (New York: Oxford University Press, 1951); *The Edge of the Sea* (Boston: Houghton Mifflin, 1955); and *Silent Spring* (Boston: Houghton Mifflin, 1962). A follow-up to *Silent Spring*, written by Frank Graham, Jr., called *Since Silent Spring* (Boston: Houghton Mifflin, 1970), details the impact of her book and describes efforts made by multinational corporations to discredit her research.

DAVID BROWER
(1912–2000)

Polite conservationists leave no mark save the scars upon the Earth that could have been prevented had they stood their ground.

—David Brower

Remembered as the "Archdruid" of environmentalism, David Brower presided over broad transformations in the twentieth-century American environmental movement—his mix of benign eminence and righteous fury conjuring the image of a real-life Gandalf. In his fifty years of activism, Brower perhaps became best known for his dynamic and sometimes reckless leadership of the Sierra Club, turning it from a genteel hiking society into a powerful force against environmental destruction. He was immortalized in a biographical book called *Encounters with the Archdruid* by writer John McPhee, who described him as the "preeminent fang" of the Sierra Club. His career followed a bumpy trajectory—radical activism and leadership, followed by sometimes bitter dissension with the more cautious elements in the movement—and one thing no one would ever accuse Brower of was docility.

Described by many as a visionary, Brower saw connections between politics, economics, and environmental destruction; in striving to spotlight those connections, Brower pushed traditional conservationism toward the more active, encompassing movement that came to be known as environmentalism. "While varying judgments have been made about David Brower, there can be no doubt that he led several victorious campaigns to save the land, helped rekindle the transcendental flame lit by [**Henry David**] **Thoreau** and [**John**] **Muir,** and played a major role in pulling the old preservationist movement out of the comfortable leather armchairs of its clubrooms and into the down-and-dirty arena of local and national policy making,"[1] wrote Philip Shabecoff. His numerous achievements in defense of the environment are virtually unmatched and include blocking the building of dams in the Grand Canyon and Dinosaur National Monument; agitating for the passage of the Wilderness Act; and founding Friends of the Earth, the League of Conservation Voters, and the Earth Island Institute. He received the UN's Lifetime Achievement Award, and was twice nominated for the Nobel Peace Prize.

David Ross Brower was born in Berkeley, California, on July 1, 1912, to Ross J. and Mary Grace (Barlow) Brower. At the age of 1, he fell from his baby carriage, knocking out most of his front teeth and mutilating his gums. Not until he was 11 did his second set of teeth fully emerge, and he spent his early childhood taunted and too shy to break into an open smile. One of his favorite places to play was on the campus at the University of California, where his father taught mechanical drawing. Strawberry Creek ran through the school grounds, and Brower spent many hours there building dams and scrambling around on the lichen-covered rocks edging the stream. Better yet, his parents frequently took their four children traveling, exploring, and camping—sometimes in the wild hills surrounding Berkeley, sometimes throughout the Sierra Nevada, and sometimes on visits to the chicken ranch where his mother had grown up in the Two Rock Valley north of Berkeley. His father built a "camping box"—a container for utensils and supplies, with one side that let down on chains to become a table—that fit onto the running board of the family's 1916 Maxwell. With the parents at the outer edges and the children sandwiched in between, the family slept on blankets laid out on the ground, imparting a sense of security that Brower treasured.

Sophisticated in literature and music, David's mother taught him to play the piano, a skill he enjoyed honing for the rest of his life. But while he was still very young, hardship struck. In 1920, David's mother went blind from an inoperable brain tumor not long after the birth of his brother Joseph. Life became even more difficult when his father lost his teaching job. The family owned two small apartment buildings in Berkeley, and David's father mortgaged them to make ends meet, spending the rest of his life managing the properties. Helping out became a family necessity, and Brower did his part by being the chief caretaker of his younger brother and by helping with cooking, washing, gardening, and apartment renovations.

Helping his mother to satisfy her love of the hills became another regular activity for Brower, and he took her on some of her longest walks after she lost her sight, sometimes up to Grizzly Peak near Berkeley, or along the edge of the Strawberry Creek watershed. He later ascribed his subtly attuned observational skills to these regular walks—his attempts to see for her sharpening his own appreciation of the details of the natural world. Collecting rocks and minerals became a hobby, but his true joy came in finding and identifying butterflies and other insects. When he was only 15, he discovered on Grizzly Peak a new butterfly species with black and white wings and green undersides, which he knew was unusual. It was eventually named after him: *Anthocaris sara reakirtii browerii.* So acute were his visual-discernment skills that—by simply noting wingbeat rhythms and glimpsing their color patterns—he could identify butterflies in flight.

Preoccupied with butterflies but wishing he had spent more time learning sports, Brower entered Berkeley High School. With a friend's help, Brower learned to play football, and though he didn't make the team, he enjoyed the social status accorded him as the team's manager. At 16 he enrolled at the University of California at Berkeley in 1929, but dropped out during his sophomore year in 1931 because of financial strain and his disillusioned sense of being an outsider. Though he professed regret later in his life at never having finished college, he also did his best to make light of this particular shortcoming, saying, for example, that he was a graduate of the "University of the Colorado River." He later told writer David Kupfer, "I think I derive my inspiration from having been a sophomore dropout from college. My wife, who graduated with a BA, thinks I've had some success because I didn't know it was impossible. I hadn't been educated to know what you couldn't do."[2]

After his fitful attempt at college, Brower took work as a clerk at the Alberta Candy Company for several years, and during his vacations he began taking long trips into the Sierra Nevada wilderness. While hiking off the trail on the slopes of Pilot Knob in the summer of 1933, Brower met a young man carrying a camera and tripod, and they stopped to chat, sharing their enthusiasm for the beauty surrounding them. The tall stranger was Ansel Adams, the renowned nature photographer and conservation activist who sat on the board of directors of the Sierra Club. When Brower joined the Sierra Club later that year, Adams would become his enthusiastic supporter within the club and would later nominate him for positions of power. More and more, Brower was giving priority to his extended wilderness jaunts, and his work ethic suffered: In 1935 Brower was fired from the candy factory for frequently failing to show up on time. That year he also published his first article in the *Sierra Club Bulletin*, a chronicle of a ten-week backpacking and climbing trip in the Sierras with a friend.

Blessedly free from the candy factory, Brower took the opportunity to find employment better suited to his temperament and habits. He got a job with the National Park Service (NPS) at Yosemite National Park, first in the accounting office, and later as publicity manager. He reveled in the chance to put his mountaineering skills to use, and during his six years of working for the NPS, he began making first ascents of peaks in the Sierra Nevada, including

Arrowhead in 1937, Glacier Point in 1939, and Lost Brother in 1941. By the time he stopped climbing in middle age, he had climbed all the Sierra peaks that are over 14,000 feet, and had made over seventy first ascents. In 1939 he led a group up Shiprock Mountain, where climbing parties had made at least ten attempts and all had failed. After closely studying photographs of Shiprock for months and months, Brower planned out a highly intricate and dangerous route up the mountain that some had called the number one climbing problem of the continent. When his attempt at Shiprock succeeded, Robert Underhill, an authority on mountaineering, called it the "finest thing ever done in rock-climbing on our continent." He also became the first person to climb Vazquez Monolith in Pinnacles National Monument, its sheer rock face having discouraged every previous climber who had ever attempted it.

In 1940, he joined other Sierra Club activists in a campaign to designate California's Kings Canyon as a national park. Home to immense trees, deep canyons, and high-alpine wilderness, the Kings Canyon area ranges in elevation from 1,500 feet to 14,491 feet and covers stunningly diverse habitats. A small portion of the area had been set aside as General Grant National Park, the third national park designated in the country, in 1890. Fifty years later, Sierra Club activists, including Brower, succeeded in convincing Congress to set aside a much larger area as Kings Canyon National Park.

Increasingly interested in finding ways to persuade the public to appreciate the natural world, Brower began getting involved in publishing. He worked with Sierra Club Books to produce an Ansel Adams book, *The Sierra Nevada: The John Muir Trail*. The experience pleased and challenged him, and it became evident that besides his formidable wilderness skills, he also had a remarkable sense of language and native editorial talents, despite his relative lack of schooling. In 1941 he took advantage of those skills and became an editor at the University of California Press. There he met a fellow editor named Anne Hus, whom he married in 1943, and with whom he would have four children: Kenneth, Robert, Barbara, and John.

As World War II broke out, Brower enlisted in the Tenth Mountain Division and served in Colorado, France, and Italy, teaching mountaineering skills to the troops, a deed for which he received a Bronze Star Medal. Being in the Alps and seeing the environmental destruction wrought by the war reinforced his commitment to protect the wilderness back home. When the war ended he returned to work at the University of California Press for several years while also devoting time to conservation through the Sierra Club. By the end of the 1940s he had become a vocal protagonist within the organization—he was editing its official publication, the *Sierra Club Bulletin*, and agitating his way through several conservation struggles, including a protest against logging in Olympic National Park and an unpopular plan to carve roads through Kings Canyon. The Sierra Club exasperated Brower by wavering on the road-building issue: Some members felt the beautiful canyons should be made accessible to cars and people alike. Brower strongly believed the wilderness should be kept roadless and eventually his side prevailed.

Founded by John Muir and others in 1892, the Sierra Club had effected dramatic preservation triumphs, such as the creation of Yosemite, Mt. Rainier, and Glacier National Parks. But in the thirty or so years since Muir's death in 1914, the organization's clout had completely dissolved due to its fraternal clubbiness and tendency to avoid conflict. More of a "posey-picking hiking society," Sierra Club had grown complacent and, in Brower's opinion, needed a shot in the arm. He overhauled the *Sierra Club Bulletin*, turning its focus from congenial chronicles of mountaineering adventures to reports of real world issues and problems conveying an insistent need to take action. "What I had already learned about mountaineering, and would learn from the *Sierra Club Bulletin* about publishing, were two of the most important influences in my life," said Brower. "Both engendered a kind of boldness that I would not otherwise have known—boldness that got me into a bit of trouble now and then, but also enabled me to accomplish a few things I would otherwise have deemed impossible."[3] In 1952 Brower left the University of California Press to serve as executive director of the Sierra Club—a sign that more and more members had come to realize that Brower's fearless political activism was becoming increasingly necessary to ward off encroaching development throughout the West. Environmental historian Hal K. Rothman described Brower's role in the changing perceptions of conservation: "By the end of the war the Sierra Club had begun to develop a politically active strain. The craggy and sometimes irascible David Brower, who would drive the transformation of conservation into environmentalism in the United States, led the way."[4]

No issues felt more urgent to Brower than wilderness preservation and land-use management. At this point, the political clout and public influence of conservationists was anemic: A limited vision of American wilderness and development impacts led to a widespread sense that all the most important areas had already been preserved. But while Brower's vision suffered no such limitations, he was still encumbered by a lack of public support and inexperience with political strategizing. His first major political battle as head of the Sierra Club was, therefore, both a challenge and a learning experience that accomplished what he later considered to be the greatest mistake of his life. Answering to the increasing demand for regional economic development plans, the Bureau of Reclamation proposed to build storage dams and hydroelectric plants in various locations throughout the West. One of these sites was at Echo Park at the intersection of the Green and Yampa Rivers within the Dinosaur National Monument on the Colorado-Utah border. (A national monument is much the same as a national park, but with looser protections.) Startled conservationists immediately raised a protest and set out to stop the project. Brower's Sierra Club began to unleash a broad publicity campaign, including lobbying and direct-mail efforts that made the dam at Echo Park front-page news. This type of public battle was one of the few tactics available to the Sierra Club, ill equipped as it was to deal head-to-head with the Bureau of Reclamation—and, to a large degree, it worked. It effectively circumvented congressional supporters of the project and put the Sierra Club in a position to negotiate.

Negotiations proceeded through years of political feints, with the conservationists continuing their refusal to budge in their opposition to the dam. Finally a deal was struck: If the Bureau of Reclamation would abandon their Echo Park project, conservationists would promise not to oppose a dam at Glen Canyon, a remote site unknown to Brower and other leading conservationists. Both sides declared victory: The bureau had a dam site, but environmental activism had scored a triumph in saving Echo Park. In June 1963, after the deal had been signed but before construction on the dam had been completed, Brower took a float trip through Glen Canyon and realized what he had traded away. "It was not easy to travel the distance without reverence, or without being grateful that an already beautiful world could here exceed itself," he wrote in sadness. "Whether you looked up at evening or in the morning at this miracle of color and design, or whether you looked at the gardens by the altar or the stream that flowed from the nave, you knew what this place meant to its setting. There would never be anything like it again."[5] Within a few years the tapestried walls and riverside willows of the canyon were under water, and visitors were greeted instead by a heartless sign: "Boaters and Skiers Please Travel Counterclockwise. Let's All Be Courteous. Let's All Have Fun!" The experience of having priceless wilderness slip through his fingers radicalized Brower. Years later, he joined a coalition lobbying for the destruction of Glen Canyon Dam, and for the rest of his life he decried compromise. "Let the people we pay to compromise—the legislature—do the compromising. . . . Every time I compromise I lose," he wrote in his autobiography, *For Earth's Sake.*

Brower had formed an important alliance during the crusade to save Echo Park—that of the aggressive lobbyist and leader of the Wilderness Society, Howard Zahniser. Zahniser believed that the Wilderness Society should join forces with other environmental organizations when fighting specific battles and had recruited Brower and the Sierra Club to help him keep the environmental movement from becoming urbane and cautious. One of their joint projects involved formulating a federal wilderness protection bill calling for the protection of over 50 million acres of wilderness from commercial activities such as mining or hydroelectric generation. They eventually drafted and redrafted sixty-six of versions of the bill, prompting scores of congressional hearings, continually renewed lobbying efforts, and many attempts at deal making over the course of nine years during the late 1950s and early 1960s. Resource development interests put up determined resistance, and government agencies like the National Park Service and the U.S. Forest Service, resenting the watering-down of their administrative powers to designate and regulate wilderness areas, also dragged their heels. But by then the idea had taken on a life of its own, and it reached fruition on September 3, 1964, when President Lyndon Johnson signed the Wilderness Act into law, creating the National Wilderness Preservation System. Sadly, Howard Zahniser died an untimely death just a few weeks before this, and never saw this hard-won victory.

As for Brower, he quickly realized that the bill was not an unmitigated triumph. The bureaucratic machine had carved away at the original proposal he and Zahniser had written, reducing their 50 million-acre request to 9.1 million acres, with provisions to review another 5.4 million acres over the next ten years. In the *Sierra Club Bulletin* he wrote, "This was no easy compromise to accept, nor are conservationists happy about it. Nevertheless, the Wilderness Bill is a major recognition of the importance of wilderness to the American people."[6] Besides the sharply reduced amount of land initially set aside by the act, Brower also cursed the difficulties involved in implementing it. Further congressional tampering, statutory technicalities, and endless reviews and field studies hindered the process.

Brower's frustrations contrasted with the mood of the broader conservation community regarding the bill's passage. Many felt that the Wilderness Act was a landmark achievement. An editorial in the Wilderness Society's *The Living Wilderness* applauded it: "For only in a civilized culture, in a climax period of man's intellectual, social, economic, and forward grace, could a wilderness preservation concept capture the national mind and be made a law of the land."[7] It created a unique legal framework for the designation of large areas of wild, beautiful, and ecologically rich land as wilderness— defined in the act's preamble as places where "the earth and its community of life are untrammeled by man, where man himself is a visitor who does not remain." Its mandate—that these lands "shall be administered for the use and enjoyment of the American people in such manner as will leave them unimpaired for future use and enjoyment"—was revolutionary in that it set aside land for no other purpose but its own preservation. As the fortieth anniversary of the Wilderness Act approached in 2004, its extraordinary legacy was even more striking: The amount of land protected under it had grown to over 105 million acres in over 660 individual parcels of public land.

Meanwhile, Brower was striding forward with ambitious projects for the Sierra Club, some of which would end up entangling him in controversy by the end of the 1960s. A master of persuasion, he began concentrating on getting his dynamic message out to a wider public by invigorating Sierra Club Books. He created the Exhibit Format Series—large, expensive editions with stunning photographs and descriptive, sometimes meditative text. First in the series was *This is the American Earth* (1960), with photographs by Ansel Adams. A later book, *In Wildness is the Preservation of the World* (1962)—a poignant anthology of New England seasonal landscapes with text taken from Thoreau—became an impressive commercial success. In all, the nineteen books in the series sold 255,000 copies in their original hardcover editions, and later a half million copies in quality paperback. Posters and eventually nature calendars and stationery began to appear, and along with the books, flooded the bookstore market with a panorama of images from America's wild heritage.

The passionate conservation ethic behind the glossy photographs was contagious, and clearly conveyed to America's college-educated, liberal-leaning, upper-middle class Brower's message that the wilderness idea was getting lost to commercialized recreation and development. Younger audiences were won over by other books put out by Sierra Club Books. One of these was *On the Loose* (1967), written by Terry and Renny Russell, two young brothers who described with humor, wisdom, and poetry their coming of age in the Sierra Nevada and enhanced the book with their own gorgeous photography. Scores of youth donned backpacks of their own and set out for the wilderness after reading it.

Brower's river of publicity also branched into smaller tributaries that reached an even broader audience. At his direction, the Sierra Club sometimes took out full-page ads in the *New York Times*, the *Washington Post*, *Los Angeles Times*, the *San Francisco Chronicle*, and other major newspapers as a pressure tactic to mobilize grassroots campaigns for environmental causes. Between June 9, 1966, and April 16, 1967, Brower placed what would become the most famous of the Sierra Club newspaper advertisements: four full-page ads in the *New York Times* (which were repeated in many other newspapers and magazines) fighting to keep dams out of the Grand Canyon. The Bureau of Reclamation had proposed two dams in the Grand Canyon itself, and, while the bill was before Congress, Brower appealed straight to the hearts of American citizens to protect this national treasure. "SHOULD WE ALSO FLOOD THE SISTINE CHAPEL SO TOURISTS CAN GET NEARER THE CEILING?" read one ad's huge headline. Another ad, written by Brower, read:

> Time and the river flowing—these created the Grand Canyon. The exquisite sculpture is now being revealed in the inner gorges as the river turns the pages it has been turning for twenty-five million years. The artificial lakes your Reclamation Bureau would back up behind the dams, in their own compulsion to invade the National Park system and to kill wild rivers, will cover the finest Grand Canyon pages with mud. A living river—nothing else—can keep the Grand Canyon alive to tell its ageless story.[8]

The Bureau of Reclamation was taken aback. They already had the dams built on paper, calling them "cash registers," and were only awaiting what seemed like certain congressional approval. The U.S. Senate passed the project proposal twice only to have it die in the House. Thanks to Brower's ads, suddenly the eyes of millions were watching Congress's every move. Telegrams and letters began drowning congressional mailboxes, and soon the plan was forfeited. With an all-out assault of clever publicity, Brower had managed, this time, to defeat the entrenched powers-that-be.

Immediately after the ads ran, a member of the Internal Revenue Service (IRS) hand-delivered a letter regarding the Sierra Club's tax-exempt status to the club's headquarters in San Francisco. Congressman Morris Udall of Arizona, objecting to the Sierra Club's single-handed obstruction of a project that would have helped his state financially, had filed a complaint with the IRS. Officially a tax-exempt non-profit organization, the Sierra Club could not legally devote money to political lobbying, which is what the highly persuasive and decisively influential newspaper ads were construed by the IRS to be. Submitting a meticulous defense of its position didn't help the Sierra Club, and the IRS officially declared that contributions to the club were no longer deductible. At first this appeared to be a severe setback, costing the club nearly half a million dollars in major contributions. But time revealed a surprising development: National sympathy and admiration for the club came pouring in, and smaller, nondeductible contributions multiplied. Membership in the club exploded—doubling between June 1966 and June 1969. Brower began to realize that the attention the club was receiving in regard to its battle with the IRS actually worked in the club's favor. "People who didn't know whether they loved the Grand Canyon sure knew whether or not they loved the IRS," he joked.

Publicity, in any form, reaches out—and Brower used it to inject repeated doses of environmental issues into practically every household in the country. Sparked by the publication of **Rachel Carson**'s *Silent Spring* in 1962, momentum was steadily building within the environmental movement during the late 1960s, and this helped give Brower's environmental message staying power. At the close of the decade, **Paul Ehrlich**'s *The Population Bomb* (1968) was an eye-opener, as were images of the flaming surface of the beleaguered Cuyahoga River, the massive oil spill at Santa Barbara, and the bewildering notion that the American bald eagle could possibly go extinct. New anxieties tugged at the sleeves of the most influential cross-section of the American public—the prospering middle class—and by using publicity, organizing skills, and pugnacious persistence, Brower created out of this nebulous energy a potent force: a constituency. For the first time, there was a phalanx of environmentalists to confront lumber, mining, development, and utility lobbyists. However, the kind of restless and agitating independence that made Brower such a brilliant leader of a movement made him a prickly and problematic executive director. Driven to innovate, to act quickly, to surprise, Brower frequently neglected to consult with the Sierra Club's board of directors, and rifts within the club were beginning to divide it.

Not only that, but the club itself became more and more difficult to manage. A hybrid of professionals and volunteers, radical environmentalists and conservative traditionalists: The Sierra Club didn't always cohere. Brower's tendency to act unilaterally only fomented unrest and controversy. Some of the board resented the loss of the club's tax-exempt status and felt it had been Brower's fault, and some were uncomfortable with his antipathy toward compromise. The leadership crisis precipitated a final showdown over the proposed location of a nuclear power plant. The Pacific Gas and Electric Company (PG&E) wanted to build the plant in an ecologically rich area in the Nipomo Dunes south of San Luis Obispo, but the Sierra Club board of directors objected; and three board members quietly negotiated an alternate location in nearby Diablo Canyon. Brower reared at this compromise; he had failed to protect Glen Canyon, and so wanted to protect the beautiful Diablo Canyon. Betrayed by his board of directors, Brower made his opposition clear, and a bitter conflict erupted. During a board meeting on May 3, 1969, the directors aired a long list of grievances against Brower—even his old friend and supporter Ansel Adams demanded that he step down—and with no other choice, Brower submitted his resignation.

Long-time member Maynard Munger tried at the time to explain the need for a change of leadership: "From 1952, when Dave took over, until now, the club has been a charismatic organization. It operated on the spirit and impetus of one man. But now, in order to return the club to the idea on which it was founded, that is, a volunteer club, it must become a rational organization, and the charisma of the one-man leadership must disappear."[9] But others felt that tempers and egos had clouded recognition of the incredible contribution Brower had made to the Sierra Club. Under his direction, the club had been transformed from a society of 2,000 "posey-pickers" and mountaineers, to a powerful political lobby representing 78,000 members, with whom he remained immensely popular. The vision of the club had expanded far beyond the ridges of the Sierra Nevada across the continent, and had been instrumental in adding nine areas to the national park system, including Kings Canyon, North Cascades, and Redwood National Parks. Brower also had turned the Sierra Club into the prototype of the modern environmental activist group, using the direct-mail campaigns, political pressure, and media savvy that would become the mainstays of any self-respecting non-profit organization. Eventually, in 1982, the Sierra Club would rethink their decision and re-elect Brower to the board, but not until they had endured thirteen years of operating in his shadow. As Robert A. Jones wrote in the *Nation* just after Brower resigned, "Maynard Munger's prediction will have become a fact: the Sierra Club will cease to be a charismatic organization and will become a rational one, but to have rationality at the total expense of vision and drive is a tragedy that should never have happened."[10]

Cast out of the organization he had been transfusing with his own tremendous energy for seventeen years—for nothing more than well-intentioned but tumultuous enthusiasm, and after winning so many unarguable successes—Brower's reputation glowed faintly with a halo of martyr-dom in the eyes of many idealists in the movement. He came to personify heroic devotion to the cause of environmentalism, made all the more com-pelling for his being "misunderstood" by his own organization. It was that same devotion to environmentalism that propelled him, hardly stopping to catch his breath first, right back into the fray: A few months after the con-flict with the Sierra Club, Brower set up a new organization. Called Friends of the Earth (FOE), it was designed as an activist environmental lobbying or-ganization, and Brower took care to avoid direct rivalry with the Sierra Club by incorporating FOE in New York City and by not sponsoring hikes and rivers trips, something for which the Sierra Club had become famous. As a partner organization, Brower also set up the League of Conservation Voters (LCV), a group he had tried and failed to get the Sierra Club to form. An in-formation clearinghouse, the LCV provides information to voters on pro-posed legislation and Congress members' environmental voting records, and also runs tough campaigns to defeat anti-environmental candidates.

In addition to these groups, Brower established the John Muir Institute, an environmental research and education center. His directorship of the John Muir Institute, along with speaking fees, provided his only income for several years. Finances were tight at FOE, and to help ameliorate shortfalls Brower worked there as an unpaid president. Often asked why he kept set-ting up additional environmental organizations rather than focusing on one effective group, Brower answered: "A single organization is too easily cap-tured. Exxon could buy it out of petty cash." His complex of organizations also allowed him a broad reach, covering three important environmental fields: legislative, political, and educational. He added litigation to that in the mid-1970s, when FOE joined lawsuits to block the trans-Alaska pipeline.

Brower's fame ratcheted substantially in 1971 when writer and envi-ronmentalist John McPhee published the classic *Encounters with the Archdruid*—a chronicle of the experiences McPhee gained in spending the better part of a year following him on lecture tours, taking long hikes with him, and watching him interact with opponents who wanted to develop in various wilderness areas. McPhee documented the potent force of Brower's leadership and listed many of his accomplishments, but also included enough humorous anecdotes to make Brower seem human. "Of all the things Brower swallows, the two he seems to like most in the world are Tanqueray gin and whipped-cream-and-strawberry-covered waffles,"[11] he wrote. *Enc-ounters* was not written as a polemic, but its presentation of Brower facing off against dam builders and developers was a compelling stimulant to the environmental movement, and copies of it began cropping up in the arms of undergraduates on college campuses coast to coast.

Building on his fame and on the swell of environmental concerns, Brower molded FOE into one of the world's leading environmental pressure groups and helped it guide America's approach to environmental activism. The now omnipresent phrase "Think Globally, Act Locally," penned by Brower, was the group's motto. But even as FOE began to gain power and recognition, Brower, in his unruliness, began hassling the group for what he saw as the increasing dilution of their radicalism. "I suffer from that common condition known as Founder's Syndrome," Brower confessed. "Because I founded the organization, I go on thinking that I can do things better than anyone else. I have had to learn to let others have their chance."[12] But letting others have their chance was not always possible for Brower to do, and he continued forging battles according to his own methods, leading to his stormy parting with FOE in 1984. Two years earlier he had been re-elected to the board of the Sierra Club, but he resigned again in disgust in 1999, finding the club to be too passive in the face of urgent environmental problems.

Brower meanwhile had begun devoting his energies to the Earth Island Institute, a San Francisco–based organization he founded in 1982 to promote conservation projects in countries around the world. He remained with the institute until he died. In rationalizing his turbulent career through which he seemed to flit from one environmental group to another, Brower explained that new organizations only retain momentum for about ten years at which point they become "afflicted" with practicality. "After that, an institution is more concerned with itself than with its mission. . . . You get comfortable where you are. You get practical. . . . But somehow I've missed that virus—I've got lots of others, but I missed that one."[13] In addition to leading the Earth Island Institute, Brower gave frequent public speeches, regaling audiences around the country with his bashful brand of earthy humor mixed with an environmental call to arms. He also continued writing. In 1995 a book he wrote with Steve Chapple—*Let the Mountains Talk, Let the Rivers Run*—was printed entirely on tree-free kenaf paper made from the hibiscus plant and introduced Brower's prescription for an environmentally stricken earth: CPR, or Conservation, Preservation, and Restoration.

Brower never let up on his crusade, doggedly ignoring health problems right up to the end of his life. A few months before his death, when Brower was fighting cancer, his doctors asked if he wanted them to intervene to prolong his life. "Hook me up to everything. I've got a lot of hard work to do," Brower replied. On November 5, two days before the unprecedented 2000 presidential election, Brower died at his home. Immediately, mournful obituaries circulated the country, calling Brower "the twentieth century's greatest environmentalist," "a latter-day John Muir," "the gold standard," and "an indefatigable champion of every worthwhile effort to protect the environment over the last seven decades." But the organizations he founded and the ideas he championed live on—as does the Kenyan proverb he made famous: "We do not inherit the Earth from our parents, we are borrowing it from our children," which is now carved in stone at the entrance to the National Aquarium in Washington, D.C. Years after he adopted the saying, Brower decided the words were too conservative for him. "We're not borrowing from our children, we're *stealing* from them—and it's not even considered a crime," he said, adding, "Let that be my epitaph, when I need it."[14]

NOTES

1. Philip Shabecoff, *A Fierce Green Fire: The American Environmental Movement* (New York: Farrar, Straus and Giroux, 1993), p. 101.

2. David Kupfer, "David Ross Brower," *Progressive* Vol. 58 (May 1994), p. 36.

3. David Brower, *Work in Progress* (Salt Lake City: Peregrine Smith Books, 1991), p. 1.

4. Hal K. Rothman, *Saving the Planet: The American Response to the Environment in the Twentieth Century* (Chicago: Ivan R. Dee, 2000), p. 96.

5. David Brower, *For Earth's Sake: The Life and Times of David Brower* (Salt Lake City: Peregrine Smith Books, 1990), p. 350.

6. David Brower, *Sierra Club Bulletin* Vol. 49 (September 1964), pp. 2–3.

7. Editorial, *The Living Wilderness* No. 86 (Spring-Summer 1964), p. 2.

8. "Who Can Save Grand Canyon?" Advertisement, *New York Times* (June 9, 1966), p. C35. Reproduced in Brower, *For Earth's Sake*, p. 367.

9. Quoted in Robert A. Jones, "Fratricide in the Sierra Club," *Nation* Vol. 203 (May 5, 1969), p. 569.

10. Ibid., p. 570.

11. John McPhee, *Encounters with the Archdruid* (New York: Farrar, Straus and Giroux, 1971), p. 41.

12. Quoted in Frank Graham, Jr., "Dave Brower: Last of the Optimists?" *Audubon* Vol. 84 (September 1982), p. 72.

13. Quoted in Bill McKibben, "David Brower: 1912–2000," *Rolling Stone* No. 858/859 (December 28, 2000–January 4, 2001), p. 36.

14. David Brower and Steve Chapple, *Let the Mountains Talk, Let the Rivers Run* (New York: Harper Collins, 1995), p. 2.

BIBLIOGRAPHY

David Brower wrote two autobiographies: *For Earth's Sake: The Life and Times of David Brower* (Salt Lake City: Peregrine Smith Books, 1990); and *Work in Progress* (Salt Lake City: Peregrine Smith Books, 1991). Other writings include *Sierra Club Bulletin* Vol. 49 (September 1964), pp. 2–3; *Not Man Apart: Lines from Robinson Jeffers* (San Francisco: Sierra Club Books, 1965); "280 Boots and 14,000 Feet," *Sierra* Vol. 86(3) (May/June 2001), pp. 42–50, 53–54; and, with Steve Chapple, *Let the Mountains Talk, Let the Rivers Run* (New York: Harper Collins, 1995). John McPhee's *Encounters with the Archdruid* (New York: Farrar, Straus and Giroux, 1971) is a compelling biographical account of Brower and has become an environmental classic. Magazine articles about Brower and his work are numerous. The following are representative: Editorial, *The Living Wilderness* No. 86 (Spring-Summer 1964), p. 2; "Battle of the Wilderness," *Newsweek* Vol. 68 (October 3, 1966), p. 108; " 'No Compromise' on Grand Canyon Dams: Sierra Club's Reply to Goldwater Plan," *U.S. News & World Report* Vol. 61 (December 12, 1966), pp.

60–61; Robert A. Jones, "Fratricide in the Sierra Club," *Nation* Vol. 203 (May 5, 1969), pp. 567–570; Frank J. Graham, Jr., "Dave Brower: Last of the Optimists?" *Audubon* Vol. 84 (September 1982), pp. 62–73; "Environmentalists in a Family Fight," *Newsweek* Vol. 107 (January 27, 1986), p. 7; David Kupfer, "David Ross Brower," *Progressive* Vol. 58 (May 1994), pp. 36–39; and John Rodden, "Earth-Sent Opportunities," *America* Vol. 172 (April 22, 1995), pp. 8–9. For obituaries, see "Death of a Legend," *Ecologist* Vol. 30 (December 2000/January 2001), p. 56; Bill McKibben, "David Brower, 1912–2000," *Rolling Stone* No. 858/859 (December 28, 2000–January 4, 2001), pp. 33, 36; and Joan Hamilton, "Passages," *Sierra* Vol. 86(1) (January/February 2001), pp. 8–9. General environmental history texts that place Brower within the environmental movement include Philip Shabecoff, *A Fierce Green Fire: The American Environmental Movement* (New York: Farrar, Straus and Giroux, 1993); and Hal K. Rothman, *Saving the Planet: The American Response to the Environment in the Twentieth Century* (Chicago: Ivan R. Dee, 2000).

DIXY LEE RAY
(1914–1994)

Warnings that in the past came from the pulpit and called for eternal punishment in the sulfurous fires of hell have been replaced by equally dire predictions that come from alarmist environmentalists, who call for spending millions of taxpayer dollars in order to avoid doom from the sulfurous effluents of industry.

—Dixy Lee Ray

A feisty and iconoclastic scientist, politician, and author, Dixy Lee Ray is remembered for her achievements in public life—rare for a woman at the time—and for her assertive independence. Her credentials are impressive: She was the governor of Washington state, the chairman of the Atomic Energy Commission, and a faculty member of the University of Washington's zoology department for nearly thirty years. The two books she co-wrote, *Trashing the Planet* and *Environmental Overkill*—both highly critical of what she termed "alarmist environmentalists"—claimed that most environmental problems are overblown or even nonexistent. She described environmentalists as "anti-development, anti-progress, anti-technology, anti-business, anti-established institutions, and, above all, anti-capitalism"[1] and famously discredited ozone depletion, the human impact on global climate, and the listing of endangered species. She was an outspoken advocate of nuclear power, holding her position even as nuclear energy became less and less popular. Throughout her career, she deplored what she perceived to be a widespread disdain for science and technology, and supported the popularization of science and a greater trust in technological advancements.

Dixy Lee Ray was born September 3, 1914, in Tacoma, Washington, to Alvis Marion and Frances (Adams) Ray. Her father came from a Tennessee family devoted to the Southern Baptist Convention; his mother, Marguerite, descended directly from Hugh Williamson, a signer of the Constitution. Dixy's mother, Frances, whose family originally came from the central states before moving to Tacoma, eloped with Alvis when she was 17 and he was 19, both still in high school. With only a few months left before graduation, Alvis left school to take a job in printing. Though he later felt he had thwarted his true calling—a career in electrical engineering—he stayed in commercial printing for the rest of his life. Frances kept the household running smoothly and raised their five girls. Though Dixy Lee was only the second born, her father had so hoped for a son that no girl names had been chosen for her, and her birth certificate read "Baby Ray, female." Eventually her parents named her Margaret, though they never called her that. Instead, they referred to her as "Little Dickens," an early hint at the headstrong personality that would later become a trademark of her political career. "Little Dickens" got shortened to "Dicks," which she transformed to Dixy, and at 16 she legally had her named changed to Dixy Lee, adding "Lee" out of her admiration for Robert E. Lee.

The family owned 65 acres of beach and woodland on Fox Island in Puget Sound, where the children grew up camping and exploring during the summers. The outdoor life enhanced Dixy Lee's interest in the natural world, especially marine life, and provided an outlet for her athletic tendencies. Later she would joke that nature did not make her willowy—she had a stout build and was very strong. Realizing her strength, her father assigned her many chores usually performed by boys, such as chopping wood and carrying heavy loads. At the age of 12 she became the youngest girl ever to climb Mount Rainier. In many ways, Dixy's personality was shaped by her father's forceful temper, his disappointment in not having a son, and his unwillingness to express emotion. She once attributed her successful career to her efforts to win the affection and admiration of her father, even though she could never be the son he always wanted. Though she worked hard to prove herself to him, he never did express his love for her.

Ray graduated from Stadium High School, Tacoma, in 1933. With the help of a merit scholarship, she enrolled in Mills College, an all-women's school in Oakland, California, and began studying zoology. Her solid physique helped her qualify for campus employment that usually went to men, such as being a janitor, and she earned enough money to pay for her own room and board. In her spare time she also indulged her love of the stage, producing a weekly show at the Emporium in San Francisco during her freshman year. She eventually added a minor in drama. In 1937 she received her bachelor's degree in zoology with a Phi Beta Kappa key. One year later Mills awarded her a master's degree in zoology and a teaching certificate.

Ray stayed in Oakland and taught biology at Oakland High School for the next four years, working to pay her student loans. Continuing with her exploration of marine science, she also worked on weekends at the Hopkins Marine Biological Station at Stanford University, in Pacific Grove, California. Her work there involved bacterial serology and the cultivation of soil amoebae. When she received a John Switzer fellowship in 1942 from the biology department of Stanford University, she was able to return to graduate study. A two-year Van Sicklen fellowship then allowed her to complete work on her Ph.D. degree in biological sciences by 1945. Later that year she joined the faculty of the University of Washington in Seattle as an instructor in zoology, and she would continue to teach there in various capacities until 1976. She also became a member of the executive committee of the Friday Harbor Laboratories, the university's marine science center on San Juan Island, a post she held until 1960.

She advanced through the ranks at the university, becoming an assistant professor in 1947, then an associate professor of zoology in 1957. In 1952 she was awarded a Guggenheim grant for a year's research on amoeba substance and its relation to serums at Hopkins Marine Biological Station. She also described a new species of free-living amoeba. Spiraling deeper into research on marine invertebrates, she then began a course of study that would become something of a specialty for her: that of organisms such as *Limnoria*, which bore through wood submerged in seawater. The Office of Naval Research gave her a grant in 1955 to compare and contrast *Limnoria* from the Mediterranean Sea and from the Washington coast. Her work proved that these organisms actually ingest the wood as opposed to simply tunneling through it, and she later obtained a patent for a treatment she developed to protect wooden undersea structures. She also organized a symposium sponsored by the University of Washington in 1957 on marine organisms' damage to dry docks, boats, and wharf pilings. After directing the symposium, she edited the collection of papers from the conference, including her own, and compiled them into *Marine Boring and Fouling Organisms*, published in 1959.

In 1958, an opportunity arose for Ray to merge her scientific knowledge and her fondness for theater: She was invited to develop a weekly series of fifteen half-hour television programs on marine biology. Her teaching experience, bold manner, and quirkiness made her an appealing TV personality. Both Ray and her "Doorways to Science" programs, which aired on National Educational Television, were a walkaway hit in Washington state. She continued to enlarge her sphere of influence in 1960 when she accepted an assignment as special assistant to the assistant director for the Division of Biological and Medical Science of the National Science Foundation, a job that meant moving to Washington, D.C. She stayed for two years, and her work there resulted in the founding of the National Center for Atmospheric Research and the National Radio Astronomy Center. She also gained two appointments with the National Academy of Sciences, one on the Committee on Oceanography and one on the Committee of Postdoctoral Fellowships (1960–1963). In addition, she was asked to serve on the Subcommittee on International Biological Stations (1962–1965).

Ray then moved back to Seattle, taking the director's position at the Pacific Science Center in 1963, which she held until 1972. The Pacific Science Center, then consisting of a cluster of six architecturally fantastic buildings, had opened the previous year as an attraction for the Seattle World's Fair, and it desperately needed strong leadership and funding. The center provided Ray the perfect venue for her guiding principle: that science should be enlightening and accessible to a large and diverse public rather than to only a small group of intellectual elites. Her years in Washington had convinced her that a wide chasm existed between the perceptions of the scientific community and those of the public, and she made it her goal to bridge the gap. Though some of her colleagues protested the idea of popularizing science, fearing it meant "dumbing down" scientific concepts, she forged ahead with her own agenda, creating fascinating and approachable exhibits, displays, experiments, and conferences on everything from the moon landing to earthquakes. She especially wanted to foster a love of learning in children, realizing that the way science was taught in school often ended up discouraging any interest a child might naturally have. Under her direction, and with the eventual financial assistance from the National Science Foundation, the state of Washington, and some seventy-five school districts in the area, the center gained national recognition, and she is credited with its survival. Now enormously respected, the Pacific Science Center bestows its prestige on others through the Arches of Science Award, which it sponsors to honor scientists who have contributed to the general public's understanding of the meaning of science.

During her years of teaching at University of Washington and acting as director of the Pacific Science Center, Ray also served on various committees and took leading roles in affiliation with several scientific and government groups. In 1964 she took an appointment to the visiting faculty at Stanford University, where she was named chief scientist for the International Indian Ocean Expedition. This undertaking, the first cooperative long-term effort to gain understanding of the Indian Ocean's processes and resources, united nations that had fought against one another in World War II. During the expedition Ray oversaw the scientific activities of Stanford University's research vessel *Te Vega*. Afterward she was invited to participate on the American Association for the Advancement of Science's Committee on Public Understanding of Science, and she also served as a member of the Smithsonian Institution's Advisory Council for the National Museum Act.

After nine satisfying years at the Pacific Science Center, Ray left in 1972 to accept a nomination by President Richard Nixon to membership on the Atomic Energy Commission (AEC), later saying "[E]nergy is at the heart of Western Civilization, and that seemed like an interesting place to be."[2] Having recently resettled herself on the family land on Fox Island in Puget Sound with her two devoted companions—a miniature French poodle named Jacques and a Scottish deerhound named Ghillie—Ray was loathe to uproot and move to the nation's capital. But she was eager to take the job, and on August 2, 1972, the U.S. Senate confirmed Ray's nomination, making her the first woman to be appointed to a full five-year term on the AEC. President Nixon reportedly was pleased to have found someone with a background in biology who would be as comfortable in the field as in the laboratory. The chairman of the AEC at the time, James Schlesinger, announced that Ray would be a valuable addition to the agency, with her ability to strike a balance between the opposing demands of energy and the environment. But Ray sensed an unspoken motive behind her appointment. "If it hadn't been for the women's liberation movement I doubt the president would have appointed me," she admitted. "I was appointed because I was a woman and that's alright with me." She also conceded that she had her homework cut out for her, as she knew little about the affairs of atomic energy.

Ray jumped feetfirst into her new job, taking on her new responsibilities with determination and ingenuity and more than justifying her appointment. Rather than flying east when she started, she chose to drive across the country in order to visit several AEC installations, and so invested in a made-to-order motor home for her journey. Once she got underway at the AEC headquarters in Maryland, her duties included minority hiring, communications, public information, and improved science education. She also wanted to encourage the advancement of nuclear medicine, a field that intrigued her. Decreasing public apprehensions about nuclear energy became a major goal for her, and she stood firmly behind this technology. She also involved herself in the AEC's public relations quagmire regarding environmental affairs. Though she acknowledged that nuclear power can have adverse impacts on the environment, she was quick to distance herself from those who warned of the ecological disasters of nuclear waste and thermal pollution, saying she wasn't the type to predict doom. "Given the clear advantage and successful operation of nuclear power, why is the nuclear power plant situation in the United States always portrayed as so dismal?"[3] she later wrote.

Temperamentally, she was well suited to the job, working well with committees and not being afraid to speak her mind. When Chairman Schlesinger left the AEC in early 1973 to head the Central Intelligence Agency, President Nixon appointed Ray to his position on February 6, making her the first woman to sit as its chair. Following a commitment to minority hiring, she chose an African American, David Jenkins, as her assistant. She would need assistance and determination in the days ahead, for the agency she inherited was entangled in a controversial history. Created in 1947, the AEC's most urgent purpose when it started was to develop nuclear weapons; with the Soviet Union busily working to develop atomic bombs, the U.S. Congressional Joint Committee on Atomic Energy exerted enormous pressure on the AEC to increase the supply of uranium ore and the production of plutonium, and to build up a nuclear weapons stockpile. It would be some time before anyone considered peaceful uses of atomic energy and before concern over waste management issues arose, and, typical of many governmental agencies, the AEC needed congressional authorization and appropriation of funds in order to accomplish anything. Many proposals for long-term disposal of nuclear waste fell victim to bureaucratic impasses, and little progress was made. By the time Ray took over the AEC, the emphasis on nuclear science had turned away from military applications toward the use of radioactivity in medicine and industry and the use of nuclear power to generate electricity. All of these activities produce waste, and public concern over nuclear safety and the mind-boggling ecological implications of nuclear-waste disposal was on the rise, creating a situation that required potent and convincing leadership from the commission.

Ray therefore played a key role in the formulation of American nuclear policies and programs. Her leadership garnered praise from some, though the AEC, which operated without public oversight, had many detractors. A small anti-nuclear movement had begun raising questions, trying to break through the agency's veil of secrecy. In 1972, several organizations including Friends of the Earth and the Union of Concerned Scientists demanded that the AEC hold hearings to examine the safety of emergency core-cooling systems. Numerous safety shortcomings, about which the AEC had been suppressing information, were exposed. While citizen opposition to nuclear power continued to mount, Ray did her best to reassure the public during her reign at the AEC that nuclear power was an unparalleled success. Impatient with what she saw as overreacting on the part of environmentalists, she became a stout advocate of nuclear energy, believing that it was safe and that it was simply misunderstood by the public. The Rasmussen Report, issued by the AEC in 1974, articulated this attitude, estimating that the accident probability of a nuclear reactor was far lower than risks people expose themselves to in daily life, such as driving a car, and that, therefore, opposition to nuclear reactors should be dismissed as irrational. This report met with severe opposition, which left Ray unfazed. She became famous for her assertion that a nuclear power plant is vastly safer than eating, since hundreds of people choke to death every year. Ray's outspoken endorsement of nuclear power earned her the nickname "Miss Plutonium" from social critic and citizen activist Ralph Nader.

Another one of Ray's tasks was to find solutions to the national fuel crisis, which only reinforced her belief in nuclear power. She orchestrated plans to speed construction of new nuclear power plants, and worked on eliminating defects in existing ones. "The fact is that we are going to have to use atomic power as our reserves of fossil fuels dwindle, and we may as well get used to it. We can't live in a Garden of Eden and still have a technological society,"[4] Ray explained. She strengthened her control of the AEC by outmaneuvering two of its most influential figures, James Ramey, an AEC commissioner and its liaison with Congress, and Milton Shaw, the director of reactor development and technology. Ray reduced Shaw's power through restructuring and paring down his job, and he eventually resigned. When Ramey's term expired, Ray did not reappoint him. Unhindered by these more circumspect voices, Ray could demonstrate her independence fully, which caused a stir in the Joint Committee: Some of the members expressed outrage, while others were pleased with her assertiveness. "Dixy Lee does what she believes in, and has brought a whole new vitality to the AEC," said one congressman.

In her personal life, Ray exhibited an equivalent nonconformist flair. Shunning the social scene in the Washington, D.C., area, she made her home in the same 8-by-28-foot motor home that she had driven cross-country. She parked it somewhere in rural Virginia, commuting to work by chauffeured limousine and keeping her "address" a secret since she was sometimes forced to move due to local ordinances against trailers. She never married, but was devoted to her eight nieces and nephews, even asking for eight souvenir pens from President Nixon at her swearing-in ceremony as AEC commissioner. Wherever she went her two dogs went too, including to her office, where they were admitted with their own photo security tags. Many visitors were startled to be greeted by the two dogs, and stories about Ray and her eccentricities were greeted with glee back in her home state.

In 1974, President Gerald Ford consolidated federal energy programs, and the AEC was absorbed in the Energy Research and Development Administration (ERDA). Ray continued her leadership responsibilities at the ERDA until early 1975, when she became assistant secretary of state in charge of a new Bureau of Oceans and International Environmental and Scientific Affairs. She stayed only six months in her new position, during which time she began a survey of all existing scientific treaties and agreements, and insisted that her office be consulted before the United States made any commitment regarding scientific, technological, or environmental affairs. When Secretary of State Henry Kissinger ignored her request, she resigned in frustration and permanently burned her bridges, saying it was impossible to get anything done under Kissinger.

Ray could not wait to leave the nation's capital and get back to what she called "the real Washington"—and her home state was glad to welcome her back. She fielded many requests for job opportunities and speaking engagements, though she had something else in mind: the governorship. She campaigned on the Democratic ticket, touring the state in her trademark kneesocks, and flaunting her famous forthrightness. She promised "honest government, open government, and responsible government," and won the election on November 3, 1976, again making feminist history, this time by becoming the first woman governor of Washington State. From the very start of what would be a controversial term of office, Ray came under fire for governing like a conservative Republican, despite having run as a Democrat.

Ray continued to champion nuclear energy, and provoked the fury of environmentalists by minimizing the dangers of nuclear waste and supporting less stringent restrictions on its disposal. Within the borders of her state lay an opportunity for her to put her policies to the test—the Hanford Nuclear Reservation in southeastern Washington, home of the largest nuclear waste dump in the nation. Public opinion was growing increasingly negative toward nuclear energy, especially after the near-catastrophe in 1979 at the Three Mile Island nuclear plant in Pennsylvania. Prompted by that accident, newspapers began investigations of radiation leaks at Hanford, where the spotlight of public scrutiny had begun to focus. Intending to force a comprehensive reassessment of national policy on radioactive waste management, Ray closed a dumping facility at Hanford, citing violations in packaging and transportation of low-level nuclear waste. A few months later she reopened it on the condition that the U.S. government attempt to find a solution to the radioactive waste–management issue, which has never fully been resolved. Many Washington voters were angered by her decision to reopen the dump site, which also allowed for nuclear waste to be trucked in from other states. The Hanford site has become one of the largest environmental cleanup projects in history and is widely considered one of the worst environmental disasters of the twentieth century.

Ray's governorship lasted only one term. She had several victories, such as balancing the state budget and bringing about full funding of basic education. But some of her views made her unpopular, as did her sometimes highhanded style. She engaged in legendary feuds with the media, famously naming the pigs on her Fox Island farm after various reporters. When she ran for re-election in 1980, she collected a massive re-election fund from timber and development interests, but lost the Democratic nomination to Jim McDermott, a state senator. John Spellman, a King County executive, eventually won the election and succeeded Ray as governor.

When she lost her re-election bid, Ray closed the door on public life and returned to her farm on Fox Island in semi-retirement. She concentrated on raising fruits, vegetables, and poultry, and took up a woodcarving hobby, inspired by her long-time interest and study of American Indian culture. She became an expert carver in cedar in the tradition of coastal Northwest Indian tribes. She also accepted invitations for speaking engagements, usually for pro-industry organizations, and served as a consultant for the U.S. Department of Energy, the Los Alamos National Laboratory, and the Lawrence Livermore National Laboratory. One of her favorite speaking topics remained energy. At one speech, delivered at an anti-environmental conference, she assured her audience: "Energy is the life blood of industrial western civilization, and environmentalists and greenie radicals hate it. . . . What is so noble about conserving energy? We know how to use it and produce it and with little impact on our environment."[5] She also was a founding board member of the Washington Institute for Policy Studies, a conservative think tank promoting a free-market approach to public policy issues such as government services and environmental solutions.

During her retirement, she authored two major books on the environment and public policy with her longtime friend and former press secretary, Lou Guzzo. In *Trashing the Planet: How Science Can Help Us Deal with Acid Rain, Depletion of the Ozone, and Nuclear Waste (Among Other Things)*, published in 1990, she aired her views of environmentalism, science, and politics. She defined her opponents as being panic-strickenly opposed to any kind of progress and argued that calm reason and alarmist environmentalism are mutually exclusive. Leaders of many national environmental organizations were described as "determinedly leftist, radical, and dedicated to blocking industrial progress and unraveling industrial society."[6] Recalling the days of her childhood, when infectious diseases were more prevalent; farm productivity was much lower without the use of chemical fertilizers, herbicides and insecticides; and life was "dirty and smelly," Ray inferred that environmentalists, by questioning the side effects of progress, were actually anti-humanity. In discussing acid rain, ozone depletion, and global warming, she acknowledged that some of the problems may be real, but argued that natural causes like lightning, decay of organic matter in swamps and wetlands, and fumes from volcanoes are much more serious than the effects of human industry. She elucidated her prevailing theme concerning the counterproductive and wasteful impact environmentalists have on society as follows: "From simple scare stories about carcinogens lurking in everything we eat, breathe, and touch to truly stupendous claims of earth-destroying holes in the sky, global changes in climate, and doom for Western society, we have been panicked into spending billions of dollars to cure problems without knowing whether they are real."[7] Following publication of the book, there was no shortage of disparaging responses from environmentalists, who faulted it with misinterpretations of data, carelessness with facts, and the use of irrelevant but scientific-sounding information to prove her point.

In her next book, also written with Guzzo, *Environmental Overkill: Whatever Happened to Common Sense?* (1993), Ray promised a common-sense approach to environmental issues such as overpopulation, global warming, and endangered species. Insisting that concern over the growing world population and its impact on natural resources hides a tyrannical need to control the private lives of citizens, she claimed that high-yield agriculture—which relies on chemical application, advanced technology, and high-input machinery—will more than provide for a growing world population. This works well with her principle that what nature cannot provide, humans must supply, and that the answers to environmental problems lie in science and technology, not in restricting consumption or regulating industry.

She went on to explain that wetland preservation has been an example of good intentions gone bad, based more on sentiment than good science. Her assertion that the ban on DDT, combined with the protection of mosquito-producing wetlands, has caused a world resurgence of malaria and other mosquito-borne diseases inflamed environmentalists and sparked rebuttals and debate. Her opponents accused her of dishonesty and gross oversimplification and pointed out that there have been no substantiated reports of an increase in malaria-infected mosquitoes in recent history. Other contentious claims included her belief that the endangered species list is a frivolous whim with no basis in fact, and that, for example, the listing of the northern spotted owl was merely a totally unjustified excuse to halt logging. In summarizing, she stated:

> In the name of environmentalism, it is no longer enough to be kind to animals, careful of wastes, and sensitive to ecosystems. According to the spokesmen for the environmental movement . . . it is necessary not only to be good stewards of the Earth and its resources, but it is essential also to reduce human impact upon the air, water, and land, and to do it immediately and by any means possible—no matter how drastic, no matter how costly. This extreme view of environmentalism is, unfortunately, the one that drives public policy.[8]

Standing firmly behind her claims, Ray found ways to make her own impact on public policy. For the last few years of her life, she served as director of the Mountain States Legal Foundation, a non-profit legal foundation created in 1976 that works to dissolve environmental protections and designations on behalf of oil, development, and timber industries. Known as the litigating agency of the Wise Use movement,[9] for which Ray became an enthusiastic spokesperson, it promotes extremist property rights and has served as a training ground for attorneys in the anti-environmental movement. In 1992, during the Earth Summit in Rio de Janeiro (which Ray called the "flat-earth summit"), she worked as **Rush H. Limbaugh**'s radio correspondent, attempting to discredit "environmental hysteria." Attempting to delegitimize the Endangered Species Act, she appeared on a religious radio station in Los Angeles in 1993, asking listeners whether they approved of $2.6 million being spent to protect the cockroach, which she claimed was listed as endangered. The theatrical cockroach example came from *Environmental Overkill*, in which she asserts that tampering with endangered species and their habitats can incur outrageous punishment. "Penalities are far more likely to be imposed for 'environmental crimes' even when committed unknowingly than for unlawful acts like burglary or aggravated assault in the criminal justice system."[10] This story was then hoisted aloft by conservative media outlets as a hyberbolic example of how the environmental movement sought to coerce huge amounts of money out of taxpayers for "worthless" causes. Under scrutiny however, her claims failed to stand up. In an investigative report, Tim Callahan revealed that Ray's statements were false.[11] The endangered species list contains no cockroaches, nor are the majority of species on the list "snails and worms and bugs," as she had also claimed.

During her long career, Ray's influence was felt far and wide—while she was heading the Atomic Energy Commission she was probably the most powerful woman in politics—and she never failed to make a lasting impression on those who met her throughout her life. She was the recipient of numerous awards, including twenty-one honorary doctoral degrees and, in 1973, the Peace Medal of the United Nations. She was named one of the Top Ten Most Influential Women in the Nation by *Harper's Bazaar* in 1977, and one of One Hundred Honored Citizens at the State of Washington Centennial in 1989.

On January 2, 1994, 79-year-old Dixy Lee Ray passed away at her home of a bronchial infection and viral pneumonia.

NOTES

1. Dixy Lee Ray and Lou Guzzo, *Trashing the Planet: How Science Can Help Us Deal with Acid Rain, Depletion of the Ozone, and Nuclear Waste (Among Other Things)* (Washington, DC: Regnery Gateway, 1990), p. 163.

2. Elizabeth Stead and Kathleen Waugh, *Dixy Lee Ray 1977–1981. Guide to the Governor's Papers* Vol. 6 (Olympia, WA: Office of the Secretary of State, 1993), p. x.

3. Ray and Guzzo, *Trashing the Planet*, p. 135.

4. Sam Iker, "Changes in Dixyland," *Time* (November 3, 1973), p. 99.

5. Quoted in David Helvarg, *The War against the Greens: The "Wise-Use" Movement, the New Right and the Anti-Environmental Movement* (San Francisco: Sierra Club Books, 1994), p. 242.

6. Ray and Guzzo, *Trashing the Planet*, p. 163.

7. Ibid., p. ix.

8. Dixy Lee Ray and Lou Guzzo, *Environmental Overkill: Whatever Happened to Common Sense?* (Washington, DC: Regnery Gateway, 1993), p. 201.

9. The Wise Use movement emerged in the late 1980s as a backlash against a surge of environmental legislation that sought to protect wilderness and endangered species and to address pollution concerns. This anti-environmental movement united resource extraction industries, ultra-conservative foundations, and property rights advocates, especially in the western United States.

10. Ray and Guzzo, *Environmental Overkill*, p. 89.

11. Tim Callahan, "Environmentalists Cause Malaria! (And Other Myths of the 'Wise Use' Movement)," *Humanist* Vol. 55 (January/February 1995), pp. 10–15.

BIBLIOGRAPHY

Dixy Lee Ray's friend and former press secretary Lou Guzzo wrote the only existing book-length biography of her: *Is It True What They Say about Dixy?* (Mercer Island, WA: The Writing Works, Inc., 1980), which contains career information and explains her personal philosophy on environmental and scientific matters. A good short biography is Janet Newlan Bower's "Dixy Lee Ray," pp. 424–432 in Rose K. Rose and Louise S. Grinstein, eds., *Women in the Biological Sciences: A Biobibliographic Sourcebook* (Westport, CT: Greenwood Press, 1997). Articles following Ray's career include Robert Gillette, "Ray Nominated to AEC," *Science* Vol. 177 (July 21, 1972), p. 246; Sam Iker, "Changes in Dixyland," *Time* (November 3, 1973), pp. 98–99; Dennis Williams and Michael Reese, "Can Dixy Rise Again?" *Newsweek* (July 14, 1980), p. 28; and "Defeat for Dixy Lee Ray," *Time* (September 29, 1980), p. 25. Two detailed articles that offer an opposing view of some of Ray's more contentious assertions are Tim Callahan, "Environmentalists Cause Malaria! (And Other Myths of the 'Wise Use' Movement)," *Humanist* Vol. 55 (January/February 1995), pp. 10–15; and Tim Callahan, "Trees and Volcanoes Cause Smog! (More Myths from the 'Wise Use' Movement)," *Humanist* Vol. 56 (January/February 1996), pp. 29–34. An overview of Ray's theories and their impact on the environmental movement can be found in Edward Flattau, *Tracking the Charlatans: An Environmental Columnist's Refutational Handbook for the Propaganda Wars* (Washington, DC: Global Horizons Press, 1998). See also David Helvarg, *The War against the Greens: The "Wise-Use" Movement, the New Right and Anti-Environmental Violence* (San Francisco: Sierra Club Books, 1994). Some of Ray's scientific papers include "Recent Research on the Biology of Marine Wood Borers," *American Wood Preservation Association Proceedings* Vol. 54 (1958) pp. 120–128; "A Biologist Looks at the Energy Crisis," *Bioscience* Vol. 24 (1974), pp. 495–497; "Acid Rain: What to Do?" *Environmental Science and Technology* Vol. 22 (1988), p. 348; and "Why We'll Need More Nuclear Power," *Fortune* Vol. 121 (1990), p. 88. Her books (written with Lou Guzzo) provide an in-depth look at her arguments and the reasoning behind them: *Trashing the Planet: How Science Can Help Us Deal with Acid Rain, Depletion of the Ozone, and Nuclear Waste (Among Other Things)* (Washington, DC: Regnery Gateway, 1990); and *Environmental Overkill: Whatever Happened to Common Sense?* (Washington, DC: Regnery Gateway, 1993).

JOSEPH COORS
(1917–2003)

[How can we stand by] inept and unorganized while the environmentalists and radicals walk all over us?

—Joseph Coors

"Brewed with Pure Rocky Mountain Spring Water." Armed with this slo-
gan, the Coors beer company expanded their brand from a small Colorado
family business founded in the late 1800s to a global corporation selling beer
in more than three dozen countries. Prior to the 1980s, when the company
began reaching for broader markets, Coors beer was a rarity, available only
in a few western states, lending it an enigmatic reputation that media pundits
called the "Coors mystique." But considering how the Coors family legacy
has been shaped by ultra-conservative beliefs, some might argue that the
Coors mystique was tarnished when third-generation company president
Joseph Coors came to the forefront of the environmental debate in the
1980s to fight environmental protections and to back one of the more influential pillars of the right-wing, the Heritage Foundation. "After the election
of Ronald Reagan foundations funded by conservative business leaders like
Joseph Coors and Richard Mellon Scaife mounted an ideological jihad
against environmentalism. It was led by the Washington-based Heritage
Foundation, with its $10-million-annual budget, which has found ways to
blame environmentalists for almost every social problem plaguing the

country,"[1] wrote journalist Mark Dowie. In 1983, thanks to his wealth and influence, and his opposition to environmental regulations, Joseph Coors was named "one of the country's leading anti-environmentalists" by *Reader's Digest*. His impact on the environment has been felt beyond the broad plane of national policymaking as well: The Coors brewery has been listed as one of Colorado's biggest polluters and has been cited on several occasions for water pollution infractions—an infelicitous twist considering the company's emphasis on the purity of its water supply.

Joseph Coors was born on November 12, 1917, in Golden, Colorado, to Alice May and Adolph Coors, Jr. His grandfather, Adolph Coors, had founded the Coors brewery in 1876 and was a millionaire by 1893. The Coors brewery was built in Golden, fifteen miles from Denver on the banks of Clear Creek, an ideal resource for brewing beer. Clear Creek's headwaters emerge among the 14,000–foot peaks of the Colorado Rocky Mountains and filter through twenty-five miles of crystalline metamorphic rock before reaching the town of Golden. Guaranteed a reliable supply of high-quality water, the Adolph Coors Company eventually would become famous for marketing its beer as "a taste of the Rockies." Wanting control over every aspect of the product that bore his name, Adolph integrated vertically, building a bottle factory, a cement factory, a 1,500-ton icehouse, and an artificial ice plant. Tragically, in the 1920s Prohibition took away Adolph's sense of purpose, and on a June night in 1929, he jumped to his death from a hotel window in Virginia Beach. His son (Joseph's father), Adolph Coors, Jr., took over running the brewery, and successfully kept it in business during Prohibition by converting it into a malted milk factory.

Adolph Jr. ruled his three sons—Joseph and his older brothers Adolph III and William (Bill)—grimly, with frosty emotional reserve and strict discipline. Since he worked such long hours at the brewery he could not be on hand to punish his sons for each offense as it occurred, so he devised a scheme whereby their mother recorded their misdeeds during the week and on Sunday he meted out the appropriate measure of spankings for each child. The brewery dominated almost all aspects of the boys' lives. As a preschooler, Joseph earned his first pay by working for the company, painting fences for 12.5 cents an hour. While his older brothers were groomed to head the brewery one day, he had slightly more freedom to explore other opportunities— though he too would ultimately end up with a career in the family business. Adolph III was the oldest, but suffered a debilitating stutter and was therefore exempted from becoming the company spokesperson. Happiest when he could be outdoors, Adolph III once confided that all he really wanted was to have a ranch. He couldn't escape the imperative of continuing in the family's quest for a beer empire, however, and even though he was (ironically) allergic to beer, he was soon ensconced in the brewery offices. Bill had dissenting ambitions as well—he wistfully dreamed of becoming a doctor or studying piano—but was instead forced to study chemical engineering and begin managerial training with his father.

Meanwhile, Joseph Coors graduated from Cornell University in 1939 with a chemistry degree, and went to work doing research engineering work for the DuPont Company in Delaware. His letters home, filled with the world outside Golden, made his brewery-bound brothers envious. In the early 1940s, he left DuPont to work for the National Dairy Products Association, which excused him from being drafted to World War II. In 1948, Coors left his job and returned to Golden with his new wife, Holly, a Philadelphia socialite. Uninterested in the process of beer making and having no taste for actually drinking it, Coors felt disinclined toward a position of authority within the brewery, so he began working for a prosperous company subsidiary called Coors Porcelain. Established before Prohibition, Coors Porcelain used the fine clay in the region to manufacture porcelain, and contributed greatly to the company's survival of the dry years. Orders came in from scientific laboratories around the country for a variety of Coors-made wares, such as mortars and pestles and crucibles.

By the mid-1950s, Joseph had settled into family and professional life. He and Holly had five sons, and he had been named president of Coors Porcelain and executive vice president of the Adolph Coors Company. Adolph III held the title of board chairman of both the Adolph Coors Company and Coors Porcelain, and Bill was president of Adolph Coors Company and executive vice president of Coors Porcelain. Around that time, the brewery made further steps toward absolute control over all facets of their operations. The company bought a nearby gas field and constructed a thirty-mile pipeline to carry gas to the plant to supply their energy needs. This set the stage for future expansions, which eventually coalesced into the Coors Energy Company, a multimillion-dollar subsidiary that owned gas fields and operated coal mines throughout the American Southwest. Adolph Coors Company also signed an exclusive contract with a can-making business, which built a factory in Golden and began making cans for Coors alone. Eventually Coors made a similar arrangement with a bottle factory, and in time Coors consolidated both factories into a massive subsidiary called Coors Container, which has never been successfully unionized.

The Coors family considered unions to be a nuisance, though they put up with them for years in order to have a union label. But by 1957, tired of labor struggles and demands, Joseph broke the union at Coors Porcelain by forcing upon it an "open-shop" provision that allowed employees to choose whether or not to join the union. When many employees chose to abandon the union, the local faltered and collapsed. Union conflicts would continue to plague the company for the next several decades, but for the time being business was good enough to ignore their influence. The year that Joseph cleared the union out of Coors Porcelain, Coors was the biggest seller of beer in the eleven states where it was distributed, and the company was making $40 million a year. In fact, the company's biggest problem was producing enough beer to satisfy demand. Known for the lightness of its flavor, Coors beer picked up nicknames like "Colorado Kool-Aid" and "canoe" beer ("it's damn near water"), but it made a good match for American tastes at the time, which generally found the bitterness of stronger beers unpleasant. Coors also introduced attractive innovations to the beer industry—in 1959 it became the first American beverage company to use aluminum cans, having perfected a process that produced delicate, lightweight, easily chilled beverage containers that didn't impart the metallic flavor steel cans did.

The family business enjoyed a great deal of prosperity in the two decades following World War II. Yet Joseph and his family lived a very modest lifestyle on a restricted allowance from his father. His kids went to public school and, well into the 1960s, had to go to a friend's house in order to watch color television. Going to visit their grandparents' mansion was the only time they caught of glimpse of the family's vast wealth. But this wealth was no secret to the outside world. Threats of kidnapping had circled the family in the 1930s, and resurfaced with tragic consequences in February 1960. When Adolph III failed to show up for a board meeting one morning, a search led to the discovery of his vehicle, still running but abandoned, on a road a few miles from his home. The morning after he disappeared, his wife received a ransom note demanding $500,000 for her husband's return. Though she complied with the note's instructions, nothing happened, and for nine months the family waited for word while the FBI conducted one of the biggest investigations in its history. That September, Adolph's body was found in a gully by a hunter. Two months later, a man named Joe Corbett was arrested for Adolph's murder and went on to serve eighteen years in prison.

Joseph faced the shocking family tragedy by plunging right back into the running of the Coors industries. His thoughts also turned increasingly toward larger social issues and their impact on his freedom to run his business as he saw fit. Coming from a strictly traditional family obsessed with a capitalistic drive to succeed, he was predisposed to a conservative viewpoint, but had never organized his beliefs into a coherent body of principles. Thus, when he stumbled across Russell Kirk's *The Conservative Mind*, published in 1953, he was gratified to find an articulation of a highly conservative ideology that he agreed with point by point. Kirk condemned labor unions and welfare, supported a clearly demarcated class structure, and argued for the sanctity of individual property rights—all provocative issues for Coors, given his desire to continue building a beer empire unhindered by intrusive governmental regulations. "Civilized society requires orders and classes. Unless we call civilization a mistake, any attempt to ignore natural inequality and propertied inequality is sure to cause general unhappiness," wrote Kirk. His definition of property rights framed them as so crucial that "the rights of property are more important than the right to life." By extension, union demands and governmental controls such as restricting a company's discharge of environmental pollution led to the decay of these rights.

Soon after Kirk's book appeared, William F. Buckley began publishing a conservative journal called *National Review*, and in 1960 U.S. Senator Barry Goldwater published *The Conscience of a Conservative*, which reiterated many of Kirk's main ideas but aroused greater attention since it was written by a national political figure. Besides so satisfyingly addressing Coors's concerns, these publications provided an ideological counterpoint to social changes that began occurring as the 1960s ushered in the civil rights and environmental movements. And Joseph Coors clung to their conservative imperatives tenaciously. Feeling that the germination of progressive ideas was causing the degeneration of the traditional values in which he believed and was spreading corruption throughout the younger generations, Coors began exerting tighter control on his workforce. He instituted a new rule: All potential new employees had to undergo a lie detector test so that he could be certain to keep his ranks free of radical liberals, homosexuals, and anyone convicted of a crime. This exemplified Coors's habit of using the brewery as a forum for the expression of his political beliefs. He often enclosed propaganda literature from the ultra-conservative John Birch Society in the pay envelopes of his employees; one year, to drive home his argument that the government encroached far too much in the lives of its citizens, he paid his workers in full—withholding no federal taxes—for two months. In the next paycheck, three months' worth of taxes were deducted to emphasize the magnitude of the government's greed.

His battle against liberal social movements led him to an interest in politics, partly because he began to realize he had sufficient influence, thanks to his money, to attract notice and even affect change. In 1964, Goldwater ran for president on the first straightforward conservative platform ever presented in a national political contest, and Coors got involved in the campaign. Goldwater sustained a resounding defeat by Lyndon Johnson, but Coors was undeterred. Confident in his ideology and developing a taste for political influence, he began to cast around for other ways to promote his worldview. He got word of a vacancy on the six-person board of regents at the University of Colorado in Boulder, thirty miles north of Golden. Believing the college to be a deep taproot of liberal politics and hoping he might influence the school's youth with his own vision of the virtues of unfettered capitalism, he decided to run for the statewide office. His campaign literature professed his ideals bluntly. "I believe that the University of Colorado should be dedicated to preserving and strengthening the cause of freedom in America. There is nothing that I want more for your children and mine than to look forward to a bright tomorrow in a free America . . . unfettered by excessive government control." He won the slot and accepted the office of regent in January 1967.

Coors grew notorious at the university for his attempts to prevent liberal social movements such as environmentalism and civil rights from "infecting" the campus. He fought to quell dissent, rebuking other regents when he felt they had been too indulgent toward student protestors. "College administrators who condone, capitulate, and make concessions to student insubordination under threat of reprisal ask for chains on their doors," he contended. He skirmished most frequently against the Students for a Democratic Society (SDS), a leftist civil rights group mobilized around an anti-nuclear focus that intensified as the environmental impacts of radioactive waste and nuclear emissions became better understood. Coors tried to offset their influence by breaking up their demonstrations and attempted (unsuccessfully) to create an academic department devoted to the study of conservative government. Sustaining his ideology was more important to him than academic freedom, and he openly admitted he would continue to countenance the beliefs he had outlined in his campaign, "even if, in so doing, so-called 'academic freedom' must be somewhat restrained." His six-year term—during which he had often been at odds with the majority of the campus—ended in 1974. Coors stepped down and opted not to run again. The university's archivist, David Hays, said later, "He was a real thorn in the side of liberals on the campus."[2]

Meanwhile, sales of Coors beer had continued to grow steadily and had in fact doubled between 1968 and 1973 despite still being sold in only eleven states. With an abundance of money and no real penchant for luxuries, Coors had the resources to champion his conservative views and bring them to a wider audience. The desire to find a legitimate outlet became an insistent pressure as Coors grew more and more aware of how the rampaging new social forces were hurting his business. For one thing, the environmental movement at the end of the 1960s and beginning of the 1970s was in a position of political ascendance. The prosperity and consumerism that followed World War II was yielding to a new consciousness of both the human impact on the environment and the impact of industrial pollution and toxins on human health. These concerns led to legislation aimed at preserving wilderness, preventing air and water pollution, and restricting hazardous and destructive industrial and agricultural practices. For example, the National Environmental Policy Act was passed in 1969, the Occupational Safety and Health Act in 1970, the Clean Air Act also in 1970, and the Federal Water Pollution Control Act Amendments in 1972. Environmental reporter Philip Shabecoff described this time as a "furious burst of bipartisan legislative activism," saying, "in its totality, the explosion of congressional activism that produced these landmark environmental statutes must be considered one of the greatest legislative achievements in the nation's history."[3]

Historical achievement or not, these measures were viewed with chagrin by Coors. There could be no escaping the fact that the production of beer involves environmental impacts from top to bottom—including from the farming of thousands of acres of barley, rice, and hops and the steady supply of millions of gallons of fresh water each year. Plus, industrial wastes from the Coors brewery, porcelain factory, and can plant—including solvents and heavy metals such as lead, mercury, arsenic, silver, and cadmium, as well as air pollution—had to be discarded. In addition, the Adolph Coors Company still had subsidiaries in oil drilling and pumping and coal mining. Coors felt that environmental regulations on these notoriously polluting and destructive interests infringed on his property rights and he endeavored to fight them.

In the early 1970s he briefly tried using television as a potential broadcast outlet for conservatives, feeling that he needed to counter what he saw as a prevailing liberal bias in the mainstream media. He funded the foundation of the New York–based Television News (TVN) Incorporated, a twenty-four-hour news service that supported line-fed video news to U.S. television stations. By 1975 he was pouring $3.2 million a year into the enterprise, but it wasn't enough to secure success, and, faced with continuing losses, he terminated the subsidiary.

Around the time he started TVN, he also wrote a letter to a Republican friend, U.S. Senator Gordon Allott of Colorado, asking for suggestions on how his money might best help the conservative cause. Given the task of responding, Allott's press secretary Paul Weyrich first thought the letter was a prank, finding it astounding that someone could be so unschooled in the ways of power that he would simply offer large amounts of unsolicited money to a politician. Once he verified the letter, however, Weyrich consulted with several colleagues to brainstorm potential worthy causes for Coors's cash. They realized that one resource available to liberals but not to conservatives at the time was an information clearinghouse. The prestigious Brookings Institution assembled research, wrote reports, and disseminated information used to brief policymakers on liberal analyses of current events. Weyrich determined that conservatives needed a counterpart. He convinced Coors to fund a small office called Analysis and Research Corporation, which soon foundered under its obscurity despite several large injections of money from Coors. But the framework had been established, and Coors had come to see the necessity for a conservative entity that could influence legislation. So in 1973, he informed Weyrich that he would finance a large-scale, tax-exempt conservative think tank on Capitol Hill, offering $250,000 upfront, with an additional $300,000 to purchase a building—mind-boggling amounts of money in the early 1970s. Coors also agreed to supply $20,000 a month during its first year.

The new organization was called the Heritage Foundation, and by the turn of the century its budget had swollen to $23 million, and it had a staff of 160, making it the premier conservative policy center in Washington, D.C. Its policies have included promoting unrestricted capitalism, fighting communism, deregulating industry, expanding the military, and proliferating nuclear weapons. The Heritage Foundation also has been a formidable influence on the environmental debate, especially during the Republican administrations of the 1980s and early 1990s. In its former research journal *Policy Review*, it wrote that it considers the environmental movement to be "extremist," and urged compatriots to "strangle the environmental movement" since it constitutes "the greatest single threat to the American economy."

His money had created a viable presence in the political life of Washington, D.C., but Coors still twitched restlessly over the perceived threat of governmental encroachments on his property and wealth. The advocacy mechanisms of the Heritage Foundation simply couldn't act quickly or decisively enough for him. Searching for a way to acquire litigation capabilities, he found inspiration in the California Chamber of Commerce, which had created the Pacific Legal Foundation in 1973 to practice law on behalf of business interests. The foundation's conservative lawyers filed lawsuits to block environmental actions and thwart regulations, and Coors wanted to bring those tactics to the Rocky Mountain region. When he had an assistant make exploratory phone calls to other wealthy business owners in the West, the response to his idea was unanimously positive. Thus, in 1976, with large infusions of money from Coors and other donors, the Mountain States Legal Foundation (MSLF) was hatched in Denver. With Coors's approval, the MSLF's first president, hired in mid-1977, was conservative lawyer and anti-environmentalist **James Watt,** whom Coors had met two years before. During the three years Watt worked for the MSLF he won the gratitude of western conservative circles by initiating many lawsuits against high-profile environmental organizations. "The Foundation [MSLF] tackled such enemies of western business interests as the Environmental Protection Agency, the Sierra Club, the Environmental Defense Fund—and the Department of the Interior. In the process the organization picked up the reputation of being anti-consumer, anti-feminist, anti-government, anti-Black, and above all, anti-environmentalist,"[4] wrote Watt biographer **Ron Arnold.** Most of these cases were funded by Coors, with additional financing from large oil, mining, agribusiness, and electric power industries in the West. In instigating the MSLF, Coors was the first to organize the previously marginalized right-wing element of American politics and to engineer a business arrangement linking this element to industry.

Coors's commitment to fighting environmental strictures and garnering political support for free enterprise was for him a natural outcome of his devotion to the family dynasty. "If we don't get involved in our government, things like this brewery won't exist anymore," he once reminded a Coors employee. But during the late 1970s, Coors business started faltering—partly due to the Coors brothers' refusal to market their product aggressively. Other beer companies had started spending barrels of money on advertising and were showing increased profits. The Coors company preferred to rely on the quality of their beer and the "Coors mystique" to attract customers. The mysterious allure of Coors beer seemed to come from the fact that it was only available in a few western states and from its reputation for obsessive dedication to quality. Bill Coors even ran full-page ads in East Coast newspapers urging easterners not to drink Coors beer, so sincerely worried was he that Coors beer that traveled that far without refrigeration wouldn't taste fresh. Though it wasn't a gimmick, the ads increased the beer's contraband appeal. In 1975, on a trip to Denver, President Gerald Ford created a minor scandal by ordering his Secret Service detail to load Air Force One with crates of Coors beer to take back to Washington, D.C.

As flattering as the Coors mystique was, it was unable to dissipate growing public disapproval of the company. Joseph's new penchant for wielding a conservative influence on the national political scene made some people uneasy. In 1975, the *Washington Post* had run a series of four stories devoted to Coors's efforts to nudge American politics to the right; and the several organizations he had created only caused more attention to be focused on him. He circled in orbits closer and closer to the highest political office in the nation—that of the president. In 1976 he jumped aboard the **Ronald Reagan** presidential campaign and went to the convention as a delegate, introducing conservative platform resolutions that opposed federal aid to public schools and day care centers. He also fought a plank supporting the Equal Rights Amendment and succeeded in striking platform language critical of oil companies. Reagan lost to Jimmy Carter, but the connections Coors had established with Reagan were still strong four years later when Reagan ran again and won. Coors was well on his way to becoming one of the most influential conservatives in America.

In 1977 Joseph Coors became co-president of Adolph Coors Company with his brother Bill. They needed to pool their energies to fight increasing criticism from activists who accused the company of violating labor and environmental laws and of discriminating against gays and other minorities. By then the union only represented 1,472 of the company's 10,000 workers. But mounting tension culminated in the Coors brothers' edging the union out of the brewery for good, as they were convinced that it had been denying them the right to manage their business. A few months later, in April 1977, union workers called a strike that would last twenty months. The Adolph Coors Company emerged victorious, but angry members of the American Federation of Labor—Congress of Industrial Organizations (AFL-CIO) retaliated by organizing a ten-year boycott that continued to hurt sales for years afterward. To survive the controversy and boost sales, the Coors brothers began to elbow their way into some of the trends shaping the brewing industry. They increased advertising, looked at expanding into new states, and introduced a reduced-calorie beer called Coors Light. Sold in shiny, unpainted aluminum cans, Coors Light was quickly dubbed "the Silver Bullet," and soon became one of the country's best-selling beers.

As 1980 approached, Joseph became one of the biggest financial backers of the Reagan presidential election campaign. Reagan had become friends with him and his wife Holly over the years, and met with Joseph and other patrons frequently to discuss their conservative vision for America. At about this time, through connections such as the MSLF, western extractive industries also were beginning to band together in opposition to labor, regulation, and environmental protections. Nicknamed by the *Washington Post* the "Sagebrush Rebellion," this group fought for the ceding of federal lands to private interests. Fully in line with these "rebels," Coors joined their ranks, which would soon include President Ronald Reagan. With the inauguration of Reagan in 1981, Coors became more powerful than ever. As a member of Reagan's "kitchen cabinet"—his close unofficial advisory group—Coors met with Reagan regularly to make staffing recommendations. His influence came through other channels as well, namely through his conservative research and legal foundations. As Jacqueline Vaughn Switzer wrote, "The Heritage Foundation is widely credited with being the organization responsible for drawing up the blueprint for President Reagan's environmental policy after his election in 1980 and for suggesting names of prominent conservatives as key appointees during the president's transition period."[5]

For potential leaders of the key offices regulating national environmental matters, Coors had several names up his sleeve. He recommended James Watt to be secretary of the Interior, and Anne Gorsuch (who later became **Anne Gorsuch Burford**) to head the Environmental Protection Agency (EPA). To the outrage of the environmental movement, Reagan followed both suggestions. Watt already had gained fame from his leadership at the MSLF, and during his tenure in the Interior Department he advocated policies that gave oil and mining interests access to ecologically sensitive public lands, wildlife refuges, and parks; and began selling public land to developers. Coors had known Gorsuch since her days in the state legislature of Colorado, where she had been known for her unconventional tactics and anti-environmental views. Having her as head of the EPA gave Coors a stratagem for meeting his needs on environmental regulatory issues, particularly in regard to waste disposal. Gorsuch hired two Coors attorneys as consultants to the EPA to advise her specifically on hazardous waste matters. As Russ Bellant wrote of this political cadre, "All were in positions to help the Adolph Coors Company with permission to dump waste in ways that many thought were hazardous to the health of area residents."[6]

Toxic-waste disposal was a source of vexation for the Coors company. The year Reagan took office, the Coors brothers learned that four of their wells, which supplied water for making the beer, were contaminated with carcinogenic solvents that were used by the can plant to clean the cans. A cracked sewer line appeared to be leaking the poisons, and probably had been for years. Although federal law required the company to report any contamination, Joseph and Bill Coors refused to entertain the idea of inspections, fines, and publicity. Quietly, they pumped the water tainted with

1,1-dichloroethylene, 1,2-dichloroethene, trichloroethylene (TCE), and other toxins into a nearby stream called Kinney Run, and also into Clear Creek, source of the company's prized Rocky Mountain water.

Meanwhile, as part of an agreement signed during the Carter administration, the Coors company faced the November 1981, closing of the dump site they used for disposing of toxic waste. Called the Lowry Landfill, the site's groundwater was so contaminated that it was considered for Superfund listing. In the years before the landfill closed, Coors had used it to dump twenty million gallons of liquid toxic waste, such as lead dross (from the can plant), flammable solvents, and cyanide solution. Rather than search for alternative sites for their waste, Joseph Coors brokered a deal through his attorneys who were also consultants at Gorsuch's EPA office to have the landfill re-opened for two weeks in 1982, giving Coors and other corporations an extra opportunity to rid themselves of toxic wastes. Congressional committees sniffed out suspicious connections between the EPA and Coors, and began pressuring the EPA for documents surrounding the case. The story went national and cast further scrutiny on the Coors company.

A few years later, employees in the can plant complained that water from the drinking fountains tasted "off." The surreptitious purging of contaminated water had come back to haunt the Coors company: The solvents had made their way from the surface water into the underground drinking-water well. Again the company refused to report the situation to the EPA or the county department of health. Health officials in the area had begun to speak up on their own around this time, having discovered that the area immediately downstream of the Coors company had double the national average of low birthweight babies and childhood cancer. A state toxicologist reported that the EPA under Gorsuch had been notified of the situation, but there had been no follow-up.

The anti-environmental forces bolstered by the support and influence of Joseph Coors had enormous influence on environmental policy during Reagan's two terms in the 1980s, and have continued to have an impact since. Many of the policy recommendations made by the Heritage Foundation were adopted by the Reagan White House. The Reagan years were marked by his determination to turn the country away from environmentalism, believing it to be politically irrelevant. Some have argued that this administration mobilized and revived the nation's largest mainstream environmental organizations—such as the Audubon Society, the Sierra Club, and the Environmental Defense Fund (all of which together with others would come to be known as "the Group of Ten")—and polished them to a new level of professionalism. As Jacqueline Vaughn Switzer wrote, "membership in the groups had skyrocketed with the appointments of Watt and Gorsuch, with some arguing that Reagan was the best thing that could ever have happened to the environmental movement. For example, the Sierra Club's 'Dump

Watt' campaign collected over a million signatures in an attempt to convince Reagan to relieve the secretary of his duties."[7] But Mark Dowie argued that the response of national environmental organizations to the conservative policies of the 1980s was "verbally loud but politically anemic," and points out that the damage to the environmental movement wrought by Joseph Coors's powerful friends was extensive. "Although Reagan's partisans rekindled some zeal among environmentalists, they inspired no imaginative strategies. . . . Some congressional opposition was created but not enough to stop Reagan from reversing two decades of environmental reform. To corporate polluters, clearcutters, and strip miners the Reagan decade was heaven sent."[8]

As the 1980s drew to a close it became apparent that Joseph and his brother were out of their depth in a beer industry that was dominated by glamorous marketing and brazen advertising campaigns. They both descended a few rungs on the corporation's ladder, letting the next generation take over the major business decisions. In 1987, Joseph Coors stepped down from his responsibilities at the brewery and also revealed that he had been having an affair for thirteen years and wanted a divorce from Holly. He remarried right away and he and his new wife, Anne, moved to California. On March 15, 2003, at the age of 85, Coors died at his home in Rancho Mirage, California. By the early 1990s, Coors beer was available in all fifty states. Today, headed by Joseph's son Peter Coors, the company remains close to the forefront of the brewing industry, with annual sales exceeding 32 million barrels.

NOTES

1. Mark Dowie, *Losing Ground: American Environmentalism at the Close of the Twentieth Century* (Cambridge, MA: The MIT Press, 1995), pp. 83–84.

2. Quoted in Dave Phillipps, "Coors Left Bitter Taste in U. Colorado's Mouth," *Colorado Daily (U. Colorado)* (March 18, 2003).

3. Philip Shabecoff, *Earth Rising: American Environmentalism in the 21st Century* (Covelo, CA: Island Press, 2000), p. 6.

4. Ron Arnold, *At the Eye of the Storm: James Watt and the Environmentalists* (Chicago: Regnery Gateway, 1982), p. 277.

5. Jacqueline Vaughn Switzer, *Green Backlash: The History and Politics of Environmental Opposition in the U.S.* (Boulder: Lynne Rienner Publishers, 1997), p. 141.

6. Russ Bellant, *The Coors Connection: How Coors Family Philanthropy Undermines Democratic Pluralism* (Boston: South End Press, 1991), p. 87.

7. Switzer, *Green Backlash*, p. 186.

8. Dowie, *Losing Ground*, p. 68.

BIBLIOGRAPHY

Joseph Coors was famously tight-lipped and rarely granted interviews or spoke to the press, so information specific to him is hard to find. Dan Baum wrote a chronicle of the Coors family history called *Citizen Coors: An American Dynasty* (New York: Harper Collins, 2000). It contains biographical anecdotes and focuses heavily on the family's business strategies, but doesn't delve into environmental issues. Russ Banham's *Coors: A Rocky Mountain Legend* (Lyme, CT: Greenwich Publishing Group, Inc., 1998) contains historical information, but is more a coffee-table book than an investigative report. For a critical look at the influence of the Coors family's political activism, see Russ Bellant, *The Coors Connection: How Coors Family Philanthropy Undermines Democratic Pluralism* (Boston: South End Press, 1991). Articles referring to Joseph Coors and his business practices or ideology are Elizabeth Peer and Philip S. Cook, "Foaming over Coors," *Newsweek* Vol. 86 (September 22, 1975), pp. 85–86; "A Test for the Coors Dynasty," *Business Week* (May 8, 1978), pp. 69–70, 72; Edward Rozek, "Joseph Coors: The Brewer of Golden," *National Review* Vol. 31 (October 26, 1979), p. 1363; and Dave Phillipps, "Coors Left Bitter Taste in U. Colorado's Mouth," *Colorado Daily (U. Colorado)* (March 18, 2003). For obituaries, see "Coors Brewery Magnate Dies at 85," *Toronto Star* (March 18, 2003), p. C16; "Joseph Coors," *Times, United Kingdom* (March 20, 2003), p. 33; and Ira Teinowitz, "Joseph Coors Made His Brand a Household Name," *Advertising Age* Vol. 74 (March 24, 2003), p. 12. Several general environmental history books are helpful for placing Coors in the environmental debate. These include Kirkpatrick Sale, *The Green Revolution: The American Environmental Movement, 1962–1992* (New York: Hill and Wang, 1993); and Mark Dowie, *Losing Ground: American Environmentalism at the Close of the Twentieth Century* (Cambridge, MA: The MIT Press, 1995); and Sharon Beder, *Global Spin: The Corporate Assault on Environmentalism,* revised ed. (White River Junction, VT: Chelsea Green Publishing Company, 2002).

S. FRED SINGER
(1924–)

Contrary to the conventional wisdom and the predictions of computer models, the Earth's climate has not warmed appreciably in the past two decades, and probably not since about 1940.

—S. Fred Singer

For the past decade, climate scientists around the world have been sending warnings about the human impact on the atmosphere, saying that global climate change wrought by fossil fuel use has already started happening and will possibly lead to increases in extreme weather events, the spread of infectious diseases, drought and crop failures, habitat destruction, species extinction, and a rise in sea level. In the face of this growing consensus, scientist S. Fred Singer stands apart. He is a prominent member of a small group of "greenhouse skeptics," who claim that evidence for human-induced global climate change is flawed and that taking steps to reduce emissions of greenhouse gases would result in enormous economic dislocation. He holds a Ph.D. in physics from Princeton and has enjoyed a high-profile career as a consultant on rocket and satellite technology, energy, and atmospheric research for numerous corporations and governmental agencies. He is a sought-after speaker on the subject of global warming and has written numerous articles, monographs, and books—including, most recently, *The Scientific*

Case against the Global Climate Treaty and *Hot Talk, Cold Science: Global Warming's Unfinished Debate.*

Global climate change has been a very slippery issue for scientists and policymakers. The world's atmosphere and weather patterns are highly complex, and while most climate scientists agree that global climate change is happening, there is some uncertainty as to the timing and severity of its impact. Highlighting these difficulties, Singer frequently makes the argument that there is too much dissent among scientists to take any action. Even though he represents a minority of opinion about global warming, his rocket science credentials and articulate manner of speaking have been convincing, and his arguments have had a disproportionate impact. For environmentalists, however, his credibility has been destroyed by the fact that he has received funding from several major oil companies, whose continued economic success is jeopardized seriously by the global warming issue. The considerable influence exerted by greenhouse skeptics like Singer and the powerful corporations that fund him creates a polarized and political environment in which it is difficult to make accurate public policy recommendations. Singer currently serves as president of the Science and Environmental Policy Project (SEPP), a research group he founded in 1990 to fight the growing consensus about global warming.

Siegfried Fred Singer was born on September 27, 1924, in Vienna, Austria. He lived in Austria and Northumberland, England, until the age of 14, when his family moved to Ohio. When he was 20 years old, he became a naturalized citizen. His father worked as a jeweler and his mother was a homemaker: Both parents encouraged his education. He attended Ohio State University in Columbus, and received his bachelor's degree in electrical engineering in 1943; he then began postgraduate work at Princeton University in New Jersey. He began teaching classes in the physics department at Princeton while he worked on his master's degree in physics, which he received in 1944. Singer then served in the armed forces during World War II, researching mine warfare and countermeasures for the U.S. Navy. Working at the Naval Ordnance Laboratory, he developed an arithmetic element for a type of electronic digital calculator, nick-named an "electronic brain," that could be used for working mathematical problems.

On his discharge from the navy in 1946, Singer took a job as a research physicist in the upper atmosphere rocket program at Johns Hopkins University in Silver Spring, Maryland. Here he began what would become a long and distinguished career in the field of rocket science. His research focused on ozone, cosmic rays, and the ionosphere, which were measured using cosmic ray balloons and instrumented rockets launched from White Sands, New Mexico, or from ships at sea. For one rocket-launching mission, he accompanied a naval operation on a trip to the Arctic, and he also conducted shipboard rocket launchings at the equator.

During this time he also worked on his Ph.D. dissertation entitled "Extensive Airshowers of Cosmic Rays"; he received the degree in 1948 from Princeton University. In 1950, he moved to London to serve in the U.S. Embassy's Office of Naval Research as a scientific liaison officer. His duties required him to keep up with and report on the latest European research on nuclear physics, astrophysics, and geophysics. In 1953 he returned to the United States and took an associate professorship in physics at the University of Maryland, where he also served as director of the Center for Atmospheric and Space Physics, conducting experiments on rocket and satellite technology, remote sensing, radiation belts, magnetosphere, and meteorites. He developed a new method of launching a rocket into space that was cheaper and safer than the previously accepted technique of using balloons: He proposed firing the rocket from a high-flying plane, either with or without a pilot. Two years later the navy adopted his new method and used high-flying aircraft to launch rockets vertically in order to conduct upper atmosphere research. Singer supervised the project.

Before he turned 30, Singer had designed an artificial satellite to launch into space for data collection. He named his satellite—about the size of a basketball—the Minimum Orbital Unmanned Satellite (MOUSE). It contained scientific instruments for recording and transmitting data on solar radiation, on the electrified layers of the ionosphere, and on fluctuations in the earth's gravitational field. For this early design of space satellites, he earned a White House Special Commendation from President Eisenhower in 1954.

Over the next two decades, Singer continued working in the atmospheric and geophysical sciences, either through various universities or through governmental agencies. He left the University of Maryland in 1962 and became the first director of the U.S. Department of Commerce's National Weather Satellite Center (now part of National Oceanic and Atmospheric Administration), where he established operational systems for managing atmosphere, land surface, and ocean data. He later considered the setting up and managing of the first weather satellite system in the country—including some of its design features—his greatest accomplishment.

Two years later he left and became the first dean of the School of Environmental and Planetary Sciences at the University of Miami at Coral Gables, Florida, where he stayed for three years. At that point, in 1967, he accepted an assignment as a deputy assistant secretary of the U.S. Department of the Interior, where he was in charge of water quality and research issues. When the U.S. Environmental Protection Agency (EPA) was established in December 1970 as the cornerstone of the emerging national environmental regulatory system, Singer became its deputy assistant administrator of policy. The creation of the EPA ushered in a new era of federal responsibility toward the environment, and as its first task it had to codify a bipartisan environmental ethic into policy, while consolidating the work of existing entities dealing with pollution-based environmental issues. It sought to implement these broad objectives energetically; according to environmental historian Robert Gottlieb, "The new agency, however, was quickly overwhelmed by its rapidly expanding regulatory responsibilities, the conflicting signals from the Nixon and later Ford administrations on how aggressively it should pursue such regulations, and effective industry maneuvering, which used scientific uncertainty in the regulatory process to delay or counter the establishment and enforcement of standards."[1]

Singer's years of government service, especially this brief experience with the fledgling EPA, gave him an insider's knowledge on policymaking, public relations, and the mechanisms of environmental regulations—all of which would serve him well in his future campaign to deflate concern over global warming. In the meantime, Singer returned to teaching. In 1971 he became a professor of environmental sciences at the University of Virginia, where for the next twenty-three years he would teach classes on global environmental issues like ozone depletion, acid rain, global climate change, the economic impacts of population growth, and public policy issues surrounding oil and energy economics.

Singer also wrote frequently on energy matters in the mainstream press. During the 1970s the topic of energy began seeing a lot more ink as the nation faced an oil embargo, rising prices, and an imminent energy crisis. The most energy-consumptive nation in the world, the United States had long relied on industrial profits made possible through the use of large amounts of fossil fuels and had come to believe that Middle Eastern oil would always be available and inexpensive. When the Organization of Petroleum Exporting Countries (OPEC) issued an oil embargo in 1973, it caused seismic changes in the world's economy and environmental history. Rising crude oil prices encouraged oil exploration and production around the globe, bringing along the environmental impacts of pipelines, spills, fires, and refineries—though high oil prices also encouraged conservation. Plus Americans had to wait in lines to fill up their cars. This inconvenience combined with the penny-pinching effects of inflation awakened a new economic and cultural climate and created new demands for renewable energy sources. Then, during the long hot summer of 1979, Iran refused to sell oil to the United States, and prices again skyrocketed. President Jimmy Carter called the battle to achieve energy independence "the moral equivalent of war," and pushed for an plan that involved conserving energy and reducing imports. Many people living in industrial nations began to realize that the reach of energy use—with the impacts of extraction and production, and the pollution it causes on combustion—had grown so overpowering that its effects had become the number one determinant of the world's environmental state. Environmentalists began to demand that ecological considerations have more weight in making economic and political decisions, and cries for efficiency in energy policy dominated almost all other environmental issues of the time.

Singer, however, did not agree with President Carter's energy plan, nor with environmentalists' interest in renewable resources. In fact, in numerous magazine articles he downplayed the energy crisis or denied there even was one. "The oil crisis is largely a media event," he wrote in the *New Republic*. In the same article he expressed his distrust of federal regulations and price controls, and said predictions of future energy shortages were based on faulty economic reasoning. "If we don't interfere too much with the natural processes of the market," he wrote, "then there will not be an oil crisis."[2] In another article, entitled "The Oil Crisis That Isn't," he disparaged government fuel allocations and again tried to anesthetize the swelling of concern over fuel shortages and consequent support for conservation. He argued that "there is no crisis, nor need there be one in the future, unless we make one ourselves. And we surely will if we resort to such controls as mandatory allocations and rationing."[3] Furthermore, in an article entitled "Living with Imports," he professed that increased oil imports "are not all bad and certainly do not imply a national disaster."[4] He also declared that conservation would take care of itself, since increasing oil prices lower demand and force the adoption of alternative sources of energy (though his suggestions for alternative sources—coal and nuclear energy—hardly satisfied environmentalists). Singer's arguments on the energy crisis illustrate his belief in "free-market environmentalism," or "market-based approaches" to environmental problems. Free-market environmentalists like Singer adhere to the philosophy that market principles and incentives are enough to spur the conservation of resources and the protection of environmental quality. This type of solution usually translates into the total deregulation of industry.

In 1989, Singer left a two-year position as chief scientist at the U.S. Department of Transportation to work for the Institute of Space Science and Technology in Gainesville, Florida. In the early 1990s, his theories made their way into a wider public discourse via a meandering route that ended with a broadcast on **Rush Limbaugh**'s radio show. Profoundly frightening evidence had been accumulating that the ozone layer—which protects the earth from destructive ultraviolet B radiation—was thinning, and that holes were appearing in the ozone over Antarctica. Since 1973—when the theory came out that chlorofluorocarbons (CFCs) break down in the stratosphere, releasing ozone-destroying chlorine—more and more scientists had become convinced of its truth. But Limbaugh, the anti-environmentalist talk-show host and best-selling author, loudly criticized the idea of ozone depletion and especially discredited the link between the ozone layer and CFCs, citing **Dixy Lee Ray**'s book *Trashing the Planet* for his facts. Ray, in turn, had cited Singer for her information on the ozone depletion "hoax." Singer had been denying that humans had any role in ozone depletion, and had declared publicly that the effects of CFCs were swamped by volcanic eruptions, which emit hydrogen chloride and thereby contribute greatly to stratospheric chlorine, which destroys ozone. But virtually all relevant research already had ruled out volcanoes as the chief source of chlorine in the stratosphere since the abundant steam also released during eruptions dissolves the hydrogen chloride and causes it to rain back down to earth.

Scientific and environmental concern over the ozone problem began to mobilize, and in 1987 the landmark Montreal Protocol enacted an international agreement to phase out the production and use of chemicals that deplete the ozone. Chemical manufacturers, who had for years relied on claims made by skeptics like Singer to argue against the theory that CFCs might damage the ozone layer, initially complained about the protocol, but soon found substitutes for CFCs. Scientific foresight and environmental concern had prevailed to prevent further ozone loss, but, unfortunately, because CFCs are so stable, they stay in the atmosphere for decades, and some of those released before the Montreal Protocol will still be disintegrating the ozone layer in 2087.

Later, Singer would take the Montreal Protocol experience and try to use it warn oil companies that they may face similar restrictions in the face of the global warming threat. He wrote to the oil industry that "it took only five years to go from . . . mandating a simple freeze of production [of CFCs] at 1985 levels, to the 1992 decision of a complete production phase-out—all on the basis of quite insubstantial science."[5] In the end, the scientific evidence turned out to be unassailable, and Singer recanted. In an article in *Science* magazine in 1993, he conceded that direct experimental data from volcanoes suggested that they play a relatively minor role and that he had become convinced that CFCs were the major problem.[6]

The process by which a scientific consensus is reached can sometimes look like a popularity contest. An idea gains credibility as more and more scientists concur with it, and the journal it gets published in may hold nearly as much weight as the idea itself. In explaining how his ideas often run counter to the majority, Singer has explained that he is above this popularity-contest aspect of science, and that he doesn't make decisions by vote. He says he simply makes observations that either confirm or deny a theory, and it just so happens that his work sometimes does not agree with current consensus. He was outside the majority with the CFC and ozone depletion theory, until he eventually retracted. He also has been outside the majority with regard to the global warming debate.

Scientists have been describing a "greenhouse effect"—caused by a build-up of greenhouse gases like water vapor, carbon dioxide, and methane in the atmosphere—for more than a century. These gases form a transparent blanket that allows solar radiation to penetrate to the earth's surface, but traps the resulting heat, working by the same mechanism as a greenhouse. This is a naturally occurring process—in fact, without it the oceans would be frozen solid—and there is no scientific dispute about its existence. Carbon dioxide, one of the principal greenhouse gases, is released in great quantities in the combustion of fossil fuels—meaning there is a human-caused element being added to the greenhouse effect. Deforestation and current agricultural practices also lead to greenhouse gas emissions. Overall, the world's output of carbon dioxide has exploded since the industrial age began, and today's levels of carbon dioxide are at their highest concentrations in 420,000 years and perhaps as far back as 20 million years. The dispute over global warming arose when scientists began to speculate about what effect this human-caused build-up of gases would have on global climate and weather patterns. Many atmospheric scientists predicted that the extra trapping of heat involved would have the potential to cause disastrous ecological consequences: sea-level rise, intense storms, record hot and cold temperatures, the spread of infectious diseases, and prolonged droughts, for example. In 1988, Dr. James Hansen, a NASA scientist, testified before Congress, saying that global climate change already had started. That same year, in response to worldwide concerns over erratic and extreme weather events, the United Nations established the Intergovernmental Panel on Climate Change (IPCC)—the largest and most stringently peer-reviewed scientific collaboration in history—to assess the threat of climate change.

Singer disagreed with all the environmentalists and scientists who believed that global warming posed a threat and that something should be done about it. He believes that radical environmentalists are hyping global warming as an alarmist melodrama to halt economic growth and prosperity. "The underlying effort here seems to be to use global warming as an excuse to cut down the use of energy," he said in an interview. "It's very simple: If you cut back the use of energy, then you cut back economic growth. And believe it or not, there are people in the world who believe we have gone too far in economic growth."[7] In 1990, Singer founded the SEPP to undermine the case for global warming preventive measures. At its inception, SEPP was an affiliate of the Washington Institute for Values in Public Policy, a think tank operated by Reverend **Sun Myung Moon**'s ultra-conservative Unification Church. It has since cut ties with Moon's organization, and now receives funding from various foundations and oil companies.

When climate change took center stage at the 1992 UN Conference on Environment and Development (also known as the "Earth Summit") in Rio de Janeiro, Singer began making frequent pronouncements in newspapers and magazines and on radio programs, spreading doubts about its validity. His Ph.D. credentials carried a significant amount of weight, and his arguments generated significant skepticism among a public that has remained relatively uninformed about the issue. Even people interested in global climate change don't purchase the computer models that predict warming trends, and very few people actually read journals of atmospheric physics or IPCC reports. Popular magazines, evening news, and radio talk shows therefore become the source of authority for a wide audience, and Singer, who writes and speaks frequently through these media outlets, can reach millions of people. Predicting that disastrous economic damage would follow any restrictions on fossil fuel use, Singer presents his own dire scenario for the public to rally against, and his skepticism makes it easy to ignore increasing warnings about the human impact on the climate.

Singer argues that the natural world and its weather patterns, atmospheric changes, and temperature trends are complex and interrelated, and not entirely understood. Little is known about the dynamics of heat exchange from the oceans to the atmosphere, or the role of clouds, for example—and recorded data leaves room for varying interpretations. In the beginning of the debate, skepticism and dissent among scientists regarding the existence of global warming was more widespread. To further his position, Singer focused on this skepticism and dissent, making the argument that more studies needed to be done before any steps were taken to curb carbon emissions.

But as the scientific community began studying the problem, and a consensus about the existence of global warming began to grow, Singer continued to downplay it. He also has criticized repeatedly the major research tool available to climate scientists: the computer model. In 1994 he entitled his regular column for the *Washington Times*, the newspaper run by the Reverend Sun Myung Moon, "Climate Claims Wither under the Luminous Lights of Science,"[8] and in it he examined and criticized the climate models that predict global warming. Using these computer models, Singer ran his own analysis and found that the temperatures it predicted for the time period between 1950 and 1980 deviated from actual temperatures from that time. From this he concluded that climate models are faulty and that global warming is not occurring. But, as scientists **Paul Ehrlich** and **Anne Ehrlich** point out in their book *The Betrayal of Science and Reason*, Singer entered inaccurate data into the models he used. He had neglected to adjust his numbers to compensate for the cooling effects of aerosols in the atmosphere, and he also failed to include the actual temperatures of the 1980s, collectively the warmest years in recorded history up to that point. "If the models had been properly represented and the actual record taken into the 1990s, the predictions would have been shown to be reasonably accurate,"[9] concluded the Ehrlichs.

Singer's efforts to stanch the tide of accumulating evidence and opinion supporting the existence of global climate change did little to turn the scientific community away from the subject. In fact, in 1995, the IPCC, which involves 2,500 scientists, issued a landmark statement revealing a level of consensus never before reached on the issue of global warming. Their report stated that "the balance of evidence suggests that there is a discernible human influence on global climate," and that climate instability would likely cause "widespread economic, social, and environmental dislocation over the next century."[10] The IPCC report was written and rigorously peer-reviewed by scientists from all over the world, independent of government interference, and had a discernable impact. The *New York Times* printed a front-page article titled "Global Warming Experts Call Human Role Likely," saying that the report showed "an important shift of scientific judgement" and "a watershed in the views of climatologists, who with the notable exception of Dr. James E. Hansen of the NASA Goddard Institute for Space Studies in New York have until now refused to declare publicly that they can discern the signature of the greenhouse effect."[11]

A few months later, Singer wrote a letter to *Science* magazine, debunking the IPCC report, saying it had omitted information and presented only selected facts. "The summary does not mention that the satellite data—the only truly global measurements, available since 1979—show no warming at all, but actually a slight cooling,"[12] he wrote. Satellite measurements are Singer's preferred data set for analyzing global temperature, and have shown no sign of global warming thus far. He admits that regular surface thermometers from weather stations around the world do show a warming trend, but he argues that the only true data for showing global trends comes from the satellites, since their measurements cover the atmosphere from pole to pole. Critics of Singer's arguments have noticed some important drawbacks to his assertions. One is that the weather satellite record only goes back to 1979, making it too short to show long-term trends. Also, researchers recently have discovered that satellite readings have failed to account for differences in measurement from the gradual decay of satellite orbits. When the readings are corrected to account for this orbital decay, they indicate the same warming trend as ground-level measurements. In late 2003, Singer was collaborating on a study to resolve the disparity between surface thermometer data—which show a warming trend in the past twenty-five years—and the weather satellite data that show no such warming. At that time, he said he had dissected the available data and was close to understanding the reason for the disparity.

Through the late 1990s, worldwide concern about the issue continued to spread. In 1997, an international convention was held in Kyoto, Japan, to negotiate a climate treaty stipulating emissions reduction levels and timetables. The outcome of the meeting was the Kyoto Protocol, in which the thirty-eight largest industrialized nations agreed to reduce greenhouse gas emissions to an average of 5.2 percent below 1990 levels by 2012. Developing countries were not legally bound to emission reduction targets since, historically, they have been responsible for only a small portion of greenhouse gas emissions. Singer believed that the premise of the Kyoto Protocol was flawed, that its policies were based on unproven theories, and that its implication that catastrophic global warming will follow from an increase in greenhouse gases was unsupported. In an interview just before the meetings in Kyoto, Singer said, "Contrary to what [global warming proponents] say, there is no global warming. And contrary to what [those proponents] say, there is no scientific consensus either."[13]

As a rebuttal to the Kyoto Protocol, Singer wrote a statement called the "Leipzig Declaration on Global Climate Change in the U.S.," which he circulated for signatures in the United States and Europe. The declaration reads, in part, "Energy is essential for economic growth. . . . We understand the motivation to eliminate what are perceived to be the driving forces behind a potential climate change; but we believe the Kyoto Protocol—to curtail carbon dioxide emissions from only a part of the world community—is dangerously simplistic, quite ineffective, and economically destructive to jobs and standards-of-living." Singer succeeded in gathering around 100 signatures, though the credentials of some of the signatories have been questioned. At least twenty of them are television weather reporters, some do not have a science degree, and fourteen are listed as "professor" with no indication of their academic specialty. A number of signers interviewed later confessed they thought they were signing a document in favor of strong action on climate change, saying that the excerpt they had been shown was misleading.

In the decade or so since global warming had first entered the arena of scientific debate, intensive research and advancing technology greatly pared down the disagreements over the fundamental questions surrounding the changing climate. The IPCC report of 1995 was the preeminent admittance of widespread agreement and concern, and increasing freak weather events around the world have only borne scientific predictions out. "There's better scientific consensus on this than on any issue I know—except maybe Newton's second law of dynamics," said D. James Baker, administrator of the U.S. National Oceanic and Atmospheric Administration. "Man has reached the point where his impact on the climate can be as significant as nature's."[14] In acknowledgment of international concurrence on the issue, a total of 165 countries agreed to the Kyoto Protocol, representing a strong effort toward taking action on global climate change. The consensus process behind the treaty provided a reminder that even though (as Singer likes to point out) scientific research should *not* be decided by vote, science-based policy decisions *should*. Nonetheless, the United States, under President George W. Bush, backed out of the Kyoto Protocol in 2001, saying that signing it was not in the United State's best economic interest. The protocol represents the only mechanism obligating nations to reduce their emissions, and without the support of the United States, the world's largest polluter, its chances of success looked grim. The rest of the world began moving forward with the process anyway, but the Bush administration, heavily influenced by the powerful fossil fuel industry and skeptics like Singer, continued to deny the impending consequences of global warming.

Both the environmental realities and economic processes of the twenty-first century are inseparable from energy regimes. Interestingly, Singer himself has pointed out the unusual situation this puts climate science in, due to the political factors and large sums of money involved in its outcome. For example, says Singer, there are no political factors or large sums of money involved in the theory of relativity, but with climate research it is more complicated. He argues that since the federal government expends millions of dollars a year in climate research, federal climate scientists are biased toward the bleakest scenarios in order to guarantee further funding. But these bleak scenarios induce policy recommendations for reducing heat-trapping greenhouse gases, which requires phasing out the use of coal and oil and shifting to renewable sources such as solar energy. No one makes a profit by selling solar energy, which comes free.

On the other hand, coal and oil companies, whose livelihoods are threatened by such policy recommendations, are among the most powerful corporations on the planet, many with annual sales larger than the annual value of the total goods and services produced by many countries. Singer's organization, SEPP, fights against the "politicization of science," and strives to document the relationship between policymaking and scientific research. But, ironically, for many years Singer has been a paid consultant for ARCO, ExxonMobil (the world's largest publicly traded petroleum company), Shell Oil Company, Sun Oil Company, and Unocal Company.[15] SEPP has received grants from ExxonMobil.[16] He claims that his paid position with these major oil companies does not influence his scientific research, despite the fact that his conclusions concur with their strong economic interest in lessening environmental regulations. Overall, industry groups, who can afford multimillion-dollar publicity campaigns, have been very successful in quelling public unease over global climate change, especially in the United States. So even if Singer's work was not "bought" by the fossil fuel industry, his opinions certainly have been given an amplified voice through expensive media campaigning. Because of his affiliation with the fossil fuel industry, Singer's research has been discredited by many in the scientific community. In a congressional hearing in 1995, U.S. Representative Lynn Rivers (D-Michigan) questioned his credibility because he had not been able to publish any work in a peer-reviewed scientific journal (except one technical comment) for the previous fifteen years. Singer did not deny the charges.[17]

Singer continues to serve as executive director of SEPP. He is also on the staff of the ultra-conservative Frontiers of Freedom Foundation, which once defined itself through its mission statement as "the antithesis to the Sierra Club and Vice President Al Gore's *Earth in the Balance*." It now lists as one of its tenets, "Property rights and economic freedom are the fertile soil in which all other rights grow and thrive. The environment is best protected and preserved where free markets thrive, capitalism is robust, and property rights are respected." Singer also continues to write and speak out against global warming. In June 2001, he gave a lecture in Washington, D.C., discrediting weather station data from around the world that shows a warming trend for the last thirty years, and insisting that satellite measurements and "proxy" data show no warming. That same year, the IPCC issued a second report, this time saying that climate change is occurring much more rapidly than anticipated: Nine of the ten warmest years on record have occurred since 1990, with the four hottest being 1998, 2002 (tied with 2003), and 2001.

NOTES

1. Robert Gottlieb, *Forcing the Spring: The Transformation of the American Environmental Movement* (Covelo, CA: Island Press, 1993), p. 129.

2. S. Fred Singer, "OPEC's Price Reduction," *New Republic* Vol. 180 (January 6, 1979), pp. 11–12.

3. S. Fred Singer, "The Oil Crisis That Isn't," *New Republic* Vol. 180 (February 24, 1979), p. 13.

4. S. Fred Singer, "Living with Imports," *New Republic* Vol. 178 (February 25, 1978), p. 37.

5. Quoted in Ross Gelbspan, *The Heat Is On* (Reading, MA: Addison-Wesley Publishing Company, 1997), p. 47.

6. Gary Taubes, "The Ozone Backlash," *Science* Vol. 260 (June 11, 1993), p. 1582.

7. Michael J. Catanzaro, "Dr. S. Fred Singer," *Human Events* Vol. 53 (November 28, 1997), p. 11.

8. S. Fred Singer, "Climate Claims Wither under the Luminous Lights of Science," *Washington Times* (November 29, 1994).

9. Paul R. Ehrlich and Anne H. Ehrlich, *Betrayal of Science and Reason* (Covelo, CA: Island Press, 1996), p. 39.

10. Intergovernmental Panel on Climate Change, Working Group II, *Summary for Policymakers: Scientific Technical Analysis of Impacts, Adaptations, and Mitigation of Climate Change* (Cambridge: Cambridge University Press, 1995).

11. William K. Stevens, "Global Warming Experts Call Human Role Likely," *New York Times* (September 10, 1995), p. 1.

12. S. Fred Singer, "Climate Change and Consensus," letter to *Science* Vol. 271 (February 2, 1996), pp. 581–582.

13. Catanzaro, "Dr. S. Fred Singer," p. 11.

14. Quoted in Joby Warrick, "Consensus Emerges: Earth Is Warming—Now What?" *Washington Post* (November 12, 1997), p. A1.

15. Gelbspan, *The Heat Is On*, p. 46.

16. Ross Gelbspan, "Bush's Global Warmers," *Nation* Vol. 272 (April 9, 2001), pp. 5–6.

17. U.S. Congress, House of Representatives, Subcommittee on Energy and Environment of the Committee on Science, Hearing on Scientific Integrity and the Public trust, Case Study 2, *Climate Models and Projections of Potential Impacts of Global Climate Change*, 104th Congress, 1st session (November 16, 1995), Report No. 31.

BIBLIOGRAPHY

Singer's many published works provide a thorough background on his views, the following being representative: *Global Effects of Environmental Pollution* (Boston: D. Reidel Publishing Co., 1970); *The Ocean in Human Affairs* (St. Paul, MN: Paragon House, 1989), which deals with ocean circulation and climate; *Global Cli-*

mate Change: Human and Natural Influences (St. Paul, MN: Paragon House, 1989); *The Greenhouse Debate Continued* (San Francisco: ICS Press, 1992), which offers Singer's critique of the IPCC science report; *The Scientific Case against the Global Climate Treaty* (Arlington, VA: SEPP, 1997); and *Hot Talk, Cold Science: Global Warming's Unfinished Debate* (Oakland, CA: The Independent Institute, 1997). For context on the OPEC oil crisis and energy issues, see Barry Commoner, *The Poverty of Power: Energy and the Economic Crisis* (New York: Alfred A. Knopf, 1976). For Singer's early position on the ozone issue, see S. Fred Singer, "My Adventures in the Ozone Layer," *National Review* Vol. 41 (June 30, 1989), p. 37; and for a broader perspective see Gary Taubes, "The Ozone Backlash," *Science* Vol. 260 (June 11, 1993), pp. 1580–1583. Ross Gelbspan's book, *The Heat Is On: The High Stakes Battle over Earth's Threatened Environment* (Reading, MA: Addison-Wesley Publishing Company, 1997), is the gold standard for deciphering the global warming issue and Singer's ties to the fossil fuel industry. Also useful are Robert Gottlieb, *Forcing the Spring: The Transformation of the American Environmental Movement* (Covelo, CA: Island Press, 1993); William K. Stevens, "Global Warming Experts Call Human Role Likely," *New York Times* (September 10, 1995), p. 1; Paul R. Ehrlich and Anne H. Ehrlich, *Betrayal of Science and Reason: How Anti-Environmental Rhetoric Threatens Our Future* (Covelo, CA: Island Press, 1996); Joby Warrick, "Consensus Emerges: Earth Is Warming—Now What?" *Washington Post* (November 12, 1997), p. A1; Michael J. Catanzaro, "Dr. S. Fred Singer," *Human Events* Vol. 53 (November 28, 1997); Ross Gelbspan, "Bush's Global Warmers," *Nation* Vol. 272 (April 9, 2001), pp. 5–6; and Sharon Beder, *Global Spin: The Corporate Assault on Environmentalism* (White River Junction, VT: Chelsea Green Publishing Company, 2002).

PAUL EHRLICH
(1932–)
and ANNE EHRLICH
(1933–)

> No geological event in a billion years—not the emergence of mighty
> mountain ranges, nor the submergence of entire subcontinents, nor the
> occurrence of periodic glacial ages—has posed a threat to terrestrial life
> comparable to that of human overpopulation.
> —Paul R. Ehrlich and Anne H. Ehrlich

In the early 1930s, when Paul Ehrlich and Anne Fitzhugh Howland were born, the world population was two billion. It is now over six billion. Population growth of this speed and volume has had an undeniable ecological impact on the earth, and Paul and Anne, now married and both teaching at Stanford University, have become the nation's best-known authorities on population and leaders of the crusade to control growth. Paul also has devoted his career to the study of human ecology, the dynamics of insect populations, the coevolution of plants and herbivores, and the evolution of human cultures. Often working in close collaboration, Paul and Anne have traveled the world doing fieldwork and studying the link between population size and environmental problems. "Around the world," they wrote in their book *Betrayal of Science and Reason* (1996), "we have watched humanity consuming its natural capital and degrading its own life-support systems." Anne prefers to work quietly to shape the policies of environmental and social organization, while Paul, with blunt outspokenness, likes to cajole decisionmakers publicly to mend their ways. Paul has written over eight hundred scientific papers and popular articles, and he and Anne have co-authored many books. Perhaps as proof of their success in reaching a mass audience, the Ehrlichs have provoked a maelstrom of criticism from anti-environmentalists and advocates of population growth. Both consider themselves to possess the one necessary qualification for being good scientists: strong curiosity.

Paul Ralph Ehrlich was born on May 29, 1932 in Philadelphia, Pennsylvania, to William Ehrlich, a salesman, and Ruth (Rosenberg) Ehrlich, a Latin teacher in the public schools. He and his sister Sally grew up there and in Maplewood, New Jersey, where the family later moved. During his childhood he exercised his interest in the natural world by chasing butterflies and dissecting frogs. As he grew into his teens and continued observing butterflies, he noticed their local habitat was being replaced by housing developments, and that he couldn't raise caterpillars on local plants because they had been treated with pesticides. During his high school years in Maplewood, he found a mentor who encouraged him to study butterflies and to publish papers on his findings. Books provided another guiding influence during those years, especially ornithologist William Vogt's *Road to Survival* (1948), which warned of overpopulation and the depletion of resources. Agricultural land throughout the world was being diminished and would not be able to produce enough food for the increasing swarms of humanity, warned Vogt, unless a protocol of conservation and population control was swiftly adopted. He also warned of the irreplaceable loss of soils, minerals, and metals—especially tin, the shortage of which he said might one day lead the country into war to ensure future access. Another book that shaped Ehrlich's views was *Our Plundered Planet* (1948), written by Fairfield Osburn, naturalist, conservationist, and president of the New York Zoological Society. He too warned of an impending population crisis, and emphasized the threat humans posed to the nation's forests, grasslands, and water resources.

Paul graduated from high school in 1949 and went on to college at the University of Pennsylvania where he took a B.A. degree in zoology in 1953. During the summers of 1951 and 1952, he worked as a field officer surveying insects in the Canadian Arctic and Subarctic. He lived and worked among the Inuit and immersed himself in their culture, even hunting walrus, dog-sledding across the sea ice, and trying to learn the Aivilikmiut Eskimo language—a life-transforming experience that he always would remember vividly.

In the fall of 1953, he began graduate studies in the department of entomology at the University of Kansas under Charles Michener, a distinguished evolutionist. For his master's research, he worked in the "Animal House," a tumbledown dwelling turned into a laboratory, from which the smell of rotting flesh emanated thanks to nearby decomposing skeletons being cleaned by a colony of scavenging beetles for display in the zoology museum. Amid the smells of decay and ether, Ehrlich spent hours sitting at a microscope and studying fruit flies to research the evolution of their resistance to the pesticide DDT. He earned his M.A. in 1955 and his Ph.D. in 1957, and he also met Anne Howland, who was studying at the University of Kansas as an undergraduate. After the Animal House, his fieldwork involved a survey of biting flies on the Bering Seacoast region of Alaska.

Anne Howland was born November 17, 1933, in Des Moines, Iowa, to Winston Howland and Virginia (Fitzhugh) Howland. Throughout her childhood she was fascinated by nature and its workings, preferring to be outside learning about wildflowers and geography than to be playing inside with dolls. Her interest in the natural world also was developed though summer camps and nature study in school. While in college, she too read Fairfield Osborn's book and was influenced by its message. She enrolled at the University of Kansas in 1952, taking a double major in art and French, and finishing in 1955.

Paul and Anne met at a bridge game in the student union. Their discussion on their first acquaintance led to the recognition that they held mutual interests in world affairs, art, science, and the environment, and they began dating. To their chagrin, while watching drive-in movies in Topeka, they sometimes would be interrupted by mosquito control operations spraying DDT directly into their car windows, an uncomfortable scene for two young people already concerned about the overuse of synthetic organic pesticides. In 1954 they married, and a year later had a daughter, Lisa Marie.

In 1957, after completing his Ph.D., Paul received a fellowship from the National Institutes of Health to investigate the genetics and behavior of parasitic mites. He conducted his research at the Chicago Academy of Science for a year, then at the University of Kansas. The Ehrlichs moved to Stanford, California, in 1959 and have lived and worked there ever since. They both took jobs at Stanford University, Paul as assistant professor, and Anne as research assistant and biological illustrator. By then, Lisa had started school and Anne was able to collaborate more closely with Paul on various projects. She dissected butterflies under a microscope, illustrating and documenting minute anatomical details for classification studies. Her meticulousness and persistence in spite of the eye-straining work repaid her with an ever-deeper interest in science. They also worked together on a handbook called *How to Know the Butterflies* (1960), which Paul wrote and Anne illustrated. Their work with butterflies usually was conducted at Stanford's Jasper Ridge Biological Experimental Area and in the Rocky Mountain Biological Laboratory at Crested Butte, Colorado. Distrustful of pesticides, Paul experimented with alternative methods of pest control, and one of his favorite subjects to study was the control of butterfly caterpillars with ants, a natural enemy.

Paul's research in ecology and evolution branched out to include reef fishes and birds in addition to butterflies. He also began working with botanist

Peter Raven, and together they developed the concept of "coevolution"—the process of interdependent, reciprocal evolutionary interactions between ecologically intertwined plant and animal species. This highly influential idea has sharpened the focus of biological work in recent decades, and there is growing evidence that plant-herbivore coevolution was a major factor in the diversification of both flowering plants and insects.

Ehrlich's research required observing species in their natural habitats, which meant a large amount of time had to be devoted to fieldwork. So, in their first sabbatical year, 1965–1966, the Ehrlichs took a trip around the world to study butterflies. As they gained a global perspective of butterfly ecology and evolution, they also paid attention to environmental degradation in different areas of the world. Some of the tropical "paradises" where they expected to find a rich diversity of birds and butterflies were being transformed. One area in the Solomon Islands had become a large coconut plantation, with all other vegetation shorn away. In the highlands of New Guinea, they saw forests that had been completely logged. Later, in Asia, as they traveled from Malaysia to Kashmir, they were hard-pressed to find native butterfly habitat. Even the celebrated high-altitude meadows of Gulmarg in Kashmir had been overgrazed to barrenness.

In 1966, the Ehrlichs visited India. One hot night in New Delhi, as Paul, Anne, and their daughter returned to their hotel in a flea-infested taxi, their intellectual understanding of overpopulation and poverty was transformed into an emotional understanding. The taxi crawled through the city on streets overwhelmed with people going through all the varied routines of daily life, without the benefit of enough food, living space, sanitation systems, or education. The noise, the heat, the dust, and the begging hands thrusting toward them gave the scene a hellish aspect. These images were etched in their memories, and propelled their efforts in a new direction. Anne, aware of how quickly their daughter was growing up, already had started shifting her focus away from working on butterflies to finding ways to ensure a livable world for Lisa. Within a few years of their trip to India, Anne and Paul's professional partnership had begun concentrating on population control and overconsumption.

By 1966, Paul had become a full professor in biology at Stanford University and also was directing the biological science graduate studies program. For him, the transition from studying populations of butterflies to studying populations of humans followed a natural extension of ecological concepts. Theories of population regulation among animals could be extrapolated to humans, helping to assess the impact of human populations on the environment. With his new grasp of the effect of unprecedented population growth on developing countries, Paul undertook a project to bring this reality home to the American public. He wrote a book that opened with a description of the dreadful taxi ride in India, went on to describe the environmental problems created by overpopulation, and warned of impending devastation if these problems were not addressed. To explain why perpetual population growth cannot be sustained forever, he echoed the argument offered in 1798 by Thomas Malthus, the English philosopher and cleric who revealed that, while population grows exponentially, food production can only grow arithmetically—which creates an inescapable scenario that places humanity on a path to self-destruction. Following this notion, Paul's book warned of the possibility of worldwide famines and advocated zero population growth. Because of the political implications in his arguments, he rushed to get his book published in time for the 1968 presidential election.

Called *The Population Bomb* (1968), the book became an almost instant best seller and created a sensation that still ripples through the environmental movement. Before his book was published, many Americans knew that the developing world might have population problems, but few people had an adequate grasp of humanity's impact on the environment. Plus, Ehrlich's book pointed out that the United States also had a population problem; because of the wealth in the nation, each American citizen consumes natural resources and causes pollution on a much greater scale. In the book's prologue he states, "As the most powerful nation in the world today, the United States cannot stand isolated. We [as enormous consumers of natural resources] are today involved in the events leading to famine; tomorrow we may be destroyed by its consequences. . . . The birth rate must be brought into line with the death rate or mankind will breed itself into oblivion."

Environmental awareness was still in an embryonic stage in the late 1960s, but had started infiltrating the American consciousness thanks to **Rachel Carson**'s book *Silent Spring* (1962). In the late 1960s, concern arose over the declaration that Lake Erie was ecologically "dead" after years of logging, industrial pollution, detergent discharges, and untreated sewage— and by 1969, when the Cuyahoga River caught fire near Cleveland, environmental awareness took on a potent sense of urgency that grew into a new political and economic force. Attuned to this new tide of public opinion, President Richard Nixon stated that the 1970s "absolutely must be the years when America pays its debt to the past by reclaiming the purity of its air, its water and our living environment. It is literally now or never."[1]

But while Americans were already primed to adopt environmental causes, the Ehrlichs still faced the challenge of showing the link between the environment and population. At the time, large families were generally considered to be desirable and were far more common than today. Many people did not even have the means to choose the size of their families. Until the June 7, 1965, Supreme Court decision in *Griswold v. Connecticut*, married couples were not even guaranteed the right to use contraceptives. That court's landmark decision struck down state laws that had made the use of birth control by married couples illegal and paved the way for the nearly unanimous acceptance of contraception Americans enjoy today. But these were novel, even revolutionary, concepts at the time of Ehrlich's book, and a shockwave of reaction and almost panic ensued in its wake. *The Population Bomb* went on to sell over three million copies, and began a serious debate over how many people the planet could support; the inequity of global resource distribution; and the consequences of social, cultural, and even religious policy and doctrine.

The popularity of Ehrlich's book won him an invitation to *The Tonight Show* soon after its publication. He spoke to an entranced Johnny Carson about his book, pleasing the crowd with his affable yet blunt speaking style. That show provoked more than 5,000 letters, the strongest response Carson had ever seen for any guest on his show, and he invited Ehrlich back again several times. Ehrlich also was deluged with requests for lectures and interviews, which he has been granting ever since. He used the public forum to announce that, after the birth of his and Anne's only daughter, he had undergone a vasectomy as his own contribution to limiting family sizes. He also used the opportunity to solicit support for a new group he had helped found. Shortly after his book came out, he and Richard Bowers, a Connecticut lawyer, and Charles Remington, a professor, created an organization that they named Zero Population Growth (ZPG). Its purpose was to spotlight the population issue in order to influence policymakers, the press, and the public—mostly concentrating on the United States. Advocating that each family restrict itself to two children, it emphasized population control techniques as matters of both personal choice and social policy. While ZPG's cause helped further the concurrent "women's liberation" movement through its support of reproductive rights, some felt that its promotion of sterilization techniques unwittingly broadcasted racist connotations: For example, ZPG struggled to dissociate itself from incidents such as the forced sterilization of two young black women in Montgomery, Alabama, in 1973.

Due in part to the success of *The Population Bomb* and ZPG, the U.S. fertility rate began undergoing amazing changes. The average total number of children per woman dropped from 3.4 in the early 1960s to 1.8 in 1975, and the doubling time of the U.S. population rose by fourteen years between 1968 and 1975. Later, Paul Ehrlich would admit to being stunned by the reproductive revolution of the 1970s. And while critics harped that Ehrlich's "predictions" of widespread famine and utter ecological devastation were exaggerations that have never come true, Ehrlich had written the scenarios as possibilities, not forecasts. Some might even say that the warnings issued by *The Population Bomb* inspired the environmental reforms that eventually staved off the worst of the potential damage. Indeed, population growth has decelerated and the immediate crisis seems to have passed—at least in the developed world. Yet the Ehrlichs still see population as a terminal threat, not only to the earth's environment, but also to modern civilization.

Six years later, Paul and Anne co-wrote a book called *The End of Affluence: A Blueprint for Your Future* (1974). It repeated the warning that nutritional disaster was on the horizon and that humans would enter an age of scarcity in which many key materials would be nearing depletion. In a show of typical Ehrlichian wry humor, the front cover reads, "To hell with ecology . . . To hell with posterity . . . To hell with the people . . . To hell with the other nations—after all, what did they ever do for us?" Underneath that it says, "If that's your motto, don't read this book!"

Population was becoming more and more a part of the national discourse, but the Ehrlichs weren't about to abandon their cause. Both continued their work at Stanford University, while also writing and pursuing other avenues of environmental advocacy. In 1975, Anne became senior research associate for Stanford's department of biology. Two years later, when President Jimmy Carter asked the Council on Environmental Quality and the U.S. State Department to prepare an interagency study projecting population and environmental outcomes that would unfold by 2000 if societies did nothing to change their current course, Anne worked as an outside consultant on the report, which was designed to serve as a framework for long-term decision making. It was completed in 1980 and published as *The Global 2000 Report to the President of the U.S.: Entering the 21st Century*. The report predicted that the world population would grow from four billion to 6.3 billion by 2000. They were remarkably close in their prediction—by the year 2000, the world population was six billion. It also projected a rise in midlatitude temperatures, significant changes in rainfall patterns, and a deforestation rate in the tropics of an acre per second. All of these projections were accurate. In 1981, Anne began teaching an environmental policy course for the Stanford's Human Biology program, and she continued co-authoring books with Paul.

Since the worst of the "doomsday" scenarios from *The Population Bomb* had yet to happen, the Ehrlichs, and Paul in particular, were goaded on occasion by "optimists"—critics who believed his book and his theories were overreactions. In 1980, Paul agreed to make a wager to prove his conviction that the world's resources were indeed running out. Perennial optimist and contrarian **Julian Simon**, an economist at the University of Illinois, offered the following gamble: He believed that humans would never run out of anything and wanted to bet any environmentalist that the prices of selected natural resources—such as grain, oil, coal, and metal—would drop, which he claimed would indicate that they were not getting any scarcer. Paul jumped at the chance, and rounded up two colleagues—John Harte and John Holdren, both from the University of California at Berkeley—to go in on the bet with him. They chose five metals—chrome, copper, nickel, tin, and tungsten—in quantities of $200 each at 1980 prices. If, by 1990, the prices had gone up, Simon had to pay the difference. If prices dropped, Ehrlich and his colleagues had to pay.

During the decade of the 1980s the world's population increased by 800 million people, but by 1990, even though the quantity of these metals in the earth's crust had not increased, their prices had dropped. In part this was due to a recession that was slowing the demand for industrial metals. Paul and his colleagues ended up paying $576.07. He later made the point that the price of metals on the stock market is not an accurate reflection of the state of environment. To expound on this idea, he and Stephen Schneider, a climatologist at Stanford University, made a new offer to Simon in 1995. They would place $1,000 per trend on fifteen "global indicators of human welfare," betting that they would worsen over the next decade. These trends were:

1. the average global temperature would rise,
2. there would be more carbon dioxide in the atmosphere,
3. there would be more nitrous oxide in the atmosphere,
4. there would be a greater concentration of ozone in the lower atmosphere,[2]
5. emissions of sulfur dioxide in Asia would be greater,
6. there would be less fertile cropland per capita,
7. there would be less agricultural soil per capita (due to erosion),
8. there would be less rice and wheat grown per capita,
9. less firewood would be available in developing nations,
10. a smaller area of virgin tropical moist forests would exist,
11. the oceanic fisheries harvest would continue its downward trend,
12. there would be fewer extant plant and animal species,
13. more people would die of AIDS,
14. sperm counts of human males would continue to decline and reproductive disorders would increase, and
15. the gap between the richest 10 percent of humanity and the poorest 10 percent would widen.

Simon refused to take the bet.

In the meantime, Paul and Anne had written a sequel to *The Population Bomb* called *The Population Explosion* (1990). It followed up on many of the ideas from the previous book, and gave updated population numbers (3.5 billion people worldwide in 1968 compared to 5.3 billion in 1990)—in much the same tone of urgency:

In 1968, *The Population Bomb* warned of impending disaster if the population explosion was not brought under control. Then the fuse was burning; now the population bomb has detonated. Since 1968, at least 200 million people—mostly children—have perished needlessly of hunger and hunger-related diseases . . . *a largely prospective disas-*

ter has turned into the real thing. . . . The Population Explosion is being written as ominous changes in the life-support systems of civilization become more evident daily.[3]

Underlying every aspect of the Ehrlich's arguments on population is their
recognition of the short-sightedness of a society that is living beyond its
means—in other words, they know that the burgeoning consumption that
typifies modern life, especially in the developed world, eventually will cause
the balance of non-renewable resources to be overdrawn. Julian Simon, conversely, tried to persuade the public that there was no need to worry about
limitations on natural resources. He maintained that the human mind is the
ultimate resource and that the world needs more people in order to have
more geniuses: Any human yet to be born might be the next Mozart or
Michelangelo, so why would anyone want to limit the birth of human beings? Rather than take precautions that would address overconsumption
and environmental deterioration, Simon believed that human ingenuity eventually would come up with solutions and the necessary technologies for coping with depleted resources and a degraded environment.

As the Ehrlichs point out, however, it requires a huge leap of imagination to expect that each new child born in Jakarta, Port-au-Prince, or
Manila—saddled with the disadvantages of malnutrition, poverty, and lack
of education—would have the same quality of life or potential for intellectual development as a middle-class child in, say, the United States. This example illustrates some of the complicating factors in population studies—the
inequity of growth between developed and developing nations and the unequal
distribution of goods and resources. The population of developing countries
(primarily in the tropics) is expected to grow from approximately 45 percent
of all people in the world to 64 percent by the year 2020, while the proportion
of people living in developed countries will drop to about one-sixth of the
world's total population. Yet developed nations control most of the goods and
resources on earth—nearly 80 percent of the global economy. When critics argue that the Ehrlichs are "people-haters" since they plead for a smaller overall
human race, the Ehrlichs point out these disparities. Their objective is not to
deprive the world of a Mozart or a Michelangelo, but to improve the standard
of living for all of humanity by ensuring adequate stores of natural resources,
a better balance of wealth and power, and the ecological well-being of the
earth's biological life-support system. They are attempting to articulate clearly
to a naturally short-sighted species—humans—the enormous environmental
losses that result from human culture.

While doing fieldwork recently in rural Costa Rica, Paul noticed that
most households, however humble, exhibit the distinctive glow of a television screen at night. According to him, television amplifies the problems
posed by the proliferation of humanity by presenting visually enticing scenarios of affluence and encouraging a culture of competitive acquisition. He

and Anne, along with their colleague John Holdren, came up with an equation that describes the impact of the human population on the biological life-support systems of the planet: $I = PAT$, where I is the overall human impact, P is population size, which is multiplied by A, affluence (measured by per capita consumption), and by T, technologies (including social, political, and economic arrangements) that foster consumption. The resulting impact, which is manifested in various ways (such as the depletion of forests, soils, and underground freshwater and the increase of CO_2 in the atmosphere), therefore comes from a combination of factors, any or all of which could be reduced to lessen the effect of overconsumption. One way to start, say the Ehrlichs, would be to stop glamorizing the fantasy versions of rich lifestyles on television, a phenomenon that inspires consumption lust in homes across the globe, even in rural Costa Rica.

The Ehrlichs believe profoundly in the idea of evolution—the premise that life evolves through genetic mutations, molded through the ages by natural selection. They even have an evolution-based explanation for the tendency of American society to ignore warnings about overpopulation and its sinister cousin, overconsumption. Human beings evolved to pay attention to the near term, to watch for immediate dangers like a leopard jumping out of a tree. Large-scale processes that occur in the "background," such as climate change and slowly increasing numbers of people, are less likely to cause a reaction of alarm in the human nervous system, designed as it is for reaction to rapid, sudden threats. As they point out in *The Population Explosion*, "[H]uman beings, besides tuning out gradual trends, do not easily recognize the need to adjust their ways of life to accommodate the needs of more than five billion fellows, most living thousands of miles away. That all people must change their behavior to permit everyone on the planet to lead a decent life is not a notion evolution has prepared us to accept readily."[4]

Three decades after their eye-opening first visit to India, Paul and Anne found slightly fewer beggars on the streets of Delhi. They also found such a choking mob of cars and motor scooters that the air was hard to breathe. India's middle class had been growing, and now—even amongst surroundings of bleak poverty—glamorous billboards advertise computer software. But this scene, notwithstanding the problematic mimicry of the consumptive excesses of the West, doesn't look like the picture of large-scale famine Paul Ehrlich envisioned for this day and age when he wrote *The Population Bomb*. Paul now admits to having a certain amount of naïveté when he wrote that book, and that his analysis of certain things, like agriculture, was off. "You show me a scientist who believes everything he believed thirty-two years ago, I'll show you a nut," he says. "Obviously I've learned a lot."[5] However, he will backpedal only to a point. His ideas about the threat of overpopulation have evolved and grown more nuanced, but he is no less passionate about them. And just because not every catastrophic possibility he outlined thirty-two years ago occurred doesn't mean that the environmental situation is in any less danger today. As the Ehrlichs have been pointing out for years, the only way society is able to support the present population is by exhausting its natural capital, and that's "a one-way street."

That concept is simple, with many implications for future generations, yet the panic set off by *The Population Bomb* has largely evaporated, and the Ehrlichs are left to wonder why more people aren't as concerned about the issue as they are. They therefore have turned their formidable understanding of evolutionary processes toward the study of human nature and culture. Cultural evolution has the power to transform the route humans take toward progress—which means it can influence society's conception of the human impact on the earth and thereby raise the level of concern for the environment. In a newer book, Paul Ehrlich explores the pull culture exerts on human ways of thinking and how this pull might be harnessed to further the environmental movement. Called *Human Natures: Genes, Cultures, and the Human Prospect* (2000), it acknowledges that human behavior is influenced by genetics, but, it argues, perhaps not to the extent that many people believe. Ehrlich argues that it has become a standard misperception that humans are so hardwired by their genes into certain behaviors and personality traits that they are virtually controlled by their DNA. But he emphasizes that culture and other nongenetic influences also have an enormous impact on personality, decision making, and all types of human behavior. His book examines questions like: Can humans change the direction of their culture to better accommodate the global environment? Can the ecosystems upon which the global economy depends be preserved, or will humans continue in their cultural evolution to take every technological opportunity to consume more? In order to achieve true cultural progress toward a more sustainable relationship with the planet's ecosystems, Ehrlich argues that people need a better understanding of the evolutionary processes that have created human culture. This paves the way for open discourse about the issue, which makes possible a conscious effort to steer cultural evolution away from problematic human tendencies.

The Ehrlichs have spent over three decades contributing to the scientific study and intellectual and emotional understanding of human and environmental well-being. Both still work for Stanford University's Center for Conservation Biology (CCB), which they helped found in 1984. Paul serves as president and Anne as policy coordinator. The CCB has become an influential research and teaching center for conservation biology, population growth, environmental deterioration, and natural resource use. Anne has also served on the boards of directors of Friends of the Earth (1976–1985), the Conferences on the Fate of the Earth (1981–1984), the Center for Innovative Diplomacy (1981–1992), and Redefining Progress (1994–1996) and on the editorial board of the *Pacific Discovery* (the journal of the California Academy of

Sciences, 1988–1994). In 1994–1995 she served on a task group of academics and scientists for the President's Commission on Sustainable Development. She currently serves on the boards of the Pacific Institute for Studies in Environment, Development, and Security (since 1988); the Rocky Mountain Biological Laboratory (since 1989), the Ploughshare Fund (since 1990), and the Sierra Club (elected in 1996). She also chaired the Sierra Club's Committee on Military Impacts on the Environment from 1985 to 1994.

In the summer of 1990, Paul won a five-year MacArthur Foundation "genius" grant for $345,000, and in September that year he went to Stockholm to share half of the $240,000–Crafoord Prize, the ecologist's version of the Nobel. In 1994 the Ehrlichs received the Sasakawa United Nations Environment Prize, and in 1998 they received the John and Alice Tyler Prize for Environmental Achievement for their individual and joint work on elucidating and publicizing the relationships between population size, resource consumption, socioeconomic equity, and the environment.

NOTES

1. *Congressional Quarterly* (October 30, 1970), p. 2728.
2. Misconceptions about ozone are common. One source of confusion is that ozone exists in two different places in the atmosphere, both having very different impacts on planetary health. Ozone in the troposphere (from 0–8 miles above earth's surface) is an ingredient in smog and can have deleterious effects on human health and on agricultural crops. The ozone layer that provides a protective shield against the sun's ultraviolet radiation is farther out in the stratosphere (8–30 miles above the earth's surface).
3. Paul R. Ehrlich and Anne H. Ehrlich, *The Population Explosion: From Global Warming to Rain Forest Destruction, Famine, and Air and Water Pollution—Why Overpopulation Is Our #1 Environmental Problem* (New York: Simon and Schuster, 1990), pp. 9–10.
4. Ibid., p. 187.
5. Natalie Angiers, "On Human Nature and the Evolution of Culture," *New York Times* (October 10, 2000), p. F2.

BIBLIOGRAPHY

Paul Ehrlich has written, co-written, or edited over thirty books and textbooks. His book with the longest impact on the conservation debate is *The Population Bomb* (New York: Ballantine, 1968), which was revised and expanded edition in 1971. Paul and Anne Ehrlich have written several books on conservation biology, including *Population, Resources, Environment: Issues in Human Ecology* (San Francisco: W.H. Freeman and Company, 1970); *The Population Explosion: From Global Warming to Rain Forest Destruction, Famine, and Air and Water Pollution—Why Overpopulation Is Our #1 Environmental Problem* (New York: Simon and Schuster, 1990); *Healing the Planet: Strategies for Resolving the Environmental Crisis* (New York:

Addison-Wesley, 1991); *Betrayal of Science and Reason: How Anti-Environmental Rhetoric Threatens Our Future* (Covelo, CA: Island Press, 1996); and, with Gretchen C. Daily, *The Stork and the Plow: The Equity Answer to the Human Dilemma* (New York: G.P. Putnam's Sons, 1995). For an interview with Paul Ehrlich, see Natalie Angiers, "On Human Nature and the Evolution of Culture," *New York Times* (October 10, 2000), pp. F1–2; and for a historical perspective on Ehrlich's population growth predictions see Andrew Ferguson, "Perceiving the Population Bomb," *World Watch* Vol. 14 (July/August 2001), pp. 36–39. A story about the resources bet with Julian Simon was written by John Tierney, "Betting the Planet," *New York Times Magazine* (December 2, 1990), pp. 52–53, 74–81. For information on Anne and Paul's collaborative work, see James K. Boyce, "The Bomb is a Dud," *Progressive* Vol. 54 (September 1990), p. 24; Jim Motavalli, "Paul and Anne Ehrlich: The Countdown Continues to the Population Bomb," *E Magazine* Vol. 7 (November/December 1996), pp. 10–12; "A Winning Partnership," *Environmental Health Perspectives* Vol. 106 (June 1998), p. A267. Gregg Easterbrook argues against the Ehrlichs' population warnings in his "Propheteers," *Washington Monthly* Vol. 23 (November 1991), pp. 43–47. The following article by Anne Ehrlich is based on her acceptance speech for the Raymond B. Bragg Award for Distinguished Service to Humanism in 1985: "Critical Masses," *The Humanist* Vol. 45 (July/August 1985), pp. 18–22, 36.

JULIAN SIMON
(1932–1998)

This is my long-run forecast in brief: the material conditions of life will continue to get better for most people, in most countries, most of the time, indefinitely. Within a century or two, all nations and most of humanity will be at or above today's western living standards.

—Julian Simon

Just before midnight on February 12, 1932, Julian Lincoln Simon was born, and his mother, Mae (Goodstein) Simon, got her wish: to have her son born on Abraham Lincoln's birthday so that his middle name could be "Lincoln." Later in life he had to confess he was proud to be named after a man who possessed such courage and love of humanity. For his part, Simon's own courage would serve him well during a career marked by unconventional ideas, irreverent attitudes, and intellectual independence. As for a love of humanity, Simon's version took the shape of a vigorous belief in unchecked population growth—he felt that the world is left richer for each person who has lived in it and that attempts to curb overpopulation are unnecessary and impede progress. He felt it was unnecessarily apocalyptic to be anxious about dwindling supplies of non-renewable natural resources in the earth's crust, since human ingenuity would always circumvent any global environmental problems. His courage also enabled him to exist as an outsider, his views sometimes far outside the mainstream, and to endure an onslaught of criticism from environmentalists who disagreed with his utopian vision of inexhaustible natural resources.

He grew up an only child in a Jewish family in Newark, New Jersey, and often felt alone and starved for affection, wishing fervently for a brother or sister. His father, Philip Mordecai Simon, had dropped out of high school to work in his parents' hardware store and later operated a small business selling sal soda for use as an industrial water softener, making enough money to keep the family comfortable during the Depression. When Julian was a toddler, his father built a screened box to put Julian in so that he could be suspended outside the second-floor window of their apartment for fresh air without his mother having to take him up and down the stairs. In adulthood, he tried to interpret this questionable system in a positive light, saying it helped him to develop self-sufficiency. Indeed, throughout Julian's childhood his mother offered him little praise, expressing instead the sentiment that he could have done better—whether in school, in sports, or in Boy Scouts. He would later joke that he was the illegitimate son of a married Jewish couple, using the term "illegitimate" not to describe his parentage but to imply that his existence was unjustified. His childhood taught him that life is a struggle and that he had to fight his own battles and look to no one but himself for help.

One of the tricks he learned for facing challenges was to make jokes: He developed a mischievous sense of humor and became known as a prankster. His aunts called him *bonditt* (Yiddish for "bandit") for the slapstick antics he pulled. From an early age Simon loved to stir things up—and it still appealed to him as an adult, especially if he could make light of a highly respectable, highly influential person. Another coping strategy Simon developed was indulging in his love of information: facts, data, figures, charts. He acquired the habit of looking up the facts from frequent arguments his father would provoke out of ignorance or just plain contrariness. If his father insisted, for example, that butter was eight cents a pound, Simon couldn't resist pointing out that butter was actually eighty cents a pound. Certain he was right, his father would refuse to listen, leaving Simon without solace until he could look up the answer in a newspaper and find the facts telling him what he had already known: He was right and his father was wrong.

In the summer of 1941, Simon's family moved to the suburb of Milburn, just outside Newark—a difficult move for him. He had to jump ahead in school to fifth grade, and from then on he always felt smaller than the rest of his class. Back in Newark he had been known and welcomed by a pack of neighborhood kids, but now he was an outsider. Additionally, not long after they moved, the United States entered into World War II, changing his life further. One impression he never forgot was the reaction of his Jewish family to the war: It was the only time he ever sensed a group of people so profoundly frightened. The war also changed his family's financial outlook by making raw materials unavailable and forcing the closure of his father's business. His father never really worked full-time again.

Simon would later admit that he had been more of a follower than a leader in school. In Boy Scouts however, his ambitions flared. He joined the Scouts in 1944, and two years later—by the time he was fourteen—he had earned the title of Eagle Scout—the highest ranking possible. During his teenage years he also developed an enterprising interest in creating businesses: He and a cousin bought a set of stencils for painting house numbers on curbstones and went door to door soliciting their painting service, actually making a fair profit. Later, in high school, he came up with the idea of using a turkey baster and some glue he had created in the chemistry lab to repair broken book spines. He spent a summer fixing books from his school's library for eight cents each, making what was then a large hourly wage.

Though he refers to his own high school performance as undistinguished, he was in the top 10 percent of his class, and when he graduated he was admitted to Harvard on a Navy ROTC scholarship. Simon enjoyed college and found his intellectual horizons expanding rapidly. The navy required him to take introductory physics, which he said turned out to be the single most valuable course he ever took. So impressed was he with it that, years later, he made his own children take it in their college years. He didn't continue studying physics however, but opted for a major in experimental psychology. The honors thesis on concept formation that he completed for his bachelor's degree—the first professional work he had undertaken—was his biggest source of pride from his undergraduate years. After graduating, he wrote up a paper on his thesis study and submitted it to a top psychology journal, but it was turned down. Confident his work was relevant and valid, Simon was unfazed by the journal's rejections. That streak of self-assuredness would carry him through many events of his future professional career, during which he frequently would position himself contrary to established beliefs.

During three of his college summers he served as a navy midshipman in various ports. After graduation from Harvard in 1953, he had to complete his military service with the navy, and because of the Korean War, his commitment was extended to three years. Life aboard a ship, though difficult, brought Simon a certain amount of satisfaction. Though he chafed under the dictatorial power structure of the navy, he enjoyed his responsibilities, and seeing foreign cities inspired him. The thrilling bustle of Hong Kong, for example, sparked his emerging belief that high-density population centers are highly desirable. But most satisfying of all was the sense of belonging, of comradeship. When he got out of the navy in 1956, he was somewhat at a loss, and wrestled with what career path to take. His dislike of elitism and distaste for authority, heightened by the hierarchical system in the military, convinced him he would never thrive in any sort of bureaucratic institution. For awhile he considered medical school, even taking an organic chemistry class to complete qualifications, but changed his mind after the course ended.

He moved back in with his parents in Millburn and, after spending a month selling *Encyclopedia Britannica*, took a job as an advertising copywriter in New York City and commuted each day into the city. Advertising inspired a certain amount of fascination in Simon, and he quickly picked up skills in market research and advertising design. Five months later Ziff-Davis Media, a publishing company, offered him a job paying double his current salary. He took the job, this time as assistant promotion manager. Working in the world of business suited Simon, and after about a year of it he was ready to go to graduate school to study business administration. He applied for a fellowship at the University of Chicago in Urbana, and got it. Once there, he took a required course in microeconomics, another course in managerial economics, and one in economic forecasting. These three courses comprised the only formal education he would ever have in economics, though he eventually would become famous in the field and actually considered himself an economist. As he saw it, his lack of training in economics worked to his benefit: He never got stuck in the mainstream mindset of the field, and never felt his imagination was limited by what others told him he could accomplish. He earned his MBA in 1959, and his Ph.D. in 1961, both from the University of Chicago. While still in Chicago, he met Rita Mintz James, a sociologist, and within months they were engaged.

After graduate school, Simon moved back in with his parents again and began a series of small mail-order businesses, including a flower delivery service called "Flowers Every Friday," a service selling gourmet coffee and tea, and one selling a booklet entitled "How to Make Your Will." Eventually he created Julian Simon Associates, a mail-order firm and advertising agency located in Hoboken, New Jersey. He employed his father in his business, and he and Rita, now married, moved to Manhattan, where he would have a quick commute. For about two years he stayed with the business, but then began to feel his talents would be more useful in another profession. Around this time he began to suffer from depression, something that would plague him for over a decade, sometimes nearly debilitating him. His work, especially once he started writing, became his only avenue of escape.

Writing turned his life toward an entirely new path. His experience in the mail-order business supplied him his first real topic, and while writing his first book, *How to Start and Operate a Mail-Order Business* (1965), he discovered that the hours he spent working on it were the only hours he enjoyed during his day. Desperate for a career change, he took the advice of a friend and contacted an economics professor at Columbia University, who immediately offered to let Simon lecture to his class. On a whim, and despite his conviction that the institutional structure of academic life would make him unfit to be a professor, he agreed. To his surprise, teaching that class on the theory of mail-order operations turned out to be exhilarating, and he decided to pursue the field further. When Simon was offered an assistant professor of advertising position at the University of Illinois at Urbana, he and his wife had a true dilemma—Simon wanted the job, but Urbana failed to impress Rita, who despaired at having to leave her good job in New York. Simon's enthusiasm was contagious though, and once they moved, Rita was offered a job with the university as well.

Starting in 1963, Simon settled in at the University of Illinois, where he would remain—teaching, researching, and writing—for the next twenty years. He also continued to fight depression and continually sought help from a psychologist. By 1966, when he had become associate professor of marketing, he had stockpiled an arsenal of teaching experience and had developed an engaging style that relied on plenty of visual aids and showcased his animated manner. His three children were born during his early years of teaching: David on November 27, 1964, and Judith on December 16, 1965. Their third son, Daniel, was born on March 27, 1968, during the family's year-long stay in Jerusalem, where Simon was a visiting professor at the Hebrew University. It was while the family was in Israel in 1968 that Simon began to study the literature of population economics. Up until then he had believed in population control, and shared the common understanding that overpopulation is a threat to economic development, quality of life, and human health. But in reading further about population growth, he became confused.

The work of a much earlier economist, Thomas Malthus, was responsible for some of Simon's previously held beliefs about population. In 1798, Malthus wrote *An Essay on the Principle of Population*—a treatise examining growth rates and the problems inherent in supplying food to more and more people over time. "Population, when unchecked, increases in a geometrical ratio," wrote Malthus. "Subsistence increases only in an arithmetical ratio. A slight acquaintance with numbers will shew the immensity of the first power in comparison of the second."[1] This means population growth eventually will outpace food production, leading to inevitable human misery. The main Malthusian premise—that population stresses the environment and humans must therefore try to live within certain limits—became an important backbone of environmental ideology. Simon once agreed with Malthusian thought and felt that population control measures should be actively implemented. In fact, the first article he wrote on the subject, entitled "Marketing Correct Methods for Promoting Family Planning," ran in *Demography* in 1968 and contributed an argument to the fight against overpopulation.

It was the following year that the humanitarian organization Population Council arranged for Simon to travel to India to study implementation strategies for a population control incentive program. But Simon's views had begun changing, and he started distancing himself from his earlier beliefs. He had come across a book by Harold Barnett and Chandler Morse called *Scarcity and Growth: The Economics of Resource Availability*, which had been published with the help of a group of conservative economists called Resources for the Future. They argued as follows: "Advances in fundamental science have made it possible to take advantage of the uniformity of energy/matter, a uniformity that makes it feasible, without preassignable limit, to escape the quantitative constraints imposed by the character of the earth's crust. A limit may exist, but it can be neither defined nor specified in economic terms. Nature imposes particular scarcities, not an inescapable general scarcity."[2]

To Simon this idea was a revelation, as was the book's argument that some natural resources were actually becoming more available rather than more scarce, using as evidence the fact that the average worker could purchase more coal or metal or food with an hour's pay than a worker in the last century. By the early 1970s, Simon had reached the conclusion that Malthus's theory was unsound, and that unchecked population growth, even with its implied drain on finite raw materials and its addition to the global burden of pollution, actually does not lower the standard of living. Concentrating on the positive impacts of humans rather than the negative, Simon came up with his own theory: People contribute to the world through their productive work hours, their investment in public infrastructures such as roads, and their creation of new technologies. In other words, Simon believed that the problem with the Malthusian focus on ecological concepts such as the sustainability of agriculture or the environmental impact of metal extraction or road building, is that it ignores the intellectual potential of humans, whom he called "the ultimate resource." The more population grows, the more ingenuity is available to solve the accompanying problems of pollution, food supply, and habitat destruction. While his arguments most often took on the utilitarian flavor of economics, there were also aesthetic and moral components. His belief—that each human has a unique opportunity to enhance the quality of life of the rest of the world—meant that it was morally wrong to make any restrictions on population size. Therefore, concluded Simon, environmentalists who worried about the capacity of the planet to support exploding populations, especially in the developing world, and who for that reason supported the idea of population restrictions, were enemies of humanity.

Simon's publicly aired analyses of Malthusian population science began drawing the first rounds of the criticism and controversy that would follow him for the rest of his life. On the first annual celebration of Earth Day, April 22, 1970, Simon was invited to speak on a panel to an audience of 2,000 people at the University of Illinois campus. All of the other panelists were environmentalists—Simon would be the token opposition. To his credit, he agreed to sit on the panel, and spoke about his optimistic vision of population and how policy cannot be based on scientific data alone, as it must rest also on values. He also made a remarkable assertion: "For the very long run I think it is safe to predict that if the population stabilizes at say 30 billion, the standard of living will be higher than if it were to stabilize at 7 billion." Applause was lukewarm. Paul Silverman, a zoologist, spoke next, disputing Simon's arguments. He questioned what kind of scientific calculations Simon must have made to come up with his assertions and said his argument lacked substance and scholarship. He also questioned Simon's implication that, because environmentalists and ecologists talk about limited resources and the negative consequences of overpopulation, their judgements don't rest on values. "It is because we are concerned about people that we are now trying to alert them to the dangers which face us," Silverman said. "Apparently, however, there is a basic difference in our value systems."[3] Simon got his revenge later by throwing a drink in Silverman's face at a faculty party.

Meanwhile, for the past thirteen years Simon had been continuing to fight serious depression, almost constantly conscious of being miserable. He viewed his work as a failure and obsessively reflected on his faults, and consulting with psychiatrists and psychologists provided little relief. But in 1975, he read about a new approach to treating depression called "cognitive therapy," which he then used to analyze the root of his own depression. In two weeks he had cured himself. Confident that his method would make a contribution to the study of cognitive therapy and could help others who were depressed, he eventually wrote a book entitled *Good Mood: The New Psychology of Overcoming Depression.* From that self-induced triumph in 1975 until his death he never suffered depression again, and even judged himself to be more joyful than most people. He later wondered if the path his career was about to take played a role in his continued cheerfulness, for during the late 1970s he experienced a breakthrough in his work, which suddenly began getting the attention he had always thought it deserved.

First, the year 1978 saw the fruition of one of Simon's brainstorms—one that illustrates the eclectic nature of his intellect. While shaving one day during the mid-1960s, he had been thinking about the public relations problems plaguing the airline industry. Airlines have always oversold flights to assure a full passenger load, but prior to 1978, if a flight ended up overbooked, some travelers had to be involuntarily bumped. Simon wondered why the airlines didn't try a reverse auction: If a flight is overbooked, ticket holders could make a bid for the lowest amount they would be willing to accept in return for waiting for another flight. The airline agent would take as many of the lowest bidders as needed and no one would be bumped involuntarily. In 1966 Simon started shopping his idea around to all the airlines, receiving nothing but rejection and frequently derision. An official at Pan American mockingly replied, "Of course we instituted the procedure immediately, after having the instructions translated into 18 languages."[4] The Civil Aeronautics Board showed no interest either. In 1968 he managed to get an article describing his scheme published in the *Journal of Transport Economics and*

Policy. But it wasn't until ten years later that his idea, with the minor modi-
fication of letting the airline set the incentive, usually a free ticket, finally
resulted in regulatory reform and the implementation of a plan that has become familiar to any air traveler today.

As for Simon's work on population issues, it soon began attracting notice
as well. In 1980, the Carter administration published a multiagency assessment of the earth's future, titled *The Global 2000 Report to the President*,
which announced that the earth's growing human population was taxing the
carrying capacity of the biological systems upon which it relies. Its forecast
that "if present trends continue, the world in 2000 will be more crowded,
more polluted, less stable ecologically and more vulnerable to disruption
than the world we live in now,"[5] earned headlines and praise around the
world, but also elicited a quick response from Simon, who said the assertions were baseless. Eventually he co-wrote with futurist **Herman Kahn** a
book refuting the report, called *The Resourceful Earth: A Response to
Global 2000* (1984). But before that he made his opposition to its findings
known in several periodicals. In a book review in *Science Digest* he called
the Global 2000 Study's report "fatally flawed," saying that "it shows no
awareness that humankind's history has been a sequence of worrisome
scarcities and resulting solutions *that left us better off than before the
scarcity arose*."[6]

He also wrote a paper unveiling his own rose-colored vision of beneficial
human progress and positive environmental trends. Entitled "Resources,
Population, Environment: An Oversupply of False Bad News," it was published in *Science* in June 1980. Global environmental "doom and gloom"
was unwarranted, he wrote. "False bad news about population growth, natural resources, and the environment is published widely in the face of contradictory evidence. For example, the world supply of arable land has
actually been increasing, the scarcity of natural resources including food and
energy has been decreasing, and basic measures of U.S. environmental quality show positive trends."[7] To prove that natural resources were not running
out, he pointed out that prices of raw materials had been consistently falling
over the years. He also said there is no evidence that population growth has
a negative effect on economic growth, in either more-developed or less-
developed countries. Occasionally his philosophy bordered on space-age
mysticism, and his lack of training in the sciences sometimes tarnished his
bold claims. When discussing why it was wrongheaded to insist that copper
is a finite resource, he wrote:

> Future quantities of a natural resource such as copper cannot be calcu-
> lated even in principle, because of new lodes, new methods of mining
> copper, and variations in grades of copper lodes; because copper can be
> made from other metals. . . . Even the total weight of the earth is not a
> theoretical limit to the amount of copper that might be available to

earthlings in the future. Only the total weight of the universe—if that term has a useful meaning here—would be such a theoretical limit.[8]

Simon's paper attracted one of the largest batches of angry letters in *Science*'s history, and because of its shock value, it was immediately reprinted in many magazines and newspapers, multiplying its impact even further. One letter of protest, written a few years later by W. Dexter Bellamy of the Institute of Food Science, said that "the views of Julian Simon are incomprehensible to many bioscientists. If Simon is to have any credibility in the scientific world, he must explain how an ever-increasing population will aid developing countries. . . . We are not living in Mr. Simon's dream world where 'copper can be made from other metals.'"[9] Conservation biologist **Paul Ehrlich** publicly wondered how such an article had passed peer-review at one of the nation's leading scientific journals, taking Simon to task for what he saw as an uninformed view of subjects that Ehrlich had spent his whole life studying: population and its impact on natural resources. He and his wife **Anne Ehrlich**, also a conservation biologist, and two energy and natural resource experts, John Holdren and John Harte, wrote their own letter to the editor, saying that, regardless of Simon's argument about increasing arable land, growing fossil fuel combustion from rising populations eventually will alter the global climate to such a degree that food production will be completely undermined. The battle lines were drawn. Ehrlich and Simon, the ecologist and the economist, would feud over these issues, sometimes bitterly, until Simon's death in 1998.

Just as when he was a child, Simon loved to stir things up. One of his greatest publicity stunts was in his 1980 piece that ran in *Social Science Quarterly*: a challenge to any environmentalist to place a bet with him on trends in prices of commodities. Insisting that it was impossible for any raw material to run out, he would let anyone pick any natural resource—grain, metals, timber, oil, or coal—and any date in the future. If the price went up, it meant the resource was getting scarcer. But Simon wagered that the price of the resource would actually go down. Ehrlich responded: "I and my colleagues, John P. Holdren (University of California, Berkeley) and John Harte (Lawrence Berkeley Laboratory), jointly accept Simon's astonishing offer before other greedy people jump in." They selected five metals—chrome, copper, nickel, tungsten, and tin—and bet $200 for each. It was October 1980 when they made the deal, and they drew up a contract to terminate it ten years later, in October 1990. If the 1990 prices of the metals (adjusted for inflation) turned out to be higher, Simon would have to pay the difference. If they fell, Ehrlich, Harte, and Holdren would pay.

The bet, which immediately became famous, was a rare event: Two highly intelligent, opinionated scholars were able to define their disagreement precisely enough that both were willing to put their money where their mouths were. In the end, thanks to a recession in the first half of the decade that slowed the demand for industrial metals worldwide, the prices of all five metals had dropped by 1990. Ehrlich wrote Simon a check for $576.07 and mailed it. The story was chronicled on the cover of the *New York Times Magazine*, and Simon felt he was finally being taken seriously. He wrote back to Ehrlich and offered to make another bet as high as $20,000 on any other resources and any future date, but Ehrlich refused. In thinking back on the whole experiment of calculating environmental problems in terms of market economics, Ehrlich would later point out that the demand for those five metals during the previous decade was not exactly a critical indicator of the state of the earth's capacity to support life. Other resources—such as soil fertility, species diversity, water supplies, and the stability of the climate— would have been more accurate trends to determine the truth of Simon's assertion that everything will only get better as time goes on.

By the time he had won the bet, Simon had made a few career changes. In 1983 he left the University of Illinois and started teaching economics and business administration at the University of Maryland. His 700-page book *The Ultimate Resource* had come out in 1981, documenting in great detail his claims on the population issue. "If the past is any guide, natural resources will become less scarce," and "population growth is likely to have a long-run beneficial impact on the natural resource situation," he wrote. As the years went by, Simon lamented the poor reception of *The Ultimate Resource*, despairing that it never showed up in citations in technical economic work. Of all his books, his do-it-yourself treatise on mail-order marketing was the most successful, selling 200,000 copies, far more than anything else he wrote.

Still, Simon had perhaps more of an effect than he often claimed. His arguments were very influential during President **Ronald Reagan**'s terms in office, impacting policy on population growth and environmental regulation. In 1984, the Reagan administration adopted Simon's position, which they termed "supply-side demographics," at the UN Population Conference in Mexico City, despite an outcry from international population control groups. That same year, environmental scientist **Barry Commoner** deplored the fact that Simon's theories were influencing policy. "The free enterprise system that Dr. Simon told us has given us all these great things is precisely the source of the policy decisions that have given us our environmental problems,"[10] he said. Later in the 1980s, Simon received an invitation to the Vatican to expound on the theory that population growth creates resources rather than uses them up, and Pope John Paul II was soon urging the world to treat people as productive assets.

Simon had access to the same data as the population ecologists who predicted global crises, but his difference in perspective and interpretation led to his becoming a scourge of the environmental movement. By framing all his arguments in terms of market forces, Simon always downplayed any discussion of biological factors and the role they historically have played in human enterprises. In his book *Hoodwinking the Nation*, published posthumously in 1999, Simon made some farfetched claims about biology, a subject outside his field of expertise, to boost his argument that biologists are more prone to erroneous judgements than economists. His declarations that "except for the study of evolution, biology is an ahistorical field of inquiry," and "biologists study individuals rather than samples of populations," for example, are both manifestly false. **Lester Brown** of the Worldwatch Institute summarized the frustration Simon evinced in professional scientists. "Most biologists and ecologists look at population growth in terms of the carrying capacity of natural systems," he said. "Julian was not handicapped by being either. As an economist, he could see population growth in a much more optimistic light."[11]

Besides the issue of population, Simon scoffed at other environmentalist warnings as well. He believed that no one could prove that the ozone layer was being depleted or that acid rain existed, and saw no reason to be concerned about global warming, calling it "the supposed greenhouse effect" and predicting it would turn out to be yet another "transient concern." He accused biologists and ecologists worried about the accelerating rate of species extinctions of basing their concerns on "nonfacts." A former advertising expert, Simon presented these arguments while adopting the pleasing and solicitous stance of "optimist"—and those who came to Simon's way of thinking were sometimes called "cornucopians," for their view of the world as an inexhaustible bounty of goods.

On the other hand, Simon accused "Malthusians" of being dour prophets of doom who couldn't even enjoy life and foresaw only a future of starvation, plagues, and war. But polarizing the debate between the cornucopians and the Malthusians gives no more of an accurate picture of the real issues of population than a soap opera gives of real life. By the 1990s, overpopulation was regarded as somewhat less of a crisis issue than it had been in the 1970s. But population scientists have not come anywhere close to Simon's level of utopian optimism regarding the future of the planet. Most experts are unconvinced, for example, by Simon's claim that current levels of population growth in the third world are going to bring those countries any long-term benefits. And environmentalists still bemoan the overconsumption of resources inherent in a growing population, and point out the fact that almost all other environmental ills, such as global warming, deforestation, habitat destruction, and species extinction have only increased as the global population has grown—and that human ingenuity has yet to fix them.

To add further dimension to the population problem, environmental justice advocates point out that growth and development (and its concomitant environmental degradation) does bring benefits to some, but imposes costs on others. The beneficiaries often tend to be rich and disproportionately male, while those who pay the cost are disproportionately poor and female. For families in the third world, and impoverished women in particular, having more children may be the only "wealth" available, even though most of the children in such situations will grow up without access to education, health care, or even adequate food.

Perhaps for these reasons, Simon never gained the affection of the general public that his sparring partner Ehrlich did. During Earth Day events in 1990, both men gave talks in Washington, D.C. Ehrlich spoke at a rally to an audience of 200,000 with heartfelt applause. Later that weekend, at a symposium of ecologists, Ehrlich spoke again of declining natural resources and criticized economists who use shortsighted, non-scientific views of the future—alluding to Simon's work by saying "the ultimate resource—the one thing we'll never run out of is imbeciles."[12] One block away, Simon delivered a very different message at a symposium sponsored by the Competitive Enterprise Institute, a think tank pursuing free-market solutions to environmental issues. Malthusians must be intellectually dishonest, he declared, because population growth actually represents "a victory over death." His audience was only sixteen people. Perhaps this disappointed him, but gesturing toward the lecture hall where Ehrlich was speaking, he said with characteristic humor and optimism, "Well, there may be more of them over there, but we're happier."[13]

Julian Simon died at his home in Chevy Chase, Maryland, on February 8, 1998, of a heart attack. At the time of his death, he was a senior fellow at the Cato Institute—a right-wing think tank founded in 1977—and a professor of business administration at the University of Maryland. Unbeknown to him, his ideas were about to see a resurgence that would cause rippling aftershocks in the environmental movement for years. A young statistician named **Bjørn Lomborg** had come across of profile of Simon in *Wired* magazine in 1997. Provoked by Simon's theories, he began conducting statistical analyses of them and claimed that he tried to disprove them but was unable to. He went on to write a book expounding on Simon's theories called *The Skeptical Environmentalist*, fueling a furious debate.

NOTES

1. Thomas Malthus, *An Essay on the Principle of Population, 1798* (New York: W.W. Norton & Co., 1976; Orig. pub. London: J. Johnson, 1798), p. 20.

2. Harold Barnett and Chandler Morse, *Scarcity and Growth: The Economics of Natural Resource Availability* (Baltimore: Johns Hopkins University Press, 1963), p. 11.

3. Quoted in Julian L. Simon, *A Life Against the Grain: The Autobiography of an Unconventional Economist* (New Brunswick and London: Transaction Publishers, 2002), p. 263.

4. Quote cited in Ed Regis, "The Doomslayer," *Wired* Vol. 5 (February 1997), pp. 136–140, 193–198.

5. Global 2000 Study, *The Global 2000 Report to the President—Entering the*

Twenty-First Century: A Report (Washington, DC: U.S. Government Printing Office, 1980), p. 1.

6. Julian Simon, "Should We Heed the Prophets of Doom?" *Science Digest* Vol. 90 (October 1982), p. 107.

7. Julian Simon, "Resources, Population, Environment: An Oversupply of False Bad News," *Science* Vol. 208 (June 27, 1980), p. 1431.

8. Ibid., pp. 1435–1436. Note that copper is an elemental metal and cannot be made from other metals.

9. W. Dexter Bellamy, "Life after 2000," letter to *Bioscience* Vol. 35 (January 1985), p. 2.

10. Quoted in Laura Tangley, "Life after 2000—The Debate Goes On," *BioScience* Vol. 34 (September 1984), p. 479.

11. Quoted in Kenneth N. Gilpin, "Julian Simon, 65, Optimistic Economist, Dies," *New York Times* (February 12, 1998), p. B11.

12. John Tierney, "Betting the Planet," *New York Times Magazine* (December 2, 1990), p. 81.

13. Ibid.

BIBLIOGRAPHY

Julian Simon's writings include *How to Start and Operate a Mail-Order Business* (New York: McGraw-Hill, 1965); *The Economics of Population Growth* (Princeton, NJ: Princeton University Press, 1977); "Resources, Population, Environment: An Oversupply of False Bad News," *Science* Vol. 208 (June 27, 1980), pp. 1431–1437; *The Ultimate Resource* (Princeton, NJ: Princeton University Press, 1981), which was republished as *The Ultimate Resource 2* in 1996; *Population Matters: People, Resources, Environment, and Immigration* (New Brunswick, NJ: Transaction Publishers, 1989); *Hoodwinking the Nation* (New Brunswick, NJ: Transaction Publishers, 1999); *A Life Against the Grain: The Autobiography of an Unconventional Economist* (New Brunswick, NJ: Transaction Publishers, 2002). With Herman Kahn, he edited *The Resourceful Earth: A Response to Global 2000* (New York: Basil Blackwell, 1984). For a debate on population issues, see Norman Myers and Julian L. Simon, *Scarcity or Abundance? A Debate on the Environment* (New York: W.W. Norton & Co., 1994). Articles about Simon's life and works include Laura Tangley, "Life after 2000—The Debate Goes On," *Bioscience* Vol. 34 (September 1984), pp. 477–479; W. Dexter Bellamy, "Life after 2000," letter to *Bioscience* Vol. 35 (January 1985), p. 2; John Tierney, "Betting the Planet," *New York Times Magazine* (December 2, 1990), pp. 52–53, 74–81; Kenneth N. Gilpin, "Julian Simon, 65, Optimistic Economist, Dies," *New York Times* (February 12, 1998), p. B11. The article that inspired Lomborg is Ed Regis, "The Doomslayer," *Wired* Vol. 5 (February 1997), pp. 136–140, 193–198. For more perspective on the famous bet, see Paul Ehrlich and Anne Ehrlich's *Betrayal of Science and Reason: How Anti-Environmental Rhetoric Threatens Our Future* (Covelo, CA: Island Press, 1996). For further studies of population issues, see Harold Barnett and Chandler Morse, *Scarcity and Growth: The Economics of Natural Resource Availability* (Baltimore: Johns Hopkins University Press, 1963); Thomas Malthus, *An Essay on the Principle of Population, 1798* (New York: W.W.

Norton & Co., 1976; Orig. pub. London: J. Johnson, 1798); and Global 2000 Study, *The Global 2000 Report to the President—Entering the Twenty-first Century: A Report* (Washington, DC: U.S. Government Printing Office, 1980). Another book that favorably presents the Simon philosophy of growth and progress is Ronald Bailey, ed., *Earth Report 2000: Revisiting the True State of the Planet* (New York: McGraw-Hill, 2000). Before his death, Simon collaborated with a former student, Stephen Moore, who had since become a colleague of his at the Cato Institute. Moore finished working on the book, which he called an index of human progress, and which showed Simon's optimistic interpretation of the quality of life in the United States: Stephen Moore and Julian Simon, *It's Getting Better all the Time: 100 Greatest Trends of the Last 100 Years* (Washington, DC: Cato Institute, 2000).

HELEN CHENOWETH-HAGE
(1938–)

America's national security is at peril unless we're able to feed and sustain ourselves. As we know all wealth comes from the land. And we either must mine, mill, or harvest from this land, or we will become a poor and third world nation.

—Helen Chenoweth-Hage

Idaho's nickname, the "Gem State," has more than one connotation. On one hand, it contains the largest roadless area in the lower forty-eight states and is home to stunning wilderness areas, such as the Sawtooth Mountains, the canyons of the Owyhee country, and the streams in the Clearwater River watershed. It is second only to Alaska in the amount of land that qualifies as wilderness but remains unprotected by law. What lends a different meaning to its nickname is the fact that gems, in their literal form, must be extracted from the earth's crust in ways that are often environmentally destructive. And Idaho's economy—especially in rural areas—is heavily resource-based, centered historically on extractive industries like mining, logging, and ranching. Idaho politics are therefore shaped by conflicting mandates to protect the landscape and to secure the state's economic stability. In general, the heavy influence of anti-environmental views and underground movements such as militia organizations have held sway in Idaho and created an antipathy toward most kinds of federal legislative intervention. Nothing has made those views more clear in recent decades than Idaho's election of Helen Chenoweth-Hage to the U.S. House of Representatives three terms in a row. As one of the "Class of 1994" (conservative Republicans who vowed, among other things, to rework Clinton-era environmental policies), Chenoweth-Hage (formerly Helen Chenoweth, née Helen Palmer) and her Republican colleagues sent up storms of protest over even the most narrowly drawn environmental initiatives at the close of the 1990s. Chenoweth-Hage frowns on environmentalism as a political mechanism that disempowers landowners, and has called for the conversion of federal lands to state, local, or private ownership. Her affiliation with the Wise Use movement and militia groups, her support of property owners, and her often uncompromising stance have won her both the idolatry of Idahoan ranchers, loggers, and miners, whose interests she upheld in Congress and the sustained and vocal criticism of environmental groups around the country. One of the standard arguments she uses in her defense is that eastern lawmakers and national environmental groups don't understand life in the West in general and in rural Idaho in particular—but her position of prominence within the federal government gave her the power to influence environmental policies far beyond the Gem State's borders.

Helen Palmer was born on January 27, 1938 in Topeka, Kansas, to Dwight and Ardelle Palmer. She and her sister Charlene spent their first years in the small farming community of Burlingame, where her parents were crop farmers. The family moved to Culver City, California, during World War II, so that Dwight and Ardelle could take jobs with Douglas Aircraft. But when the war ended, they returned to their agricultural roots, this time in Grants Pass, Oregon, where the family operated a dairy farm. Her parents exerted a powerful influence on her and instilled in her a strong set of values and a respect for other people. Her father also made sure to keep his daughters engaged in current events by introducing political debates into the dinner conversation. An apparent effect of this fostering of debate and discussion was that Helen and her sister grew up thinking for themselves—in very different directions. Eventually Charlene would become a Peace Corps volunteer and a political liberal, while Helen would become a champion of political conservatism.

Helen went to Whitworth College in Spokane, Washington, on a double scholarship of basketball and music: She played the string bass in both the concert band and the marching band. At Whitworth, she met Nick Chenoweth and decided to quit school and get married, which they did in 1958 in Grants Pass. Three years later they moved to Orofino, Idaho, and they spent their early married years there, mingling with the town's flourishing conservative crowd, reading **Ayn Rand** novels and discussing restrictive governmental controls and capitalism. She and Nick ran a ski shop on nearby Bald Mountain for a few years and raised their two children (one born in 1960, the other in 1961)—taking them floating on the Clearwater River during the summer months. Starting in 1964, she worked as a self-employed consultant in medical and legal management, a job she held until 1975. During those years she also frequently gave lectures on management and political issues, served as a guest instructor at the University of Idaho School of Law, and got involved in local politics. By the mid-1970s, she was GOP county chairman.

In 1975, Chenoweth's life underwent some major changes, beginning with a divorce. In the midst of this personal upheaval, Idaho Senator Jim McClure approached and asked her to be the next state executive director of the Idaho Republican Party. Agreeing that she was ready for something new, she moved to Boise and took the position. After two years of leading the state Republican Party, she was hired as chief of staff and then campaign manager for conservative Republican Steve Symms, who was running for a U.S. Senate seat. He won election in 1980 and, in the words of David Helvarg, "would become the voice of the anti-environmental movement on Capitol Hill."[1] Chenoweth left Symms's office in 1978 and founded Consulting Associates, Inc., a consulting firm that specialized in energy policy, natural resource use, environmental policy, and government contracts. Following the oil crisis of the mid-1970s, drastic changes in national energy policy were at hand, giving Chenoweth's firm plenty of clients. The year she started the firm, President Jimmy Carter signed the National Energy Act, aiming to reduce American dependence on foreign oil. One of the bills under the act, the Public Utility Regulatory Policies Act (PURPA), encouraged the development of small, independent power projects. In response to this new national mandate, developers began working on small-scale hydroelectric projects in the region, and Chenoweth's consulting firm worked closely with them to promote these projects over the next few years. Though hydroelectric power had long been seen as preferable to coal, oil, and nuclear power, environmentalists were beginning to rethink their earlier acceptance of hydropower as a benign energy source. In testimony before a U.S. House of Representatives subcommittee in 1985, Russell Shay of the Sierra Club said, "[F]isheries in California and the Pacific Northwest face disasterous effects from the unprecedented numbers of small hydro projects which have been proposed for our western waterways."[2] New construction of hydroelectric plants, with which Chenoweth's firm was involved, was condemned as particularly destructive. "We were required to meet all the same environmental regulations that big projects did," she later lamented. "Because of the environmentalists, this program just evaporated."

Lobbying and working with the Idaho legislature on behalf of her clients brought Chenoweth into an ever-widening circle of influence. She also was becoming an active member of the greater Boise community—making contacts and connections while participating in events, such as the American Cancer Society's "Jail and Bail" fundraiser, and serving as deacon at the Capitol Christian Center. By the time she announced her decision to run for Congress, she had support from groups like the Christian Coalition, the

Idaho Citizens Alliance (which works to deny civil rights for homosexuals), Idahoans for Term Limits, and Ross Perot's United We Stand. Her growing exposure and the spread of her conservative message dovetailed with the emergence in the late 1980s of the Wise Use movement, an alliance that includes disparate types—such as loggers, rural landowners, industry groups, and even top government officials—all held together by their belief that natural resource protection laws are a threat to private property rights. Arising out of response to the environmental awareness that had been simmering for the past three decades, the Wise Use movement sought to undermine environmental regulations and promote industrial and agricultural access to public land. Their argument that environmental regulation costs jobs, weakens the economy, and threatens private property rights has become a commonly heard response in any environmental debate in recent years. In fact, these arguments provided Chenoweth with the ideological backdrop for her future congressional career.

Chenoweth decided to run for a U.S. House of Representatives seat in 1994, and her campaign exhibited her characteristic flair for publicity and disregard for "political correctness." She ran against two-term incumbent Democrat Larry LaRocco on a platform reflecting her belief that the American West was under siege by President Bill Clinton's administration. Clinton's proposed policy changes—such as mining reform, higher grazing fees on public land, and restricted logging on federal lands—were labeled by Chenoweth and other conservative western lawmakers as a "war on the West." "We westerners depend on the exports of agriculture, mining, and timber. It's our way of life and we have a personal stake in it. When the administration calls for a 'balance in the timber industry' and maintaining forests instead of developing portions of them, they're talking about our jobs,"[3] she said.

During her campaign, she held a fundraiser dubbed the "endangered salmon bake," where she served salmon that she jestingly said was endangered to illustrate her dismissal of the notion that her state's Snake River sockeye salmon runs were in jeopardy. As she saw it, an animal that's on the endangered species list should not be available for consumers to purchase, and since salmon is sold in cans in every supermarket, its populations must not be threatened. The ploy paid off in terms of publicity and immediate name-recognition. But the problem with her argument, as many have since pointed out, is that the salmon sold in stores is not from endangered populations. Idaho's Snake River population of sockeye salmon, which has to migrate past four dams in order to reach its spawning grounds, has been reduced to a trickle in the past few decades. In 1991, it became the first Idaho salmon to be listed under the federal Endangered Species Act. That year only four fish returned to their spawning grounds at the headwaters, and in 1994, the year of Chenoweth's endangered salmon bake, only one sockeye salmon made it to the headwaters. Her argument that "it can't be endangered if it's for sale" was seen widely to be an oversimplification that ignored several issues: the differences in salmon species, the fact that much of what is bought in stores is domestically raised on farms, and the fact that Idaho hadn't been able to have a regular salmon fishing season in over fifteen years. Still, whether her salmon bake was in poor taste or not, Chenoweth's concern over the significance accorded to salmon recovery was a legitimate issue for someone running for Congress in Idaho. Many blame the dwindling of Idaho's salmon on the dams on the Snake River, but the removal of those dams could have considerable impact on irrigation, hydropower, shipping, ranching, and recreation—all major foundations of the Idaho economy. Those industries were clearly more of a priority for Chenoweth than salmon restoration; in fact, she liked to say that "the white Anglo-Saxon male" was the real endangered species.

LaRocco, who had tried and failed to add wilderness to the 4 million acres already protected in Idaho, and who advocated measures to re-establish endangered salmon runs in Idaho, represented exactly the sort of "big government" that Chenoweth felt was threatening the western way of life. To her, more wilderness designation would mean fewer logging jobs in a state where logging and mining activity already had been seeing a drop in recent years. She blamed environmentalists and their increasing restrictions for the drop, though her opponents argued that it was overharvesting that left fewer forests to cut and that falling mineral prices were responsible for the mining slump. At any rate, when she promised to "fight like a badger" for industry, to work to allow silver mining in Idaho's Sawtooth National Recreation Area, and to fight any future wilderness designations, resource-based communities in Idaho were listening. And when LaRocco aired radio ads warning of the impact of Chenoweth's right-wing stance on environmental issues, she countered by linking him to the Clinton administration's "war on the West" land-use proposals and spotlighted his support for a 1993 deficit-reduction bill that raised taxes. In the end she defeated him with a resounding 55 percent of the vote.

Representing the Boise-based First District of Idaho, Chenoweth went to Washington, D.C. as part of the Class of 1994: a wave of seventy-three Republicans elected to the House of Representatives in a backlash against taxes, spending, and "big government." After four decades of a Democratic majority in the House, Republicans took control in what was the largest transfer of power from a majority party to a minority party in twentieth-century U.S. politics. In a conservative "Contract with America," they promised major reforms and outlined goals such as term limits, increased national security, capital gains tax cuts, cuts in spending on welfare and other social programs, and reductions in government staff positions. Chenoweth's agenda for Idaho matched well with the Contract for America, and to remain true to its term-limit goals, she pledged to limit herself to only three two-year terms of office.

Efforts to strengthen or expand the scope of environmental laws in the years following the 1994 elections became challenging in the face of the GOP-controlled Congress, and Chenoweth played her part in creating logjams for environmental legislation. There was never any doubt about where she stood on environmental issues: After being elected, she decorated her office in Idaho with boxes of "Spotted Owl Helper," a ribald spoof on Hamburger Helper mixes. In her office beside the U.S. Capitol in Washington, D.C., she displayed a baseball cap that read, "Hug a logger today," and she soon became famous for publicly wearing a t-shirt reading "Earth First! We'll Log the Other Planets Later." When she arrived in office, she prepared to scale back environmental restrictions on industry, small businesses, and private landowners. She won seats on both the Agriculture and Natural Resources Committees, strategic positions from which she could effect decisions on resource policy. In addition, House Speaker Newt Gingrich appointed her to the Endangered Species Act task force.

But polls were beginning to show that the public disapproved of the slate of anti-environmental attacks on everything from clean water to the Endangered Species Act and that, in fact, the majority of Americans supported wilderness designations and stronger environmental laws. As the 1996 election approached, support for Chenoweth began to seem shaky. Many Idahoans had grown concerned over her insistence on turning public lands over to state control. But any hopes that Republican contender William Levinger, an anesthesiologist from Nampa, would defeat Chenoweth in the May 28 primary were spectacularly dashed when Levinger had an apparent mental breakdown on April 17 during a Boise television interview. Levinger told the reporter that he was only running for Congress because he couldn't swim to Hawaii, and, as if that weren't bizarre enough, he proceeded to display wads of money to the camera and offered a reporter $5,000 to kiss him on the air. When he stripped down to his underwear on the air, police showed up and escorted him to a mental hospital. Interestingly, despite spending most of the remaining six weeks of his campaign in a mental hospital, Levinger still got 32 percent of the vote in the Republican primary. Chenoweth then faced Democratic challenger Dan Williams, a 32-year-old trial lawyer. Though she won re-election, her margin was much smaller this time: fewer than 7,000 votes out of more than 258,000 cast.

During the next term in office, she continued her fight to rid the country of the "intrusive bureaucracy" of federal environmental policy. While serving on the House Subcommittee on National Parks and Public Lands, she protested President Clinton's establishment of the Grand Staircase-Escalante National Monument in Utah in September 1996. Clinton explained the reasons for his designation of the area, which includes regions of winding canyons, natural bridges and large arches of brilliantly hued sedimentary rock, in a proclamation: "Spanning five life zones from low-lying desert to coniferous forest, the monument is an outstanding biological resource. . . .

The blending of warm and cold desert floras, along with the high number of endemic species, place this area in the heart of perhaps the richest floristic region in the Intermountain West." National monument designation protects an area from private development and mining—basically the same as a national park, but with looser restrictions. The following spring, during an oversight hearing, Chenoweth expressed her grave misgivings over what she saw as the president's unilateral action in creating the Utah monument. She then introduced two bills to fight it. The first, H.R. 596, would prohibit further extension or establishment of any national monument without an express act of Congress. The second, H.R. 597, was the same bill, but only applicable to Idaho. The House took no significant action on either bill.

In a display of her leadership skills, Chenoweth became chair of the House Subcommittee on Forests and Forest Health in 1997, the first Idaho House member to chair a subcommittee in fifty-four years. This position allowed her to influence decisions on grazing rights, salmon restoration efforts, old-growth forest protection, and endangered species. It also allowed her to go toe-to-toe with some of the Clinton administration's most environmentally active policymakers, Secretary of the Interior Bruce Babbitt and Environmental Protection Agency Director Carol Browner. To no one's surprise, Chenoweth vowed that Babbitt and Browner would be put under oath any time they testified before her subcommittee—a clear sign of her mistrust of their agendas. During the few years she headed the subcommittee, she made every effort to undermine environmental protection legislation. When President Clinton announced the American Heritage Rivers Initiative, a showcase of America's rivers that would enhance local conservation efforts and promote tourism, Chenoweth reacted with characteristic rhetorical zeal, calling it "a bold and shocking attempt by the administration to usurp individual water rights, private property rights, and state sovereignty,"[4] and arguing that the Heritage River designation would create yet another tool for use by environmental extremists. Despite the broad-based support of Clinton's initiative, and despite the fact that the program is entirely voluntary and locally driven, she introduced a bill (H.R. 1842) to terminate the American Heritage Rivers program. The House Resource Committee passed the bill by a voice vote in November 1997, but it never reached the House floor. Chenoweth persisted. The following month, she was a lead litigant in a lawsuit challenging the Clinton administration's authority to implement the plan, but the case finally was dismissed the following March.

Sympathy with private landowners and suspicion of federal power has underlain much of Chenoweth's approach to policymaking. Whether arguing against federal enforcement of the Endangered Species Act or fighting the creation of a federally administered national monument, her tactics always attempted to bring the scale of power to a lower level. In keeping with this tactic, another program she fought was the United Nations World Heritage Treaty. Signed by the United States in 1972, the treaty designates selected landmarks as World Heritage Sites for their "outstanding universal value" (i.e., cultural, historical, or natural significance) and mandates their international protection. The treaty is implemented by the World Heritage Committee under the direction of the United Nations Environmental, Scientific and Cultural Organization (UNESCO). Yellowstone National Park was America's first World Heritage Site in 1978, and since then 68 percent of all U.S. national parks, monuments, and preserves have earned the designation. Chenoweth's concern over the program's overarching power structure impelled her to action in 1995, after the United Nations listed Yellowstone a "World Heritage Site in Danger" in response to the Crown Butte Mining company's proposal to develop a gold and silver extraction operation three miles from the boundary of the park. In part because of the international attention gained by the UN's listing and in part because of rampant opposition throughout the United States, the mining project had to be abandoned. Concerned over the UN's encroachment on the authority of Americans, Chenoweth became a leading co-sponsor of a bill (H.R. 901) called the American Land Sovereignty Protection Act, which would require the executive branch to obtain congressional approval before designating any site on American soil as a World Heritage Site. As she urged passage of the bill, Chenoweth participated in tense arguments in committee meetings with those who opposed it. In October 1998, the House of Representatives passed H.R. 901 by a 236–191 vote, but the Senate never acted on it.

Another action Chenoweth took that winter included introducing a bill in response to concern over global climate change, which proposed to accelerate clearcutting of forests and then to replant them with young trees. An article in *Earth Island Journal* derided the proposal as a thinly disguised excuse to boost the logging industry, saying, "congressional anti-environmentalists came up with a spectacularly disingenuous bill (H.R. 151) designed to 'send a message' to the White House in advance of the Kyoto summit on climate change. Instead of requiring polluting industries to cut CO_2 emissions, Rep. Helen Chenoweth (R-ID), chair of the House Subcommittee on Forests and Forest Health, and Don Young (R-AK) proposed that the country's forests be 'managed' to reduce greenhouse gases."[5] Since it has become widely accepted that deforestation reduces the capacity of the planet to absorb carbon dioxide (CO_2), and in fact actually causes the release of this greenhouse gas, this bill stood no chance of passing.

During Chenoweth's 1998 re-election campaign, environmental issues again played a significant role. Ever since the 1996 elections, when environmentalists voted in seventeen eco-friendly members of Congress, GOP leaders had started sending party members the message that the American public would no longer tolerate blatant anti-environmentalism, and that conservatives needed to re-work their tactics. Since her uncompromisingly pro-industry position had earned her labels such as the "cream of the extreme," and "environmental public enemy number one," Chenoweth had to backpedal a bit in order to follow the advice. She did, for example, begin making suggestions that there were some areas of Idaho forests that were too fragile for logging. But while she may have curbed some of her more incendiary rhetoric, her pro-logging position had barely budged. Efforts to defeat her mobilized a wide array of organizations and people, from the League of Conservation Voters, which donated more than $200,000, to movie stars like Tom Cruise, Nicole Kidman, Michael Douglas, and Hollywood director Rob Reiner—all of whom attended a Democratic Party fundraiser devoted to ousting her. She of course had her own sources of support for her campaign, and, backed by such heavyweights as Idaho Forest Products, Potlatch, Bennett Lumber, Hecla Mining Company, the cattle industry, and Idaho Power, she won re-election a second time and headed into her third and final term.

Her last term saw some of her greatest battles over issues of national forests and forest health. Early in 1998, Michael Dombeck, chief of the U.S. Forest Service, ordered an eighteen-month moratorium on any additional road building in pristine national forest areas, which effectively placed 32 million acres of unbulldozed land temporarily out of reach of the timber industry. Over 370,000 miles of road already had been carved into national forest lands, necessitating huge inputs of money for maintenance and environmental mitigation. In the previous decade alone, Chenoweth's native state of Idaho had lost a million acres of potential wilderness to logging and road building on its national forestland. But Chenoweth condemned Dombeck's act and geared up to fight environmentalists on the issue, saying that they just can't relate to the rural lifestyle of her constituents back home. "I will continue to fight against this moratorium until hell freezes over, and then I will fight it on the ice,"[6] she said. The debate escalated with President Clinton's announcement on October 13, 1999, of his Roadless Initiative, in which he directed the U.S. Forest Service to review 43 million acres of national forest lands for increased protection. Less than 20 percent of national forests in the United States are permanently protected, with much of the existing roadless area on Forest Service–land characterized by rugged terrain, low-value timber, or ecologically sensitive areas—and public sentiment strongly supported protection of the biological diversity, wildlife habitat, and forest quality they contain. Dombeck applauded Clinton's action: "This is an unprecedented time for our country and the Forest Service. By using the best science available, and giving careful consideration to public review and comment, the conservation legacy initiated by **Theodore Roosevelt** and **Gifford Pinchot** will extend into the 21st century."[7]

The Forest Service began preparing an Environmental Impact Statement to analyze an appropriate course of action, and eventually advocated the complete prohibition of road construction and logging on these roadless lands, which they amended to include 58.5 million acres of national forest. When Chenoweth's Subcommittee on Forests and Forest Health held a hearing on the issue, she made her opposition clear: "We have doubts because of evidence reported by this subcommittee in previous hearings that shows extreme environmental organizations—many of whom are on record as being opposed to many forms of forest recreation—have had and continue to have a special insider's role in formulating many of the policies which appear to be driving the agency rulemakings."[8] She and other Republican lawmakers objected to the fact that organizations such as the Pew Charitable Trusts and the Turner Foundation had donated money to environmental organizations to help them promote the Roadless Initiative.[9] However, Chenoweth and her allies had little recourse since the donation process is legal, and in fact many conservative organizations receive money from other foundations in the same manner. The U.S. Forest Service proceeded—with wide public support—to submit the final Roadless Area Conservation Rule to the Federal Register in January 2001. That May, Idaho U.S. District Judge Edward Lodge issued an injunction against it. Currently, President George W. Bush's administration has decided not to appeal the injunction.

Chenoweth meanwhile had taken a brief respite from congressional imbroglios for a private celebration. On October 2, 1999, in a wedding ceremony in Meridian, Idaho, to which over 11,000 people were invited, she married Wayne Hage, a property rights activist and a rancher operating a 759,000-acre ranch in the Monitor Valley of Nevada. They had met when she was on a lecture circuit in 1991, at around the time when Hage had run into trouble with the U.S. Forest Service, which had repeatedly charged him with grazing violations. Eventually the Forest Service confiscated and sold 108 head of his cattle, and Hage retaliated with a lawsuit. Several years later, Hage and Chenoweth met again, and this time the relationship became romantic. Considering their ideological similarities—with both espousing the view that the federal government holds too much power over land in the West—it was unsurprising when the *Las Vegas Review-Journal* reported that "friends said it was the perfect union between two of the biggest Sagebrush Rebels from the west."[10]

Chenoweth-Hage's reputation as a fighter of federal land laws and environmental protections had become firmly established by this time, and she was quick to lend her badger-like feistiness to help fight for local property rights causes beyond her Idaho base. One such cause had been stirring thirty miles west of Ohio's capital city, Columbus, since 1997, when the U.S. Fish and Wildlife Service proposed the creation of a new wildlife refuge in the Little Darby Creek area. The Little Darby Creek watershed, a national and state scenic river, harbors one of the most biologically diverse assemblages of wetland species in the Midwest. But drainage of wetlands and clearing of native forests and oak savanna for agricultural purposes and development have threatened the watershed's diversity of flora and fauna. The proposed refuge would provide protection for the area's nineteen state-listed endangered animal species and eleven state-listed threatened or endangered plants. In a Draft Environmental Assessment of the Little Darby Creek area, the Fish and Wildlife Service wrote, "Historically, the Darby Creek Watershed encompassed the easternmost wetland/tallgrass prairie/oak savanna ecosystems in the United States. This unique landscape was important for its diverse, abundant plant life and for its grassland and wetland-dependent bird species. Overall, the area has been broadly defined as 'Prairie Peninsula' and part of the larger mid-continent tallgrass prairie ecosystem, of which less than 1 percent of its original 25 million acres remains."

The Fish and Wildlife Service hoped to purchase 23,000 acres in the watershed from willing buyers, and to buy the development rights of an additional 26,000-acre buffer zone that would be kept for farming. But the plan met with intense debate, which evolved into outright revolt from area landowners. Chenoweth-Hage joined the fight, which spanned three years of studies, hearings, and rallies. In September 2000, she gave an impassioned speech at a protest dubbed the "Darby Farmland Rally." She began by expressing her disapproval of national environmental policy on federal lands: "We don't want to see that kind of waste, ruin, and destruction come to this most blessed and beautiful and productive farmland, and I join you in fighting to preserve it. Not preserve it by government edict, but preserve it from the ravages of government control." To Chenoweth-Hage, the issue at stake was not the preservation of a unique ecosystem that was quickly disappearing at the hands of human activity, but the preservation of the property rights of those who lived there. The notion of setting aside land to exist in its natural state for the benefit of the plants and animals that evolved there was, to her, a waste of that land's potential and a danger to human prosperity. She continued in her speech: "Now, what does the Fish and Wildlife Service want to do? They want to return it to mosquito infested farmland, mosquito infested wetlands. . . . It doesn't meet the test of common sense, does it, that we would want to take good farmland out of production and give it to the mosquitoes? . . . [T]he fact is that America will become much weaker." In the end, after putting heavy pressure on members of Congress, local opposition triumphed, and the refuge proposal was officially withdrawn.

When her term ended in 2000, Chenoweth-Hage kept her promise to limit herself to three terms and left office, though she plainly admitted she would have liked to continue to serve. She explained that she didn't regret taking the term-limit pledge, she just regretted signing on for only three terms. Given the complexities of the job and the learning curve, she realized that ten to twelve years would have been a more appropriate length. When asked what she wanted to be remembered for as a congresswoman, she answered, "[T]hat I have been true to real Republican principles." In other words, she defended individual rights, American sovereignty, and private property.

Leaving office didn't mean Chenoweth-Hage gave up the fight for those principles, however. She and her husband have remained active property rights advocates, touring and giving lectures and seminars around the country. The lawsuit that Hage had filed in 1991 against the U.S. Forest Service after having his cattle confiscated in a grazing permit dispute was finally decided in his favor in 2002. Chenoweth-Hage and Hage want to use that judicial victory as an example for other property owners, and have given seminars explaining the limits of federal law enforcement jurisdiction, and how to prevent government usurpation of property rights. They continue to make their home on their ranch in Nevada.

NOTES

1. David Helvarg, *The War against the Greens: The "Wise-Use" Movement, the New Right and Anti-Environmental Violence* (San Francisco: Sierra Club Books, 1994), p. 67.

2. U.S Congress, House of Representatives, Subcommittee on Energy, Conservation and Power, of the Committee on Energy and Commerce, Hearing on Hydroelectric Relicensing, 99th Congress, 1st Session (Washington, DC: U.S. Government Printing Office, 1985), p. 124.

3. "Chenoweth vs. LaRocco," *Human Events* Vol. 50(30) (August 5, 1994), p. 16.

4. Charles Pope, "Maelstrom of Opposition Hurts 'Heritage Rivers' Plan," *Congressional Quarterly Weekly Report* Vol. 56(20) (May 16, 1998), p. 1279.

5. "GOP Climate Plan: 'Cut the Trees!' " *Earth Island Journal* Vol. 13(1) (Winter 1997/1998), p. 17.

6. "Idaho's Own Natural Resource," *Congressional Quarterly Weekly Report* Vol. 58(20) (May 13, 2000), p. 1082.

7. U.S. Forest Service, "U.S.D.A. Forest Service to Implement President's Roadless Initiative," Press release (October 13, 1999).

8. Helen Chenoweth-Hage, "Forests and Forest Health," Federal Document ClearingHouse Congressional Testimony (April 4, 2000).

9. Pew Charitable Trusts gave nearly $3.5 million to the Heritage Forests Campaign, which promoted the Roadless Initiative. Chenoweth-Hage and her colleagues also protested input from other environmental groups, such as the Wilderness Society, Natural Resources Defense Council, U.S. Public Interest Research Group, Earth Defense Legal Defense Fund, Audubon Society, and the Sierra Club.

10. Andrew DeMillo, "The Final Frontier," *Las Vegas Review-Journal* (September 27, 1999).

BIBLIOGRAPHY

Chenoweth-Hage has been featured in several editions of the *Who's Who* series from Marquis Publications, including the *Who's Who of American Women* (19th–22nd editions) and *Who's Who in the West* (26th–30th editions). Several articles from newspapers and magazines contain useful biographical information, insight on her political ideology, or general overviews of the Class of 1994; these include Jennifer Babson and Bob Benenson, "Helen Chenoweth," *Congressional Quarterly Weekly Report* Vol. 53(1) (January 7, 1995), pp. 58–60; Paul Rauber, "Eco-Thug: Helen Chenoweth," *Sierra* Vol. 81(3) (May/June 1996), p. 28; Charles Pope, "Maelstrom of Opposition Hurts 'Heritage Rivers' Plan," *Congressional Quarterly Weekly*

Report Vol. 56(20) (May 16, 1998), p. 1279–1281; Timothy Egan, "Teddy Roosevelt is Rolling over in His Grave," *Sports Afield* Vol. 220(2) (August 1998), pp. 84–89; Daniel Coyle, "Are You Trying to Seduce Me, Mrs. Chenoweth?" *Outside Magazine Online*, November 1998. http://outside.away.com/magazine/1198/9811chenoweth.html (accessed May 11, 2004); Dana Millbank, "Whatever Happened to the Class of 1994?" *New York Times Magazine* (January 17, 1999), p. 36; Andrew DeMillo, "The Final Frontier," *Las Vegas Review-Journal* (September 27, 1999); John Grizzi, "Politics 2000," *Human Events* Vol. 56(17) (May 12, 2000), p. 18. For transcripts of Chenoweth-Hage's remarks during various congressional hearings, speeches, and press briefings, a good resource is the Federal Document ClearingHouse (FDCH), which offers primary-source government material and transcripts online. FDCH documents are archived in EBSCO research databases. Remote online access to these databases is permitted to patrons of participating libraries. Specific documents containing material by Chenoweth-Hage include "Forests and Forest Health," FDCH Congressional Testimony (April 4, 2000); "Conservation Bills," FDCH Congressional Testimony (May 24, 2000); "Forest Service Rulemaking," FDCH Congressional Testimony (June 22, 2000); "Lessons of Private Conservation," FDCH Congressional Testimony (September 14, 2000); "Potential Energy Crisis in the Winter of 2000," FDCH Congressional Testimony (September 20, 2000); and "Future of the Forest Service," FDCH Congressional Testimony (September 21, 2000).

JAMES GAIUS WATT
(1938–)

We will mine more, drill more, cut more timber.

—James Watt

In the American West of the late 1970s, an uprising against governmental interference sought the transfer of federal land to the states, conjuring up images of tobacco-chewing, power-hungry cattlemen facing off against controlling, regulation-hungry politicians. This uprising, called the Sagebrush Rebellion, began making loud footsteps down the halls of power in 1981, when James Gaius Watt became President **Ronald Reagan**'s secretary of the Interior. As such, he wielded enormous influence over the allocation of U.S. public land and its natural resources, and he quickly made his land management ideology very visible. Believing that the private sector should be allowed much more room to profit from public lands, he pushed policy ideas that differed markedly from the reigning value system, which held that land in the public trust should be maintained as a heritage for future generations. Watt, who insisted that federal ownership of land was an ill-advised idea that did not put the land to its best use, strove to make public land more freely available to private developers and business interests, with the fewest possible regulatory restrictions. His favorite land-management principles—disposal, development, and deregulation—meshed perfectly with Sagebrush Rebellion principles and caused an uproar of controversy within the conservation movement. Watt never compromised his position, and he came to be remembered as much for his inflammatory policies as for his personality, which often landed him in conflict with other politicians, the media, and the public. Zealous and self-assured, Watt loved making decisions and exerted a hard-driving determination not to duck even the most difficult ones. What the conservation movement found so infuriating about his stance was that he opposed them not just politically, but personally—believing that he was fighting a moral battle over right and wrong. Eventually, when he had become a virtual lightning rod of criticism within the Reagan administration, Watt's overbearing manner forced him from office and he resigned. He later would say that his administration had brought about a revolution and that he had restored America's greatness; even though a number of his programs were never implemented successfully, he had tamped a trail for his successors to follow in terms of policy. On the other hand, by inflaming those who opposed him, his ideas and proposals mobilized environmental groups. During the two and a half years he served as Interior secretary, his influence reverberated in all corners of the political world, and within the conservation movement, the consequences of his leadership would be felt for many years to come.

James Gaius Watt was born on January 31, 1938, in Lusk, a small county seat in the prairies of eastern Wyoming. His father, William, homesteaded a ranch while also building up a substantial law practice. From the time James was small, he grappled with endless outdoor chores, such as mending fence or caring for the cattle. He would later say that those early experiences gave him a unique understanding of the American West and the way of life there. His perceptions also were shaped by the conservative viewpoint modeled for him by his father. Resentful of the "left wing," which he perceived to be taking over the country, William Watt often expressed passionate anger at election outcomes and what he saw as rampant idealism in the public schools.

When James was in eighth grade, his family moved to Wheatland, a town of 2,300 in southeastern Wyoming, where his father had become the new lawyer in town, and where his mother, Lois, would manage the thirty-room Globe Hotel. Already nearly six feet tall with curly reddish-blond hair, he always used the name James, never Jim or Jimmy, and always signed his name "James G. Watt." When schoolmates asked what the "G" stood for he would smile and drawl, "Guess," a cunning mispronunciation of his actual middle name, Gaius. James met Leilani Bomgardner in Wheatland, and she would be the only girl he ever dated. They spent their high school years together, where James was a varsity athlete and a member of the school honor society. As a senior, he was elected governor of the Wyoming's Boys State, and also won the title of prom King, with Leilani as the queen.

After graduating from high school they went to the College of Commerce and Industry at the University of Wyoming together, where James aimed to make himself known to important business and political leaders in the state.

Three weeks before Leilani's nineteenth birthday, James proposed to her, with the stipulation that he first be allowed to live in a fraternity house long enough to establish his presence and qualify for future fraternity leadership. Two months later, on November 2, 1957, they married, taking one day for a honeymoon before returning to classes. Both adhered to strict Christian beliefs and aspired to a moral life beyond reproach.

Already constantly driven toward aspirations of leadership, Watt served as president of the Honor Society in his sophomore, junior, and senior years of college. He received his B.S. degree and graduated with honors in 1960, and immediately applied to the university's College of Law, where he would soon become the editor of the *Wyoming Law Journal*. During the summer before law school started, Watt worked for the Small Business Administration and the University of Wyoming, developing strategies to help local businesses overcome problems. During his law school years, he also taught business law and real estate part time at the university, as well as serving as a research assistant for the Wyoming Legislative Statue Revisions Committee, recommending modifications to the state's public school laws.

In 1962, after finishing law school and passing the Wyoming state bar, he became the personal assistant to Milward L. Simpson, the Republican governor of Wyoming, who was campaigning for a U.S. Senate seat. When Simpson won, Watt was asked to serve as his legislative assistant, and he and Leilani moved to Washington, D.C. He held that post for four years, during which time he also was admitted to the bar of the United States Supreme Court. Also while in Washington, D.C., in a momentous event which would influence many of his future decisions, he attended his first gospel meeting, reaffirming his religious beliefs and establishing himself as an ardent born-again Christian.

Watt began wielding influence on the nation's land and water resources during the three years he served as secretary to the Natural Resources Committee and the Environmental Pollution Advisory Panel of the U.S. Chamber of Commerce (1966–1969). In this capacity, basically as a lobbyist for business and development interests, Watt challenged the environmental initiatives that were just starting to work their way through Congress. During a 1967 debate over air quality legislation, Watt argued for state rather than federal control over setting pollution levels (which would ultimately result in more lenient restrictions nationwide). He supported a similar scheme for strip-mining. While honing his pro-development philosophy, he influenced many U.S. Chamber of Commerce's policies regarding public lands, energy, and pollution.

Watt once remarked that he never wanted to hold a particular job for more than a few years, so that he could continue to embellish his resume. Following this ambition, Watt left his lobbying job in 1969, when the new Nixon administration brought him on to coordinate its transition team. As part of his transition team duties, Watt was assigned to be a special assistant to former governor of Alaska **Walter J. Hickel,** whom Nixon had just nominated as secretary of the Interior. Watt's job was to make sure the less-than-sophisticated Hickel got confirmed: and he did successfully guide Hickel through the nomination hearings, though not without opposition. The environmental movement, just beginning to gain political clout, put up a fight against the conservative Hickel, who, in Watt's opinion, mistakenly attempted a moderate stance. "He tried to show the liberal environmentalists that he was one of them," Watt later said. "Watching him, I learned one could not outrun environmentalists to the political Left."[1] Hickel retained Watt as a consultant for several months, where he earned $98.00 a day to serve as Hickel's "eyes and ears on oil," as one trade journal put it.[2]

Hickel's association with Watt, who was already known for being a former business lobbyist opposed to conservation measures, prompted skepticism from some who feared that the relationship jeopardized any concern Hickel, as Interior secretary, might have for environmentalist causes. Watt was unbothered by the criticism, though after only a few months he left the consulting job for a yet another appointment: deputy assistant secretary of the Interior Department, with responsibility for the Bureau of Reclamation and other Interior Department agencies involving water and power resources. The Nixon administration, gritting its teeth, was facing the growing importance of environmental issues to American voters. But with Watt as spokesperson on water resource issues—such as dams, power plants, reservoir operations, irrigation, and desalination technology—business and development interests still enjoyed an advantage, especially in the arid West, where water issues are at the root of power. All but ignoring the Reclamation Act—which was created by **Theodore Roosevelt** in 1902 to limit to 160 acres the landholdings of anyone receiving federal irrigation subsidies (and thereby preventing land monopolies)—Watt gave the first hints of the anti-governmental-control philosophy that would form the backbone of the impending Sagebrush Rebellion.

Watt stayed at that post for three years, from 1969 to 1972, before being promoted to head the Interior Department's Bureau of Outdoor Recreation. His supervisor, an assistant Interior secretary, clashed with him and eventually refused to work with him. Watt's responsibilities included administering $300 million a year in federal matching funds for the acquisition and development of recreational lands. He also oversaw land-use planning at the local, state, and federal levels; instituted a new financial plan for the Interior Department; and produced the country's first nationwide outdoor recreation plan. The appropriateness of this would seem somewhat ironic a few years later, when Watt admitted that he doesn't like hiking or boating, and, in fact, seemed to consider wilderness as more of a warehouse for raw materials than as a national treasure to be enjoyed for generations.

Watt left the Interior Department in 1975 when he was appointed by President Gerald Ford to be a commissioner on the Federal Power Commission

(FPC). For the following two years, he helped to regulate interstate aspects of the electric power and natural gas industries, pushing for removal of all price controls on natural gas, which was newly discovered. Though the FPC was unable to bring about deregulation, Watt's efforts helped to triple the price ceiling for natural gas, which he considered to be a production-boosting free-market approach. President Jimmy Carter's Department of Energy eventually absorbed the FPC. In his final few months there, from January to July 1977, Watt served as the FPC's vice chairman and created a dispute by overruling his staff members and voting to allow the construction of a hydroelectric dam on the Blackwater River in West Virginia. This project, vociferously resisted by conservation groups, brought on several lawsuits against the FPC, including one by the Interior Department (then headed by Cecil Andrus).

On leaving the FPC, Watt took a job that brought him the most controversy to date and cemented his notoriety as an anti-environmentalist: He became president and chief legal officer of the Mountain States Legal Foundation (MSLF), a conservative law firm specializing in promoting business and in reserving natural resources like water, oil, gas, and farmland for private use in the name of free enterprise. It was founded in 1976 by right-wing beer baron **Joseph Coors,** who handpicked Watt to become its first president. Watt and his family moved to Denver, where he began loudly backing the MSLF cause, making him a hero of the emerging Sagebrush Rebellion. At that time, the federal government owned 760 million acres of land—the majority of which fell in western states and Alaska—and held title to the substantial oil, gas, and mineral reserves on that land. Moneyed interests in the West argued that federal ownership and regulation of western land and its resources were infringing on the rights of individuals and industry there, and that the land could be better utilized through profitable extrapolation of its resources. These "Sagebrush Rebels" were incensed by efforts made by the Carter administration, namely Cecil Andrus as secretary of the Interior, to enforce the Reclamation Act laws, which would limit federal water projects that subsidized the irrigation of almost 12 million acres of western farmland. Wanting both the exclusive right to extract resources from federal land and the continued federal irrigation subsidies, the Sagebrush Rebels had their hands full with legal battles to establish the rationale for their position. Watt, born and cultivated in the West, with his native roots and confrontational temperament, became the unofficial spokesperson for the independent-minded Sagebrush Rebels, fighting for grazing rights on public lands, reduced air pollution regulations, gas and oil leases on public lands, and reduced federal restrictions on strip-mining. During the three years Watt worked for the MSLF, the foundation fought forty-seven lawsuits, thirteen of them against the Interior Department (which Watt would soon lead). These cases were funded by Coors, with additional financing from large oil, mining, agribusiness, and electric power industries; the issues they involved often seemed obscure to those in the East, where there is much less federal land.

Even before campaigning for president, Ronald Reagan had been espousing support for the Sagebrush Rebellion; once he was elected, he began to look for ways to implement their policies. The most important element in his plan would be his choice of head of the Interior Department. The Reagan team ran through several other choices before Watt's name was recommended by Senator Paul Laxalt from Nevada. After submitting to a peremptory interview conducted by Laxalt, Watt got the final nod of approval, and on December 22, 1980, President-elect Reagan designated him to be secretary of the Interior. Considering the opposition Watt would face from environmental groups and the stubborn disposition it would take for him to promote his unpopular ideas, it is unsurprising that Senator Alan Simpson, in recommending Watt, would say, "This is a bear of a job, and it will take a grizzly to do it."[3]

Watt's reputation preceded him, and his confirmation hearings drew on an already deep well of dissent. Suspicion over Watt's history of anti-environmentalist, pro-industry activities lent opponents a loud voice in their arguments against his nomination, though Watt maintained that he would be a good steward of the land and support controlled and systematic development of resources. Also problematic were Watt's fundamental religious beliefs, which some felt he imported into his politics in inappropriate ways. But, in spite of widespread resistance, Watt was confirmed by the U.S. Senate on January 22, 1981, and was sworn in as the forty-third secretary of the Interior the following day. He also was given the position of chairman of the Council on Natural Resources and the Environment, which gave him some authority over the Department of Energy and the Environmental Protection Agency.

Watt's ascendancy gave members of the Sagebrush Rebellion a bold optimism. Responsible for administering all federal land, Watt controlled the National Park Service, the Bureau of Land Management, the U.S. Fish and Wildlife Service, the Bureau of Reclamation, the Bureau of Indian Affairs, and the Office of Surface Mining. In effect, Watt had become the nation's chief environmental officer, and considering his faithful ties to the Sagebrush Rebels, who demanded the relinquishment of federal control over the land and resources in question, it is not surprising that questions were being raised regarding the appropriateness of having Watt as caretaker of lands in the public domain. He was soon being referred to as the "fox guarding the chicken coop," and, seeming to revel in the ire of his opponents, he installed a photograph of a fox in his new office. He also flaunted his ideology by turning the bison on the department's seal to face right instead of its traditional position facing left. These acts sent an unsurprising message out to the conservation movement—that Watt would not be taking a moderate stance—and the battle over wilderness and management of public lands quickly became polarized.

One of the most unsettling aspects of Watt's stewardship ethic was his Christian fundamentalism. Following the mandates of the Scriptures, Watt saw nature as an extraneous entity separate from human life and he felt that his responsibility was to occupy the land until the Second Coming. When testifying before the House Interior Committee soon after taking office, he in effect dismissed the idea of preserving resources for future generations, saying "I do not know how many future generations we can count on before the Lord returns."[4] Also infuriating to his opponents was his moral absolutism and his portrayal of the struggle over public land management as a war between right and wrong: In other words, between the good Christians, who use the resources of the land, and the "leftist pantheists," who worship the land and natural objects. In frustration, columnist Colman McCarthy wrote in the *Washington Post*:

> If I get the theological drift of Watt's pastoral vision, the land of milk and honey overseen by the Department of the Interior . . . is now under divine mandate to be bulldozed, leveled, drilled, mined, and leased down to the last holy square yard. . . . As a born-again Scripture-quoter, Watt can doubtlessly leap to the altar with favorite subdue-the-earth texts that make it seem as if God created the earth just for Mobil Oil or Consolidated Coal.[5]

Upon taking office, Watt restructured the Interior Department and got rid of all but one appointed official—replacing them all with pro-development conservatives. He cut the staff of the Office of Surface Mining—which enforces strip-mining laws—from 1,000 to 600, claiming that this would effectively place control in the hands of the states; in actuality it threw the office into a state of chaos and greatly reduced its power. Another part of his reorganization involved dissolving the recreation agency he had once directed (formerly called the Bureau of Outdoor Recreation, but since changed to the Heritage Conservation and Recreation Service) and merging it with the National Park Service, a move that disappointed many outdoor enthusiasts. In addition, he placed a moratorium on the acquisition of more national park land, saying that money should instead be spent on development of infrastructure within existing parks. He also pushed for more development on wildlife refuge land.

A severe blow to the morale of conservationists came when Watt attempted to reverse a decision made by the previous interior secretary, Cecil Andrus, involving offshore drilling by oil companies in four Pacific Ocean basins. These basins, lying in valuable fishing grounds and bordering some of California's most treasured beaches, were removed from a lease sale list by

Cecil Andrus a week before the 1980 election. Watt's plan proved immensely unpopular, with Californians of widely diverse walks of life unified against it, and it brought Watt a warning from the state Republican Party: This could cost them the governorship in the next year's election. Congress passed a moratorium on drilling in the area, which was eventually permanently protected as a sanctuary, but Watt already had earned the reputation by some as an exploiter of resources. By the end of his term he had freed more federal acreage for oil, gas, coal, and geothermal exploration than any Interior secretary before him.

Land-management policy already had undergone a long evolution in the United States—from the Homestead Act of 1862, which doled out 160 acres of frontier to any settler who would inhabit it for five years, to a gradual shift toward an emphasis on conservation. By the turn of the twentieth century, with the establishment of the first national parks and new regulations protecting grasslands and forests, the prevailing view was that the land was valued as a national asset to be preserved and carefully managed. During the 1970s, concern over the deterioration of the environment accelerated, prompting Congress to form a strong bipartisan coalition that began enacting many landmark environmental laws. The federal government had begun to look like an active and dominant force for protecting the environment and regulating polluting industries, and the environmental movement enjoyed a bit of camaraderie with political power. In his emphasis on replacing federal action with state and local control, Watt was attempting to grind to a halt the momentum gained by the environmental movement during the 1970s and to return to the nineteenth-century practice of disposing of public land. The Reagan administration, in a decision led by Watt, announced their immediate intention to sell 307 parcels of federal land totaling 60,000 acres and their further hopes of disposing of 35 million more acres (a land area equal to Maine, New Hampshire, Vermont, and Massachusetts combined) over the next five years. Watt and Reagan held the view that the U.S. government owned far too much land, and they wanted to change the role of government in property management.

Watt's idea—that land in the public domain was a wasteful form of social welfare—marked a dramatic change, one that raised questions regarding the value of public land and that sparked a highly antagonistic battle. He felt that the land would be better put to use by the private sector, free from federal oversight and thus free from any environmental regulations. Opponents feared that relinquishing federal ownership and responsibility for public land would leave it open to unmitigated exploitation by a narrow group of business interests. The Wilderness Society made an official statement in protest of the land sale: "American history has demonstrated that the public is not well served, in the long run, by turning over commodity lands to private interests. The aim of business is short-run profits, not long-run preservation—and experience has shown that conservation of resources is critical to

sustaining a high standard of living—or living at all."[6] Major legal and political obstacles immediately plagued Watt's privatization plan. Conservation
groups filed lawsuits demanding environmental impact statements, and resistance spread. Even real estate agents lobbied in protest of the land sale, fearful of that much property being suddenly dumped on the open market. One
year after the land sale was announced, only 4,600 acres of public land had
been sold. Watt's ambitions were dashed, and the large-scale privatization
program was abandoned.

Watt always had felt that the conservation movement held too much political control and that it was his duty to win the land back from the greedy
preservationists. Boasting of this, he once said, "[T]hey realize they've lost
the keys to the front door. I opened up the door to everyone." But thanks in
part to Watt's ambitions, conservation groups were getting more and more
savvy about legal matters, public relations, and organizational skills. In this
way his provocations actually served to empower his opponents, even as he
strove to defeat them. A growing number of people regarded Watt and his
programs as a threat to their interests, and environmental quality issues suddenly were making the news and gaining more attention. As a consequence
of Watt's leadership within the Department of the Interior, conservation organizations experienced a large upsurge in membership and donations. During the three-year span from 1977 and 1980, the Sierra Club had gained
only 3,000 members to reach 181,000. But by 1983, after another three
years, it had grown to 346,000 members. Other groups like the wilderness
Society and the Audubon Society experienced similar unprecedented growth.
Previously Watt's tactic had been to portray environmentalists as a narrow
special interest group that could be dismissed as extremist. But he underestimated how many Americans were embracing the concept of conservation.
Steve Greenberg's cartoon that ran at the time in the *Daily News* of Los Angeles in 1981 showed Watt threatening a small gathering of his opponents,
saying "You environmentalist extremists are gonna toe the line!" The staid
and decidedly mainstream group consisted of Bambi, Smokey the Bear,
Johnny Appleseed, and Hooty Owl.

Ironically, the mainstreaming of environmentalism catalyzed the formation of the first truly radical activist groups in 1981. Earth First! gained
fame with its "no compromise" stance and confrontational direct-action
tactics, which they called "ecotage," for ecological sabotage. They chained
themselves to trees, aggressively blocked bulldozers, and drove metal spikes
into trees intended for harvest—forcing loggers to forfeit them for fear of in-
jury. Earth First! was founded by **Dave Foreman** and a cohort of fellow activists who felt that mainstream environmentalism was not accomplishing as
much as it should. Perhaps Watt was thinking of Earth First! when he characterized environmentalists as extremists, but considering his own extreme
right-wing ideology, it seemed as the two sides provided a reasonable counterbalance to each other. At any rate, the extremism of Earth First! only

made higher-brow conservation organizations seem more acceptable. As Hal K. Rothman pointed out, "Even Watt could have civil discussions with some environmentalists, it seemed, especially if the alternative was having people whom the secretary regarded as long-haired crazies running around his woods."[7]

When attempting to marginalize the environmental movement did not achieve the desired results, Watt tried the divide-and-conquer approach. Conservation has always been subject to partisan politics, but Watt's pro-development, pro-industry revolution polarized the issue further and thus threatened the bipartisan consensus that had been forged by the environmental movement. Driving the wedge in every chance he got, he pitted environmentalists against hunting and fishing groups by hyping issues such as road access or management of game animals, the few issues on which the mostly like-minded groups might disagree. And he never hesitated to argue that environmentalists were responsible for the loss of blue-collar jobs.

Watt did succeed in antagonizing the environmentalists and polarizing the debate, but his actions failed to fracture permanently the foundation upon which the environmental movement stood. In fact, he was losing credibility. Jokes and bumper stickers cropped up across the nation, such as "Q: How much energy would it take to destroy our environment? A: One Watt." In the White House, Watt was still held in high esteem for his views, his determination, and his energy. But, even before the conflagration that led up to his resignation, there were hints that he was a potential political liability to the Reagan administration. Having become a magnet for public criticism, Watt's personality sometimes overshadowed his actions and got in the way of the political process, and he almost constantly was deeply embroiled in controversy. So, in the fall of 1983, when Watt joked about a study commission he headed, saying, "I have a black, a woman, two Jews, and a cripple," it tipped the scales completely, erasing any hope he had of a political future. Though this insensitive and nasty remark offended many, President Reagan stood steadfastly by Watt—easily the most adversarial member of his cabinet— saying he did not want a "lynching." After fleeing to California to consider his options, Watt decided to resign. In a letter to President Reagan he acknowledged that a new leader was needed for the Interior Department, but maintained pride in his work: "The restoration of our national parks, refuges and public lands is well under way. . . . Balance is being restored. I leave behind people and programs—a legacy that will aid America in the decades ahead."[8] President Reagan wrote back, saying, "It is with great regret that I accept your resignation as Secretary of the Interior, effective at noon on November 8, 1983. I believe that history will call you one of our very best Secretaries of the Interior. . . . Our nation needs both wilderness areas, faithfully preserved, and appropriate resource development. . . . You have understood the need to balance these two goals and have done so with dedication and success."[9]

After bowing out of public life, Watt, along with Doug Wead, wrote a book called *The Courage of a Conservative*. In it they traced the decline of American morality to the middle of the nineteenth century, when grammar school textbooks were purged of Biblical verses, leading to the gradual progress of the "intellectual vacuum" of liberalism that had come to control government. Portraying himself as a victim of a conspiracy-hungry liberal press, Watt wrote of the personal sacrifice involved in his service to his country and described gaining strength from a framed plaque on his office wall that said, "nothing takes the place of persistence."

Watt's tenure as secretary of the Interior was consequential to public land management, environmental policy, and the conservation movement. Though he resigned in a cloud of disgrace, his work while in office had carved pathways for his immediate successors to follow, which they largely did. William P. Clark served for a year, followed by Donald Paul Hodel, both of whom continued to pursue much the same agenda as Watt, though with greater political finesse. Thus, though his term as Interior secretary was brief, the land still bears the marks of his actions through changes in perceptions of the role of government in overseeing federal land, and through the rise of the Sagebrush Rebel philosophy. Watt's influence on the conservation movement has been felt powerfully, as well, and has lead to dramatic and lasting changes. Conservation groups welcomed the swarms of people who objected to Watt's principles, and so expanded their constituency. But money had entered the picture as well: large amounts of it backing conservation groups and making them vulnerable to the same corruption of which they accused the business lobby. In addition, after hearing President Reagan repeatedly define himself as an environmentalist, a fog of disillusionment was spreading. From then on, cynicism was an ingredient in any discourse on politics, even regarding environmental issues.

While Watt was partly to blame for the cynicism that began growing in the American public—eroding trust in governmental officials and the political process—one thing he was never accused of was being a cynic himself. As Jay Hair, the executive vice president of the National Wildlife Federation said at the time, "This man is absolutely sincere. He just has a different vision of what stewardship of the public lands should be. We define stewardship as using our natural resources in ways that assume they can be restored over time. His definition is taking the resources and changing them irreversibly."[10] Watt truly believed that his leadership had improved the quality of the people's land, saying again and again that he had restored the greatness of America.

He now lives in Jackson, Wyoming, and works as a private consultant. In 1995 he was indicted on twenty-five criminal counts in connection with influence peddling at the Department of Housing and Urban Development on behalf of developers. He maintained his innocence, but copped a plea to a single misdemeanor charge and was sentenced to five years of probation and 500 hours of community service. He and Leilani have two grown children, Erin Gaia and Eric Gaius.

NOTES

1. James G. Watt and Doug Wead, *The Courage of a Conservative* (New York: Simon and Schuster, 1985), p. 199.

2. Ronald Brownstein and Nina Easton, *Reagan's Ruling Class: Portraits of the President's Top 100 Officials* (Washington, DC: The Presidential Accountability Group, 1982), p. 111.

3. Leilani Watt, *Caught in the Conflict: My Life with James Watt* (Eugene, OR: Harvest House Publishers, 1984), p. 32.

4. Quoted in Philip Shabecoff, *A Fierce Green Fire: The American Environmental Movement* (New York: Farrar, Straus and Giroux, 1993), p. 208.

5. Colman McCarthy, "James Watt and the Puritan Ethic," *Washington Post* (May 24, 1981), p. L5.

6. Peter Stoler, "Land Sale of the Century," *Time* Vol. 120 (August 23, 1982), p. 21.

7. Hal K. Rothman, *Saving the Planet: The American Response to the Environment in the Twentieth Century* (Chicago: Ivan R. Dee, 2000), p. 173.

8. Leilani Watt, *Caught in the Conflict*, pp. 179–180.

9. Ibid., p. 182.

10. Ibid., p. 81.

BIBLIOGRAPHY

James Watt's book, co-authored with Doug Wead *The Courage of a Conservative* (New York: Simon and Schuster, 1985), contains almost no biographical information and is more of a treatise on his conservative philosophy. His wife Leilani's book, *Caught in the Conflict: My Life with James Watt* (Eugene, OR: Harvest House Publishers, 1984), is mainly a personal account of her experience in dealing with the public outcry over her husband's policies, and contains little political information. A helpful analysis of Watt's impact on land management is found in Ronald Brownstein and Nina Easton, *Reagan's Ruling Class: Portraits of the President's Top 100 Officials* (Washington, DC: The Presidential Accountability Group, 1982). For a look at the religious aspects of Watt's stewardship ethic, see Susan Power Bratton, "The Ecotheology of James Watt," *Environmental Ethics* Vol. 5 (Fall 1983), pp. 225–236. Watt's role in the campaign against the environmental movement is discussed in the following: Philip Shabecoff, *A Fierce Green Fire: The American Environmental Movement* (New York: Farrar, Straus and Giroux, 1993); David Helvarg, *The War against the Greens: The "Wise-Use" Movement, the New Right and Anti-Environmental Violence* (San Francisco: Sierra Club Books, 1994); Jacqueline Vaughn Switzer, *Green Backlash: The History and Politics of Environmental Opposition in the U.S.* (Boulder: Lynne Rienner Publishers, 1997); and Hal K. Rothman,

Saving the Planet: The American Response to the Environment in the Twentieth Century (Chicago: Ivan R. Dee, 2000). See also Colman McCarthy, "James Watt and the Puritan Ethic," *Washington Post* (May 24, 1981), p. L5; Jerry Adler, William J. Cook, Mary Hager, and Tony Fuller, "James Watt's Land Rush," *Newsweek* Vol. 97 (June 29, 1981), pp. 22–32; Peter Stoler, "Land Sale of the Century," *Time* Vol. 120 (August 23, 1982), p. 21; and Melinda Beck, Mary Hager, Jeff B. Copeland, Darby Junkin, Shawn Doherty, and Peter McAlevey, "Battle Over the Wilderness," *Newsweek* Vol. 102 (July 25, 1983), pp. 22–30.

ROSS GELBSPAN
(1939–)

In the United States the truth underlying the increasingly apparent changes in global climate has largely been kept out of public view. As a result, what most Americans know about global warming is obsolete and untrue.

—Ross Gelbspan

Since abrupt changes in the global climate could lead to food and fresh water shortages, severe storms, and disrupted access to energy supplies—which could, in turn, incite widespread famine, rioting, and even war—strategic planners at the Pentagon began grappling with the national security threats of global warming early in 2003, commissioning a detailed report that studied the issue closely. An article in *Fortune* magazine discussed the implications of the Pentagon's decision to take global warming seriously: "At least some federal thought leaders may be starting to perceive climate change less as a political annoyance and more as an issue demanding action. If so, the case for acting now to address climate change, long a hard sell in Washington, may be gaining influential support, if only behind the scenes."[1]

This is quite welcome news to former journalist and author Ross Gelbspan. After a distinguished thirty-year career of reporting and editing for daily newspapers, including the *Philadelphia Bulletin*, the *Washington Post*, the *Village Voice*, and the *Boston Globe*, Gelbspan retired. But not long into his retirement he began to wonder how global climate change had come to be so shrouded in confusion in the United States. His dedication to intellectual honesty wouldn't let him ignore the question, and when he began to investigate further—aided by his journalistic skill at tweezing the truth out of complex situations—he uncovered a widespread campaign of misinformation promulgated by the oil and coal industries and intended to assuage public concern. Gelbspan then helped launch a crusade to disclose the truth about the global addiction to oil and coal and the environmental damage this causes through the greenhouse effect, presenting the facts with integrity and elegance in numerous magazine and newspaper articles. His book, *The Heat Is On: The High Stakes Battle over Earth's Threatened Climate* (1997) definitively brought home the imminence of climate change, which already has propelled the earth's weather patterns into instability and which exacerbates virtually every other environmental problem. *The Heat Is On* also documented the attempts of a small but highly vocal group of "scientific skeptics" to distort the nature of the debate and raise doubts in the public mind, and exposed their financial backing by major coal and oil companies. Though he still relies on his journalistic talents, Gelbspan has entered a new métier—activism—as he works to promote the idea of a complete transformation of the twenty-first century's energy regime of oil and coal. He remains undaunted by the enormous challenge of convincing the general public to grasp the catastrophic consequences of global warming, and while he takes heart in any tiny step the U.S. government makes toward acknowledging the severity of the problem, he knows that radical changes must occur in the not-too-distant future.

Ross Gelbspan was born on June 1, 1939, to Ruth and Gene Gelbspan in Chicago, Illinois, where he grew up with one sister. He received his BA in political science and English from Kenyon College in Gambier, Ohio, in 1960, then began a two-year course of studies in international relations at the Johns Hopkins School of Advanced International Studies in Washington, D.C. After one year of graduate school, he was offered a reporting job at the *Philadelphia Bulletin* and left school to take the opportunity. He briefly switched to the *Washington Post* before moving to New York City to work for the *Village Voice* during the late 1960s and early 1970s. In 1971, he wrote a series on the Soviet underground, a series for which he spent a month in the Soviet Union interviewing dissidents and human rights advocates: This series was reprinted later in the *Congressional Record*.

He began reporting on environmental affairs in the early 1970s when he did a story for the *Village Voice* based on a study by an MIT team (Donella Meadows, Dennis Meadows, Jorgen Randers, and William Behrens III) that used a computer simulation model to look at population, industrialization, food production, natural resources, and pollution, and stressed the environmental consequences of limited resources being consumed at an exponential rate. The study was later published in the groundbreaking book,

The Limits to Growth.[2] Then, in 1972, the *Village Voice* sent him to Stockholm, Sweden, to report on the first United Nations Conference on the Environment (now known as the "Earth Summit"). The Stockholm conference ushered in the modern system of international environmental negotiations and triggered a flurry of regulatory activity at national and international levels as countries responded to emerging challenges of environmental management. At the time, Americans also were riding the crest of the new cultural and political wave known as the "environmental movement," and they were becoming increasingly concerned about pollution, population, and nuclear waste. While at the Stockholm conference, Gelbspan began to gain an understanding of the ill effects that result from the extravagant burning of oil and coal. It was also there that he met Anne Charlotte Brostrom, whom he married in 1973.

Gelbspan left the *Village Voice* and worked for a time as the national news editor for Scripps Howard News Service, based in New York City, while also teaching journalism as an adjunct professor at Columbia University. But before long, a job offer came from the *Boston Globe*, and in 1979, he and his family moved to Massachusetts, where he became the *Globe*'s senior editor. In his capacity as special projects editor there, he edited a series of articles on job discrimination against African Americans in Boston-area corporations, universities, unions, newspapers, and state and city government offices. This series, an exercise in public service that investigated some of Boston's most honored institutions—including the *Boston Globe*—won a Pulitzer Prize for specialized local reporting in 1984. In the Pulitzer tradition, the prize listed the names of the main reporters and the newspaper itself, but since it was Gelbspan who had conceived of and directed the project, the *Globe* chose him to be named the recipient. This became an issue later when the fossil fuel industry attacked his character and accused him of lying about having received a Pulitzer.

His investigative work led to another project, this one involving the suppression tactics used by the U.S. Federal Bureau of Investigations (FBI) to conduct anti-leftist operations in Central America during **Ronald Reagan**'s presidency (1981–1988). Groups such as the Committee in Solidarity with the People of El Salvador (CISPES)—made up of peaceful protestors of Reagan's policies in Central America—were labeled terrorist organizations, and the FBI was ordered to track them down. Gelbspan's digging exposed FBI alliances with right-wing U.S. groups like the John Birch Society, and documented the FBI practices of harassment, domestic surveillance, and break-ins that led to the blacklisting of 100,000 political and religious activists on the FBI's terrorism files. He presented his findings to the public in his book, *Break-Ins, Death Threats, and the FBI: The Covert War against the Central America Movement* (1991). The Massachusetts Civil Liberties Union voted Gelbspan the recipient of a Distinguished Service Award for this work, which he regretfully declined out of a journalistic conflict of interest, since he might someday have been required to cover the Civil Liberties Union for a story.

Turning his gaze again toward the public's interest in environmental matters, Gelbspan wrote a series of articles about a decaying nuclear power plant in western Massachusetts, contributing to the community awareness that led to its eventual closure. Much of his coverage at the *Globe*, in fact dealt with environmental issues—a beat for which he became known. He wrote articles on recycling, ozone depletion, problems with trash-burning incinerators, European pressure on the United States to control carbon dioxide emissions, and the clean-up of hazardous waste sites in Massachusetts, for example. Then, two decades after the first UN Conference on the Environment, Gelbspan reported on the 1992 Earth Summit in Rio de Janeiro. In the days leading up to the conference, he co-authored with Dianne Dumanoski a four-part front-page series on it for the *Globe*. Their series began with a projected newscast from the year 2030:

> Next on the 11 o'clock news for Aug. 22, 2030: Food riots erupt in Boston . . . Damage from superhurricane Edward may hit $1 billion . . . Nature helps avert a water war between New York and Pennsylvania . . . In world news, India threatens nuclear force to fend off Bangladeshi refugees . . . Scenarios like these are being forecast by more and more scientists. Unless skyrocketing rates of pollution and population growth are reduced soon, they warn, many biological systems needed to sustain humans will collapse within the lifetimes of today's children.[3]

Their articles alluded to the inertia that had impeded progress during the contentious run-up to the summit, when an effort to get a head start on negotiating international treaties was thwarted by the tendency of nations to adhere to their own self-interests. Gelbspan and Dumanoski wrote:

> Many observers say the effort was especially hampered by the posture of the United States, which is the only remaining military superpower as well as the world's largest polluter. . . . Alone among the leaders of the industrialized nations, President Bush was unwilling to set specific targets for limiting the heat-trapping gases linked to global warming. That brought widespread condemnation from other world leaders, a sharp turnaround for a nation that was once an undisputed world leader in the environmental arena and a major force for environmental reform at a pioneering UN conference in Stockholm 20 years ago.[4]

Debate over global warming in the United States was still subdued and lukewarm, partly due to the administration's obvious lack of alarm—though environmentalists, informed by news coverage such as Gelbspan's, were becoming much more alert to the issue. Thus, when the Earth Summit commenced, American environmentalists were frustrated and embarrassed by the U.S. delegation's deliberate evisceration of the global warming treaty and its misguided declaration that forests in developing countries were "sinks" for the carbon emissions of wealthy nations.

The articles on the Earth Summit were the last Gelbspan would submit as senior editor. Immediately after they ran, he retired, opting to accept the voluntary buy-out that the *Globe* offered as a way to cut costs. With his new free time he turned to creative writing and started a novel. But in 1995, a doctor on the Intergovernmental Panel on Climate Change (IPCC)—which the UN had formed in 1988 to address the climate crisis—approached him with a series of articles he had written for the British medical journal the *Lancet* examining the impact of global warming on human diseases. Drawn in by them, Gelbspan agreed to collaborate on a piece for the popular press outlining the link between climate change and the upswing in the spread of infectious diseases. Later that year, when the article appeared in the *Washington Post*, it was well received, and Gelbspan thought he had washed his hands of the issue and could return to his novel. But the article coaxed numerous responses from readers, who wrote or called him, telling him he was overreacting and that there was no proof of global climate change. Gelbspan asked after their source of information, attempting to ascertain how they had reached such a level of certainty on the issue, and several people referred him to the work of a few scientists who disputed global warming's validity. As he probed the politics surrounding the issue more deeply, Gelbspan quickly discovered the main reason for the public confusion.

Following the recent Earth Summit, which had amplified international awareness of global climate change, a band of several high-profile "greenhouse skeptic" scientists had upped their efforts to buttress the widespread public belief that the issue was filled with uncertainties and hardly cause for alarm. Following the tips he had received from readers of the *Washington Post*, Gelbspan read everything he could find by the main skeptics. Somewhat to his relief, their work appeared sound and persuasive, and he told his wife he was finished with his research: The issue was mired in scientific uncertainty. But he already had arranged interviews with a few other climate scientists and felt obligated to keep these appointments. When he did, he got the rest of the story: The scientists informed him that the skeptics were distorting the mainstream opinion of science and were very much in the minority. Gelbspan's principles of journalistic integrity were offended:

> What that did for me was that it really made me quite angry because my reaction was, Gee whiz, these folks were taking our reality away from us. In a democracy, I believe very strongly that we need honest information to make our decisions and our choices. When that information is not available to us, we are not able to exercise our rights in a

democracy. We are not able to respond to threats. We are not able to deal with policy questions. So, what really got me much more upset than anything else was the usurpation of our reality by disinformation.[5]

He was hooked, and set to work, unearthing the truth behind global warming science and the skeptics' campaign to anesthetize public concern over it.

In 1995 he wrote an engrossing and eye-opening essay that appeared in the December issue of *Harper's Magazine*. Bringing home the fragility of the earth's blanket of air that makes up the atmosphere, he reminded readers that the outer edge of it lies only twelve miles above earth and that industry pumps six billion tons of carbon dioxide into this narrow space every single year. Carbon dioxide and the other greenhouse gases act like the panes of glass on a car parked in the sun: They let the heat of the sun in and then trap it. The article traced an outline of increasing extreme weather events in recent years, plus insect infestations and disintegrating ice shelves in the Antarctic—all indirect effects of unchecked burning of oil and coal. And even though the ten hottest years in recorded human history up to 1995 had occurred since 1980, most people remained unable to comprehend the reality of global warming, their fears soothed by the tiny group of greenhouse skeptics. Gelbspan's article disclosed the fact that many of these skeptic scientists receive fuel industry funding; the five front-runners—Dr. **Richard Siegmund Lindzen,** Dr. Pat Michaels, Dr. Robert Balling, Dr. Sherwood Idso, and Dr. **S. Fred Singer**—all have taken money from coal and oil companies like Exxon, Shell, Unocal, ARCO, Sun Oil, and the Western Fuels Association (a multimillion-dollar consortium of coal interests). They claim that their research is uncorrupted by these infusions of money; the immense industry-funded publicity they enjoy, however, means that their message dwarfs the message of mainstream science and hugely boosts the weight of their opinions. "By keeping the discussion focused on whether there is a problem in the first place, they have effectively silenced the debate over what to do about it," Gelbspan explained. He also described the enormity of the task of bringing the dangers of global warming to light: "We live in a world of man-size urgencies, measured in hours or days. What unfolds slowly is not, by our lights, urgent, and it will therefore take a collective act of imagination to understand the extremity of the situation we now confront. . . . What too many people refuse to understand is that the global economy's existence depends upon the global environment, not the other way around."[6]

Gelbspan took the main ideas from this article, which was nominated for a National Magazine Award, and expanded them into a book called *The Heat Is On: The High Stakes Battle over Earth's Threatened Climate* (1997). The book wastes no time equivocating about the reality of human-induced changes to global climate: "Environmentalists have been warning us about global warming for years. What is news is that global warming is no longer merely a future possibility. The heat is on. Now. Its early impacts, in the form of more extreme and unstable climate, are being felt even as I write."[7] Ever since the Industrial Revolution, a combination of fossil fuel combustion and deforestation[8] has allowed carbon to be released into the lower atmosphere, trapping heat and causing increasingly erratic weather patterns around the world. As Gelbspan pointed out, global temperature records already were bearing witness to climate change: 1997 had just replaced 1995 as the hottest year ever recorded, the five hottest consecutive years on record up until 1997 began in 1991, and the eleven hottest years in recorded history had occurred since 1980. Other consequences of alterations in the atmosphere included shifts in drought and rainfall patterns, more record-high and -low temperatures, and more severe storms. Interspersed with Gelbspan's discussion of the politics of climate change, he gave examples of escalating extreme weather events such as flooding in Bangladesh, the worst drought in Brazil in a century, severe wildfires in the North American West, devastating hurricanes, and malaria epidemics—anecdotal cases that don't "prove" global warming by themselves, but that provide a small sample of what the future may have in store for the planet.

While the general public may not yet relate the conflagration of strange global weather events to climate change, leading climate scientists recognize them as the unsurprising early symptoms of the rise in the average global temperature. In *The Heat Is On*, Gelbspan affirmed that scientific opinion is virtually unanimous in agreement that industrial activity is having an effect on the earth's atmosphere. The 2,500 members of the IPCC—the unprecedented international collaboration of rigorously peer-reviewed scientists—published a decisive report in 1995 indicating that global warming is happening and that it is not simply a factor of the natural variability of the climate: It is human caused and will lead to a whole host of ecological disasters if not stanched. The United States is the only nation in the world that remains agnostic on the issue.

This is largely because the truth linking the coal- and oil-dependent economy with global warming and recent record-setting weather events has been kept carefully submerged in the United States by powerful forces. Gelbspan devoted much of his book to examining the campaign of deception by coal and oil companies—which, together, constitute the biggest single industry in history—that keeps many people in this country confused and misinformed. He expanded on the affiliation between the greenhouse skeptics and the coal and oil industries; in 1993 the American Petroleum Institute spent nearly the same amount on public relations as the entire combined expenditure budgets of the nation's five major environmental groups that focus on climate change. Besides seemingly limitless funding, the fossil fuel industries enjoy another advantage, one that arises from a misuse of the standard rule of journalism requiring that arguments on both sides of an issue be presented together. "This canon causes problems when it is applied to issues of science," wrote Gelbspan. "It seems to demand that journalists present competing points of view on a scientific question as though they had equal scientific weight, when actually they do not. . . . As a result, ideology disguised as science can contaminate the debate."[9] In other words, misled by a misunderstanding of journalistic balance, reporters too often confuse opinion with fact and give equal ink to global warming skeptics, even though they are but one drop in an ocean of scientific consensus on the issue. Dr. Steven Schneider, a leading atmospheric researcher with the National Center for Atmospheric Research in Boulder, Colorado, agrees with Gelbspan: "It is journalistically irresponsible to present both sides as if it were a question of balance. Given the distribution of views, with groups like the National Academy of Science expressing strong scientific concern, it is irresponsible to give equal time to a few people standing out in left field."[10] The skeptics' views are given further credibility by their Republican allies in Congress, who have called on them to testify on an equal footing with leading federal climate scientists. After hearing from skeptic Dr. Pat Michaels, U.S. Representative Dana Rohrabacher, Republican from California and chairman of the House Science Subcommittee, pronounced that concern over global warming scenarios was based on "unjustified scare scenarios," and recommended deep cuts in federal spending on climate research.

In the public debate over global warming, Gelbspan has found that journalistic ethics also are being compromised by withholding certain important pieces of information: funding disclosures. He argues that the funding behind scientific research and opinion pieces should always be identified, giving an example of an Op-Ed piece that appeared in the *Wall Street Journal* by skeptic Dr. Robert Balling, who claimed concerns over global warming were overstated. While it might seem reassuring to read such claims, especially since Balling was identified as a climatologist from Arizona State University, readers might form a different impression if they knew that some of Balling's work had been underwritten by coal interests and the government of Kuwait.

Having spent a major portion of his life dedicated to journalism, Gelbspan has gained perspective on the ways in which the profession has changed in the last forty years and how those changes are affecting the quality of information available to the public on issues such as global warming. News organizations used to be small businesses (many of them family owned) dedicated to journalism. Over the years, through mergers and takeovers, media outlets have become large conglomerations that are much more driven by the demands of Wall Street. To compete for investment and larger profit margins, many media corporations have sought ways to cut costs, some by reducing staff—which means there are fewer reporters with less time to investigate the issues they cover. In the case of climate change, which is a complex issue hidden behind a smoke screen of oil and coal public relations, having fewer reporters digging for the facts is a huge hurdle in bringing the debate up to an appropriate level in the United States. Furthermore, the culture of journalism has become very political, and when climate change does get mentioned, it is most often in a political context, such as when President George W. Bush withdrew from the Kyoto Protocol. Overall, says Gelbspan, coverage of climate change has been influenced negatively by the transformation of news organizations and by the trend away from "real" news toward crowd-pleasing, celebrity-driven news.

In direct contrast to the oblique and equivocating coverage of climate change in the news media, Gelbspan's *The Heat Is On* discussed some of the likely consequences of climate instability around the world in what are perhaps the most startling sections of the book. Besides environmental disasters—devastating weather events, spreading diseases, sea level rise, population explosions of insects, and melting ice caps—there will be social, political, and economic consequences, too. North America boasts rich resources, access to expensive technologies, and an unshakable tradition of democracy and personal freedom. But impoverished parts of the globe, which are also the most environmentally vulnerable areas, don't have those advantages. Faced with disruptions in water sources, food supplies, and human health, nations in the developing world—where democratic traditions are already precarious—will likely revert to totalitarian governments with increased violence and chaos. In addition, frustrated with being consigned to a life of desperation, people in politically volatile areas may take desperate measures. Four years before September 11, 2001, Gelbspan wrote, "The United States, like any open society, is vulnerable to terrorism. A significant surge in terrorism is the likeliest result of the desperation that is overtaking many people in environmentally disrupted countries."[11] To Gelbspan, global warming is more than an environmental problem, it is a civilization problem.

His book carried a powerful and influential message, and, not surprisingly, it became the subject of attacks by the fossil fuel lobby. Soon after its publication, the book began attracting attention and praise from several media outlets, including the *Minneapolis Star-Tribune*, the *Boston Globe*, and the *Washington Post*. To counter that, the Western Fuels Association—the coal industry lobby group—took out full-page ads in the *Washington Post* and the *Washington Times* (the newspaper owned by ultra-right-wing Reverend **Sun Myung Moon**'s Unification Church), discrediting the book and implying that its publisher had paid for all the favorable publicity. Greenhouse skeptic Dr. S. Fred Singer, who receives fossil fuel industry funding, joined Western Fuels in accusing Gelbspan of lying about his credentials, declaring that he had never been a co-recipient of the 1984 Pulitzer Prize. While Gelbspan's name was not listed on the prize itself, because he was the editor and not a reporter, the *Boston Globe* had chosen him to receive the prize because he had come up with the idea and directed the entire series.

Gelbspan now laughs about the incident, saying he felt good about their attempt to smear his reputation, as it meant they hadn't been able to find anything wrong with his book.

Since the book's publication, Gelbspan has been extensively traveling and speaking on global climate change—giving forty talks and year, writing fifteen articles a year, and meeting with activist groups. He has appeared on *ABC News Nightline* and the National Public Radio shows, *All Things Considered* and *Talk of the Nation.* In 1998 he was invited to the World Economic Forum in Davos, Switzerland, where he addressed heads of state, government ministers, and leaders of multinational corporations. Later in 1998 he began taking an even more proactive role, and, with Dr. Paul Epstein of Harvard Medical School and the IPCC, Gelbspan brought together a group of people to work out a set of solution strategies to help lead the world away from the current destructive energy regime that relies on fossil fuels. This group, which includes scientists, energy company presidents, economists, and other specialists, came up with the World Energy Modernization Plan, a set of three interacting prescriptions. The first element of the plan involves the $25 billion in U.S. government subsidies currently given to the fossil fuel industry. If these subsidies were transferred to a renewable energy industry—which could be overseen by oil companies—oil prices would not be deflated artificially and excess consumption would be discouraged. Additionally, oil companies would have the financial incentives to develop a renewable energy infrastructure. The second element involves the use of revenues from a miniscule tax on international currency transactions to finance the development of alternative energy technologies for developing nations. And the third element proposes to set up a fossil fuel efficiency standard that would become more and more stringent every year, placing restrictions on oil and coal emissions by degrees, while renewable energy sources—such as wind, solar, and fuel cells—would be simultaneously gaining ground.

The World Energy Modernization Plan is Gelbspan's answer to the recalcitrant fossil fuel lobby's argument that renewable energy systems would bankrupt the global economy. The plan would actually increase wealth worldwide, allowing poor countries to develop their economies sustainably, without further pollution, and would create millions and millions of jobs through the labor-intensive production of renewable energy technologies. These cost-effective solutions could help both stabilize the climate and reverse the gross economic inequities that inflame hostility toward the United States in the third world. Also, the United States would boost its own national security by gradually reducing and eventually eliminating dependence on Middle Eastern oil.

Through lectures and articles, Gelbspan continues to promote the World Energy Modernization Plan. He and the other creators of the plan presented it at a conference in Buenos Aires in 1998, and were then invited by the United Nations Development Programme to host a conference on these strategies in Bonn, Germany, in June 1999. He also presented the strategies in May 2000, at a conference he keynoted in Cairo, and later that year he presented them to a group of senators and congressmen from the G-77[12] at a round of climate talks in The Hague. The strategies have been endorsed by large non-governmental organizations in India, Mexico, Germany, and Bangladesh, and by a large following of environmentalists, economists, and energy specialists both in the United States and abroad. He also discusses them in depth in his most recent book entitled *Boiling Point*.

Gelbspan's work to accelerate international climate negotiations became even more critical when George W. Bush became president in 2001. Once in office, President Bush reneged on a campaign promise to cap carbon emissions from power plants; called for the construction of at least 1,300 new power plants in the next twenty years; and reduced air pollution restrictions for power plants. But it was his announcement in early 2001 that the United States would be withdrawing from the 1997 Kyoto Protocol that provoked worldwide disappointment, though it was perhaps unsurprising, considering the extent of funding the Bush campaign received from the fossil fuel industry. The Kyoto Protocol—a treaty negotiated by over 100 countries—calls for the world's largest developing nations to reduce their greenhouse gas emissions by an average of 5 percent below 1990 levels by the year 2012. It represents the only set of rules obligating industrial countries to reduce their emissions, and, in order to be legally binding, it must be ratified by a minimum of fifty-five countries responsible for at least 55 percent of global emissions. Without the participation of the United States, which alone contributes at least 20 percent of the world's greenhouse emissions, ratification of the treaty faces a precipitous battle. Nevertheless, President George W. Bush pulled out, stating that conforming with the accord is not in the United States's best economic interest.

However, economic self-interest becomes irrelevant in the face of climate instability and the international political unrest that could result. The IPCC has insisted that emissions must be cut 70 percent as soon as possible for the atmosphere to stabilize. The Kyoto Protocol sets limits far below 70 percent—in fact, its goal of reducing greenhouse gases to slightly below 1990 levels is actually almost negligible. But, says Gelbspan, the treaty is simply intended to be a first step toward forging international cooperation—a difficult process. Just like the Montreal Protocol—the international convention that eventually phased out ozone-destroying chlorofluorocarbons—the Kyoto Protocol sets manageable low goals, but with the stated intention of ratcheting restrictions upward as climate scientists dictate. It represents an extremely important diplomatic platform that provides a mechanism for approaching the issue of global climate change. International consternation regarding the U.S. refusal to address the issue has been mounting, and many countries, including Japan, Brazil, Russia, New Zealand, and the European Union, have indicated already their willingness to proceed without the leadership of the United States. Actually, explains Gelbspan, other countries might even find it easier to promote more aggressive approaches to alleviate climate change without the foot-dragging participation of the United States.

Since the publication of *The Heat Is On* in 1997, the United States has come under terrorist attack, started a volatile war with oil-rich Iraq, and endured a power outage of an unprecedented size in the Northeast. While most of the country may not consider these events to be related to the issue of global warming, Gelbspan is quick to point out that the country would be better served by promoting a switch to smaller-scale, renewable sources of power around the world; this would reduce the vulnerability inherent in large, centrally operated power systems; cut back on greenhouse emissions; and allow the United States to become a constructive rather than destructive influence in the Middle East. Other trends have made news since Gelbspan's book came out, including increasingly bizarre and extreme weather events. During the summer of 2003, Europe experienced an all-time record-breaking heat wave that killed as many as 10,000 people in France. In May 2003—the warmest May on record for land temperatures—the United States saw 562 tornadoes, setting a new record; in September, the enormous Hurricane Isabel, a record-breaking storm in terms of speed and swath, left record numbers of people without power. The year 2003 tied 2002 as the hottest year ever recorded; the five hottest years on record have all occurred since 1997, and the ten hottest since 1990. It has been 225 months since the world recorded a colder-than-normal month.

Gelbspan has been working for nearly a decade to make the issue of global warming an urgent one—to "get it out of the ghetto of environmental issues," as he puts it—and to bring the discussion of solutions up to an appropriate scale. President George W. Bush still sidesteps the issue, but this short-sightedness may end up leaving him behind. Concern for the atmosphere has infiltrated even some of the biggest names in industry and caused a shift of focus. An indication of this came in March 2000, when Ford, Daimler-Chrysler, Texaco, the Southern Company, and General Motors all announced that they were cutting ties with the Global Climate Coalition (GCC)—the lobbying group representing fossil fuel, automotive, and heavy-industry interests that has spent more than $63 million to stall constructive discussions of global climate change and to promote a false optimism. This followed the defections from the GCC a year earlier by British Petroleum and Shell, which have both taken major steps toward acknowledging the reality of climate change in recent years. British Petroleum has become the world's largest producer of solar energy systems, and Shell has started a $500 million renewable energy company.

More recently, renowned Department of Defense Advisor Andrew Marshall—who has held substantial sway over U.S. military policy for the past three decades—became concerned enough over the national security implications of global climate change to commission a report on it. The Pentagon report—written by Peter Schwartz, a CIA (Central Intelligence Agency) consultant and former head of planning at Royal Dutch/Shell Group, and Doug Randall, a consultant with the Global Business Network (a think tank based in California)—was released late in 2003 and explored how abrupt climate change could potentially cause disruption and conflict around the globe. To help planners think about coping strategies, the report sketches a dramatic but plausible scenario of what might happen as weather patterns spiral into extremes over the next few decades. "Such change would probably cause cooling in the Northern Hemisphere, leading to longer, harsher winters in much of the U.S. and Europe," wrote David Stipp in an article on the Pentagon report. "Worse, it would cause massive droughts, turning farmland to dust bowls and forests to ashes. Picture last fall's California wildfires as a regular thing. Or imagine similar disasters destabilizing nuclear powers such as Pakistan or Russia—it's easy to see why the Pentagon has become interested in abrupt climate change."[13]

Gelbspan tried to retire once, before making his life into a whirlwind of research, writing, lecturing, and advocating the wholesale change of the global energy regime. Progress is being made, and his efforts have been a large part of that; but he hopes someday to get back to writing his novel. He and his wife Anne make their home in Brookline, Massachusetts. They have two grown daughters, Thea and Joby.

NOTES

1. David Stipp, "The Pentagon's Weather Nightmare," *Fortune* Vol. 149 (February 9, 2004), p. 106.

2. Donella H. Meadows, Dennis L. Meadows, Jorgen Randers, and William W. Behrens III, *The Limits to Growth: A Report for the Club of Rome's Project on the Predicament of Mankind* (New York: Universe Books, 1972). The study was commissioned by the Club of Rome, a non-profit, non-governmental think tank seeking interdisciplinary solutions to global problems pertaining to the environment, demography, and development.

3. Ross Gelbspan and Dianne Dumanoski, "Racing to an Environmental Precipice: Fear of Future on Deteriorating Planet Sets Agenda for Rio de Janeiro Summit," *Boston Globe* (May 31, 1992), National/Foreign section, p. 1.

4. Dianne Dumanoski and Ross Gelbspan, "Summit Goal Has Daunting Barriers," *Boston Globe* (June 1, 1992), National/Foreign section, p. 1.

5. "An Interview with Ross Gelbspan," http://www.evworld.com/ archives/ interviews/gelbspan1.html (September 5, 1998) (accessed May 11, 2004).

6. Ross Gelbspan, "The Heat Is On," *Harper's Magazine* (December 1995), p. 36.

7. Ross Gelbspan, *The Heat Is On: The High Stakes Battle over Earth's Threatened Environment* (Reading, MA: Addison-Wesley Publishing Company, 1997), pp. 6–7.

8. Deforestation contributes to greenhouse gas emissions in two ways: Living trees absorb carbon dioxide through their leaves and sequester it. Cutting a tree down stops this process. Secondly, the burning of trees as firewood (more common in de-

veloping countries) releases the stored carbon dioxide into the atmosphere, where it accelerates the pace of warming.

9. Gelbspan, *The Heat Is On*, p. 58.

10. Quoted in Gelbspan, "Racing to an Environmental Precipice," p. 1.

11. Gelbspan, *The Heat Is On*, p. 165.

12. The G-77 refers to a group of seventy-seven developing countries that formed a coalition in June 1964 to promote collective economic interests and enhance a joint negotiating capacity. It is the largest third world coalition in the UN, and has increased to 135 countries, though it retains its original name due to its historic significance.

13. Stipp, "The Pentagon's Weather Nightmare," p. 100.

BIBLIOGRAPHY

Gelbspan's *The Heat Is On: The High Stakes Battle over Earth's Threatened Environment* (Reading, MA: Addison-Wesley Publishing Company, 1997) is the preeminent general-audience source for deciphering the global warming issue and the campaign of misinformation by the fossil fuel industry. The book was published in paperback in 1998 as *The Heat Is On: The Climate Crisis, the Cover-up, the Prescription* (Reading, MA: Perseus Books). He has also written *Break-Ins, Death Threats, and the FBI: The Covert War against the Central America Movement* (Cambridge, MA: South End Press, 1991); "The Heat Is On," *Harper's Magazine* (December 1995), pp. 31–37; "Bush's Global Warmers," *Nation* Vol. 272 (April 9, 2001), pp. 5–7; "Beyond Kyoto Lite," *American Prospect* Vol. 13 (February 25, 2002), pp. 26–27; and "Rx for an Ailing Planet," *Boston Globe* (April 22, 2003), op-ed page. Articles about Gelbspan and his work include Sarah McCoy, "The Battle over Earth's Climate," *Sierra* Vol. 82 (September 1, 1997), pp. 60–65; Tim O'Riordan, "Betrayers of a Global Truth," *Nature* Vol. 389 (October 16, 1997), pp. 685–687; and Joan Hamilton, "Truth Hugger," *Sierra* Vol. 86 (May/June 2001), p. 10. To read about the Pentagon report on global climate change, see David Stipp, "The Pentagon's Weather Nightmare," *Fortune* Vol. 149 (February 9, 2004), p. 106.

HELENA NORBERG-HODGE
(1946–)

> Ultimately we are talking about a spiritual awakening that comes from making a connection to others and to nature. This requires us to see the world within us, to experience more consciously the great interdependent web of life, of which we ourselves are among the strands.
>
> —Helena Norberg-Hodge

Helena Norberg-Hodge thought she understood the notion of progress—the gradual betterment of humankind, achieved through technology, development, and economic growth. Then in 1975, her work as a linguist took her to Ladakh, sometimes called "Little Tibet"—a very remote land in the northern Indian region of Kashmir. When she arrived she found a harsh and very arid landscape under the steep snowy peaks of the Himalayas. Ladakhis lived there with almost no money, raising yaks and other farm animals and living a very simple life almost completely cut off from the outside world. She was charmed and fascinated: Who were these people who had never had or even seen designer sunglasses, cars, radios, factory-made shoes, or cigarettes, let alone fast-food restaurants and Hollywood movies? One of their greatest daily pleasures, in fact, was a local green tea brewed with salt and yak butter. And yet, in such a barren land, with such limited resources, they had managed for hundreds of years to live harmoniously on the land and enjoyed remarkable happiness. Any adverse condition or situation, from the smallest social snub to a wolf killing one of their calves, was met with equanimity. "Chi choen?" they would say: What's the point of being upset? The deep contentment of the Ladakhis and the health of their land made them a compelling model for sustainability—a model that brought Norberg-Hodge back to Ladakh year after year.

As she continued to study the Ladakhi people, language, and culture, she also watched as Western influences such as technology, a money-based economy, and homogeneous cultural standards began to infiltrate the region. Broad and dramatic changes began transforming life there, as outside economic and social forces pushed Ladakhis away from their subsistence tradition and toward Western notions of prosperity. The foundations of Ladakhi society began to erode under this pressure, their incredible peace of mind to recede. Seeing this, Norberg-Hodge's understanding of concepts like "progress" and "standard of living" were turned upside down, no longer based on development and material wealth, but based on qualities of life that go much deeper: the consolations of living in sustainable balance with the natural world, strong community interconnections, and abundant cultural self-esteem, for example. Her role in Ladakh gradually changed from outside observer to concerned activist, and for the past twenty years, she has been helping the Ladakhis respond to such pressures—to create place-appropriate and renewable developments instead of unsustainable Western technologies, and to preserve ecological and cultural diversity.

Due to the political volatility of the Kashmir region where she works and to the fact that she has received death threats, Norberg-Hodge prefers not to give out extensive information on her personal backgroud. Helena Norberg-Hodge was born on January 10, 1946, to a Swedish-German mother and a Swedish-English father. She had relatives in Sweden, Germany, and England, and spent time in each country as she grew up. For most of her childhood she lived in Sweden, and she then attended college in Germany and England. She studied philosophy, psychology, and art history in college, but an interest in languages further drove her to travel. By the time she was 25, after years spent traveling through Italy, France, and Mexico, she could speak six languages. During the early 1970s she worked in Paris and London as a linguist, and in 1975, on the strength of her skills, she was invited by a German anthropological film team to go with them to Ladakh to make a documentary.

High up under the western Himalayas in the Kashmir region of northern India, Ladakh captures only four inches of rain a year and endures eight months of harsh winter, when temperatures can drop to as low as forty degrees below zero. As Norberg-Hodge discovered, however, it also possesses a subtle beauty. She describes the journey into Ladakh as follows: "Ahead of you, in the parched rainshadow of the Himalayas, the earth is bare. In every direction are mountains, a vast plateau of crests in warm and varied tones from rust to pale green. Above, snowy peaks reach toward a still, blue sky; below, sheer walls of wine red scree fall to stark lunar valleys."[1] Despite the starkness, the harsh climate, and the relative dearth of natural resources, Ladakhis had lived for over a thousand years in this area characterized by almost complete inaccessibility—and thus completely free from the trappings of Western civilization. And yet they have enjoyed a surprisingly high standard of living with no concept of poverty. During her first visit, Norberg-Hodge became immediately fascinated by the culture of Ladakh and by its language, which is one of the most complex and difficult languages in the world. The language had never been studied or documented, so Norberg-Hodge decided to study it herself. For the next two years, she trekked into the remote valleys throughout the region, learning to speak Ladakhi and collecting folk stories. Her language skills enabled her to become fluent in Ladakhi after only one year, making her the first European in recent times to gain a nuanced understanding of the culture and of the inner workings of Ladakhi society. She left Ladakh after two years to study linguistics under Noam Chomsky at Massachusetts Institute of Technology, and eventually did a thesis on the Ladakhi language.

In 1978, Norberg-Hodge returned to Ladakh with the man she would later marry, an English barrister named John Page. This time, she began looking more closely at the remarkable self-sufficiency of Ladakhis and studying the traditional knowledge that allowed them to achieve a culturally rich life in the midst of scant resources and no modern conveniences. Inventive agricultural practices allowed the barren dusty land to become the vibrant green oases of Ladakhi villages, where the people had evolved the skills to grow barley and vegetables at 12,000-foot elevation in a very short growing season. At slightly lower elevations, there were orchards of apricots and walnuts. Irrigation was achieved through channels that were built carefully hundreds of years before and that tap meltwater from glaciers. The channels sometimes wound through rock and steep mountainsides for several miles before branching out into intricate, well-maintained networks in each village; and all the villagers, even the young children, were skilled at regulating the flow of water in the channels, using a delicate sense of timing. Animals such as yaks, goats, donkeys, horses, and, in particular, the local hybrid cross between a cow and a yak, called a *dzo* provided labor, wool, milk for butter and cheese, meat (occasionally), and dung—which was carefully dried and was the Ladakhis' main fuel source.

Ladakhi houses were built using local materials, namely, stone and mud. The mud was dug up locally and formed into bricks, which were left to dry in the sun for several weeks. Clothing was made from woven wool, and warm and sturdy footwear was made from yak skin. As a whole, Ladakhi society operated under a well-functioning and sustainable system that knew no waste and ran smoothly without the exchange of money. The only necessities they lacked were salt, tea, and a few metals for cooking utensils and tools, and they traded amicably for these goods outside the community. Immersed in this culture, Norberg-Hodge began to comprehend fully some of the fundamental differences in land ethic and resource use between Western and Ladakhi cultures. She explained this dawning knowledge:

> I was also beginning to learn the meaning of the word *frugality*. In the West, *frugality* conjures up images of old aunts and padlocked pantries. But the frugality you find in Ladakh, which is fundamental to the people's prosperity, is something quite different. Using limited resources in a careful way has nothing to do with miserliness; this is frugality in its original meaning of 'fruitfulness': getting more out of little. Where we would consider something completely worn out, exhausted of all possible worth, and would throw it away, Ladakhis will find some further use for it. Nothing whatever is discarded. What cannot be eaten can be fed to the animals; what cannot be used as fuel can fertilize the land.[2]

But perhaps even more striking than the remarkable resourcefulness of the Ladakhi people were the deep contentment, generous cultural pride, and overall happiness they exuded. Norberg-Hodge noticed immediately that it was impossible to spend any amount of time in Ladakh without being won over by contagious laughter. They enjoyed a secure sense of their own worth, perhaps in part due to their awareness of being inextricably connected to one another and to the land that sustains them. Large extended families provided a sense of mutual interdependence and unconditional emotional support. Particularly touching to Norberg-Hodge was the abundant self-esteem evident in the children: Unlike in Western society, there was no such thing as "alienated youth." In fact, teenagers—both girls and boys—played important roles in family life, and were unashamed to be openly nurturing and affectionate toward babies and the elderly alike. Though they had no "formal" (i.e., Westernized) education, children were involved in all aspects of daily life, and learned a large variety of skills adapted to the traditional way of life.

As one of the last cultures on earth to come into contact with Western industrialization, Ladakh provided Norberg-Hodge with a unique chance to study the impact of the infiltration of modern culture on the lives of the people in the region. And as the only foreigner who could speak their language, Norberg-Hodge became a sort of ambassador from the Western world. Having witnessed the unique Ladakhi *joie de vivre*, self-sufficiency and cultural pride, she quickly grasped the threat posed by seductive Western culture, with its dazzling technologies and its emphasis on material acquisition and monetary (as opposed to spiritual or emotional) wealth. She took her role as ambassador seriously and began working to protect some of the ancient traditions and the overall gentle pace of life from the inevitable steamroller of development. At the same time, she avoided presuming that Ladakhis would want to retain their primitive living conditions once they became aware of some of the comforts and conveniences modern technology had to offer.

Negotiating a delicate balance, she began to work toward helping the Ladakhis understand that they could choose to adopt some of the more sustainable Western technologies without having to abandon their own culture.

With these thoughts in mind, she met with the Indian Planning Commission in 1978 to request permission to create a small pilot project for demonstrating the use of solar technologies—an elegant energy solution for a region that receives sunlight for more than 300 days a year. Ladakhis already had begun buying government-subsidized coal and wood at prices they could ill afford in order to enjoy a little heat in the winter—a situation that was not sustainable in the long run. But solar power exemplified a way in which Ladakhis could enjoy an entirely renewable resource. They could heat their houses in the bitter winter and also make possible the use of greenhouses and solar ovens. Through Norberg-Hodge's project, a system was discovered that worked particularly well for heating houses. Named the "Trombe wall" after its French designer, it involves a double layer of glass built into a south-facing wall and painted black to absorb the sun's rays—and it easily could be adapted to traditional architecture and available materials.

Through the solar technology project, Norberg-Hodge brought changes to Ladakh. But bigger changes, caused by much more powerful external forces, already had started happening in the region. Its location in India between Pakistan and Tibet makes it a highly strategic zone that's vulnerable to Pakistani and Chinese incursions. In 1974, India decided to establish a stronger foothold in Ladakh and began making efforts to develop the region for tourism. Development centered on Leh, a city of about 10,000 and the main population center in Ladakh (though the majority of Ladakhi people lived outside Leh in traditional villages). This included building roads, hotels, and restaurants and installing hydroelectric power stations, a court, banks, and radio and television stations. Subsidies on imports eventually were implemented, making imported wheat, rice, sugar, firewood, and other consumer products cheap compared to local resources. As traffic, tourism, and a consumer economy descended upon Ladakh, widespread and disturbing changes began to occur among the people who lived there.

Several of the changes were predictable and obvious. For example, the importing of foods and consumer goods brought into the region many more products than Ladakhis had needed previously. Waste, pollution, and litter began to proliferate. Norberg-Hodge watched as trash—such as gaudy plastic containers, rusting metal, broken glass, and flaking paint—became part of the village scenery, and as urban blights—such as monotonous housing colonies—ate into the green fields. Electricity poles and wires began to punctuate the dusty plateau, and billboards advertising powdered milk and cigarettes began to block the surrounding mountains from sight. The introduction of a money-based economy caused Ladakhis, who always had been very conscious of the limits of local resources, to think differently.

Money seemed to have no limits: Its acquisition and accumulation appeared to be independent of the limits, laws, and rhythms of the land. In addition, money changed the way people interacted. Instead of helping neighbors, bartering local goods, and trusting one another, they began to see relationships in terms of potential exploitation for monetary gain. Money also changed how they perceived themselves as a culture. Tourists, who began traveling through Ladakh, could spend hundreds of dollars in a single day, amounts of money Ladakhis wouldn't have spent in a whole year. Suddenly their fruitful frugality looked to them like poverty, and cultural pride began to erode. The consumer culture of the West can be alluring, especially when filtered through television and advertisements or hinted at by glamorous transient tourists—and Ladakhis, especially the children, began to feel that their way of life was inferior and backward. This was reinforced when Western education, based on a British curriculum, was brought to Ladakh. Children were taught in English and forced to learn British literature and other subjects totally disconnected from the living cultural context and local resources of Ladakh. Implicit in this version of education is the message that Ladakhi culture is wrong and "uncivilized." And after spending years gaining Eurocentric knowledge, the youth of Ladakh graduated without any location-specific skills, such as how to build a house out of mud or how to farm with *dzos*, and many ended up leaving the area for office jobs in the city.

Modernization brought less predictable changes as well. For one thing, the constant stream of imported goods and resources that began to flow in discouraged a close responsibility toward the limits of the natural environment; and the population of Ladakh began to grow beyond its normally stable level, causing the beginnings of urban sprawl. Also, perhaps surprisingly, the encroachment of "civilized" Western society led to a loss of individuality as Ladakhis became self-conscious and felt a pressure to conform to an idealized image. Finally, modernization, with its emphasis on wealth and power (and therefore competition), has exacerbated ethnic and religious rivalries. Conflicts have arisen among groups that had lived together in peace for centuries, and social breakdown has become evident. "Progress" has divorced the people from the earth, from their sense of community, and ultimately from themselves.

Seeing how Western ways were transforming Ladakh, Norberg-Hodge began an effort she called "counter-development," to promote and popularize a new, creative, and more humane definition of progress that revolves around the idea of place-appropriate technologies based on local resources and local knowledge. She embarked on a series of lecture tours and seminars in Europe and in North America, hoping to give Western audiences a glimpse of the social and ecological balance that had existed in Ladakh and thereby inspire them to visions of a more sustainable and harmonious way of life. By 1980, her work in Ladakh and the West coalesced into a small international organization called the Ladakh Project, which creates ecological and community-based solutions to counteract money-driven development. By running workshops and lectures and producing videos and publications, the Ladakh Project has been successfully encouraging discussion on development pressures and environmental destruction in Ladakh. These issues are also pertinent beyond Ladakh's borders, and Norberg-Hodge has used the lessons learned there at the local level to examine global trends in agriculture, energy, and health. Thus, as the Ladakh Project became a powerful resource within Ladakh, it also became an important educational tool for all developing countries.

One of Norberg-Hodge's greatest challenges lay in convincing Ladakhis not to succumb to the pressure to conform to Western images of luxury and sophistication as seen through the mass advertisements that began filtering into Ladakh. These glittery visions "are not accompanied by warnings about toxic wastes, the erosion of farmlands, acid rain, or global warming," she says. "People in the developing countries are also unaware that in response to such problems, many individuals in the industrialized parts of the world are seeking to regain a balance with the earth."[3] Modernization has not necessarily turned Westerners into happy people. In fact, faced with a society so obsessed with appearances and wealth, many Westerners are so busy commuting and working in offices that they have little leisure time, are forced to join health clubs to fight the effects of a sedentary life spent mostly indoors, and feel disconnected from a larger sense of community and the rhythms of the natural world. These are the side effects of modern development, says Norberg-Hodge, as are pollution, psychological stress, drug addiction, and homelessness.

In collaboration with a Ladakhi friend, Norberg-Hodge turned to theater to bring her message across. She wrote a play called *Ladakh: Look before You Leap*, which tells the story of a young Ladakhi who rejects the old culture, ridicules his parents for being backward, and starts smoking cigarettes, listening to loud Western music, and wearing designer jeans. When his grandfather falls sick, young Rigzin persuades his parents to call in a Western-trained doctor who had just come from America. To his surprise, the doctor informs Rigzin that he's actually lucky to have been born a Ladakhi. "In America," the doctor informs him, "the most modern people eat something they call stoneground wholemeal bread. It's just like our traditional bread, but there it's much more expensive than white bread. People over there are building their houses out of natural materials, just like ours. It's usually the poor who live in concrete houses. . . . So much that is modern in America is similar to traditional Ladakh."[4]

Norberg-Hodge's commitment to raising awareness of the cultural and environmental damage brought by development led some of Ladakh's leading thinkers to band together and search for a more sustainable approach to modernization. In 1983, Norberg-Hodge helped organize the group officially as the Ladakh Ecological Development Group (LEDeG), and it began working closely with the Ladakh Project to develop numerous small-scale renewable-energy technologies, such as hydraulic pumps for lifting irrigation and drinking water, solar water heaters, photovoltaic power for lighting, and small wind turbines for electricity production. The group also published the first book in the Ladakhi language on the subject of ecology. Renewable energy has become widely accepted in Ladakh, thanks largely to these efforts. For her work as director of the Ladakh Project, Norberg-Hodge shared the Right Livelihood Award (also known as the "alternative Nobel Prize")[5] with LEDeG in 1986. LEDeG, headquartered in Leh with its current staff of over 100 Ladakhis, has become the most influential non-governmental organization in the region. In 1993, when Ladakh was granted semi-autonomous status by the Indian government, three out of five members of the new governing body were former LEDeG directors.

Ladakh was one of the last subsistence economies to survive untouched into the mid-twentieth century, yet its reaction to the process of development has been anything but unique. Its transformation is only one example of changes that have taken place all around the world in response to development and globalization. To reflect the global relevance of the work she has done in Ladakh, Norberg-Hodge founded the International Society for Ecology and Culture (ISEC) in 1991, which absorbed the Ladakh Project. Though she continues her work in Ladakh, she also uses ISEC to protect biological and cultural diversity around the world—a more and more pressing need as globalization threatens to hasten the impoverishment of the poor and to ransack the environment. In 1993 ISEC organized the Women's Alliance of Ladakh (WAL) with the twin goals of strengthening local culture and agriculture and raising the status of rural women. Some of WAL's work includes throwing annual festivals that celebrate local skills like traditional spinning, weaving and dyeing, and the preparation of indigenous foods. Other programs include regular cleanup campaigns, encouraging community responsibility for the local environment. In 1998, WAL successfully banned the use of plastic bags. In an effort to counter the negative effects of Western culture, WAL sponsors "No TV" weeks.

Tourism has become a part of the Ladakhi economy, and the Ladakh Project recognized the need to impart to tourists a clear understanding of their impacts, as well as the impacts of economic globalization. To provide tourists with information on how to contribute to positive change, the Ladakh Project instituted the Tourist Education Program, which offers a daily showing of the video-version of Norberg-Hodge's book, *Ancient Futures: Learning From Ladakh*, followed by discussions of conventional development and the global economy. Further and more life-changing outreach is accomplished through the Farm Project, which welcomes volunteers from all over the industrialized world to live and work on small family farms in Ladakh during the growing season. The farm-stay experience not only allows participants to witness the strengths of a traditional culture, but also fosters self-respect amongst Ladakhis: When Westerners ask how to milk a cow or irrigate a field, Ladakhi children have an opportunity to show off their skills proudly. Similarly, any interest visitors show in traditional forms of entertainment, like storytelling and live music, allows villagers to view their culture in a more positive light.

Fighting the trend toward globalization may seem to be an impossibly daunting challenge. The industrial model pushed by multinational corporations and Western governments exerts a powerful psychological pull, and the concept of unity has tremendous appeal, symbolizing cooperation and international harmony. Since there is little publicity regarding the environmental destruction and community disintegration caused by economic unification, resistance to it can look impractical or utopian. But Norberg-Hodge's ideas for long-term solutions require a range of small-scale, regionally diverse initiatives adapted to local cultures and environments—ideas that in their simplicity become feasible and even attractive.

In introducing a reader or an audience to her arguments against globalization, Norberg-Hodge always starts with food and its systems of production and distribution. "There is almost nothing more important than the localization of food," she says. "Every human being has to eat three times a day, so to call a system efficient that separates people further and further from their source of food is nothing short of madness."[6] In typical supermarkets around the world, foods come from around the world through a process of global trade that relies on massive transportation subsidies. This makes possible a situation that allows people in Kenya to purchase butter from Holland at half the price of locally produced butter and people in England to purchase butter from New Zealand that is far cheaper than the local product. In Mongolia, which has produced its own milk products for thousands of years and still has twenty-five million milk-producing animals, shops mainly carry German butter. Norberg-Hodge questions how it could be possible that something that has traveled thousands of miles could compete in price with a local product. But her question is one that is not often asked. Long-distance transport of food raises little concern with the general population since, as a rule, the costs inherent in this system are hidden. For one thing, people largely are unaware that most of the money they spend on food actually goes to corporate middlemen, not the farmers who raised it. In a book that Norberg-Hodge co-wrote with Todd Merrifield and Steven Gorelick, called *Bringing the Food Economy Home: Local Alternatives to Global Agriculture*, the United States is cited as an example: Distributors, marketers, and input suppliers get 91 cents out of every food dollar spent in America, while farmers receive only 9 cents. But it isn't just the money exchanged at the checkout line that perpetuates this system—millions of tax dollars also are spent on subsidizing the transportation networks, researching industrial agricultural inputs like pesticides and biotechnology, and maintaining the energy infrastructure the system requires.

Other hidden costs of long-distance food transport include the damage accrued to the environment. The modern centralized system of agricultural trading forces the amassing of huge quantities of single crops that can be mass-produced cheaply enough to be sold on the world market for profit. So instead of producing diverse food crops to feed local communities, farmers must create immense monocultures that require copious doses of pesticides, herbicides, and fertilizers—not to mention the elimination of biodiversity, erosion of the soil, and poisoning of the surrounding waterways. Furthermore, the long-distance shipment of those crops to trading centers has a high environmental cost arising from the colossal pollution and greenhouse gas emissions inherent in fossil fuel combustion. In the United States, food shipments make up over 20 percent of all commodity transport, resulting in at least 120 million tons of carbon dioxide being released into the atmosphere each year. Norberg-Hodge scorns the argument that this type of global trade is necessary to maintain a certain standard of living, since the system actually encourages countries to import and export the same commodity simultaneously, as if the goal were trade itself rather than a rich and nourishing supply of food.

According to Norberg-Hodge's argument, increased local self-reliance in terms of food production would alleviate many of the environmental and even social problems that already have begun to arise from globalization. Shifting toward options that favor smaller, more local enterprises has benefits beyond environmental ones: the creation of local jobs and a more equitable distribution of resources. Furthermore, Norberg-Hodge does not consider the ultimate solution to be the elimination of trade, but simply to reduce unnecessary transport. Things that can be grown and produced locally should be, and should be cheaper than imports. In America, for example, products not available domestically, such as tea, cacao, coffee, and spices—which humans have been trading for centuries and which are dry, relatively light, and cheap to transport—should still be imported, but with appropriate tariffs so that the cost involved in shipping is incorporated. The new trend toward farmer's markets and community-supported agriculture, in which households can contract directly with local farmers for regular deliveries of fresh produce, is, in Norberg-Hodge's eyes, evidence that people are beginning to follow their dissatisfaction with the impersonal homogenized supermarket culture toward a new goal of connectedness. To encourage this trend, ISEC helped implement the enormously successful Food Links program at the Soil Association—the leading campaigning and certification organization for organic food in the United Kingdom. The program has helped establish over 450 farmer's markets across the United Kingdom. ISEC also has established community-supported agriculture schemes in both Europe and the United States, and, in addition to this type of grassroots organizing, has set up two major agriculture conferences and is a member of several farming coalitions.

Recently, certain events have supported further Norberg-Hodge's notion that not everyone is as pleased with globalization as large corporations and governments may wish. When the World Trade Organization attempted to have a meeting in Seattle, Washington, in December 1999, wild demonstrations broke out and a state of civil emergency was declared. The demonstrations represented a very broad opposition to corporate control and the spread of consumerism around the globe. Norberg-Hodge feels the demonstrations marked a turning point in modern industrial history:

> The demonstrations came about as a result of a build-up of awareness by millions of people worldwide that the root cause of escalating unemployment and environmental breakdown wasn't what they'd been led to believe. It wasn't dark-skinned immigrants taking their jobs away. It wasn't a question of right or left politics. It wasn't the result of some sort of evolutionary "progress," innate human greed, or even a propensity to overpopulate. It was a result of institutional structures that had been imposed by governments.[7]

Six months later, at a Washington, D.C., meeting of the International Monetary Fund and the World Bank (two organizations that have been active in advancing globalization), large crowds of demonstrators again protested the effects of globalization and the role of these organizations on the world stage. But though she found reason to be optimistic about the protests and their widespread media coverage, Norberg-Hodge also believes that protests are only a "last resort" type of activism. The most vital way to affect change, she says, is to become economically literate: to understand the meaning of economic policies and their impact and to get involved on a community level to strengthen local currencies, establish community land trusts, and institute a local food movement.

Another critical component of creating stronger local connections that goes beyond economics involves nurturing a sense of connection to the place one lives. An unfortunate result of the homogenization of culture and information is that regional ways of life look contemptible in comparison with globalized glamor. Children who can touch a button on the television and see African wildlife, hyped-up adventure tales, and colorfully packaged and promoted toys can then become easily bored with their immediate surroundings as soon as the television is off. Engendering a sense of place, says Norberg-Hodge, means encouraging children (and adults) to see the living environment around them: for example, learning some of the local, native plant life; reconnecting with their sources of food; and recognizing and celebrating the cycles of seasons. Instilling a sense of connection with neighbors and the larger community also can create a healthy sense of close social ties and interdependence.

Norberg-Hodge's experiences in Ladakh gave her a deep understanding of a sustainable community. When she had arrived in 1975, the concepts of "sustainability" and "ecology" were merely textbook terms to her, but over the years, as she experienced the Ladakhis' traditional culture and saw how connected they were to the land, she saw more clearly the meaning of those words. Such revelations caused her to rethink the Western lifestyle in which she had grown up. Still, she is not against progress; she just wants to redefine it in more meaningful terms. "I'm not advocating asceticism. I'm advocating wealth, richness, joy, culture," explains Norberg-Hodge. "The modern-day mantra 'we cannot go back' is deeply ingrained in our thinking. Of course we couldn't go back even if we wanted to, but our search for a future that works is inevitably bringing us back to certain fundamental patterns that are in greater harmony with nature—including our own human nature."[8]

NOTES

1. Helena Norberg-Hodge, *Ancient Futures: Learning from Ladakh* (San Francisco: Sierra Club Books, 1991), p. 9.

2. Ibid., p. 25.

3. Ibid., p. 158.

4. Ibid., pp. 170–171.

5. The Right Livelihood Award was established in 1980 by Jakob von Uexkull, a Swedish-German philatelist who sold his valuable postage stamps to create the original endowment. He felt that Nobel Prizes ignore much of the work and knowledge vital to the future of the planet and wanted to honor and support those who have made contributions toward environmental sustainability. Right Livelihood Awards are presented annually in the Swedish Parliament.

6. David Leser, "Global Warning," *The Good Weekend (Sydney Morning Herald Magazine)* (May 27, 2000).

7. Ibid.

8. Jay Walljasper, "Helena Norberg-Hodge," *Utne Reader* (November/ December 2001), p. 71.

BIBLIOGRAPHY

Norberg-Hodge's *Ancient Futures: Learning from Ladakh* (San Francisco: Sierra Club Books, 1991) tells the story of her years working in Ladakh, and gives an in-depth view of the changes to the Ladakhi culture and environment brought by rapid industrialization. She also has co-authored several books that explore more global environmental issues: Peter Goering, Helena Norberg-Hodge, and John Page, *From the Ground Up: Rethinking Industrial Agriculture* (London: Zed Books, 1993); Edward Goldsmith, Martin Khor, Helena Norberg-Hodge, and Vandana Shiva, *The Future of Progress* (Devon, England: Green Books, 1995); and Helena Norberg-Hodge, Todd Merrifield, and Steven Gorelick, *Bringing the Food Economy Home: Local Alternatives to Global Agriculture* (Bloomfield, CT: Kumarian Press, 2002). For articles on Norberg-Hodge and interviews with her see: Tracy Barnett, "Tibetan

Society Bridges the Future," *Progressive* Vol. 51 (April 1987), p. 15; Robert Gilman, "Ladakh: Helping a Culture Choose Its Future," *In Context Quarterly* No. 17 (Summer 1987), p. 18; Susan Moon, "View from the Mountain," *Mother Jones* Vol. 16 (January/February 1991), p. 16; Mark Mardon, "Cultural Revival," *Sierra* Vol. 77 (March/April 1992), pp. 23–24; Robert Gilman, "Strands in the Web," *In Context Quarterly* No. 31 (Spring 1992), p. 36; Andrew Kimball and Donald Davis, "Globalisation and Food Scarcity," *Ecologist* Vol. 29 (May/June 1999), pp. 185–186; David Leser, "Global Warning," *The Good Weekend (Sydney Morning Herald Magazine)* (May 27, 2000); Jay Walljasper, "Helena Norberg-Hodge," *Utne Reader* (November/December 2001), pp. 70–71. A good biographical sketch can be found in Mary Joy Breton's *Women Pioneers for the Environment* (Boston: Northeastern University Press, 1998).

DANA ALSTON
(1951–1999)

For us, the issues of the environment do not stand alone by themselves. They are not narrowly defined. Our vision of the environment is woven into an overall framework of social, racial, and economic justice. It is deeply rooted in our cultures and our spirituality. It is based in a long tradition and understanding and respect for the natural world. The environment, for us, is where we live, where we work and where we play.

—Dana Alston

People of color often have been disproportionately at risk of environmental pollution in their workplaces and neighborhoods. For example, there are more than 6,000 industrial plants in the United States that produce dangerous chemicals, and their waste disposal facilities are often sited in economically disadvantaged communities with high percentages of people of color. Also, minorities typically face the worst of workplace hazards such as pesticides and industrial chemicals. As Deeohn Ferris of the Lawyers' Committee for Civil Rights expressed it, "We're all in the same sinking boat, only people of color are closest to the hole."[1]

Meanwhile, the mainstream environmental movement always has been indisputably white in leadership, staff, and image; it has courted a reputation as an elitist pursuit made possible by social ease and comfort. African American, Native American, and Latino social justice advocates have been fighting for years against toxins and industrial pollution, and yet have not identified with or felt included by mainstream environmentalism. Not until environmental justice activists like Dana Alston began promoting the marriage of social justice with environmentalism did the environmental movement succeed in drawing people of every color out of the shadows and into a more cohesive political constituency. The environmental justice movement envisions a world where the traditional environmental agenda broadens enough to integrate and promote social justice issues and to recognize that the protection and preservation of the environment demands the protection and preservation of the people who make their home there.

Instead of operating on a foundation of financial security and professionalism like the large national environmental groups, this movement is built around the work of small, low-budget organizations and dedicated individuals like Alston. Her activist work—directing various foundations, fundraising, and giving memorable public speeches—defined the soul of the environmental justice movement and gave prominence to a new kind of environmental politics. During her relatively short life, Alston came to be known and loved for her irreverence for paternalistic systems of power, her temerity, and her impatience with token solutions.

Dana Ann Alston was born in Harlem on December 18, 1951, to Garlen and Betty Alston. During the mid-1960s she became active in the black student movement, concentrating particularly on apartheid and on racial issues surrounding the Vietnam War. When reports came back that blacks serving in Vietnam were incurring disproportionately high casualties in 1965–1966, angry civilians like Alston protested. Responding quickly to these dissenters, the Pentagon enforced a reduction in numbers of black soldiers on the front lines as the war progressed, which eventually lowered casualty rates until they corresponded evenly with the percentage of blacks serving in the army.[2]

While studying at Wheelock College in Boston, Alston served as president of the Black Student Organization and agitated fellow black students to demand more courses in African American studies and more black faculty members. She graduated with a B.S. in 1973, and began pursuing an interest in the link between public health and social and economic justice. This led to graduate work at the School of Public Health at Columbia University, where she completed a master's degree in occupational and environmental health in 1979.

Intent on improving the quality of life for low-income people of color, Alston took a series of jobs during and after graduate school with organizations directed toward those efforts. Her approach to raising the standard of living for minority communities involved her recognition that racial and social discrimination sometimes intersected with environmental problems in these areas. But her definition of environmental issues differed from those of the major national environmental organizations, which she found to be interested predominantly in leisure, recreation, wildlife, and wilderness preservation. She was more concerned with environmental problems that posed a direct threat to the health of minorities living in low-income areas—problems that were going ignored by the mainstream environmental movement.

A study published in 1975 by economist William Kruvant for the Energy Policy Project of the Ford Foundation had shown a close parallel between poverty, low occupational status, segregation, and air pollution. This relationship is not one of cause and effect. In other words, the economically disadvantaged people living in these areas were not the cause of the air pollution plaguing their homes. In fact, there is a positive correlation between income level and fuel consumption. As Kruvant pointed out, "[Poor and minority-group persons] are largely victims of middle- and upper-class pollution because they usually live closest to the sources of pollution—power plants, industrial installations, and in central cities where vehicle traffic is heaviest. Usually they have no choice. . . . Living in poverty areas is bad enough. High pollution makes it worse."[3] It was exactly this type of relationship between the exploitation of the natural environment and exploitation of people in poor communities that Alston strove to tease apart and reform.

For a while she worked for the Red Cross, where she confronted community contamination issues associated with toxic wastes and nuclear testing. Alston began asking questions about hazardous waste, namely, where does it go? She saw the pattern repeated time and time again—waste disposal sites are placed where people are poor, where people are powerless, and where people are not white. Robert Bullard, a sociologist and environmental justice activist with whom Alston eventually would collaborate, summarized the situation: "Whether they be landfills, incinerators or hazardous waste dumps, it is very clear that the siting of these facilities follows the path of least resistance. Historically, this has meant poor communities and communities of color—African Americans, Latinos, Asians, and Native Americans."[4] Nuclear testing presented similar problems, but was so buried by the apparatus of public relations that even the socially progressive anti–nuclear movement was not recognizing its inherent racial discrimination. Alston looked deeper into the issue and connected the dots: The Soviets tested bombs on an Asian republic, the British tested bombs on aboriginal land in Australia, the French tested their bombs in Algeria and in the South Pacific; and America tested its bombs on Shoshone land in the western United States. She considered these practices to represent colonialism and racism and lamented the fact that environmentalists and peace activists were doing nothing to stop it.

During the late 1970s and early 1980s, Alston worked at an organization called Rural America, where she helped farmworkers deal with pesticide issues. While much has been made of the dangers of pesticide residues on food, and while the environmental movement strives to keep these poisons from endangering wildlife, little attention had been devoted to the health risks faced by farmworkers and their families. In an article entitled "Beyond White Environmentalism," Hawley Truax and Gail Chehak wrote,

"According to the U.S. Department of Labor, our nation's three to four million farmworkers have the highest rate of exposure to toxic poisoning of any occupational group in the United States. The source of this poisoning is, of course, pesticides."[5] Eighty to 90 percent of the migrant workforce on farms is Chicano—with African Americans comprising the next largest group, followed by Haitians, Filipinos, Vietnamese, and other minorities. Farmworkers have no protection from pesticide hazards through any sort of federal law, and they usually are excluded from state laws such as workers' compensation. While there are national "re-entry" standards that require workers to wait a certain length of time after pesticides are sprayed before re-entering the fields, these standards are weak and no attempt is made to enforce them.

"Pesticides have only one purpose—to kill or harm living things," said Dr. Marion Moses on the subject. "Farmworkers and their families cannot avoid exposure to these toxic chemicals. Pesticides are on the crops they harvest, in the soil, in the air, in the water, even in the fog."[6] Moreover, migrant farmworkers typically receive no education or training in safety precautions. Often those who are assigned to spray the pesticides speak and read only Spanish, which renders the English safety instructions on the containers worthless. There also exists an unspoken fear among workers of creating a fuss and jeopardizing their job. They come to accept the rashes, headaches, dizziness, and nausea as part of their job, and very rarely, if ever, seek medical attention.

While working at Rural America on these issues, Alston met Larry Kressley, who was working in the same office on a community development project. Kressley left in 1981 to become a program officer at the Public Welfare Foundation, but a decade later he would still remember Alston's leadership qualities and dedication, and would recruit her to work for his office. In the meantime, Alston also left Rural America and went to work for the National Black United Fund in New York City, eventually becoming the group's president. Working at the National Black United Fund gave Alston the opportunity to fulfill one of her big goals: to increase funding for organizations committed to grassroots environmental justice. To this end, she supervised a lawsuit that resulted in making it possible, for the first time, for workers to donate to black-led charitable funds. She also worked on development and grant-making with the National Committee for Responsive Philanthropy—a network of progressive foundations—and for TransAfrica Forum, a non-profit dedicated to educating the general public about the economic, political, and moral ramifications of U.S. foreign policy in Africa, the Caribbean, and Latin America.

By the end of the 1980s, the divergent grassroots efforts that made up the environmental justice movement began to coalesce and receive public attention. In 1987, Benjamin Chavis of the Commission for Racial Justice coined the phrase "environmental racism" when presenting a report at the National Press Club in Washington, D.C. The press greeted the phrase with skepticism and even anger. But it wasn't until the expression made it into the newspapers that the environmental justice movement started getting some of the attention it desperately deserved. The following year, several studies indicated that while the black middle class had begun to prosper economically and workplaces had become more integrated since the 1970s, other parameters reflecting quality of life for blacks were still showing little or no improvement. In 1988, black unemployment was more than double that of whites, and blacks' median income hovered around 58 percent of whites' median income. Added to this daunting poverty were high illiteracy rates and housing scarcities, all of which contributed to the segregation of blacks and other minorities to low-income housing—often concentrated in inner-city neighborhoods where risks from industrial pollution are greatly elevated.

Additionally, the older, substandard housing in these areas incurred higher risks of exposure to lead and asbestos. Primarily a brain poison, lead can build up slowly in the bloodstream, leading to damage to the nervous system and causing developmental disorders and even impaired and antisocial behaviors. Lead can be harmful even in small amounts. The primary sources of exposure are chipped and flaking housepaint, auto exhaust, industrial pollution, and contact with soil that has been contaminated with paint chips, lead-based insecticide, or highway pollution. It had long been known that black urban children had disproportionately high blood levels of lead. But lamentably, not until 1984, when studies confirmed that suburban children were also at risk of lead poisoning, did the EPA begin taking action to force oil refiners to reduce the lead content of gasoline.[7] Even that regulatory action was not enough to alleviate the problem in black communities. A benchmark study released in 1988 by the Agency for Toxic Substances and Disease Registry reported that 44 percent of urban black children are at risk from lead poisoning—four times the rate of white children.[8] Two years later, another report announced that over 700,000 inner-city children were suffering from lead poisoning: Fifty percent of them were black.[9]

The early 1990s were busy years for Alston. In February 1990, she joined the staff of the Panos Institute, an independent policy studies organization that works to help journalists cover sustainable development issues that are often overlooked or misunderstood—particularly those that traverse national boundaries. For Panos she developed the Environment, Community Development, and Race Project, which seeks to increase public understanding of the environmental threats faced by people of color by promoting coverage of these issues in the media. As her first task, she solicited and edited a collection of articles and interviews about the environmental justice movement; the collection was published in 1990 as *We Speak for Ourselves: Social Justice, Race, and Environment.* In her introduction to the collection, she described the importance of reconceptualizing the definition of environmentalism to make it more inclusive: "Communities of color have often taken a more holistic approach than the mainstream environmental movement, integrating 'environmental' concerns into a broader agenda that emphasizes social, racial and economic justice." She concludes the introduction by quoting Charles Lee, author of the groundbreaking study released in 1987 called *Toxic Wastes and Race in the United States*. "Charles Lee . . . puts it bluntly: 'Can there truly be a healthy environment without justice?' " she wrote. "The answer to this question will undoubtedly become one of the critical issues of the 1990s."[10]

Featured in the collection were a sample of stories about those struggling for environmental justice, including inner-city youth in Brooklyn who were rallying to rid their neighborhoods of hazardous materials; the history of environmental destruction and human rights abuses inflicted on Shoshone Indians in Nevada; the collective actions of the SouthWest Organizing Project, a multi-ethnic organization based in New Mexico that is devoted to racial and gender equality and to social justice; and the attempts of waste management companies in the United States to dump hazardous wastes in politically and economically less-powerful nations overseas, such as South Africa, Haiti, and the Congo.

Throughout her career, Alston's own activism was just as wide-ranging as the collection of stories in *We Speak for Ourselves*. Her work supported a diverse venue of grassroots environmental justice groups and transcended geographical boundaries. Both rural and urban struggles commanded her attention, from the slums in New York City to the Indian reservations in the Southwest, to segregated black communities in the South. Her energies also were focused beyond the borders of the United States: She had remained active in the solidarity movement to promote racial equality in South Africa and actively campaigned for the movement that eventually helped dismantle apartheid. When Nelson Mandela was released early in 1990, after being imprisoned for twenty-seven years for his political affiliations, Alston was part of the working group that organized his historic visit to the United States a few months later.

It was proving up to be a momentous time for the environmental justice movement in the states as well. In January 1990, a startling letter was sent to the chief executive officers of each of the mainstream national environmental organizations in the so-called Group of Ten (these were the National Wildlife Federation, Friends of the Earth, the Wilderness Society, the National Audubon Society, the Sierra Club, the Environmental Policy Institute, the Natural Resources Defense Council, the Environmental Defense Fund, the National Parks and Conservation Association, and the Izaak Walton League) by the Gulf Coast Tenant Leadership Development Project. Led and staffed mainly by people of color, the Gulf Coast Tenant group organizes communities in Louisiana's "Cancer Alley," a twenty-eight-mile corridor of hazardous industries between Baton Rouge and New Orleans that is inhabited largely by the direct descendants of former slaves. Their letter accused the big organizations of racist hiring practices. Signed by three prominent civil rights leaders and several environmental activists, it was a stinging indictment. It requested that "every environmental organization, yours included, cease operations in communities of color within sixty days, until you have hired leaders from those communities to the extent that they make up 35–40 percent of your entire staff."

Two months later, a second letter, from the SouthWest Organizing Project (a predominantly Native American and Latino group) delivered a second blow to the Group of Ten. The second letter was similar in tone to the Gulf Coast Tenant letter and was signed by more than 100 activists and representatives of community-based groups. Sociology professor Dorceta Taylor described the underlying sense of exasperation that had prompted these letters: "It is crystal clear that diversity in nature is superior to homogeneity. Why isn't it obvious to people advocating this position that such diversity is also desirable in human communities? Why isn't it understood that diversity is necessary for this movement to grow and progress?"[11]

The effect of the letters has been a lasting one. "These documents have generated a great deal of soul-searching in the environmental movement. Long-accustomed to seeing themselves as the voice of a more enlightened morality, most environmentalists are simply not accustomed to being the target of the kind of confrontational rhetoric usually hurled at Japanese whaling fleets,"[12] wrote Paul Ruffins, a senior editor of Washington, D.C.'s Black Networking News. Sierra Club Director Michael Fischer called them a "wakeup call," while Catherine Verhoff at the Natural Resources Defense Council responded by warning her mainstream environmental colleagues that ignoring this message incurred the risk of becoming obsolete. In the aftermath of the letters, most national environmental organizations mounted diversity campaigns, with varying degrees of success.

While the January and March letters were galvanizing the mainstream environmental movement, the environmental justice movement was gearing up for a major affirmation of their growing strength and reach. A People of Color Environmental Leadership Summit was being organized, and Alston was invited to be a part of its planning committee. Its official goal was to reshape and redefine the environmental movement:

> The Leadership Summit is not an independent event, but a significant and pivotal stop in the crucial process whereby people of color are organizing themselves and their communities for self-determination and self-empowerment around the central issue of environmental justice. It is living testimony that no longer shall we allow others to define our people's future. It is our intention to build an effective multi-racial environmental movement with the capacity to transform the political landscape of the nation around these issues. The very survival of all communities is at stake.[13]

On October 25, 1991, along with other environmental justice leaders—including sociologist Dr. Robert Bullard, Patrick Bryant of the Gulf Coast Tenant Leadership Development Project, Benjamin Chavis, Charles Lee, Donna Chavis, and Richard Moore of the SouthWest Organizing Project—Alston convened the First National People of Color Environmental Leadership Summit. Held in Washington, D.C., over the course of four days, the event attracted hundreds of representatives of environmental justice organizations led by people of color. On the first day, 300 delegates from all over the United States—including Latino Americans from the Southwest, African Americans from "Cancer Alley" in Louisiana, and Asian Pacific Americans—met to set an agenda. None of the delegates were white. On the second day, they were joined by 250 representatives of sister organizations like civil rights, community development, church, and public health groups.

Representatives of mainstream environmental organizations were also invited to attend the last half of the summit. Michael Fischer, executive director of the Sierra Club, and John Adams, executive director of the Natural Resources Defense Council (NRDC), both gave speeches. Alston, known for being a thoughtful public speaker, was chosen to follow their speeches with a keynote address welcoming the mainstream organizations and explaining the principles of the environmental justice movement to them. Michael Fischer went first, and openly admitted that the Sierra Club had been "conspicuously missing from the battles for environmental justice. We regret that fact sincerely. We are here to reach across the table and build the bridge of partnership with all of you. We are not the enemy," he insisted. "We know it is in our enlightened self-interest to be fully involved in seeking environmental justice or we risk becoming irrelevant."

Next, John Adams spoke. He expressed his conviction that the summit marked a major turning point for the environmental movement. "The NRDC has come to realize that the issues of racism, poverty, and environmental degradation are intertwined and inseparable. The environmental movement cannot solve one without solving or attempting to solve the others," he said. But his attempt to foster a sense of unity occasionally fell conspicuously short. "You can't win this battle alone,"[14] he continued, evidently not feeling comfortable enough to use the word "we."

It was then Alston's turn to take the podium. Assigned the task of responding to the speeches of Fischer and Adams, she faced a tricky diplomatic challenge: to accept their offers of help and partnership while also addressing criticisms the environmental justice movement had long harbored toward mainstream environmental organizations. As she began to speak, she told the summit audience that she had decided not to respond to the platitudes offered by the major environmental groups. "Our movement is not a reaction to the environmental movement," she said. "We have come here to define for ourselves the issues of the ecology and the environment. We have to speak these truths that we know from our own lives to those participants and observers whom we have invited here to join us. We have come for you to hear our understandings from our mouths directly, so there will be no confusion and no misunderstandings." The audience, hungry for these assertions of independence and self-definition, responded loudly as Alston continued. She spoke of a sense that the environmental movement was floundering and casting about for a new and more comprehensive vision. The environment had become one of the chief concerns of the general public, she asserted, and yet environmental groups seemed to be having little success in tapping into that concern and making meaningful changes in people's lives. "The environment affords us the platform to address the critical issues of our time: questions of militarism and defense policy; religious freedom; cultural survival; energy and sustainable development; the future of our cities; transportation; housing; land and sovereignty rights; self-determination; and employment," she said.

Eventually she turned to the mainstream environmental leaders and acknowledged their offers of support. "We are interested in making a partnership and a relationship," she said. But "what we seek is a relationship based on equity, mutual respect, mutual interest, and justice. We refuse narrow definitions. . . . We refuse a paternalistic relationship. We are not interested in a parent-child relationship." Her words made clear the fact that the dynamic between the environmental justice movement and established environmental organizations was sometimes an uneasy one. She made reference to the fact that the actions and policies of these organizations have a drastic impact on the life and health of the communities she advocates for—and that, in fact, she and her colleagues had sometimes engaged in direct conflict with some of the boards of directors of certain environmental groups. As an example, she mentioned the fact that Waste Management, Inc.—a company known for dumping poisonous materials in communities of people of color and for being one of the chief perpetrators of environmental injustice in the nation—had representatives on the boards of two Group of Ten organizations. "We know that company well," she said, wryly. "What we don't know is why they're on the boards of the National Wildlife Federation and the National Audubon Society."

She concluded her speech by exhorting the mainstream environmental leaders to raise these uncomfortable issues with the rest of the movement. "We will continue our challenge from the outside," she said. "You must confront the situation within yourselves and your colleagues." Alston's moving and passionate speech resounded throughout the summit, astutely capturing the sense and purpose of the environmental justice movement. It continues to be quoted widely.

Before the summit adjourned, the delegates formulated and ratified seventeen Principles of Environmental Justice. The first one asserts the fact that environmental justice is not just about hazardous wastes and urban landscapes, but is deeply intertwined with the same ethos that sustains environmentalists: "Environmental justice affirms the sacredness of Mother Earth, ecological unity and the interdependence of all species, and the right to be free from ecological destruction." Other principles include affirming the right of all workers to a safe and healthy work environment, demanding equality in decision-making processes, and opposing the destructive operations of multinational corporations. Additionally, they demand the cessation of the production of toxins, call for universal protection from nuclear testing, and demand that public policy be based on mutual respect and justice.

The questions raised at the summit changed the face of the environmental movement forever, and gave the environmental justice movement a sense of bedrock beneath their feet. One of the delegates said of the summit, "We were able to come together with a unity that I have not seen in all my years of activism." Conference Coordinator Charles Lee said simply, "It was an indelible experience." The summit inspired several more regional environmental justice meetings around the country, including one in New Orleans in December 1992, that brought together over 2,000 people. Immediately after the summit, then-Senator Al Gore created the Environmental Justice Act, and when Bill Clinton took office as president in 1993, Dr. Robert Bullard was asked to serve on the Clinton transition team—an unprecedented gesture to the environmental justice grassroots community. That the summit had an immediate and lasting impact on the environmental movement was hard to deny. As journalist Mark Dowie put it, "If there are temporal turning points in the history of American environmentalism, the period between October 25 to October 27, 1991, is certainly one of them."[15]

Alston's forward momentum after the event did not taper off. In 1992, she led a delegation of environmental justice leaders to the Earth Summit and Global Forum meetings in Rio de Janeiro, where she called on nations to fight racist and exploitative economic systems that endanger public health. She carefully made the point that the environmental justice movement must be an international struggle. The impoverished minority communities around the world that receive risky technologies, non-sustainable development projects, and banned pesticides from developed countries must educate, organize, and mobilize resistance to these practices. Her vision of a multiethnic, multiracial, multicultural commitment to environmentalism was a powerful incentive. As one supporter said of her leadership in Rio de Janeiro, "Dana was magnificent." Upon return, she was rewarded a well-deserved sabbatical through the Charles Bannerman Memorial Fellowship, a grant that recognizes the work of social justice activists. She took the opportunity to visit South Africa and rest and reflect on her work.

Later that year, she was approached by Larry Kressley, her former colleague at Rural America. He had risen to the executive directorship of the Public Welfare Foundation (PWF) and had a vacancy for a senior program officer for the PWF's environmental program. He wanted Alston to fill it. He later recounted her reaction: " 'Well, you know Larry,' " she said, " 'I'm an activist and I always will be, and I'd want to continue that activism if I was at the Foundation.' And I said to her, 'Well, that's the reason I want you to come and be with us. I don't want to change you; I want to change what we do on the environment.' " Alston agreed to come, and ran the PWF's Environmental Initiative—a premier grant-making program that supports environmental justice programs—until her death. While working there, she also encouraged other philanthropic foundations to support the environmental justice movement. In 1994, she contributed to an influential open letter to funders explaining the environmental justice cause and describing some of its leaders and the work they were doing.

On August 7, 1999, Alston died in San Francisco, California, while being treated for kidney disease in the aftermath of a stroke she had suffered two years prior. She left a young son, Khalil. Mourning friends and family honored her memory by establishing the Dana A. Alston Fund for the Bannerman Memorial Fellowship—a sabbatical fund that recognizes the fact that grassroots social activism entails long hours with low pay and that supports the need to escape and rejuvenate once in awhile. Alston's constant outpouring of energy and hard work certainly exemplified the need for such chances for renewal.

Alston was a giant among environmental justice leaders. Part of her legacy includes the success she had in articulating the need to reshape environmentalism—to define it in ways that reflect the connections among the various movements for change and in ways that include the natural landscape as well as the human one. The work she accomplished during three decades of activism continues in her wake. After two years of planning and several false starts, the Second National People of Color Environmental Leadership Summit was convened in October 2002. The four-day meeting drew over 1,200 delegates from grassroots and community-based environmental justice organizations. In an awards ceremony dedicated to Alston, twelve women were honored for their outstanding efforts in environmental justice activism. One of these "sheroes," Hazel Johnson, received a special "Dana Alston award" for her integrity, resilience against opposition, dedicated leadership, and passion to serve. The evening was a remarkable and fitting tribute to Alston, and a way for her influence and energy to live on.

NOTES

1. Quoted in Mark Dowie, *Losing Ground: American Environmentalism at the Close of the Twentieth Century* (Cambridge, MA: The MIT Press, 1995), p. 125.

2. Gerald David Jaynes and Robin M. Williams, Jr., eds., *A Common Destiny: Blacks and American Society* (Washington, DC: National Academy Press, 1989), p. 72–73.

3. Quoted in Julian McCaull, "Discriminatory Air Pollution: If Poor, Don't Breathe," *Environment* Vol. 18 (March 1976), p. 31.

4. Robert Bullard, "Dumping in Black and White," p. 6 in Dana Alston, ed., *We Speak for Ourselves: Social Justice, Race, and Environment* (Washington, DC: Panos Institute, 1990).

5. Hawley Truax and Gail E. Chehak, "Beyond White Environmentalism: Minorities and the Environment," *Environmental Action* Vol. 21 (January/February 1990), p. 20.

6. Quoted in Nicole Brown, "Pesticides and Farmworkers," p. 28 in Dana Alston, ed., *We Speak for Ourselves: Social Justice, Race, and Environment* (Washington, DC: Panos Institute, 1990).

7. Dowie, *Losing Ground*, p. 155.

8. Truax and Chehak, "Beyond White Environmentalism," p. 21.

9. Nicole Brown, "Heavy Facts about Lead," p. 27 in Dana Alston, ed., *We Speak for Ourselves: Social Justice, Race, and Environment* (Washington, DC: Panos Institute, 1990).

10. Dana Alston, ed., *We Speak for Ourselves: Social Justice, Race, and Environment* (Washington, DC: Panos Institute, 1990), p. 3.

11. Dorceta Taylor, *Proceedings of the Michigan Conference on Race and the Incidence of Environmental Hazards* (July 1990).

12. Paul Ruffins, "Mixing a Few More Colors into the Green," *In Context Quarterly* Vol. 25 (Late Spring 1990), p. 33.

13. Charles Lee, ed., *The First National People of Color Environmental Leadership Summit: Proceedings* (New York: United Church of Christ Commission for Racial Justice, 1992), preface.

14. Hawley Truax, "Environmental Justice for All," *Environmental Action* Vol. 23 (November/December 1991), p. 6.

15. Dowie, *Losing Ground*, p. 151.

BIBLIOGRAPHY

Much of the work in the environmental justice movement goes unnoticed by the larger society, and there is relatively little published information on Alston's life. There is a short but good biographical sketch of Alston in Anne Becher, ed., *American Environmental Leaders: From Colonial Times to the Present* (Santa Barbara, CA: ABC-Clio, 2000) Vol. 1, pp. 20–22. Also see Robert Gottlieb, *Forcing the Spring: The Transformation of the American Environmental Movement* (Covelo, CA: Island Press, 1993); and Mark Dowie, *Losing Ground: American Environmentalism at the Close of the Twentieth Century* (Cambridge, MA: The MIT Press, 1995) for information on Alston, particularly her role at the First National People of Color Environmental Leadership Summit. Her publication for the Panos Institute is Dana Alston, ed., *We Speak for Ourselves: Social Justice, Race, and Environment* (Washington, DC: Panos Institute, 1990). Her famous speech is printed in Charles Lee, ed., *The First National People of Color Environmental Leadership Summit: Proceedings* (New York: United Church of Christ Commission for Racial Justice, 1992), and is currently available online at http://www.ejrc.cau.edu/dana_speech.htm. For background information on the environmental justice movement and the summit, see Julian McCaull, "Discriminatory Air Pollution: If Poor, Don't Breathe," *Environment* Vol. 18 (March 1976), pp. 26–31; Ronald B. Taylor, "Do Environmentalists Care about the Poor?" *U.S. News and World Report* Vol. 96 (April 2, 1982), pp. 51–52; Robert Gottlieb and Helen Ingram, "The New Environmentalists," *Progressive* Vol. 52 (August 14, 1988), pp.14–15; Dick Russell, "Environmental

Racism: Minority Communities and Their Battles against Toxics," *Amicus Journal* Vol. 11 (Spring 1989), pp. 22–32; Hawley Truax and Gail E. Chehak, "Beyond White Environmentalism: Minorities and the Environment," *Environmental Action* Vol. 21 (January/February 1990), pp. 19–23; Paul Ruffins, "Mixing a Few More Colors into the Green," *In Context Quarterly* Vol. 25 (Late Spring 1990), p. 33+; Karl Grossman, "Environmental Racism," *Crisis* (April 1991), pp. 14–17, 31–32; Julia Flynn Siler, "Environmental Racism? It Could Be a Messy Fight," *Business Week* (May 20, 1991), p. 116; Hawley Truax, "Environmental Justice for All," *Environmental Action* Vol. 23 (November/December 1991), pp. 5–7; Robert Bullard, ed., *Confronting Environmental Racism: Voices from the Grassroots* (Boston, MA: South End Press, 1993); Robert Bullard, J. Eugene Grigsby III, and Charles Lee, eds., *Residential Apartheid: An American Legacy* (Los Angeles: Center for Afro-American Studies Publications, 1994). One of the first in-depth studies of environmental racism is Charles Lee, *Toxic Wastes and Race in the United States: A National Report on the Racial and Socioeconomic Characteristics of Communities Surrounding Hazardous Waste Sites* (New York: United Church of Christ, 1987). For a study of black social, political, and economic trends, see Gerald David Jaynes and Robin M. Williams, Jr., eds., *A Common Destiny: Blacks and American Society* (Washington, DC: National Academy Press, 1989).

VANDANA SHIVA
(1952–)

I think there's nothing as exhilarating as protecting that which you find precious. To me, fighting for people's rights, protecting nature, protecting diversity, is a constant reminder of that which is so valuable in life. . . . But frankly, I also absolutely get thrills from taking on these big guys and recognizing how, behind all their power, they are so empty. . . . Each of these balloons does deflate. I've seen a lot of balloons get deflated in my life.

—Vandana Shiva

Aranyani, Goddess of the Forest, has been worshipped in India for centuries as a representation of the highest expression of life and fertility. In Indian culture, the primary measure of enlightenment lies in humankind's capacity to consciously incorporate her rhythms into the everyday practices of tribal and peasant society. Ecologist, author, physicist, and Indian environmental activist Vandana Shiva describes the importance of forests as a foundation of Indian culture: "The diversity, harmony and self-sustaining nature of the forest formed the organizational principles guiding Indian civilization; the *aranya samskriti* (roughly translatable as 'the culture of the forest' or 'forest culture') was not a condition of primitiveness, but one of conscious choice."[1] Locating the source of life in diversity and creativity as embodied by a female forest deity illustrates an intimate link between women and the environment—

a link that Vandana Shiva has been exploring and nurturing for decades, earning her the title of "ecofeminist." She believes that the special female relationship with the environment can be a rich foundation of ecological knowledge. Though she is sometimes described as a feminist militant, Shiva's compassion encompasses the whole human race—as she says it, her heart is with the people. It just so happens that her answer to the environmental degradation, social injustice, and cultural erosion she sees in the world lies in the empowerment of women as instinctive caretakers of the earth and in the simultaneous preservation of biodiversity as the earth's source of fertility and regeneration. Her work—which involves agricultural development, forest preservation, globalization, water rights, biotechnology, and seed conservation—features women's rights and ecology at the heart of every solution and has won her an affectionate international reputation as an environmental hero. "I want Vandana Shiva to be president of the world,"[2] said environmental crusader and founder of the Earth Island Institute, **David Brower.**

Vandana Shiva was born on November 5, 1952, in the town of Dehra Dun in northern India. Her father worked as a forester, and she spent much of her childhood traveling with her parents and sister by foot, horse, or mule through the forests of the Himalayan foothills. With her mother composing and singing songs about the wilderness they saw, they hiked from bungalow to bungalow, carrying all they needed on their backs and often eating only dal and potatoes. Those experiences became a source of very fond memories and profound satisfaction for Shiva, and out of them she grew to love and appreciate the Himalayan forests and mountains.

Her parents had a profound and positive influence on her life. Her mother, a pioneering feminist, had been involved in the Indian independence movement against British colonialism, and believed that only women could bring peace to the world since men's egos and greed led to violence and tension. She had been one of the few women from her community to become highly educated, and had enjoyed a prestigious governmental career as an inspector of schools before deciding to become a farmer instead. She made sure to raise her two daughters without any of the gender discrimination inherent in their native culture, and Vandana grew up assured that she never needed to hold herself back from any aspiration just because she is a woman. Her mother also shared her dedication to Gandhian concerns for India's social and economic welfare with her daughters. For example, for her sixth birthday, Vandana wanted a new nylon frock like she had seen other girls wearing. Her mother left the decision up to her, saying, "I'll buy you a nylon dress. But you know, if you buy nylon, some industrialist will get another Mercedes. But if you buy *khadi* [Indian homespun cotton], some woman's kitchen fire will get lit." Worried about depriving a poor family of their livelihood, Shiva changed her mind about the nylon dress—and remembers her mother's lesson to this day.

Intellectually precocious, Shiva began teaching herself higher mathematics and physics so that she could get into college, since these subjects were not taught at the convent where she went to school. Her ultimate goal was a real, comprehensive understanding of nature, and she believed she could reach that goal through physics, the foundation of all sciences. She immersed herself in the subject, graduating from Punjab University in 1973 with a master's degree in nuclear physics. While working on the research for her degree, she sometimes experienced pangs of doubt about nuclear science and the radiation hazards it poses to humans. In her training she had been taught the foundations of nuclear physics, everything from energy transformation to how to create chain reactions in nuclear material, but she had been taught nothing about the effects of radiation on living systems. Only through her sister, who had become a doctor, did she learn about the dangers to herself and others inherent in her line of work. When senior physicists told her not to worry about such safety issues, she only became more determined to come to an understanding of the ethics behind the situation.

Continuing to grope with these questions, Shiva went to the University of Guelph in Ontario, Canada, and enrolled in a Foundations of Physics program, where issues like these were being explored. In 1976, from the University of Guelph, she received a second master's degree, this one in the philosophy of science. On completing her degree, she sought an escape from academia and felt an urge to return to a beloved spot to which her father used to take her in the Himalayan foothills: a sunny oak forest that embraced a beautiful stream where she used to swim. Returning home with quiet anticipation, she hastened to the place only to find that the oaks had been destroyed by logging and that the stream had become a trickle. Locals told her that entrepreneurs with World Bank funding had cut down the oak forest in order to plant apple orchards—a venture that never even turned a profit.

The Himalayan foothills have a long history of commercial logging, dating back before the area was incorporated into British India in the early nineteenth century. But during British colonization, road building and railroad construction increased logging in the area, incurring severe environmental damage. After India's independence from Britain in 1947, deforestation accelerated in the region, spurred by government policies that encouraged rampant extraction of natural resources. Local villages bore the brunt of the forest destruction and were rapidly losing the important, life-giving resources that made them dependent on the forests: fuel, fodder, and medicinal supplies. Logging practices also destroyed their springs, meaning that village women had to walk farther and farther to find water.

After finding her own favorite forest logged into oblivion, Shiva soon connected with a remarkable movement of peasant women who were taking action to stop deforestation in the Himalayan foothills. Called "Chipko women," they had begun organizing in earnest in 1974 to protest the planned commercial harvest of 2,500 trees in the forests near the village of

Reni in Uttar Pradesh. When the loggers began trying to cut down the trees, the women of the village, led by a 50-year-old matriarch, forced them to turn back. Their basic strategy—hugging trees that lay in the path of chain saws and bulldozers and using their bodies as barricades—led to the name Chipko, which means "to embrace." Through word of mouth, the strategy and message spread from village to village and began involving more and more women. Shiva volunteered to help the Chipko women through a loosely structured network called "Friends of Chipko." She found she could make the most effective contribution to the movement by calling on her scientific credentials. Whenever scientific reports criticizing the movement were released, Shiva and her colleagues banded together and issued scientifically based "counter-reports" in favor of the Chipko cause. Doing her part to broadcast the message, she also helped organize speaking tours around the country for the movement's leading voices and rallied students to join the movement. These tree-embracing women were protesting more than just environmental degradation and a longer walk for water: logging posed a direct threat to the lives of local villagers. In 1978, a few years after Shiva joined their cause, the potential threat materialized when an entire logged mountainside fell into the Ganges River, creating a four-mile-long lake that burst and created a massive flood in the Ganges basin.

Hundreds of thousands of Chipko women participated in these nonviolent but powerful protests, which eventually radiated throughout the northern regions of India, and continued through the 1970s until a logging ban in the Himalayas was enacted in 1981. Shiva's interaction with the women in the movement formed the first step in a chain reaction that would propel her into environmental activism. "It was their perceptions and their beliefs that were the really rich foundations of my knowledge of ecology. They offered me a new sensibility about relationships. . . . All my theory-building has come out of this nature-centered and woman-centered action,"[3] she maintains.

Though India's environmental impoverishment had started compelling more and more of her attention, Shiva had not yet finished her studies in physics. She went back to Canada to re-immerse herself in the subject, this time at the University of Western Ontario, though she returned to the Chipko movement every summer to write counter-reports and document the devastation from deforestation. In 1978 she received her Ph.D. with a dissertation entitled "Hidden Variables and Non-Locality in Quantum Theory." Finished with school, Shiva sought work that would incorporate her scientific background as well as her interest in protecting the natural world. This led to a job conducting interdisciplinary research in science, technology, and environmental policy, first for the Indian Institute of Science and then for the Indian Institute of Management. Her research attracted the notice of India's Ministry of the Environment, which recruited Shiva to study the environmental impact of mining in the Doon Valley of northern India. Two years later, India's Supreme Court banned mining there as a result of her report.

Her work began attracting notice for more than just the high quality of her research and reports. In 1981, as part of her work for the Institute of Management, Shiva started a study on social forestry and conducted research on the consequences of a World Bank–financed plan to convert food-growing land into eucalyptus-growing land for pulp production. Her findings incited an uproar among peasants and farmers, who started to uproot the eucalyptus trees in these heavily subsidized plantations. As the first major challenge to a World Bank–backed project in India, these protests catalyzed a major debate over industrial forestry. Though she certainly could enjoy the gratifying sense that her work was making a difference, Shiva was disheartened by the reaction of her director. Worried that the institute would lose World Bank support, he apologized to visiting World Bank representatives about Shiva's enthusiasm and activism. Knowing she could not longer work for such a bureaucracy, she left the institute to follow her conscience.

Shiva returned to her native village of Dehra Dun in 1982 and made plans to start her own research institute. Her parents gave her their full support, even handing over the family resources for her venture. Converting her mother's cowshed into an office, she founded the Research Foundation for Science, Technology, and Ecology (RFSTE) and began to dedicate her efforts toward environmental issues such as biological diversity, forest and water conservation, genetic engineering, and food production. Increasingly concerned about initiatives proposed by multinational corporations and global development agencies like the World Bank, Shiva wanted to concentrate on finding solutions on a community level. The institute's location in her mother's cowshed proved highly appropriate, as it gave her immediate access to local peasant communities and their traditional and ecologically sustainable ways of life.

One of the first issues she devoted herself to was liberating farmers from the far-reaching consequences of the Green Revolution, which arrived in India in the late 1960s. Dependent largely on plant breeding and mechanization, the Green Revolution was a technical, industry-based, agricultural package exported from developed countries to developing countries beginning after World War II but not hitting its stride until the 1960s and 1970s. Its promoters believed that India's food shortages could be solved by planting laboratory-designed, high-yield varieties of wheat and rice. As these new methods—developed by multinational corporations mainly in the West—were implemented, they started replacing the carefully honed and complex rotational system, involving wheat, maize, millet, legumes, and oil seeds, that local farmers had developed through forty centuries of experience. The new system also required copious use of fertilizers, pesticides, and irrigation, and its overall impact was sudden and substantial. Under its rule, India reduced food dependence to such a degree that it actually became a food exporter. But the larger costs of the Green Revolution have undermined the health, well-being, and security of life for billions of people. As environmental historian J. R. McNeill wrote, "It reduced family and regional autonomy, enmeshing farmers in a world of banks, seed banks, plant genetics, fertilizer manufacturers, extension agents, and water bureaucrats. . . . It sought to harness nature tightly, to make it perform to the utmost, to make it maximally subservient to humankind."[4] Ecological balances were quickly upset by Green Revolution techniques: The heavy irrigation led to waterlogging and salinization, which then rendered the land in question unfarmable. Also, it encouraged monoculture, which invites pest infestations, which this reduced yield and forced farmers to apply heavier and heavier doses of toxic pesticides.

The social impacts of industrial agriculture were especially devastating for women. Before the Green Revolution in India, women were an integral part of agriculture and had made huge and innovative contributions to cultivation practices, livestock care, and food-gathering methods—in fact, as Shiva points out in her book, *Staying Alive: Women, Ecology, and Development*, women were the world's original food producers. In the sustainable agriculture systems traditionally used in India prior to the invasion of modern technologies, women played a major role in keeping the soil fertile, nurturing the cows and other animals, and managing mixed and rotation cropping. Shiva maintains that the industrial agriculture model began replacing this kind of feminine expertise with the theories of male-dominated corporations—resulting, ultimately, in the devaluation of women. As she explains in *Staying Alive*:

> Contrary to received views that modernization would liberate women from old discrimination and domination, the modernization of agriculture in India is deepening old prejudices and introducing new biases and violence. The assumption of the sustainability and dispensability of nature and women that results from the dichotomies and dualisms of economic and scientific reductionism is the underlying cause for the desertification and death of soils on the one hand, and the deprivation, devaluation, and death of women on the other.[5]

Shiva had long recognized that science and technology were not gender neutral—that, in fact, the exploitative dominance of humans over nature, which had been shaped by reductive Western science since the sixteenth century, was closely connected to the oppressive relationship between men and women. During the early to mid-1980s, a new movement that sought to unravel these exploitative relationships was taking shape and gaining force. Called "ecofeminism," it called for overthrowing all the social structures of domination. "Part theoretical construct, part literary expression, and part social movement . . . ecofeminism emerged as an amalgam of different perspectives and approaches about the human/nature relationship and the integration of feminist, ecological, and antimilitarist ideas,"[6] says environmental historian Robert Gottlieb. Shiva embraced the ideas behind the movement, and eventually wrote a book with the German sociologist Maria Mies called *Ecofeminism*. In the book they underline the importance of women's participation in the preservation of life and biodiversity, pointing out that women everywhere, as mothers and nurturers, were almost always the first to protest against environmental destruction. "The reason is that women have a distinctive perception of what life is, a sense of what is really vital, which colours their view of what is at stake in the world,"[7] says Shiva. As she and Mies state in the book's introduction, "Th[e] capitalist-patriarchal perspective interprets difference as hierarchical and uniformity as a prerequisite for equality. Our aim is to go beyond this narrow perspective and to express our diversity and, in a different way, address the inherent inequalities in world structures which permit the North to dominate the South, men to dominate women, and the frenetic plunder of ever more resources for ever more unequally distributed economic gain."[8]

As one of the world's most celebrated voices of ecofeminism, Shiva's views have had a broad impact in the United States and elsewhere. Her condemnation of "scientific reductionism" became a preeminent part of the global ecofeminist movement as it evolved and grew. And as with any flowering social cause, the larger it grew, the more tendrils it had to support. Ecofeminism attracted many different voices from various backgrounds of race, class, age, and ethnicity, and came to represent varied and sometimes conflicting viewpoints and agendas. Accommodating the diverse approaches— which included spiritual arguments for women's special relationship to the earth, direct-action protest such as the anti-nuclear and anti-toxins campaigns, strict emphasis on issues of environmental justice and social equality, and the focus on modern technology and its impact on reproductive rights— became unwieldy and challenging.

Shiva has discussed some of the ways in which ecofeminism seemed to diverge. She noticed that ecofeminists in the United States seemed to put greater emphasis on the spiritual realm than ecofeminists in Europe or the Third World. For women in the Third World, who struggle for the conservation of their survival base, a preoccuation with spirituality is a luxury they can barely comprehend. The ecofeminism of these women overcomes the dichotomies between spirit and matter, and economics and culture, and represents a counterbalance to the ecofeminist views of the United States. Alternative views such as these have been influential in the recent American effort to redefine the conceptual basis for both environmentalism and feminism, and have helped break new ground in the traditionally male-dominated environmental movement.

Some critics of the movement see it as pitting women against men—dividing when it should be uniting. In their book *The Stork and the Plow*, environmental scientists **Paul Ehrlich, Anne Ehrlich,** and Gretchen Daily discuss *Ecofeminism* by Shiva and Mies:

> Just when cooperation between sexes and among races is more than ever essential to resolve the human predicament, Maria Mies and Vandana Shiva lump women, nature, and foreign peoples and countries together as 'colonies' of white men. . . . The sad thing is that, although some of their diagnosis is correct, such broad-brush condemnation is not a helpful contribution to solving a set of global problems that threatens the futures of both men and women.[9]

While Shiva does tend to accentuate the plurality inherent in colonization, whether of women, nature, or developing countries, she does so only in an attempt to draw up possible alternatives that will create a better balance of power—one with the potential to unify men and women of different heritages and backgrounds in a common goal of fighting global capitalism and supporting a community- and ecology-based economy.

In addition to its degrading impact on women, other aspects of the industrialization and commodification of agriculture began warranting Shiva's attention. Globalization and technological advances are sharpening the tactics of the Green Revolution and complicating their consequences. In the late 1980s, the World Bank had begun pressuring the Indian government to allow multinational agribusinesses to promote their seeds and chemical supplies to Indian farmers. This opened the door to agricultural companies like Cargill, which began persuading farmers to switch to their laboratory-developed seeds. But many of those seeds are not self-reproducing and are also chemical-intensive, leaving farmers dependent on multinational companies for seeds, pesticides, and fertilizers. An example of this is Monsanto's Roundup Ready soybean, which has been genetically engineered to tolerate high doses of Monsanto's herbicide Roundup. Not only do farmers have to use more herbicide (and they are contracted by Monsanto to use only Roundup and no other brand), but they are also expressly forbidden to save seeds from one crop to plant the next crop with. They must continue to purchase seed from Monsanto, which can send company officials to investigate a farm to see if any seeds have been saved. If so, the farmer can be arrested for infringing on Monsanto's property.

As a result of these developments, many biologically diverse traditional crops started disappearing. Since Shiva's approach to ecology is grounded in the idea that human prosperity and survival depends on biological diversity, the disappearance of these ancient varieties of food crops in her native land alarmed her. Calling seeds the "last resource of the poor," she recognized the social evils inherent in appropriating such a primary element in the process of growing food for sustenance. Seeds always have been considered precious by indigenous cultures, so precious that, even in the face of starvation, they were kept off-limits as food. But since the Green Revolution, multinational companies have been gaining more and more control over seeds and seed production, especially in developing countries in the Southern Hemisphere, which are home to the world's richest stores of natural biodiversity. Between 1968 and 1988, Shell acquired over sixty independent seed companies, and Ciba-Geigy bought twenty-six. Today, an ominously named company called Imperial Chemical Industries is among the top ten seed producers in the world. For Shiva, this is a clear example of a conflict between the interests of technology and those of ordinary people. "Ecologically and economically inappropriate science and technology can become causes of underdevelopment and poverty, not solutions to underdevelopment and impoverishment,"[10] she wrote in *Monocultures of the Mind*.

To counteract these trends, Shiva began working to preserve a particular Indian tradition involving a ritual many farmers once practiced with their neighbors. Each family planted nine seeds in a pot on New Year's Day, and nine days later everyone compared the vigor of their seedlings to those of the other families. This allowed everyone to discover whose seeds were best and to exchange seeds to optimize the village's food supply. In 1991, Shiva began working through the RFSTE to create a seed conservation and exchange program, called "Navdanya" (literally, "nine seeds"), to encourage farmers to use traditional varieties of food crops to combat genetic erosion (loss of genetic diversity). Navdanya has since grown to include twenty community seed banks that have collected and preserved more than 2,000 rice varieties as well as other crops, such as millets and pulses (peas and beans). More than 60,000 farmers have become members, and they help further the cause by spreading Navdanya's ideas and methods to neighboring villages and cities. One farmer, Darwan Singh Negi, switched to organic farming in 1997 with Navdanya's aid: He grows six types of rice on his 3-acre farm in Uttaranchal, and, though he spends almost 70 percent less than his non-organic neighbors on fertilizers, pesticides, and seeds, his yields are similar to theirs.

This program has been hugely successful and has branched out since its inception, but Shiva has not stopped there. Traditional plant varieties, biodiversity, and the social welfare of farmers continue to be threatened with extinction as biotechnology makes advances in the world of genetic engineering and patenting. Shiva believes patenting to be a particular threat. Large corporations can travel to other countries, scope out information on a certain native medicinal plant or find a unique variety of seed a local farmer uses, return home and claim it as an innovation, get a patent on it, and then hold exclusive rights on the use of the products or processes associated with that knowledge. Cary Fowler and Pat Mooney, in *Shattering: Food, Politics, and the Loss of Genetic Diversity*, describe some of the insidious consequences of patenting for farmers in developing countries:

Farmers may not wear white coats or use fancy equipment, but they observe variation, note mutations, practice selection, and engage in breeding and seed multiplication—the basic activities of their plant breeder counterparts in the North. The difference is that in industrialized countries, laws are designed to recognize the achievements of individualized work. The "inventor" gets a patent or patent-like protection. The Third World system of innovation is more informal and communal in structure, hardly conducive to our formalized patent system. Thus, the contributions of farmers go unrecognized, unrewarded, unprotected—even denigrated.[11]

Shiva calls patenting "biopiracy" and likens it to a slave trade, since what's being traded is the knowledge that makes survival possible for 80 percent of the people in the world. A good example of biopiracy at work is a dispute in the 1990s over basmati rice—a staple of Indian food and part of India's national heritage. A Texas-based company called "RiceTec" attempted to patent variants of basmati rice, and an initial patent was granted to them in 1997. When the government of India failed to act in defense of basmati biodiversity and indigenous knowledge, Shiva and the RFSTE launched a global campaign against the patents. Individuals and organizations barraged the U.S. Patent and Trademark Office with protest letters demanding that the basmati patent be rescinded. As a result of protests, RiceTec withdrew fifteen of its eighteen patent claims, and on August 14, 2001, the U.S. Patent and Trademark Office struck down large sections of the basmati patent. Shiva saw this as a victory, saying, "Rice . . . to many of the people of Asia, is life itself. This is why the ongoing corporatization of rice varieties is such a tragedy. Rice must be owned and controlled by the small farmers—the people—and not by foreign corporations."[12]

Another fight over patenting involved the neem tree, an omnipresent resource in India that has hundreds of uses: Its leaves are used to fertilize the soil, its oil is used as a contraceptive and as lamp oil, its pulp is fed to livestock, and its wood is used for timber. It is also used for medicinal purposes and as a natural pest control agent, since it disrupts reproduction in insects. Women since ancient times have placed neem leaves in seed-storage containers and in clothing boxes to keep pests out. For these and other reasons, the neem tree is sacred in India, and its uses have evolved through centuries of women's learning and handing down of knowledge. In the early 1970s, the neem tree's beneficent properties intrigued an American timber exporter visiting India. He returned to his company headquarters in the United States with a sample of neem wood and began to test its pesticidal properties. Using a neem extract, he developed a compound he called "Margosan-O," the patent of which is now owned by a transnational chemical company called "Thermo Trilogy." Thermo Trilogy began to manufacture neem products in

India for export, which greatly increased demand for neem seeds. Consequently, the market price for neem seeds in India has risen over 1,000 percent in the past twenty years, making a once-universal staple unaffordable to Indians. Currently thirty-three patents exist on the neem tree, exemplifying its unique multifaceted usefulness, but also invoking a loss of accessibility of this resource to the native Indian peasants who first shared their knowledge of it with the world.

Shiva has compiled a four-page list of some of the patents multinational corporations have taken from the soil of tropical countries for the production of chemicals and antibiotics. Pfizer, for example, took out a patent for the production of antibiotics from microorganisms taken from India's soil without asking permission and without offering any form of compensation. Some economists argue that the roots of genetic erosion and environmental destruction can be traced to the fact that natural resources like biodiversity are "free," and that they should be given a measurable value so that they can be protected through a free-market system of economics. But Shiva points out a mistake inherent in this line of thinking: It falsely assumes that value can be defined as price. This is one of several reasons Shiva and many other environmentalists oppose free-trade treaties like the North American Free Trade Agreement (NAFTA) and the General Agreement on Tariffs and Trade (GATT). GATT was first signed in 1947 to provide an international forum that encouraged free trade by regulating and reducing tariffs. It served as the basis for the multilateral trading system until major revisions were made to the agreement in 1994, ultimately leading to the formation of the WTO on January 1, 1995. Meanwhile, NAFTA was implemented in January 1994, a radical experiment that merged the United States, Canada, and Mexico into an economic bloc that eliminated trade barriers between the three nations.

These agreements promote and perpetuate the globalization of a massive consumer-based economy that puts the protection of ecosystems around the world up for negotiation among multinational corporations and powerful governments. A majority in the United States opposed NAFTA, but that did not stop the agreement from proceeding. Fully aware of what these treaties mean in terms of local control of resources and protection of the environment, and aware that—in the case of NAFTA—the will of the people had been ignored, Shiva has called free-trade agreements "the most significant crisis in the world today." In a speech called "Biodiversity and Biopiracy" that she delivered in Seattle in 1996, Shiva said,

> The relationship between the human species and other species had to be decided on ethical terms. It cannot be decided on commercial terms, but of course ethics is a barrier to free trade. And that is what industry has been so organized in removing. . . . It is time we recognize that we are no more ruled by governments, nor by our congresses,

nor by our parliaments, nor by elected leaders—we are ruled globally by corporations.[13]

The strategic compromises brokered by these transnational corporations on issues of environmental protection open the system up to vast inequities: Economically powerful entities can afford to pay high prices for resources, leaving the less well-off to bear the costs of resource scarcity and environmental degradation.

Perhaps ironically, one of the first battles Shiva began fighting with the WTO involved its inclusion of "green clauses" intended to impose environmental standards on the free-trade process. When reading the fine print, she discovered that the environmental clauses were one-sided and heavily favored northern corporations at the expense of poorer nations. Plus, says Shiva, the environmentally friendly–sounding green clauses potentially could be hiding a secret agenda, deflecting attention away from the environmental and social impacts of free trade by creating a thin screen of green rhetoric. Also particularly troublesome to Shiva is the agreement's section on Trade-Related aspects of Intellectual Property (TRIPs), which came into effect on January 1, 1996. "Intellectual property" refers to the legal status accorded patents on intangible entities such as plant and animal forms, including seeds. What is problematic to Shiva is that TRIPs is an endorsement of patents on living beings and requires member countries to enforce protection of these "rights." By removing ecological and cultural goods from the hands of people and communities, the private rights of corporations are hoisted above the rights of local communities, and the protection of ecosystems, public health, and traditional cultures are undermined. Shiva has been a vocal opponent on these issues on the international diplomatic stage ever since their emergence, and, through the RFSTE, she also works to demystify for farmers the implications of free-trade agreements and TRIPs.

The type of Western scientific and economic development that has led to the patenting of what used to be the common heritage of the native populace, Shiva describes as patriarchy and simply a new form of colonialism. This type of developmental vision, in her view, arises out of "the exploitation or exclusion of women, . . . the exploitation and degradation of nature, and . . . the exploitation and erosion of other cultures."[14] In spite of her strong advocacy for women's rights, the environment, and traditional cultures, however, one thing Shiva does not want to do in her work is to exclude anyone. Her belief is that the recovery of the vivifying forces of nature and women will be beneficial to all humans by supporting nurturance over domination, sustainability over destruction, and experienced, tangible knowledge over detached, profit-driven knowledge. She sums up the passion with which she pursues this belief in the Hindi word *satyagraha*, in which *satya* means "truth" and *graha* means "anguished, deep-rooted fight for your rights." In 1993, Shiva received a Right Livelihood Award for her environmental activism.[15] She continues to direct the RFSTE, which has relocated to New Delhi, and to keep up a hectic schedule of prolific writing and speaking engagements.

NOTES

1. Vandana Shiva, *Staying Alive: Women, Ecology, and Development* (London: Zed Books, 1989), p. 55.

2. Quoted in David Kupfer, "David Ross Brower," *Progressive* Vol. 58 (May 1994), p. 38.

3. Judithe Bizot, "Vandana Shiva Talks to Judithe Bizot," *Unesco Courier* Vol. 54(12) (December 2001), p. 37. Reprinted from the March 1992 issue.

4. J. R. McNeill, *Something New under the Sun: An Environmental History of the Twentieth-Century World* (New York: W.W. Norton & Company, 2000), p. 227.

5. Shiva, *Staying Alive*, p. 120.

6. Robert Gottlieb, *Forcing the Spring: The Transformation of the American Environmental Movement* (Covelo, CA: Island Press, 1993), p. 232.

7. Quoted in Bizot, "Vandana Shiva Talks to Judithe Bizot," p. 37.

8. Maria Mies and Vandana Shiva, *Ecofeminism* (London: Zed Books, 1993), p. 2.

9. Paul Ehrlich, Anne Ehrlich, and Gretchen C. Daily, *The Stork and the Plow: The Equity Answer to the Human Dilemma* (New York: G. P. Putnam's Sons, 1995), pp. 133–134.

10. Vandana Shiva, *Monocultures of the Mind: Perspectives on Biodiversity and Biotechnology* (London: Zed Books, 1993), p. 135.

11. Cary Fowler and Pat Mooney, *Shattering: Food, Politics, and the Loss of Genetic Diversity* (Tucson: University of Arizona Press, 1990), p. 145.

12. Andy Steiner, "Vandana Shiva: Indian Physicist Who Fights for Small Farmers," *Utne Reader* No. 108 (November/December 2001), p. 72.

13. Vandana Shiva, "Biodiversity and Biopiracy," speech, Seattle, WA, 1996. Quoted in Mary Joy Breton, *Women Pioneers for the Environment* (Boston: Northeastern University Press, 1998), p. 212.

14. Breton, *Women Pioneers for the Environment*, p. 213.

15. The Right Livelihood Award was established in 1980 by Jakob von Uexkull, a Swedish-German philatelist who sold his valuable postage stamps to create the original endowment. He felt that Nobel Prizes ignore much of the work and knowledge vital to the future of the planet and wanted to honor and support those who have made contributions toward environmental sustainability. Right Livelihood Awards are presented annually in the Swedish Parliament.

BIBLIOGRAPHY

Vandana Shiva has written over twenty books on environmental and feminist issues; these include: *Staying Alive: Women, Ecology, and Development* (London: Zed

Books, 1989); *The Violence of the Green Revolution: Third World Agriculture, Ecology and Environment* (London: Zed Books, 1993); *Monocultures of the Mind: Perspectives on Biodiversity and Biotechnology* (London: Zed Books, 1993); *Biopiracy: The Plunder of Nature and Knowledge* (Cambridge, MA: South End Press, 1997); *Stolen Harvest: The Hijacking of the Global Food Supply* (Cambridge, MA: South End Press, 1999); *Tomorrow's Biodiversity: Prospects for Tomorrow* (London: Thames and Hudson, 2001); *Protect or Plunder? Understanding Intellectual Property Rights* (Cambridge, MA: South End Press, 2002); *Water Wars: Privatization, Pollution, and Profit* (Cambridge, MA: South End Press, 2002). With Maria Mies she wrote *Ecofeminism* (London: Zed Books, 1993). And she is also a co-author with Edward Goldsmith, Martin Khor, and Helena Norberg-Hodge of *The Future of Progress* (Devon, England: Green Books, 1995). For interviews with Shiva see David Barsamian, "Vandana Shiva," *Progressive* Vol. 61 (September 1997), pp. 36–39; and Judithe Bizot, "Vandana Shiva Talks to Judithe Bizot," *Unesco Courier* Vol. 54(12) (December 2001, reprinted from the March 1992 issue), pp. 36–39. Other articles on Shiva and her work include Elizabeth Larsen, "Vandana Shiva: Champion of Indian Ecofeminism," *Utne Reader* No. 44 (March/April 1991), p. 44; Vicky Hutchings, "Green Gauge," *New Statesman and Society* Vol. 8 (October 6, 1995), p. 30; Barbara Leiterman, "Vandana Shiva Simply Wants to Change the World," *Ms.* Vol. 7 (May/June 1997), pp. 30–33; Andy Steiner, "Vandana Shiva: Indian Physicist Who Fights for Small Farmers," *Utne Reader* No. 108 (November/December 2001), p. 72; and Meenakshi Ganguly, "Seeds of Self-Reliance," *Time* Vol. 160(9) (August 26, 2002), p. A34. A good biographical sketch can be found in Mary Joy Breton's *Women Pioneers for the Environment* (Boston: Northeastern University Press, 1998).

J. MICHAEL FAY
(1956–)

I want to show the world that in Central Africa there remains a vast wilderness, sparsely populated, with the natural environment mainly intact, where biodiversity is overwhelming. . . . Most of all, I want to help preserve as much of this magical world as possible.

—Michael Fay

Forsaking suburban comforts such as king-sized beds, fast food, and television, Michael Fay plunged into the heart of the most inaccessible tropical forests in central Africa and spent over a year walking, trudging, and swamping through its jungles—not once sleeping under a roof. "After three or four months your body gets hard and you don't feel the bug bites and footworms and you start seeing nature," said Fay later. And that was one of his primary intentions as he planned and executed this trek, which he called the "Megatransect"—to cover, on foot, nearly 2000 miles of uninhabited wilderness in the Congo Basin in order to see and document its wildlife and plants and to gain a better understanding of the ecosystems. The purpose of the trek, however, was not simply to further scientific understanding. As Fay explained, "Our objective is conservation, not science, not education, not exploration. If all these things we are doing—including science—do not lead to our goal, which is conservation, then we shouldn't be doing them."[1] Fay possesses a truly adventurous spirit, teeth-gritting determination, and a galvanic sense of purpose, and by the time he emerged from the jungle after 456 days, he had lost thirty pounds, endured foot-worms, leeches, legions of mosquitoes, and malaria. He and his crew had also seen things no other human had ever seen and had recorded data on countless plant, bird, insect, and animal species to aid future conservation efforts.

The Megatransect was not Fay's first contribution to saving African wilderness. By the time he started it in 1999, he already had been working on the ground in the forests of the Congo Basin for twenty years to integrate national resource stewardship into the mind-set of the local communities and governmental bodies as they sought a framework for sustainable indus-try. His land-use model does not call for abolishing development. Fay be-lieves that humans, in all their entrepreneurial brilliance, should be allowed to use the land and its resources, but that the use must be governed in such a way that it maximizes both the benefit of local communities and the health of the landscape. One example of such a solution is the establishment of na-tional parks, which not only become national treasures, but also potential resources for alleviating poverty (through tourism) and promoting health, education, human rights, and biodiversity.

J. Michael Fay was born on September 19, 1956, in Plainfield, New Jersey. He grew up in New Jersey and in Pasadena, California. A self-described nature boy, Fay was happiest when collecting wildlife and hiking through the San Gabriel Mountains around his California home. For his high school senior the-sis project, he conducted a botanical and ornithological survey of the Rincon Mountain range in Arizona. He went to college at the University of Arizona in Tucson, studying ecology and evolutionary biology and working as a techni-cian for the U.S. Department of Agriculture, first in their Bee Research Labo-ratory and later in their Plant Materials Center. During his college years he became smitten with the vast landscapes of Alaska, where he had been doing fieldwork on plants and birds, and he thought he would end up there. But in 1978, the same year he received his bachelor's degree with honors, he joined a scientific affiliate of the U.S. Peace Corps and was sent to Tunisia to study botany and ornithology in Ichkeul National Park. Steamy and breathtakingly beautiful, Ichkeul is home to the last remaining lake in a chain that once ex-tended across North Africa and is a major stopover for hundreds of thousands of migratory birds, who come to feed and rest there. Fay embraced opportuni-ties such as this, and it fed his desire to get as deeply into the wilderness as pos-sible. Though the Peace Corps prides itself on being "the toughest job you'll ever love," and offered distinctly unglamorous conditions and barely any pay, Fay went beyond the usual two-year commitment and stayed on for six years, continuing botany work. He never made it back to Alaska.

On finishing his initial two-year stint at Ichkeul National Park in 1980, Fay requested to be sent to central Africa. His request granted, he spent his final four years with the Peace Corps in the Central African Republic— eventually ending up at a new national park called Manovo-Gounda St.

Floris, which protected an expansive stretch of savanna abounding with elephants, black rhinos, cheetahs, gazelles, and leopards. Fay fell into the restless
habit of sticking around base camp long enough to complete his scientific duties, and then, lured by wilder places and itching to explore, borrowing a
Suzuki trail bike and venturing farther afield. His exploratory adventures took
him off the roads, sometimes for up to fifty miles across expanses of savanna
where no one else had ever been, sometimes for up to two weeks at a time.

In the mid-1980s, Fay returned to the states to attend school at Washington University in St. Louis, Missouri, where he spent several years working
on his master's degree on the western lowland gorillas of the Central African
Republic. On completing his master's in 1987, he began work on his Ph.D.,
a continuing study of the ecology of lowland gorillas that necessitated
months of fieldwork in Africa. To collect estimates of gorilla abundance, he
conducted line transect surveys: straight trails cut through a small representative sample area of forest that were walked repeatedly to tally gorilla nests.
But his preferred study method, which he called the "group follow," involved sneaking behind a group of gorillas at a discrete distance, observing
their behavior continuously without disturbing them. On one such trek, Fay
and his Pygmy tracker followed these skittish creatures for twelve straight
days on foot, a method of travel that suited Fay better than the Suzuki and
allowed him better access to forbidding terrain.

As he became familiar with the natural history and habits of the gorillas,
he also learned more about the local villagers. He found that, in general,
gorillas who live in a habitat completely free from human contact live in
peace, but that, at the interface between wildlife and human villages, a more
warlike attitude is common. To illustrate this, Fay tells a story about a male
gorilla—cast out of his family group to find his own territory—who began
loitering near a village. Startled villagers feared he would try to challenge the
humans and possibly hurt someone, but Fay convinced them to be patient
and see what happened. When, over time, it became clear the gorilla harbored no such aggressions and, in fact, showed little fear of humans despite
what appeared to be a machete scar on his face, the villagers eventually
adopted him as a local character. They named him Ebobo and became his
fiercest defenders. One of Fay's continuing goals is to counter local attitudes
that are based solely on fear of wildlife or on the mercenary incentives of
poaching. He seeks opportunities such as the one provided by Ebobo to
nudge local communities toward an understanding of local wildlife and the
ecosystems that sustain it, and thereby create a following for conservation—
a foreign concept to most natives. But with the looming likelihood of losing
90 percent of the forests in central Africa to logging and development in
the next few decades, Fay must impart a sense of concern, if not urgency,
among local tribes. These forests, which have bestowed wood and food to
the Pygmies in central Africa for millennia, seem deceptively invincible to
those who have never ventured beyond their charmed borders. When asked

how they would feel if roads were built through the jungles, leading to the destruction and death of the forests and animals like Ebobo, they scoffed, saying no on could kill off the forest, it is just too big.

Fay completed the necessary fieldwork in Africa and returned to school in St. Louis to begin writing his dissertation. No sooner had he begun than he was asked by Richard Barnes, a respected elephant biologist, to survey forest elephants in the northern part of the Republic of Congo. The survey area consisted of three virtually inaccessible ecosystems in the sweltering core of the Congo Basin rainforest—including vast swampland and uninhabited forest—and would have to be surveyed on foot. Nothing could be more irresistible to Fay: He abandoned work on his dissertation and returned to Africa. One of the survey areas, called Ndoki (its meaning in Lingala—"sorcerer"—conjures the aura of mystery surrounding this impenetrable forest), presented Fay an especially enchanting prospect. Barriers to human habitation surround the area: Swamps to the south and east, hills to the north, and the Ndoki River, unnavigable even to local Pygmies, to the west. This remoteness and lack of human presence make the region an extremely rare ecological treasure—an intact ecosystem that has remained in a pristine state for millennia. Fay completed surveys in all three areas, but it was to the primeval Ndoki region that he returned the following year for more exploration. He would continue conducting elephant surveys in the region for years, eventually learning to fly and acquiring a rebuilt Cessna (a surplus from the Central Intelligence Agency, complete with bullet holes) to conduct aerial surveys in addition to ground searches.

Almost immediately after perceiving the ecological pricelessness of the area, Fay began laboring to protect it. Intensive logging in other northern Congo forests had begun in the mid-1980s despite bringing in relatively little income to the Congolese government. In fact, many of the logging operations were actually losing money and frequently neglected to pay off debts to state-owned companies. But logging companies continued to grab up land as fast as they could, and Fay feared the Ndoki forests would fall prey to them within a few years. In 1989 he began pulling together such disparate entities as the U.S. government, Japanese researchers, conservation organizations, and the World Bank, to put pressure on the Congolese government to create a Ndoki reserve. His proposal delineated a core area that would receive absolute protection, with a buffer zone in the more accessible areas surrounding it that would allow for tourism, carefully controlled subsistence hunting, and sustainable logging.

The plodding footsteps of the diplomatic process took time. But by 1991, the Congolese government was collaborating with local, national, and international authorities toward the establishment of a park. The Wildlife Conservation Society created the Nouabalé-Ndoki National Park project in 1991 to oversee the effort, with Fay as its director. Although the growing list of responsibilities that came with this new post kept him preoccupied, he still managed to make occasional expeditions into the forest. One such trip involved a fifteen-day hike—across the Ndoki River and into the interior of the forest—to search for two elephant clearings that had shown up on aerial maps but that he had failed to locate on an earlier trip. The elephants create these open beach areas along rivers in the midst of dense forest as they trample and dig for salt in the mineral-rich mud. Some clearings are used by as many as 3000 elephants, as well as by a wide variety of other wildlife, making them indispensable but poorly studied habitats. One night during the trek, termites found Fay's one t-shirt and reduced it to shreds, giving him the chance to try a new approach to jungle attire: nothing but a pair of shorts and river sandals. This enabled him to dry off more quickly after swamping through a flooded forest or a stream and worked so well that it became his uniform of choice for fieldwork. Fay and his crew found the elephant clearings, but also found disturbing evidence that humans are affecting this forest from afar. Certain water-loving trees appeared to be dying and failing to regenerate. Fay believes widespread deforestation in other parts of Africa has changed the continent's weather patterns, inducing a long dry spell that threatens this tree and other rainforest species.

Human impact is a never far from Fay's mind, especially as he himself enters untouched wilderness and, even more consequentially, pushes for the establishment of national parks there. On an investigative trip to the jungle to write an article on Fay, journalist Eugene Linden wondered if perhaps the Ndoki should simply be left alone. "It has been protected for milleniums by its inaccessibility. Should there not be somewhere on earth where nature can be safe from the heavy hand of humanity? Journalists, explorers and scientists can inadvertently set in motion the destruction of the places they are trying to protect,"[2] he wrote. Fay's response is simple: In no way would the Ndoki be safe if simply left alone, given recent macroeconomic trends that make logging more profitable in central Africa. In his fight to preserve the Ndoki as a national park, Fay faced the frustrating position of the Congolese government: That the priority of the Republic of Congo is development for its people, even if it means the destruction of the country's forests. African nations don't have the resources of a wealthy country like the United States, which can afford to heavily subsidize its national parks, and the Congolese government was unwilling to establish a park without funding from outside sources. In a testament to both his conservation ethic and his sheer determination, Fay managed to secure the necessary outside funding from the Wildlife Conservation Society, the World Bank, and the U.S. Agency for International Development—and in December 1993, the Nouabalé-Ndoki National Park (NNNP), a 1 million-acre area of lush and virgin wilderness, was created. Now recognized as a conservation area of international significance, the NNNP hosts a biologically diverse abundance of life, including elephants; western lowland gorillas; chimpanzees; leopards; red river hogs; slender-snouted crocodiles; innumerable kinds of monkeys; nine species of forest antelope, including the elusive sitatunga and the exquisitely beautiful bongo; and over 300 bird species and 1,000 species of plants. Its misty landscape of forests, open spaces of marshy grassland, and dense swamps is heavy with the weight of unaltered evolutionary history—and so rich with life that there is always the unnerving sensation of being watched.

Throughout the rest of the 1990s, Fay managed the Nouabalé-Ndoki National Park and continued his efforts to shift inherited local attitudes away from resource extraction and toward resource conservation. Area villagers were still poaching elephants and selling their tusks despite an international ban on the sale of ivory in 1989, and despite the fact that it pulled in scarcely any money. Fay approached the villagers, explained the ecological aspects of the problem, and offered instead to hire them as game wardens to protect the elephants, paying more in wages than they would have made in ivory sales. This trade-off, besides offering legal, sustainable jobs for villagers, resulted in a sharp drop in the number of elephants being killed.

Guiding Fay's work in the forests of the Congo Basin is a simple model of land use that puts natural resource stewardship at the forefront of development policy. He believes, as **Theodore Roosevelt** did 100 years ago, that without conservation and sustainable management of natural resources, all other aspirations of a nation eventually will be doomed. In the United States, land-management issues almost always involve debate, but Fay would say this shows a remarkable achievement on the part of the conservation movement. Trained as a biologist to see an evolutionary perspective, he understands the human instinct to extract any available resources from the environment in order to survive. "That's kind of what humans are programmed to do," he says. "And to do the opposite of that, to conserve, I think is a very difficult thing for people to even comprehend, let alone enact. It's kind of counter-evolutionary, and I think it takes a lot of education and a lot of foresight." For that reason, the level of serious debate that has entered land-use decisions of the past century proves how fully integrated the idea of stewardship has become in the process of policymaking in the United States. Fay hopes that his efforts will help to introduce that same level of awareness and debate into resource-management policy in central Africa.

Fay addressed these issues in a testimony he gave before a U.S. House of Representatives subcommittee in March 1997, when he asked for the involvement and support of the U.S. government in achieving his goal of encouraging sustainable management of central African forests. He chronicled the catastrophic consequences of the rapid expansion of the logging industry in every forested country in Africa. He described the current land rush in central Africa, exacerbated by the depletion of forest resources in Asia, and the globalization of industries in the 1990s. In fact, Fay explained to the committee, if allowed to continue, the rush to acquire and log remaining large forests in Africa, where there are few regulatory constraints, would lead to greater environmental alteration there in the next ten years than has occurred over the past 2,000 years. He also described the effect of resource exploitation on the local communities. The Pygmy people, who have lived in these forests for thousands of years, often take jobs in logging camps, leading to the erosion of the traditional social fabric of their lives. When a logging operation ends, there are no more jobs, and the forests, which provided the only home they have ever known, are also destroyed. Raising the awareness of the local population about the effects of this type of boom-and-bust logging could reduce the chances that they would continue to allow a land-use practice that only leads to social turmoil and ecological destruction.

For several years, in between congressional hearings, running the national park, and finally completing work on his Ph.D. (which he received in 1997), Fay had been making careful plans for a new expedition, this one on a much grander scale than anything he had done before. The germ of this idea was born during the hundreds of hours he had spent flying over forests, creeks, valleys, and clearings in remote central Africa monitoring elephants. His aerial perspective revealed that there were major intact ecosystems that actually connected to form a vast wilderness the size of Florida, the largest expanse of wildland remaining in central Africa. The scope of this undefiled wilderness beguiled him, and the idea began to take shape: To conduct a thousand-mile survey through this area, far from human habitation, to document the life of the forests.

Plotting out a route that would be continuous in space and time and as far from human encroachment as possible, Fay traced a winding 2,000-mile path starting in Bomassa and going through northern Congo and then across Gabon to the Atlantic coast at Gamba. As someone who had once earned the nickname "Concrete" from Pygmies for his toughness in the face of jungle hardships, he had long-been accustomed to spending unplanned nights outdoors and had become somewhat nonchalant in his own approach to planning outings. However, now he could leave nothing to chance. He would need a crew to help carry supplies, chop a trail through the thick vegetation, and help with various measurements. This meant he would be responsible for the safety and well-being of a dozen or so Pygmies, a source of major anxiety for him in light of dangers they would face—snakes, tropical diseases, charging elephants, swollen rivers—all made more dangerous by the remoteness of their surroundings. Organizing the necessary details—the scientific equipment, the notebooks he would use to record observations, a Global Positioning System (GPS) unit to determine their exact location, maps, food, and medical supplies, not to mention networking to secure financial backing from the Wildlife Conservation Society and the National Geographic Society—took years of intricate calculation.

Fay's focus during the endeavor would be to gather an abundance of data on everything from the species and sizes of trees and plants, to the presence of elephant or gorilla dung piles, to insects and bird songs. His familiarity with the jungle meant that he was good at ascertaining overall biological richness: He had become skilled at seeing the many interwoven connections that make an ecosystem function. "The system I have developed is a quantified natural history walk," he said. "Just wandering around in the woods, you can piece things together. But if you quantify as you go and force yourself to intensively observe a wide number of variables simultaneously—which is very tiring, it's like being an air traffic controller—all of a sudden it starts to make sense."[3] Unlike most scientific studies, where only one thing is surveyed at a time, Fay's project would be more of an ecological overview of the state of Congo Basin forests, and while the results could not be analyzed in the same way as standard scientific studies, they would still be useful for guiding management decisions. To distinguish his undertaking from the conventional line transect technique and to give an idea of the immensity of his journey, Fay named it the Megatransect. In his enthralling and in-depth chronicle of the Megatransect for *National Geographic*, writer David Quammen compares Fay's journey to the expedition of Lewis and Clark in the early 1800s. "That journey was, of course, America's own first and greatest megatransect," he wrote. But there was one important difference: "Lewis and Clark's enterprise was premised upon the goals of commercial exploitation and easy travel for traders, whereas Fay's Megatransect has a drastically different goal: Protecting big areas of rich forest from reductive human impact."[4]

On September 20, 1999, one day after his forty-third birthday, Fay embarked on the Megatransect along with Ndokanda, a Pygmy guide who had aided in previous explorations, nine other Pygmy crew members, and a handful of other helpers—including a camp boss, a cook, and a photographer. A week into their journey, they passed through what Fay called a "gate," after which point humans were no longer the dominant species in the landscape. They emerged into a realm of elephants, gorillas, fruit bats, cobras, and splendorous birds such as blue turacos, chocolate-backed kingfishers, and olive sunbirds. They walked under a high canopy of green filigree, the clamorous undergrowth tamped down by elephants in intricate and well-planned highway systems. Some trails were as wide as boulevards, and each one led to an important destination—one to a grove of fruit trees, another to a river crossing, and another to a bathing site. It became evident that the animals here had never seen a human before. Most chimpanzees across Africa are hunted heavily and therefore fearful when they encounter humans, but Fay began seeing chimpanzees who were entirely unwary. Instead of running away, they reacted out of intense curiosity and interest, staring openly and hooting.

Conditions were tough in the jungle, as Fay knew they would be. The thorny brush left everyone gashed, and as they waded through a constant succession of streams and wet mud, the skin on their feet was rubbed nearly raw under their sandal straps. For this they relied on the universal problem solver—duct tape—which they used as a second skin. But while it alleviated abrasion, it couldn't protect them from footworms, a parasite that travels from elephant dung into the skin on the feet or toes, burrowing in only to die and potentially cause infection. For Fay, these were minor irritants that receded into background static as his observational skills became more and more highly tuned. Without the distractions that accompany electricity, and the sensory overload from radio, television, the ringing phone, cars, and other sounds of commerce, Fay's remarkable "air traffic controller" level of concentration reached its highest amperage.

During the first three months, the team crossed through Nouabalé-Ndoki National Park, through pristine forest, and through some timber concessions and logging camps along the lower Ndoki River. Fay's policy was always to follow the path of least resistance, so as to ease the task of walking and to minimize the impact of their passage through the jungle. He often led the team along elephant trails, but where there were none, they had to hack a trail with a machete. By December they had settled into this rhythm, when gradually they found themselves pressing into a dismal swamp of overwhelmingly dense vegetation. It was a solid wall of marantaceae, a tropical plant that had grown into a stultifying thicket. Having no other choice, they started chopping their way through, but had no way to know how long it would last. As Fay described it, "[I]t's an environment which is completely claustrophobic. It's like digging a tunnel except there's sunlight."[5] The going was unbearably slow: They would spend an entire ten-hour day cutting a trail, only to crawl one mile. Fresh flowing water grew very scarce, making it necessary for the team to survive on puddles of swamp water. Fay and his crew had to muster an inhuman amount of patience and inner calm to push through the thicket, an effort that ultimately took an endless ten weeks. Fay later called it the "Green Abyss," and said the ordeal was the most trying thing he had ever done in his life. Furthermore, since their progress had been so unexpectedly hampered, their food supply came precariously close to running out before Fay could arrange via satellite phone an extra airdrop of supplies: cans of sardines and manioc powder.

As the weeks passed and they neared the Gabonese border, a new development threatened the success of the project: One of the Pygmy crew, a man named Mouko, contracted hepatitis and became dangerously ill. Though Fay felt almost maniacally driven to stick to his intended route, he made the decision to veer off course in order to evacuate Mouko to a town with a hospital. This was the only time he would stray, and it cut about twenty miles from his original plan. But to Fay's credit, Mouko survived. Meanwhile, the rest of his Congolese crew was exhausted—and to complicate matters, a border dispute smoldered along the Congo-Gabon line. So Fay sent his crew home and started over on the Gabonese side, recruiting a new, energetic crew.

After a few chaotic days, the new team eventually accustomed itself to the strange rigors of the Megatransect as they worked their way through Gabon's Minkébé forest. Gabon contains some of the least exploited wilderness on the African continent, with highly diverse rainforests that shelter forest elephants; sixteen primate species, including lowland gorillas; and myriad other jungle animals, plants, and birds. But with Africa's swelling population, the natural resources of the region were becoming vulnerable to development. Gabon's oil reserves were running out, leaving the government looking toward the wood industry as a source of foreign exchange. When Fay's team started exploring the Minkébé forest area, he found a spectacular ecosystem, virtually undisturbed by humans, and wrote in his trip report of wanting desperately for this forest to survive. Fortunately, a section of the Minkébé forest recently had been designated a protected reserve by the Gabonese government, and three adjacent parcels were being considered for protection as well. Fay knew these areas were well worth protecting, even at great cost, since they would otherwise soon cease to exist. Yet, as always, he knew he had to be pragmatic: There must be a way to encourage sustainable industry and a healthy economy for the human population of the region. The solution Fay envisioned was ecotourism, which would combine neatly the goals of both industry development and conservation. And once the team reached the end of the Megatransect at the Gabonese coast, Fay resolved, he relentlessly would begin pursuing this idea with the Gabonese government.

In the meantime, there were other puzzles to solve. Though the forest they passed through was large, healthy, and rich with jungle species, there was a mysterious absence of gorillas and chimpanzees. In the seven weeks it took Fay and his team to walk across this forest, they found only one gorilla dung pile, an indication of a drastic reduction in gorilla numbers. Fay suspected the Ebola virus. Named after the Ebola River in Congo, where it was discovered in 1976, Ebola is a viral disease that causes an often fatal hemorrhagic fever in humans and apparently in other primates as well. In the mid-1990s, when Ebola outbreaks killed dozens of people in the Minkébé forest region, scientists also documented the disappearance of gorillas there. Since that time, epidemics of Ebola in humans in northwestern Congo and northeastern Gabon have coincided with documented deaths of gorillas in the areas, and the presence of the Ebola virus has been confirmed from gorilla and chimpanzee carcasses. Fay conjectures that the opening of forests to logging in central Africa could explain the spread of diseases like Ebola and AIDS, which follow working populations into logging camps and along transport routes. Early in 2003, another epidemic in northern Congo killed 100 people and nearly wiped out a population of gorillas living in a nearby sanctuary. Primatologists have started to use terms like "catastrophic" when describing the threat Ebola poses to remaining gorilla populations in central African forests. The information Fay collected on his Megatransect helped to track the path of the disease and to reinforce growing evidence of the devastating impact it is having on humans and primates alike.

After some 450 days of walking, recording data, and living with only the jungle canopy for a roof, Fay and his crew finally began to hear the surf of the

Atlantic Ocean off the Gabonese coast. On December 18, 2000, at 12:39 P.M., they emerged from the forest onto the beach. Bewildered by this gigantic river of salt with no beginning or end, the Pygmies had to be coaxed out of the forest to where the waves spilled onto the sand. The Megatransect, which ended up being 2,000 miles long, was completed. They had challenged the extremes of physical endurance, and everyone under Fay's responsibility had survived. It was an overwhelming experience to have reached the ocean, and the team was awash in a mixture of relief, accomplishment, and sadness that it was over. After walking through the magnificent trees in the deepest jungle day after day, Fay was extremely daunted by the thought of having to re-enter the world—to hear the sound of a car again.

But his first priority was to save the forests he had just gotten to know so intimately, and if that meant returning to civilization then he would do it with characteristic determination. Back in the United States, he began organizing the data he had crammed into thirty-nine waterproof notebooks and a video camera, and started his mission to get the word out about the imperative of protecting the forest. He met with the president of Gabon, El Hadj Omar Bongo, in the Palace Hotel in New York City, and showed him pictures of the wildlife and the forest habitat he had encountered on his trek. President Bongo was astonished. He had very little idea of the richness of wildlife in his country and was also largely unaware of the impact the logging concessions were having on the forests. Even though logging represents only 7 percent of the gross national product of Gabon, it has a highly destructive influence on the forests. Fay offered President Bongo persuasive arguments for giving Gabon's forests a more prosperous future by shifting the focus from logging to conservation and its lucrative partner, ecotourism.

Thanks in part to Fay's persistence, support for this type of land-use model is growing. In September 2002, at the United Nations World Summit on Sustainable Development in Johannesburg, President Bongo announced his decision to create thirteen new national parks in Gabon. Over 7.5 million acres will be protected, or almost 11 percent of the country's land, including the Minkébé forest preserve and many other highly critical areas. At the same summit, the Congo Basin Forest Partnership (CBFP) was launched with an address by U.S. Secretary of State Colin Powell, who then traveled to Gabon to show support of the inauguration of its new national parks. By joining together several conservation projects, regional governments, and international organizations, the CBFP seeks to promote economic development, alleviate poverty, and improve local governance through natural resource conservation programs. Partners include the United States, several central African countries, Japan, Germany, France, the United Kingdom, Canada, South Africa, the World Conservation Union, the World Bank, World Wildlife Fund, the Wildlife Conservation Society, and various forestry associations. The initial plan of the partnership is to focus on eleven endangered landscapes in six Congo Basin countries to create a network of sustainably managed national parks, to stop illegal logging and illegal trade of wildlife, to implement programs to improve forest management, and to help local communities to derive forest-based livelihoods through eco-tourism.

The Congo Basin Forest Partnership is a legacy of Fay's vision to create a new platform of ideas regarding these forests and their global significance. In light of this achievement and the cautious but growing optimism for conservation in the central Africa, there can be little doubt of the impact of Michael Fay's historic Megatransect. More than any other event, it has brought to light both the stunning ecological richness and the dangerous vulnerability of the forests of the Congo Basin. Its objective—to call attention to the state of wild areas in central Africa and to create a debate that would change local ideas about conservation and management—has been met. However challenging it may be for international conservation groups, with their resources and influence, to shift the balance of ideas from resource exploitation to resource conservation, from unregulated development to sustainable development, it is indomitably more difficult for one person to bring about those changes. Yet Fay accomplished that on his own, largely through the sheer momentum of his will. His personal goal for conservation has become larger than himself, and because of his efforts and the publicity surrounding them, it is now the common goal of many. Amidst the wave of reaction that has spread from his story, some who have heard Fay talk about his trek and seen the breathtaking photos of the jungle have voiced the same concern raised by journalist Eugene Linden: that all the attention will serve only to encourage trampling droves of people to visit these undisturbed areas. But Fay, who found in these forests a home he had been looking for his whole life, repeats that the answer lies not in keeping them a secret. His response reflects his pragmatic and realistic land-use ethic that conservation should also enhance and sustain the local population—in other words, people have to visit the forests for them to survive.

NOTES

1. Joshua Brown and Jennifer Esser, "Mike Fay," *Wild Earth* Vol. 12 (Fall 2002), p. 26.

2. Eugene Linden, "The Last Eden," *Time* Vol. 140 (July 13, 1992), p. 63.

3. Joshua Brown and Jennifer Esser, "Mike Fay," *Wild Earth* Vol. 12 (Fall 2002), p. 26.

4. David Quammen, "End of the Line: Megatransect Part III," *National Geographic* Vol. 200 (August 2001), p. 95.

5. David Quammen, "The Green Abyss: Megatransect Part II," *National Geographic* Vol. 199 (March 2001), p. 9.

BIBLIOGRAPHY

Two accounts of Fay's earlier work in the Ndoki region are Eugene Linden, "The Last Eden," *Time* Vol. 140 (July 13, 1992), pp. 62–69; and Douglas Chadwick, "Ndoki," *National Geographic* Vol. 188 (July 1995), pp. 2–42. A comprehensive and fascinating account of the Megatransect was written in three parts by David Quammen for *National Geographic* as follows: "Megatransect," Vol. 198 (October 2000), pp. 2–29; "The Green Abyss: Megatransect Part II," Vol. 199 (March 2001), pp. 2–37; and "End of the Line: Megatransect Part III," Vol. 200 (August 2001), pp. 74–102. For Michael Fay's personal perspective of the journey, see an article he wrote, "Walk for Wildlife," *Wildlife Conservation* Vol. 104 (September/October 2001), pp. 36–43. For an interview with Fay in which he discusses his conservation ethic, see Joshua Brown and Jennifer Esser, "Mike Fay," *Wild Earth* Vol. 12 (Fall 2002), pp. 22–28. Other articles about Fay and his work are Elizabeth Royte, "Out of the Woods," *New Yorker* Vol. 77 (May 14, 2001), p. 50; Andrew Curry, "J. Michael Fay," *U.S. News and World Report* Vol. 131 (August 20–27, 2001), pp. 60–61; Aliette Frank, "Incredible Journey," *National Geographic World* Issue 313 (September 2001), pp. 26–29; and James Barron, "At Home in the Wild, but Evicted by a Beast," *New York Times* Vol. 152 (February 9, 2003), p. 41. For transcripts of testimony given by Fay before congressional hearings the Federal Document ClearingHouse (FDCH) offers primary-source government material and transcripts online. FDCH documents are archived in EBSCO research databases, which are accessible to patrons of participating libraries. Specific documents containing Fay's testimonies include "Logging, Forest Ecosystems and People in Northern Congo," FDCH Congressional Testimony (March 19, 1997); and "Save the Congo Basin," FDCH Congressional Testimony (March 11, 2003).

.

BJØRN LOMBORG
(1965–)

I think it's a shame when I hear a mother worrying about pesticides in food while forgetting to tell her son to wear a cycle helmet when he goes out on his bike. Understanding statistics is to understand the true nature of risk. The end of the world, I'm pleased to say, is not nigh.
—Bjørn Lomborg

Skepticism is a necessary component of any scientific inquiry. The scientific method actually thrives on adversity and dissent: If a theory is solid, it will withstand challenges; if it is not, it should be discarded or reconceptualized. In addition to making science more robust, skepticism and dissent make science an exciting source of news for popular media outlets. For example, while the vast majority of climate scientists agree that global warming is a grave problem that needs to be addressed, it is more dramatic for the media to report on those few who disagree. One of those few contrarians is Bjørn Lomborg, a Danish statistician who wrote a book, *The Skeptical Environmentalist*, that argues that the current litany of environmental disasters— global warming, species extinction, pollution, overpopulation, and exploitation of natural resources—is nothing more than overzealous hype on the part of activists and scientists. But while skepticism is a central tenet of scientific inquiry and, for the same reasons, of environmental debate, Lomborg's brand of skepticism was not welcomed by the environmental movement for several reasons. For one thing, many environmental scientists accused Lomborg of misrepresenting their work and undermining the general public's understanding of their research. Also a problem was the media frenzy Lomborg inspired, which occurred partly because the controversy boosted ratings and partly because Lomborg himself made for great footage—he is photogenic, charming, and affable. His background made great copy, too: He's a former Greenpeace member who believed all the common perceptions of human-caused environmental degradation before converting to his optimistic view. Finally, the environmental community lamented the fact that Lomborg's message was accepted by a wider audience than might have been expected, given that environmental consciousness seems to have become almost mainstream. Lomborg professes to being amazed at how many people on both sides of the issue got so fired up over what he considers to be a "fairly common point," namely, that trends indicate overall improvement. But to the environmental researchers who have devoted their lives to the study of these trends, Lomborg's point seems far from common and deserves every bit of debate, dissent, and refutation it has received.

Bjørn Lomborg was born on January 6, 1965, in Copenhagen, Denmark, to Jorgen and Birgit Lomborg. His father, who came from a gardening family and worked as a florist, died when Bjørn was 1½ years old. His mother raised him as an only child while working as a primary school teacher. When Bjørn was 10, they moved to Aalborg, Denmark's fourth largest city, situated on the banks of the Limfjord River in northern Jutland. He studied mathematics and physics in high school, and spent his spare time learning about music and computers. He later described himself as having been a "very academic teenager, clever in a slightly nerdy way, awkward, the kind of guy who would always be picked last for the football team."[1]

Lomborg spent his freshman year of college (1983–1984) in the United States at the University of Georgia in Athens, where he enjoyed the opportunity to gain perspective on American culture and improve his English-speaking skills. During that time he became more open and adventurous, came to terms with being gay, and had what he describes as a political awakening. "I didn't have big academic aspirations at the time, and became very caught up in the peace movement," he told Jason Cowley for the *New Statesman*. "I was worried about nuclear weapons, [and] I wanted to change the world." When he returned to school in Denmark he became heavily involved in protests against the North Atlantic Treaty Organization (NATO). During these politically active days, he also joined Greenpeace, one of the best-known direct-action environmental organizations in the world.

He received his master's degree from the University of Aarhus in 1991, and his Ph.D. at the University of Copenhagen in 1994, both in political science. His interest in political science veered toward the study of statistics, and in 1994 he took a job that combined both disciplines: He became an assistant professor at the Department of Political Science at the University of Aarhus, teaching students to apply statistics to problems in political science. His own research involved fairly obscure topics such as game theory, which involves theorizing about how people act in situations where strategy is involved. As he explains it, "[W]hen you decide whether to bring an umbrella on your next walk, you don't have to consider any strategic consequences: forgetting the umbrella does not make the weather 'want' to douse you. On the other hand, a decision to dress up for a social meeting does entail strategic consequences: the others may not have dressed up, leaving them feeling uncomfortable, whereas you not dressing up may lead them to think you are sloppy."

In 1996, Lomborg published a paper on game theory that conservative scientist Matt Ridley described as "obscure but brilliant,"[2] and which earned him an invitation to give a talk at a conference on computable economics in Los Angeles. When he attended the conference in February 1997, he stumbled upon an event that totally altered his career path and led to years of international attention. Waiting for a flight at the Los Angeles airport, he picked up a copy of *Wired* magazine. It contained a profile of "The Doomslayer," a nickname for the conservative economist **Julian Simon**, then a senior fellow at the Cato Institute and professor of business administration at the University of Maryland. Simon's arguments—that the environmental situation was actually improving, that global warming was nothing to worry about, and that natural resources need not be conserved since humans will just figure out new technologies to replace them—rankled Lomborg. "When I read the article I thought 'hell, no,'" Lomborg remembered later. "I thought that obviously the environment is getting worse. But Simon said one irritating thing: go check the facts."[3]

When he returned to Denmark, where he had since risen from assistant to associate professor at the University of Aarhus, he formed a study group among his students to begin disproving Simon's claims through a rigorous application of statistics. He assumed it would be easy to debunk Simon's arguments as products of narrow-minded conservative American thinking, and he thought it would be fun to show how wrong Simon actually was. But somehow his study group ended up verifying many of Simon's statements. "What we discovered changed my life forever," he said. "For much of what Simon said about the environment was true and much of what we as greens believed was false—that for instance, the air in the developed world is becoming less, not more polluted. I realized that if I was wrong in what I believed about the environment, I was not the only one."[4] Growing more and more intrigued, Lomborg contacted the left-leaning Danish daily newspaper *Politiken* and offered to write a series of articles on his findings. His professed aim was not to denounce environmental activists, but to help them analyze the issues more accurately and to start a discussion. Lomborg's four lengthy *Politiken* articles resulted in a surge of protest. Environmentalists throughout Scandinavia vented their views in over 400 articles in major metropolitan newspapers, some calling Lomborg a fanatic and an apologist for capitalist decadence. A website was created to discredit him.

If it were not for the fact that he had called into question issues that environmentalists and scientists had been researching and crusading on for decades, Lomborg would appear to be an unlikely target for the fury he was generating. Friendly, informal, and with a disarming grin and a fashionable blond shock of hair, he looks more like a progressive urban hipster than a fanatic. Being raised in Denmark—a liberal country with a long history of socially progressive governments—Lomborg had grown up surrounded by what he describes as a "global, we-need-to-take-care" sense of the environment. For example, Denmark levies very high taxes on cars—about 200 percent—to encourage people to find alternative transportation. Lomborg believes in this type of policy and has never owned a car himself, preferring to ride his bike everywhere. He also lives the kind of wholesome lifestyle one would not expect of an apologist for capitalist excesses: He describes himself as a "liberal leftist," doesn't drink alcohol or smoke, and is a vegetarian. But whether his outward appearance and lifestyle seem deceptive or not, Lomborg was not terribly troubled by stirring up such controversy, and in fact began working on expanding the four *Politiken* articles into a book.

The book was published first in Denmark in 1998 as *Verdens Sande Tilstand* (literally: "The True State of the World"), and generated further hype. But when it was eventually published in 2001 by Cambridge University Press and released in the United States, Lomborg's *The Skeptical Environmentalist* raised such a maelstrom of criticism from green activists and environmental scientists that any previous furor seemed anemic in comparison. Weighing in at over 500 pages, including 2,930 footnotes and more than 1,800 references in the bibiliography, *The Skeptical Environmentalist* covers a broad spectrum of topics and is heavily loaded with statistics. It also contains 173 figures and nine tables. Its subtitle, *Measuring the Real State of the World*, deliberately plays off the annual *State of the World* reports issued by the Worldwatch Institute, a fortress of environmentalism. Founded by **Lester Brown** in 1974, the Worldwatch Institute uses the *State of the World* reports to raise public awareness of environmental threats to a level sufficient to encourage effective policy response. These reports have been warning the world about the environmental damage caused by current agricultural practices, overpopulation, pollution, climate change, and unsustainable use of natural resources since 1984. The overall message of *The Skeptical Environmentalist*, on the other hand, is that the environmental movement has been overreacting and that many of its most fundamental concerns, which he calls "The Litany," are grossly exaggerated. He states in the first chapter:

> We are not running out of energy or natural resources. There will be more and more food per head of the world's population. . . . Global warming, though its size and future projections are rather unrealisti-

cally pessimistic, is almost certainly taking place, but the typical cure of early and radical fossil fuel cutbacks is way worse than the original affliction, and moreover its total impact will not pose a devastating problem for our future. . . . Acid rain does not kill the forests, and the air and water around us are becoming less and less polluted. Mankind's lot has actually improved in terms of practically every measurable indicator.[5]

The main text of the book is devoted to statistical analyses of virtually every environmental concern—world hunger, global warming, forest depletion, species extinction, loss of non-renewables, acid rain, as well as water and air pollution—and concludes that in each case things have improved or are better off than scientists claim. Environmentalists and their scientific allies, Lomborg suggests, deliberately portray the commonly heard alarmist scenarios in order to ensure continued funding for their own research.

At first, most environmental scientists dismissed the book as a non-scientific polemic and very few of them spent any time or effort responding with arguments. But, much to their dismay, several popular media outlets lauded it. The *Washington Post* called it "the most significant work on the environment since the appearance of its polar opposite, **Rachel Carson**'s *Silent Spring* in 1962."[6] A review in the *Economist* said:

> This is one of the most valuable books on public policy—not merely on environmental policy—to have been written for the intelligent general reader in the past ten years. Its target is environmental pessimism, the defining mood of the age. By the end, fair-minded readers will find that most of the concerns they had about the future of the planet have given way to fury at the army of dissembling environmentalists who have dedicated themselves to stirring up panic by concealing the truth.[7]

The *New York Times* and the *Wall Street Journal* also published favorable reviews. Other media outlets began to spin stories about how Lomborg had "exposed" environmentalists as being wrong in all their arguments. After a couple months of this, the environmental science community realized they needed to respond, "or else watch Lomborg's claims confuse legislators and regulators, and poison the well of public environmental information,"[8] said Richard Bell in a *World Watch* magazine commentary. The World Resources Institute, a Washington, D.C., environmental research and policy group, published a list of "nine things journalists should know about *The Skeptical Environmentalist*," making the case that Lomborg lacked the scientific credentials to carry out a proper and accurate analysis of the state of the environment.

In the midst of the upsurge of controversy, Lomborg remained implacably loyal to the claims he had put forth in his book, rescinding nothing and budging not an inch. Tempers began to run high. In September 2001, at a reading in an Oxford bookstore, Mark Lynas, a journalist writing a book on the impacts of climate change around the world, pushed a whipped cream–loaded pie into Lomborg's face, saying later he intended it as "a relatively light-hearted way to bring pompous and powerful people down a peg."[9] His face covered with white glop, Lomborg maintained his good-natured charm. "I was stunned," he admitted. "But at least the pie tasted good." Already on his way to becoming a media darling, he began working the talk-show circuit in the United States and touring college campuses, insisting he was being misinterpreted. "I'm not some free-market demon that wants to dismantle all the things that environmentalism has achieved," he said. "But we only have so much worry to go around, and I would argue that we overworry about the rainforest and underworry about other pressing issues in the world, like the lack of clean drinking water, basic sanitation, and food for the developing world."[10] Conservation biologists took offense at this argument, which pits concern for the environment against concern for basic human-survival needs, ignoring the fact that all of humanity depends on the environment for survival and that, in fact, billions of people suffer when ecosystems are impoverished.

In late 2001, *Nature* printed a review of *The Skeptical Environmentalist* by Stuart Pimm, a conservation biologist at Columbia University in New York, and Jeff Harvey, an ecologist at the Netherlands Institute of Ecology in Heteren. The review pilloried Lomborg's book and his analytical methods. They compared the book to a poorly written term paper and condemned Lomborg for selecting and highlighting data that furthered his polemical argument while ignoring research that failed to support it. They also pointed out that of the nearly 2,000 references in the bibliography, about 5 percent came from news sources and about 30 percent from web downloads, which are frequently not peer reviewed. On the implications of the debate surrounding the book they concluded, "[C]ertainly, controversy is part of science, but extraordinary claims require the extraordinary scrutiny that comes from competent peer review—something that appears to be missing in this case."[11]

The most excoriating attack yet on *The Skeptical Environmentalist* came in the shape of a twelve-page group of articles in *Scientific American* in January 2002. In an introductory note, editor-in-chief John Rennie called the book a failure, saying that "it is hard not to be struck by Lomborg's presumption that he has seen into the heart of the science more faithfully than have investigators who have devoted their lives to it; it is equally curious that he finds the same contrarian good news lurking in *every* diverse area of environmental science."[12] Several essays written by environmental scientists followed, each examining in detail some of the problems they saw in Lomborg's book so that readers could understand some of the fundamentals of the disagreement it provoked. Stephen Schneider, a climatology researcher and lead author of several chapters in IPCC[13] reports, explained why Lomborg's assertions on global warming were fatally flawed. First of all, Lomborg's prediction that the overall warming trend will turn out to be relatively mild is based on a misunderstanding of the literature. Second, Lomborg asserted that renewable energy technologies eventually will crowd fossil fuels off the market; but, as Scheider pointed out, Lomborg opposes the very policies that would allow the initial investments in these alternative energy systems. Finally, and most crucially, Lomborg believes the Kyoto Protocol to be a waste of money since its baseline carbon dioxide emission caps are too low to affect a long-term amelioration of the greenhouse effect. But the real purpose of the Kyoto Protocol is not to cure global climate change forever, said Schneider, but to initiate the difficult and delicate process of international cooperation and to provide the framework for future policy.

In another essay, John Holdren, an environmental science and public policy professor at Harvard, examined Lomborg's treatment of energy issues. Lomborg framed the issue as one of depletion, saying environmentalists worry too much that certain energy resources are running out. But, as Holdren explained, "[W]hat environmentalists mainly say on this topic is not that we are running out of energy but that we are running out of environment—that is, running out of the capacity of air, water, soil, and biota to absorb, without intolerable consequences for human well-being, the effects of energy extraction, transport, transformation, and use."[14]

A third essay, written by Thomas Lovejoy, chief biodiversity adviser to the president of the World Bank and senior adviser to the president of the United Nations Foundation, discussed how Lomborg's analytical methods and use of statistics portray a misleading picture of habitat loss and species extinction rates. For example, Lomborg opens his chapter on biodiversity by repeating an estimate that biologist Norman Myers made in 1979; that 40,000 species were being lost every year. This estimate, strictly a preliminary and exploratory assessment designed to advance the issue of extinction onto scientific agendas, was proven to be too high. Lomborg used this as proof that scientists exaggerate claims of mass extinction, yet he ignored the more than eighty papers written by Myers in the twenty years since 1979, which gave revised and updated information on mass extinction and biodiversity. Questions of biodiversity aside, Lovejoy incidentally pointed out what may be the most devastating hole in *The Skeptical Environmentalist*'s entire thesis, namely, that many of the improvements Lomborg lauds are in fact the result of years of environmental policy. In other words, some of the very parameters Lomborg uses to prove that "doomsday" environmental claims are exaggerated—such as reduced air pollution in cities and cleaner rivers—do indeed show improvement, but only *because* of the efforts of the environmental movement.

In the month following the appearance of the *Scientific American* essays, sales of *The Skeptical Environmentalist* quadrupled. Cambridge University Press, the book's publisher, denied stirring up controversy as a deliberate marketing strategy, but there could be no denying that the continued debate boosted Lomborg's profile. This became even more evident when Lomborg was tapped for a high-ranking position within Denmark's government. In February 2002, Prime Minister Anders Fogh Rasmussen announced that Lomborg would head Denmark's new Environmental Assessment Institute (EAI), which had been set up to conduct cost-benefit analyses of environmental issues and to trim public spending. The conservative Rasmussen had come to power in November 2001, taking over a position held by Social Democrats since 1920. He believes in a free-market approach to environmentalism, assuming that economic principles and incentives are all that are needed to protect environmental quality, which usually translates into the total deregulation of industry. He soon announced plans to let local authorities build houses in state forests previously protected from development, abolished plans for three offshore windpower parks, and decided to cut one in five jobs at the Danish Environmental Protection Agency.

Soon after Lomborg took his new post, the EAI challenged Denmark's new program for recycling aluminum cans and other disposable packaging. In a report, the EAI questioned whether the money invested in the program was being well spent and suggested a cheaper scenario in which aluminum cans would be incinerated. The Danish Environmental Protection Agency (EPA) studied the EAI report and concluded it was mistaken, namely because aluminum cans do not burn. The deputy director general of the Danish EPA issued a statement calling the EAI's report "too hasty in its criticism" of the can recycling plan, and saying that "the analyses are too theoretical, and therefore reach the wrong conclusions." Based on these criticisms, the EAI studied the issue in greater detail and discovered that in two-thirds of Danish incineration plants, burning aluminum cans causes difficulties. They revised their report to incorporate the higher costs incineration plants would face in trying to mitigate these difficulties, and then stuck with their original conclusion. Despite the cost to the environment of not recycling aluminum[15] and the complications incineration plants would face, the EAI still argued that Denmark's aluminum recycling program should be aborted to save money. They also issued reports arguing against other environmentally friendly policies such as paper recycling and wind power. With a conservative prime minister making significant changes in environmental regulation, and with Lomborg heading the EAI, some worried that Denmark's reputation as a pioneer in the environmental movement would be compromised.

The debate over Lomborg's version of environmental skepticism, which had so far existed on the pages of journals and magazines and in the controlled atmosphere of TV studios, took a more serious, career-jeopardizing turn for him in the early spring of 2002, when a group of scientists, including Stuart Pimm and Jeff Harvey, reported Lomborg to the Danish Committee on Scientific Dishonesty (DCSD). Set up in 1992 by the Danish Research Agency, the DCSD is the first European body to provide oversight on issues of scientific misconduct. Its mandate requires it to consider any complaint whatsoever—arising from the public or private sector—about any scientist. Though Lomborg's credentials are in political science and statistics, not science, the DCSD decided it had the authority to hear his case since he had presented his book as a scientifically researched argument. In addition to Pimm and Harvey's complaint, two other cases were lodged against him, the three of them totaling over 650 pages of arguments, counts, and deliberations. Given the positive reviews *The Skeptical Environmentalist* had received and the media storm it had caused, the DCSD recognized the social and political influence of the book—particularly on U.S. environmental policy—and took its duty seriously. As they expressed in their seventeen-page formal written judgement: "The U.S.A. is the society with the highest energy consumption in the world, and there are powerful interests in the U.S.A. bound up with increasing energy consumption and with the belief in free market forces. The U.S.A. is also responsible for a substantial part of the research into this and other areas dealt with by Bjørn Lomborg." At the very least the Danish (and American) public deserved to know whether Lomborg's arguments were based on solid science or not. But perhaps even more relevant to the DCSD's mandate, Lomborg held a politically powerful position at Denmark's Environmental Assessment Institute. If his scientific credentials were shaky, the institute's authority was in danger, especially since its own statutes insisted on a director with appropriate research experience.

The DCSD's written report summarized the accusations leveled at Lomborg: "In the three complaints, B.L. is accused of fabricating data, selectively and surreptitiously discarding unwanted results, of the deliberately misleading use of statistical methods, consciously distorted interpretation of the conclusions, plagiarization of others' results or publications, and deliberate misrepresentation of others' results." In judging whether or not these accusations were justified, the DCSD relied primarily on the analyses published in the *Scientific American* article in January 2002. After six months of review, the DCSD announced its judgement in January 2003: Lomborg was found to have been scientifically dishonest, though he was not guilty of gross negligence. In other words, his scientifc methods were flawed, but it had not been a deliberate attempt to mislead the public. The formal report concluded:

> On the basis of the material adduced by the complainants, and particularly the assessment in *Scientific American*, DCSD deems it to have

been adequately substantiated that the defendant, who has himself insisted on presenting his publication in scientific form and not allowing
the book to assume the appearance of a provocative debate-generating
paper, based on customary scientific standards and in light of his
systematic onesidedness in the choice of data and line of argument, has
clearly acted at variance with good scientific practice.

Though many scientists on the international front praised the decision,
Lomborg's defenders were quick to attack the ruling, calling it censorship
and criticizing the investigators for relying on published critiques of *The
Skeptical Environmentalist* (namely, the *Scientific American* articles) instead
of thoroughly analyzing it themselves. Lomborg, too, resented the final decision. "They simply said that if the four critical scientists in *Scientific American* said I was an idiot, then I must be,"[16] he lamented. It looked to some as
if, in this case, the dissent and skepticism that makes for scientific rigor was
being unfairly squashed by a "green witch-hunt." Reviewer Richard Fisher
had made a similar point earlier: Though he thought the book was deeply
flawed and disagreed with most of it, he felt it had been of some benefit to
science by emphasizing the need for critical analysis of data. "All that Lomborg has accomplished is to try, without much success, to expose the soft un-
derbelly of science,"[17] he wrote.

But there were also those who saw Lomborg less as a skeptical environmentalist than as someone who is just wrong. This camp saw broad ethical
implications in the way in which Lomborg's message had been presented to
the public, which they considered to be a campaign of disinformation. As
conservation biologist **Paul Ehrlich** wrote, "The notorious Lomborg affair
highlights serious ethical problems for biologists in balancing concerns
about freedom of speech with the way power and privilege can be used to
control what people know."[18] One problem Ehrlich outlines is the fact that
The Skeptical Environmentalist gained prestige by being published by Cambridge University Press. This could give the false impression that the book
had been scientifically peer reviewed. "The question about Lomborg is not
whether he should be allowed to voice his views, but whether he should be
granted venues that suggest support and approval from communities that
neither support nor approve his views. The ethical question is one of truth in
packaging,"[19] concluded Ehrlich.

The DCSD ruling propelled Lomborg back into the spotlight at a time
when publicity surrounding him had begun to dim. It also triggered a
backlash of political maneuvers and further inquiries. The Danish Parliament reacted to the ruling by asking a panel of experts to investigate the
eight environmental analyses conducted by the EAI, one of which was the
aluminum recycling report. Five independent Scandinavian scientists studied the reports and concluded that "none of these reports represent scien-

tific work or methods in the traditional sense." On the other side, a group of social scientists in Denmark called for the DCSD to be disbanded, prompting the Danish Science Minister Helge Sander to ask the Danish Research Agency to organize an independent working group to review DCSD policies and procedures. In response, some 600 scientists in Denmark signed a petition in support of the DCSD and presented it to the Danish Research Agency.

To top it off, in February 2003, Lomborg lodged two formal complaints against the DCSD with the Danish Ministry of Science, Technology, and Innovation. The ministry embarked on its own investigation and, nearly a year later, in December 2003, they pronounced Lomborg vindicated. They found fault with the original ruling, saying, "[T]he DCSD has not documented where [Lomborg] has allegedly been biased in his choice of data and in his argumentation, and . . . the ruling is completely void of argumentation for why the DCSD find that the complainants are right in their criticisms of [his] working methods."

Even before this apparent victory over the DCSD ruling, and in the face of constant and nearly unanimous negative reviews from the scientific community, Lomborg's book and its message have remained popular. Some of his critics are dumbfounded by this, but the reason for his popularity may not be so elusive. In fact, the public response to Lomborg's book has pinpointed one of the most fundamental problems the environmental movement faces in trying to recruit the general public—bad news, often repeated and intensified, tends to cause a sense of despair. In his book on global warming called *The Heat Is On*, **Ross Gelbspan** recounts a Harvard seminar on climate change in which the magnitude of the problem became so evident that it drove students away. "The material was compelling, they said, but it engendered overwhelming personal reactions. The problems were so great—and the ability of the students to affect them so remote— that they could deal with their feelings of frustration and helplessness and depression only by staying away."[20] A seemingly well-reasoned set of arguments, published by a respected academic press and written by a charming, media-savvy liberal, might go a long way toward assuaging one's sense of guilt over environmental issues. Paul Kingsnorth wrote about this phenomenon in relation to Lomborg's book, saying how seductive the skeptics' arguments can be:

> For it's not just nasty fat cats and politicians who want to believe their message; we all do. Deep down, we all want to believe that everything will be fine—because deep down, we know it won't. We can see our streets gridlocking, our fields disappearing under waves of Barratt Homes, fish stocks collapsing, farmers hemorrhaging from the land, politicians giving up, markets taking over. . . . [W]e hate,

with a secret passion, anyone who tells us what we quietly know already: that one day soon we are all going to have take responsibility for our actions.[21]

Lomborg's book got attention and continues to sell in part because his message makes environmental disasters like global warming seem less overwhelming. With his reassurances that everything is getting better, that the end of the world is not nigh, and that there's no need to panic, Lomborg offers a despairing public absolution, with an entertaining dose of controversy and debate on the side.

Lomborg lives in Copenhagen, Denmark, and continues to work for the Environmental Assessment Institute.

NOTES

1. Jason Cowley, "The Man Who Demanded a Recount," *New Statesman* Vol. 132 (June 30, 2003), p. 31.

2. Matt Ridley, "The Profits of Doom," *Spectator* Vol. 288 (February 23, 2002), p. 10.

3. Jim Giles, "The Man They Love to Hate," *Nature* Vol. 423 (May 15, 2003), p. 216.

4. Cowley, "The Man Who Demanded a Recount," p. 28.

5. Bjørn Lomborg, *The Skeptical Environmentalist: Measuring the Real State of the World* (New York: Cambridge University Press, 2001), p. 4.

6. Dennis Dutton, "Greener than You Think," *Washington Post* (October 21, 2001), p. 01. Dutton, who was identified in the byline as "a professor of philosophy who lectures on the dangers of pseudoscience at the science facilities of the University of Canterbury in New Zealand," is a supporter of Julian Simon's work and promotes the Global Climate Coalition, a consortium of oil and coal interests.

7. "Doomsday Postponed," *Economist* Vol. 360 (September 8, 2001), p. 29.

8. Richard Bell, "Media Sheep," *World Watch* (March/April 2002), p. 11.

9. Mark Lynas, "Natural Bjørn Killer," *Ecologist* Vol. 33(2) (March 2003), p. 26.

10. Keith Kloor, "Eco-Provocateur," *Audubon* (January/February 2002), p. 18.

11. Stuart Pimm and Jeff Harvey, "No Need to Worry about the Future," *Nature* Vol. 414 (November 8, 2001), p. 150.

12. John Rennie, "Misleading Math about the Earth: Science Defends Itself against *The Skeptical Environmentalist*," *Scientific American* (January 2002), p. 59.

13. The IPCC was established by the World Meteorological Organization and the United Nations Environmental Program in 1988 to assess current information on human-induced climate change. It is the largest and most rigorously peer-reviewed scientific body in history and has completed three assessment reports.

14. John P. Holdren, "Energy: Asking the Wrong Question," *Scientific American* (January 2002), p. 65.

15. Aluminum provides perhaps the premier illustration of the environmental benefits of recycling. According the the U.S. Environmental Protection Agency, using recy-

cled aluminum to make new cans uses only 5 percent as much energy as using virgin bauxite ore. To make aluminum from "scratch," the ore must be mined, shipped to a refinery, subjected to a high-voltage electrical current, and formed into ingots, whereas recycled aluminum is simply melted and recast.

16. Giles, "The Man They Love to Hate," p. 218.

17. Richard M. Fisher, "Skeptical about *The Skeptical Environmentalist*," *Skeptical Inquirer* (November/December 2002), p. 51.

18. Paul Ehrlich, "Bioethics: Are Our Priorities Right?" *Bioscience* Vol. 53 (December 2003), p. 1212.

19. Ibid., p. 1213.

20. Ross Gelbspan, *The Heat Is On: The High Stakes Battle over the Earth's Threatened Environment* (Reading, MA: Addison-Wesley Publishing Company, 1997), p. 172.

21. Paul Kingsnorth, "Eat Your Greens," *Ecologist* Vol. 33 (March 2003), p. 31.

BIBLIOGRAPHY

Following the publication of Lomborg's *The Skeptical Environmentalist: Measuring the Real State of the World* (New York: Cambridge University Press, 2001), a multitude of book reviews, articles about Lomborg and reviews of the controversy have been published in the popular press. For positive reviews of Lomborg and his book, see "Doomsday Postponed," *Economist* Vol. 360 (September 8, 2001), pp. 28–30; Dennis Dutton, "Greener than You Think," *Washington Post* (October 21, 2001), p. 1; "The Litany and the Heretic," *Economist* Vol. 362 (February 2, 2002), p. 75–77; Matt Ridley, "The Profits of Doom," *Spectator* Vol. 288 (February 23, 2002), pp. 10–11; and Jason Cowley, "The Man Who Demanded a Recount," *New Statesman* Vol. 132 (June 30, 2003), pp. 28–31. Opposing views are found in Stuart Pimm and Jeff Harvey, "No Need to Worry about the Future," *Nature* Vol. 414 (November 8, 2001), pp. 149–150; John Rennie, "Misleading Math about the Earth: Science Defends Itself against *The Skeptical Environmentalist*," *Scientific American* (January 2002), p. 59, with additional articles by Stephen Schneider, John P. Holdren, John Bongaarts, and Thomas Lovejoy, pp. 60–71; Keith Kloor, "Eco-Provocateur," *Audubon* (January/February 2002), p. 18; Richard Bell, "Media Sheep," *World Watch* (March/April 2002), pp. 11–13; Daniel Simberloff, "Skewed Skepticism," *American Scientist* Vol. 90 (March/April 2002), pp. 184–187; Richard M. Fisher, "Skeptical about *The Skeptical Environmentalist*," *Skeptical Inquirer* (November/December 2002), pp. 49–51; Paul Kingsnorth, "Eat Your Greens," *Ecologist* Vol. 33 (March 2003), p. 31; Mark Lynas, "Natural Bjørn Killer," *Ecologist* Vol. 33(2) (March 2003), pp. 26–30; Jim Giles, "The Man They Love to Hate," *Nature* Vol. 423 (May 15, 2003), pp. 216–218; and Paul Ehrlich, "Bioethics: Are Our Priorities Right?" *Bioscience* Vol. 53 (December 2003), pp. 1207–1217. For articles about the Danish Committee on Scientific Dishonesty ruling see Andrew Revkin, "Environment and Science: Danes Rebuke a 'Skeptic'," *New York Times* (January 8, 2003), p. A7; Alison Abbott, "Ethics Panel Attacks Environmental Book," *Nature* Vol. 421 (January 16, 2003), p. 201; "More Heat, Less Light on Lomborg," *Nature* Vol. 421 (January 16, 2003), p. 195; Debora MacKenzie, "Book Puts Danish Institute in the Spotlight," *New Scientist* Vol. 177 (January 18, 2003),

p. 8; Fred Pearce, "Call off the Witch Hunt," *New Scientist* Vol. 177 (January 18, 2003), p. 23; Alison Abbott, "Social Scientists Call for Abolition of Dishonesty Committee," *Nature* Vol. 421 (February 13, 2003), p. 681. Ross Gelbspan's *The Heat Is On: The High Stakes Battle over the Earth's Threatened Environment* (Reading, MA: Addison-Wesley Publishing Company, 1997) discusses the disinformation campaign regarding global climate change and the general tendency to resist news of overwhelming environmental disaster.

CHRISTOPHER SWAIN
(1968–)

I believe that if I get into that river, I can put the river in the public eye, I can highlight threats and solutions, I can become something of a champion for the Columbia River. And folks who might not know that that most contaminated of beauties, the Columbia, is slipping away might get the word. And who knows? They might come to her aid.

—Christopher Swain

Athlete and advocate Christopher Swain jumped into the headwaters of the Columbia River in British Columbia on June 4, 2002, to undertake an unprecedented quest: to swim the river's entire 1,243-mile length. The ecosystem of the Columbia River has been rendered nearly impotent by pollution and cement—dammed in fourteen places and filled with agricultural runoff, radioactive waste from the Hanford Nuclear Reservation, sewage, chemical slurry from sawmills, and heavy metals—and Swain wanted to plead its case. Believing that much of the American public has grown desensitized to panicked reports of environmental problems, he decided that, in order to call attention to the shameful state of the Columbia River, he had to get wet. He made it personal, exposing himself to frigid water, pollution, and pounding waves and testing his physical and mental endurance. In July 2003, he made it to the Pacific Ocean at Astoria, after thirteen months of swimming, fundraising, and reaching out to more than 13,000 people, including 8,000 schoolchildren.

In addition to immersing himself in every inch of the waterway's length, he also found himself immersed in a media buzz that was impossible to control. His situation illustrates the delicate and precarious balance that must be struck when dealing with certain types of environmental advocacy in the mass media: He needed to capture the limelight in order to raise discussions of water quality and to breathe life into the potential for Columbia River restoration, but he was regularly accused of getting too much attention and of caring more about his own fame than the fate of the Columbia River watershed. Swain grew increasingly frustrated by these accusations, especially since he had little control over what reporters chose to print. Issues like pollution or the effect of dams on salmon runs often came as a second thought after crowd-pleasing details like what he ate while swimming or how his wife felt about his being gone so much. Although it was these personal details that cast the river's plight in human terms and made Swain's story compelling to the thousands of people he spoke to along the way, it sometimes seemed as if his star status tarnished the purity of his cause. "Beware the cult of personality," warned Darryl Cherney, an Earth First! activist. Others, however, are less critical of high-profile advocacy, seeing it as an effective tool in an age of ever-escalating media buzz. "Only punk anarchists are against environmental celebrities," says **Dave Foreman**, co-founder of Earth First! "The naysayers are fools and they are cutting their own throats. We need heroes who symbolize the movement to the public as a whole."[1]

Christopher Swain was born in New York, New York, on February 24, 1968. He comes from a lineage of sailors, including both grandfathers; his father, who is also a corporate lawyer; and an uncle. His mother worked at a children's center in New York, but left to raise her three children: Christopher and his sisters Amanda and Eliza. His grandparents were a close and positive influence in his life, fostering his interests in competitive sports and the natural world. Sports and the outdoors were early passions for Swain and, given his natural affinity for swimming, he looked for chances to be in or near water. In his favorite childhood dream he plunged deep into the ocean, opened his mouth, and discovered he could breathe underwater and was miraculously able to explore the aquatic world as long as he liked. When he was 7 years old he won his first sailboat race—five years later, as a requirement for a sailing class, he accomplished his first open-water swim in the Atlantic Ocean. To pass the test, he had to jump, fully clothed, into the water; strip down to a swimsuit; and then swim unassisted to the beach, a quarter of a mile away. With the safety of dry land appearing impossibly far, 12-year-old Christopher fought worries that he wouldn't make it and that the entire town would ridicule him. But as he glided through the chilly water, he concentrated on calming his strokes into a steady rhythm until, before he knew it, his feet pulled him onto the firm sand.

Swain went to high school at the Waring School, a private school in Beverly, Massachusetts, graduating in 1986. While in college at Wesleyan University in Middletown, Connecticut, he competed on the rowing team and then branched out into cycling—applying himself with such determination that he ended up a nationally ranked bicycle racer. In 1990 he graduated from Wesleyan with a bachelor's degree in film studies and French literature, and sometime that year had a revelation regarding his athletic strivings. "While I was recovering from a biking accident, I did some soul searching and determined that competition for competition's sake was empty. And in the process of looking for what I cared about, I discovered that I had to align my athletic efforts with my deepest aspirations," he said later.

In testing this new resolution, he summoned the endurance he had been building up during seven years of training and, in December 1991, successfully completed one of the most unfathomable tests of human will: the Apache Run for the Sun initiation, which no non–Native American had attempted ever before. As the rules dictated, he ran up trails in the mud and snow of the Rocky Mountains, cradling a gulp of water in his mouth that he was forbidden to swallow, until nine miles later when he reached a ceremonial hole in the earth where he finally spit out the water and pledged to live a life of harmony for himself, for all people, and for the earth. Over ten years later, during his Columbia River swim, he would reflect on that pledge and consider his goal of advocating for the ecological and cultural restoration of the river to be meeting that challenge of harmonious living.

Acting on a similar aspiration combining environmental and social concerns, Swain conceived of an idea to help children living in difficult circumstances. He wanted them to see something utterly alien to their experience, like a mountain valley, to potentially inspire in them a new perspective. In 1993, he founded the non-profit Children's Forestry Project (CFP), which gave under-privileged youth hands-on experience planting trees on degraded forestland in Colorado, Connecticut, and Massachusetts. The CFP's work won acknowledgement from many circles, including the American Film Institute and the Shatse Gaden Monks of Tibet. Two years later, Swain started another non-profit organization—the Human Rights Company (HRC)—which sought to promote awareness of the Universal Declaration of Human Rights, the treaty adopted by the General Assembly of the United Nations in 1948 to affirm the inherent dignity and rights of all humans. The HRC provided outreach to local schools, organized a Walk for Human Rights across Massachusetts, and provided the inspiration for Swain's first advocacy swim. In 1996, to promote universal human rights, he swam the lower 210 miles of the Connecticut River—from Vermont to the Atlantic Ocean—in seventeen days. During the swim he met a woman named Heather who read about the swim in a newspaper, came out to meet him, and even swam with him for a day. A few months later they got back in touch, and eventually married in September 1998.

The Connecticut River Swim for Human Rights showed Swain how media-friendly such an event could be. He discovered that people were fascinated by the intimacy of his relationship to the river and wanted to hear him talk about it. Swimming in it day after day, he became very in tune with the rhythms of the river, its currents, the clack of gravel on the riverbed, its smell—and he concluded that "tasting every mile of a river is a great way to build the credibility to speak on its behalf." When he reached the Atlantic, his overwhelming feeling was not the elation of accomplishment, but sadness that his time in the river was at its end. Unknown to him as he completed the Swim for Human Rights, the next time he would undertake an advocacy swim—on the Pacific Northwest's Columbia River—he would be advocating for the river itself.

But first Swain succumbed to the temptation of taking his athleticism back into the realm of competition. He began training for distance running and completed the Portland Marathon in Oregon in 1997, the same year he received a master of acupuncture degree from the New England School of Acupuncture in Watertown, Massachusetts. Poised now with his experience in swimming, cycling, and distance running, Swain took the obvious step for someone committed to pushing himself to the heights of endurance: the sport of triathlon. In 1998 he qualified for the U.S. Triathlon National Championships, and the next year he competed in the first IRONMAN USA Lake Placid Triathlon, finishing thirty-third in his division.

Swain's wife Heather grew up in Oregon, and while visiting there to run the marathon and visit her relatives, he got his first glimpse of the Columbia River—actually somewhat of a disappointment. He had envisioned a wilder, more freely flowing river rich with salmon, but found what he termed "a contaminated beauty." Distressed by the disconnect between the pristinely clear and ecologically rich river described by Lewis and Clark at the beginning of the nineteenth century and the polluted, dammed-up, brown chain of slack water that exists today, he began researching. He studied pictures of the river from before dams were put in, learned lists of pesticides that had been detected in the river, and read about the Hanford Nuclear Reservation, which looms ominously off the banks of the Columbia in Washington state.

The Columbia River, comprising the fourth largest watershed in the United States, makes a major contribution to the economy of the Pacific Northwest and is intricately embedded in the region's culture and history. While its importance to over nine million people is incontrovertible, it is precisely this human dependence on the river that puts its ecological health at risk. Threats to Columbia River and the people living along it include twenty different pesticides, bacteria, polychlorinated biphenyl (PCB), and heavy metals including arsenic, aluminum, lead, selenium, mercury, and many others. Dioxins, some of the most toxic and carcinogenic substances known, were detected in every sediment sample taken in a study of the lower Columbia in 1991, and industries continue to dump them into the river.[2] All of these substances have been detected at levels considered unsafe for either drinking or for water recreation (including swimming) and have rendered fish or shellfish from the river too harmful for human consumption. Swain later summed up his reaction to some of his research:

> We've got a finite amount of water in the Columbia River Basin. Sometimes it helps me to remember that all the water in the Columbia Drainage is continuously cycling through. No "new" water molecules are entering the system. . . . Now that we have messed up so much of that water, our way of life is at risk. Here in Portland, for instance, it is not safe to eat the fish, or swim, or drink from the river. These are traditional forms of use and enjoyment that are no longer available to us. My hope is that they will be available to our great-grandchildren.[3]

Fourteen dams also compromise the health of the river. Their construction has destroyed riparian habitat and created devastating problems for salmon survival by obstructing their migration to and from spawning grounds. Dams slow the flow of water—thereby increasing water temperature, sometimes up to levels lethal to salmon eggs—and kill fish directly in their turbines.

Some of the most unsettling research involved the Hanford Nuclear Reservation, which spreads out over 560 square miles of southeastern Washington desert. From the 1940s through the 1960s, in the process of producing plutonium for nuclear weapons, the Hanford plant released over 400 billion gallons of liquid radioactive and chemical waste into the soil column, while hundreds of billions of gallons of wastewater were discharged directly into the Columbia River. In the 1960s, Oregon's Public Health Division declared the Columbia River, which borders the Hanford site for fifty-one miles, the most radioactive river in the free world. The contaminated groundwater underneath Hanford creeps in toxic plumes until it reaches the Columbia, where it has raised the levels of uranium and other substances beyond acceptable drinking water standards. At Hanford, millions of gallons of high-level, very corrosive chemical and radioactive wastes are still stored underground in 177 underground tanks, sixty-nine of which are acknowledged to be leaking. Since the production of plutonium ceased in the late 1980s, Hanford's only mission has been to clean up, but, in spite of its Superfund listing, the cleanup process has been slow and hampered by bureaucratic tangles, and the site remains one of the most grossly contaminated areas in North America and possibly the world.

The more Swain learned, the more upset he became, and he continually mulled over the injustices suffered by the Columbia River. In 1999, he and Heather moved to Portland to be closer to Heather's family. The fall of the following year, returning home from a trip to the East Coast, Swain drove west into the rainy Pacific Northwest, entranced by the Columbia, unrolling alongside the highway. As he thought again about the history of the human impact on the river, his native passion for water and his desire to see the Columbia run clean culminated in a sense of purpose, and at that moment he committed himself to making the advocacy swim happen. As he began to search for sponsors and to get the word out, he also surrendered to a brutal training regimen of endless lap swimming, lake swimming, weight lifting, and hill running, to discipline his body. That winter, in December 2000, Heather and Christopher's first child, a daughter named Rowan, was born.

After almost two years of preparation, on June 4, 2002, at Canal Flats in British Columbia, Swain got into his dry suit and dove into the southern end of Columbia Lake, the headwaters of the Columbia River. Before spending the next seven hours swimming the eight-mile length of the lake, 100 local elementary students saw him off, toasting him with goblets of pure Columbia Lake water. Swain himself drank straight from the lake, the only drinkable water in the entire 1,243 miles of the swim. The years of training and planning had reached fruition, and, by tasting the water at its source, he reminded himself of his vision for a purer, healthier future for the rest of the river.

Swain's long days of swimming soon blurred into weeks. Accompanying him on the water was a crew person in a 1974 Zodiac inflatable boat loaded down with equipment: tarps, camping gear, cook stoves, spare swim gear, Ibuprofen, mosquito netting, maps, a cell phone, and lots of food. Running on a no-frills budget, he and his support person camped out at night or stayed with local families or at sponsoring inns. In addition to the grueling effort of propelling himself through miles of water each day, Swain strove to juggle the logistics of this fledgling endeavor—often staying up late into the night making sandwiches for the next day, working on fundraising, paying bills, or keeping up with his online swim journal.

For water over 55 degrees, Swain wore a wet suit, sleek and hydrodynamic. But in colder water he relied on a more protective dry suit (or as he called it, a "damp suit"). He also wore neoprene gloves, socks, boots, and hood, and covered all exposed skin with SPF 36 sunscreen and his lips with SPF 45 zinc oxide. As final protection against the microorganisms in the water that could make him sick, he gargled with a 1.5 percent hydrogen peroxide solution every time he took a break to eat or drink anything. Keeping himself stocked with the calories necessary to swim for up to nine hours a day while regulating his body temperature in frigid water required a good deal of planning—and food. Every fifteen minutes he would swim over to the support boat to eat pretzels, Clif Bars, Goldfish crackers ("I'm the guy who's introduced the invasive species of cheddar cheese goldfish cracker into the upper Columbia River," he joked), peanut butter and jelly sandwiches, and energy drinks. Even when he did not feel hungry he had to continue to supply his working muscles with fuel, or he would get cold and his stamina would suffer.

He also drank hot tea during his calorie stops, and that also helped keep him warm. But Swain claimed it was the people he met along the way that really kept him going—school groups, parents, mayors of riverside communities. He focused most of his outreach on schools, finding children to be the most enthusiastic supporters of cleaning the river. They were fascinated with his equipment and by the daily facts of how he eats and where he sleeps, and they were charmed when he admitted to falling in love with the river. After promising one school group that he would inspect the river to ascertain the best possible ways to start cleaning it up, he later said he would rather drown than fail them. Many of the towns Swain passed through rely on industries that have a negative impact on the river's health, yet he found only support for his cause and affection for the Columbia. His driving motivation during the endeavor was stoked by the encouragement he got from river communities. He told them that he lived on the same river, which made them neighbors, and that he intended to come back when he had finished to continue entreating them to restore the river. "Almost invariably, people smile when I say this," he wrote in his swim journal. "I imagine that most of them think I'm nuts. But I also imagine that some of them are wondering what would happen if a 259,000-square-mile neighborhood decided to clean up its local river."

During that summer among the glorious mountains of southern British Columbia, Swain pushed his way through water sometimes as cold as 44 degrees. He swam past small mountain towns and through the longest contiguous stretch of wetlands in North America. Most of the way he was helped along by the current, though in early July he had to muscle his way—against a prevailing wind—through the slack waters of Kinbasket Lake for 80 miles. The untainted waters of the first 100-or-so free-flowing miles of the river, tasting of reeds and glacial silt, faded into memory as he approached the slack waters behind the first few dams, where he began tasting sewage, chainsaw bar oil, sawdust, and slag from metal smelters.

By the end of July, with 180 miles to go before crossing the U.S. border, he had swum over a quarter of the way to the Pacific and already had portaged around two dams. He then entered the Arrow Lakes, which had been flooded into a reservoir when the Keenleyside Dam was built in 1968. The Arrow Lakes were naturally nutrient poor, meaning that trout and kokanee salmon were hard-pressed for food there. But after the dam went in, these fish were further beleaguered. In 1999, BC Hydro—the company that had built the dam—started throwing nitrogen/phosphorous fertilizer pellets off a ferry in an attempt to increase nutrients in these lakes. Monitoring studies have yet to determine what effect the fertilizer is having on the phytoplankton and microbial communities in the lakes.

The effects of the Keenleyside Dam range beyond the hardships of the local fish populations. Swain met and talked with people who once lived in Burton City, which was flooded by the dam. BC Hydro bought off the farms and houses of families living there, and those who refused faced eviction threats. Also uprooted was the Sinixt tribe, which was declared "extinct" right before the dam went in, and thus was stripped of its legal status as the waters buried its ancestral lands. Many locals harbor deep resentment over the destruction of their valley, and as Swain swam over flooded orchards, houses, roads, and farms, he imagined that the water felt heavier for the burdensome displacement of hundreds of people.

During the fall and winter, Swain broke his journey into legs, swimming as much as weather, health concerns, and logistical issues allowed. As always, he kept his eyes open for threats to water quality as he went. One such potential menace involved Teck Cominco, a company that operates one of the world's largest fully integrated zinc- and lead-smelting and refining complexes at Trail, British Columbia. In preparation for swimming through this industrial site in early October, Swain asked for a tour of the facility, wondering how much poison runs into the river from their outflows. The officials showed him their experimental plots where they employ natural agents like botanicals to remove heavy metals from the soil. They emphasized their environmental policies and showed him the location of the three outfalls that discharge effluent into the Columbia River. The next day, as he swam past the Teck Cominco facility, he noticed liquid draining into the river from a pipe that didn't correspond to any of the three outfalls pointed out to him. When he asked about it, the company informed him that all those pipes were officially sealed and suggested he was perhaps confused about what he had seen. But a few weeks later he received a letter from the company admitting that his observation had been accurate after all. They explained that the "inactive" pipe was being used for preventive maintenance, which involves flushing it out with bypass cooling water, and that apparently Swain had happened to swim by during one of the scheduled discharges. Swain gave the company the benefit of the doubt, but left with the conviction that it is a good idea to be vigilant and ask questions about what is being discharged into one's waterway.

On October 3, 2002, Swain reached the U.S. border near Northport, Washington. Maneuvering away from the turbulence of the merging Pend D'Oreille River, he managed to battle the current and make shore, where he met with a U.S. customs inspector, showed his passport, had his peanut butter and jelly sandwiches inspected, and was free to continue his journey. As he progressed, he readied himself for the approaching Grand Coulee Dam and the arduous stretch of slack water that would precede it. Before he got there he would have to brave already-plunging temperatures (it got down to eighteen degrees on October 14) and the sometimes-fatal rapids of the Little Dalles below Northport.

Claiming title as the largest concrete structure in North America, the Grand Coulee Dam is considered one of the wonders of the engineering world. Work on the dam began in 1933, and, once complete, it flooded an enormous canyon in eastern Washington, creating Lake Roosevelt, the reservoir that contains 9 million-acre-feet of water and stretches over 150 miles—nearly to the Canadian border. Inundation of the valleys above the dam disrupted the lives of local Indian tribes, particularly the Colvilles, eliminating much of the prime riverside farmland on their reservation and destroying or curtailing access to established hunting grounds. No fish ladders were included in the dam's design, resulting in a loss of access to 1,140 miles of upriver spawning grounds for salmon, thus completely eliminating them above the dam. In addition, the upper section of Lake Roosevelt is currently being considered as a federal Superfund site thanks to the load of heavy metals and other pollutants that have been trapped behind the dam. On January 20, 2003, in nearly freezing water, Swain stroked his way to the halfway point on the river—621.5 miles equidistant from the starting and ending points. By early February, he had reached the Grand Coulee Dam.

Winter temperatures made the river too cold to swim in for any length of time, so Swain spent more time at home during the coldest months, which was a relief since the time away from his wife and young daughter wore away at him emotionally. During the winter, Swain continued doing outreach, maintained an buzzing undercurrent of publicity, worked part-time on odd jobs like trimming trees and moving boxes of shoes at a warehouse, and managed to get back to the river to swim a few days a month. In March, he traveled to New York City to receive the International Earth Day Award at the United Nations, which had declared 2003 the International Year of Fresh Water, making Swain a perfect candidate for the award. In spite of a continuing battle with an ear infection, he swam across the frigid polluted waters of the East River from Roosevelt Island to Manhattan in honor of the cause before receiving his award that evening.

A month later he faced what had been his biggest source of dread—the stretch of river that washes through the Hanford Nuclear Reservation—and he completed it in two nervous days. Uneasy about entering water poisoned with the unquantified spoils of the Atomic Age, Swain tried to get a test for background radiation levels in his body for before and after the Hanford stretch, but authorities at the U.S. Department of Energy, which manages the cleanup operation at the site, denied his request. Swimming through Hanford was surreal. "It was just achingly beautiful—pelicans, elk, wild horses," said Swain. "You turn your head one way, and you see these white bluffs. You turn your head the other way and you see Reactor B, where they made the plutonium for the bomb we dropped on Nagasaki."[4]

On May 15, 2003, he reached the Oregon state line and made for the scenic Columbia River Gorge, where Lewis and Clark had found thriving Native American tribes building a culture and economy around the plentiful salmon runs in the river. Salmon have decreased precipitously in the Columbia, and Swain sees this as an example of how environmental problems are closely tied to human problems. Swain describes past management decisions regarding dams and salmon as "Faustian bargains" that have caused declines in the quality of life of those who live closely entwined with the river. One particularly troubling example involves Celilo Falls—a vital spiritual and commercial site for fourteen native salmon-based cultures—which was flooded by the construction of the Dalles Dam in 1957. The destruction of Celilo Falls, now commonly regarded as one of the great tragedies of the American West, is a story Swain tells repeatedly in interviews in order to give it as much attention as he can. He wants to rouse a sense of responsibility toward the injustices of the past and to create a meaningful debate that could lead to the restoration of Celilo Falls—for the sake of the salmon runs, overall river quality, and cultural heritage. Inevitably, in discussions of dam breaching, the usual arguments arise: the economic burden, the inconvenience it would pose to river traffic, and the loss of hydropower from the dam's generators. But Swain wants to tip the scales toward another point of view, one that takes into account both the ecological value of a free-flowing river and the common cultural heritage of the people who evolved with the river.

Dodging six- and eight-foot waves, ferocious winds, and massive container ships in the gorge, Swain made his way past Portland, Oregon, and on to the Pacific Ocean. By the end, he just wanted to finish. His wife was expecting their second child, his finances had bottomed out, and he was tired. On July 1, 2003, he battled the ten-foot swells at the mouth of the river and tried to take in the fact that he was finished. As he wrote in his swim diary, "Here at statute mile zero, the river finally gives itself to the sea. I rode it all the way. 1,243 miles. I am sad and elated. Done and yet not done."

While still absorbing the realization that thirteen months' worth of courage, determination, and hard work were over, and simultaneously trying to gauge whether his mission accomplished all he hoped, Swain headed into a media storm. His endeavor created a buzz because it was an extraordinary accomplishment and a sensational story that generated human interest, and because Swain was media savvy and persistent. The success of environmental celebrities is measured by their recognition, and in fact depends on it. Swain realized that any media attention increased the chance that an apathetic citizen might find inspiration in the story and join the cause. "And there lies the difference between Swain and the purist greens," wrote journalist Bruce Barcott. "In a world cluttered with noble causes, it may take a book deal, or a pretty face—or hey, maybe six months of waterlogged fingers—to get the public behind you."[5]

When publicity is all-important, even negative press can further the cause. Over the winter, journalist Doug Clark from the *Spokane Spokesman-Review* had taken a tour in the crew boat while Swain swam alongside through Lake Roosevelt. He eventually wrote a contemptuous piece in which he called Swain a lunatic, cast doubt on whether he would even complete the swim, and accused him of environmental scare-mongering. "There are dumber ways to make a name for yourself, I suppose," wrote Clark.

"No one has ever pushed a macadamia nut with his nose to the top of Mt. Rainier, for example."[6] As letters to the editor volleyed back in protest of the article, Swain triumphed in the exchange. "While we run the risk of absorbing a few personal hits in our attempt to put the river in the public eye, I also think it makes for healthy exchange and spirited discussion," he wrote in his swim diary. "Any way I look at it, I have to smile: everybody's talking about cleaning up their dirty river."

But when the press started accusing Swain of doing the swim for purely egotistical reasons, it became harder to see the publicity in a positive light. One article called Swain an "environmental action figure," another an "eco-performance artist," and an editorial in the Portland *Oregonian* ridiculed the "unflinchingly enamored" media attention. "Gag me with a spoon of Columbia River's neuro-toxin soup," it read. "Here's a guy who's good at only one thing: Finding causes that get attention."[7] While some people felt that Swain's ego left no room for his conservation message, he himself regularly bemoaned the reluctance of the media to grapple with industrial pollution issues. He pointed out a story that had run in an eastern Washington newspaper that had covered his swim, but had neglected to mention the nearby Hanford Nuclear Reservation despite his repeated mentions of it.

At any rate, by the end of the swim Swain was tired of being labeled and even started to bristle at being called an environmentalist. After exposing himself to sewage, heavy metals, DDT, class IV rapids, heavy boat traffic, bacteria, frigid temperatures, extreme physical exertion, ear infections, swollen lymph nodes, and sunburn, he had become quick to distance himself from those less personally involved in environmental issues. "I am more impatient with the 'desk jockeys' in the environmental movement than ever before. I don't think people have any business advocating for waterways that they don't regularly use and enjoy. On the contrary, I think they have a professional responsibility to get wet,"[8] he said in an interview. Furthermore, he believes the term "environmentalist" has outlived its usefulness. He worries that this loaded term causes divisions and polarizes groups of people instead of bringing them together:

Many of the folks who use and enjoy waterways the most—hunters, fishermen, and boaters—have been alienated by their brethren in the environmental movement. It is a sorry state of affairs when we alienate those who might become our strongest allies. . . . I still hope that the swim might result in the formation of an unlikely, extraordinary, informal coalition of people from every side of the clean water debate. These folks would hold in common only their affection for the river, and would base their protection and restoration initiatives firmly upon that common ground.[9]

Ironically, since he refuses to be called an environmentalist, while also criticizing those who believe in protecting the river but are too leery of its miasmic pollution to "get wet," Swain himself runs the very risk of the alienation that he deplores—only in his case it is the environmentalists who might feel slighted.

Regardless, it is clear that he succeeded in bringing attention to the Columbia River. The severity of the river's condition was highlighted and made compelling by Swain's willingness to endanger his own health by immersing himself in its entire polluted length. This opened the public's eyes to the fact that the Columbia River breaks every rule of the Clean Water Act: For the majority of its length it is not safe to fish, swim, or drink from its waters. Most people have come to accept that these sources of pleasure and sustenance are no longer available, never thinking to question how or why this must be so. But Swain, by the simple act of swimming, made this a question again. He plans to return to the towns he visited along the river and to continue the dialogues he started about the river's health. But he will make sure that, whatever he does, he incorporates his role as a parent and husband. He now has two daughters to spend time with: Eleven days after he finished the swim, a second daughter was born to Swain and his wife, and they named her Celilo.

To continue educating and advocating on behalf of the Columbia River and to put his network of connections to good use, Swain started a new foundation, the Columbia River Conservancy. He continues to speak and give presentations promoting a comprehensive river cleanup and a restoration of its natural flows. As one example of the influence of Swain's swim, the mayor of the town of Trail, British Columbia, where Swain had spoken about water quality at a public reception, wrote to him later with the news that the town planned to reduce or eliminate the use of pesticides and herbicides on all city land, thereby cutting down on toxic runoff into the river.

NOTES

1. Quoted in Bruce Barcott, "Voyage of the Man-Fish," *Outside* (May 2002), p. 24.

2. Tetra Tech, *Reconnaissance Survey of the Lower Columbia River, Task 6 Reconnaissance Report,* prepared for Lower Columbia River Bi-State Program (Redmond, WA: Tetra Tech, Inc., 1993).

3. John Richen, "Reflections on a 1,243 Mile Swim: A Conversation with Christopher Swain," (December 2, 2003), http://www.smokebox.net/archives/interviews/swain1202.html (accessed May 11, 2004).

4. Ben Jacklet, "Man, Overboard," *Portland Tribune* (June 20, 2003), p. A3.

5. Barcott, "Voyage of the Man-Fish," p. 24.

6. Doug Clark, "Swimmer May Be Missing Boat," *Spokane Spokesman-Review* (December 12, 2002), p. B1.

7. S. Renee Mitchell, "Media All Wet for Buying Story: Hook, Line, Sinker," *Oregonian* (July 9, 2003), p. B2.

8. Richen, "Reflections on a 1,243 Mile Swim."

9. Ibid.

BIBLIOGRAPHY

Swain's odyssey has been covered solely by the popular media: periodicals, radio interviews, and newspaper articles. The best source of information available is the Columbia Swim website, which includes Swain's detailed swim diary and press releases—see http://www.columbiaswim.org/. For articles about Swain, see Bruce Barcott, "Voyage of the Man-Fish," *Outside* Vol. 27 (May 2002), pp. 20, 24; Barry Espenson, "Swimmer Takes 1,242-Mile Dip for River Restoration," *Columbia Basin Bulletin* (June 21, 2002); Patty Wentz, "The Long Haul," *On Earth: Environmental Politics, People* Vol. 24 (Fall 2002), p. 24; Doug Clark, "Swimmer May Be Missing Boat," *Spokane Spokesman-Review* (December 12, 2002), p. B1; Hal Bernton, "Swimmer Makes 1,243-Mile Journey to Save River," *Seattle Times* (June 16, 2003); Ben Jacklet, "Man, Overboard," *Portland Tribune* (June 20, 2003), pp. A1, A3; Blaine Harden, "He Loves Salmon So Much that He Swam Their River," *Washington Post* (July 6, 2003), p. A2; S. Renee Mitchell, "Media All Wet for Buying Story: Hook, Line, Sinker," *Oregonian* (July 9, 2003), p. B2; Amy Roe, "Mouth of the Columbia," *Willamette Week* (July 16, 2003), p. 13; and John Richen, "Reflections on a 1,243 Mile Swim: A Conversation with Christopher Swain," (December 2, 2003), http://www.smokebox.net/archives/interviews/swain1202.html. For technical information on water quality in the Lower Columbia River, see Tetra Tech, *Reconnaissance Survey of the Lower Columbia River, Task 6 Reconnaissance Report*, prepared for Lower Columbia River Bi-State Program (Redmond, WA: Tetra Tech, Inc., 1993).

APPENDIX: BRIEF BIOGRAPHIES

Arnold, Ron. Born August 8, 1937, Houston, Texas, to Dixie and Leniece Arnold Brown, adopted by John Andrew (a transit inspector) and Carrie Arnold (his grandparents). He attended the University of Texas, 1954–1955, and the University of Washington in Seattle, 1965. In the mid-1960s, Arnold worked as a graphic designer at the Boeing plant in Seattle. During those years he was a Sierra Club member, but became disenchanted with the group over issues of private property rights and the use of natural resources. In 1971, he started his own graphics company and began producing slide shows for timber companies. In 1977, he fought the expansion of Redwood National Park on behalf of three timber companies. Two years later, in a series of articles for *Logging Management* magazine, he proposed a need for an anti-environmental movement to counter the efforts of environmentalists. Together with **Alan Merril Gottlieb**, Arnold did just that; the two became founding leaders of the Wise Use movement. Since 1984, he has divided his time between managing Northwoods Studio, a private communication consulting firm; running the Center for the Defense of Free Enterprise, a pro-business think tank; and writing a newspaper column. The center's publishing division, the Free Enterprise Press, has published several of his books, including *Ecology Wars* (1987); *Trashing the Economy: How Runaway Environmentalism Is Wrecking America* (written with Alan Gottlieb, 1993); *Ecoterror: The Violent Agenda to Save Nature: The World of the Unabomber* (1997); and *Undue Influence: Wealthy Foundations, Grant-Driven*

Environmental Groups, and Zealous Bureaucrats that Control Your Future (1999). *Bibliography:* Helvarg, David. *The War against the Greens: The "Wise-Use" Movement, the New Right and Anti-Environmental Violence.* San Francisco: Sierra Club Books, 1994. Switzer, Jacqueline Vaughn. *Green Backlash: The History and Politics of Environmental Opposition in the U.S.* Boulder: Lynne Rienner Publishers, 1997.

Austin, Mary. Born in Carlinville, Illinois, on September 9, 1868; died Santa Fe, New Mexico, August 13, 1934. Attended Blackburn College in her hometown, where she studied math and science and was elected class poet. After graduation, she moved with her family to the desert on the edge of the San Joaquin Valley in California. The arid western landscape was a source of constant fascination to her and eventually became a literary inspiration as well. After she married in 1891, she and her husband moved to the Owens Valley, California, where Austin taught school and wrote about the natural world, particularly the land and people of the American Southwest. Her best-known work, a collection of essays, is *A Land of Little Rain*, Boston and New York: Houghton Mifflin, 1903. She eventually published several works of fiction, an autobiography, and other nature essays—honing her perspective on ecology, the spiritual-human connection to the land, and a non-anthropocentric vision of the natural world. Her books created a foundation for science-based nature writing and had a lasting impact on the deep ecology movement. *Bibliography:* Austin, Mary. *Earth Horizon.* Boston: Houghton Mifflin, 1932. Fink, Augusta. *I—Mary: A Biography of Mary Austin.* Tucson: University of Arizona Press, 1983. Pearce, T. M. *Mary Hunter Austin.* New York: Twayne Publishers, 1965.

Bailey, Ronald. Born November 23, 1953. Bailey is the author of *Eco-Scam: The False Prophets of the Ecological Apocalypse* (1993), which challenges many widely held views of environmentalists. He also edited *Earth Report 2000: Revisiting the True State of the Planet* (2000), which argues that environmental problems are overstated. He has produced several documentaries for PBS, including the series *Think Tank* and *Techno Politics*. He was been a staff writer for *Forbes* from 1987 to 1990 and has written anti-environmental articles for the *Wall Street Journal*, the *Washington Post*, *Smithsonian Magazine*, the *Washington Times*, and *National Review*. A popular speaker, he has lectured widely, arguing against ecology and for economy. He is the science correspondent for *Reason*, a conservative monthly magazine, and an adjunct scholar at the Competitive Enterprise Institute and the Cato Institute, both of which are think tanks that oppose environmental legislation. *Bibliography:* Beder, Sharon. *Global Spin: The Corporate Assault on Environmentalism.* Revised edition. White River Junction, VT: Chelsea Green Publishing Company, 2002.

Bari, Judi. Born November 7, 1949, Baltimore, Maryland; died March 2, 1997, Willits, California. Judith Bari became active in politics while studying at the University of Maryland, becoming so involved in the anti–Vietnam War and labor union movements that she gave up school to dedicate herself to activism. She joined Earth First! activities in 1988, and participated in non-violent resistance tactics. Concern for loggers led her to support a moratorium on tree spiking, and she sought to balance the safety and stability of loggers' jobs with environmental goals. Despite her sympathy with loggers, she began receiving death threats for her activism. On May 24, 1990, as she and fellow Earth First! member Darryl Cherney began driving to a protest, a car bomb placed under her seat blew up, nearly killing her and injuring Cherney. After six painful weeks of rehabilitation, Bari finally could walk again. She continued her activism and was a key organizer of the Earth First! movement until her death from breast cancer.

Bartram, William. Born April 9, 1739, Kingsessing, Pennsylvania; died July 22, 1823, Kingsessing. Both William Bartram and his father John Bartram were botanists and explorers—the first to collect and describe indigenous American plants. Father and son traveled throughout New England and the American Southeast on botanical expeditions, keeping detailed notes on the plants and animals they saw. In 1773, William embarked on his own four-year journey. His journal from the trip, entitled *Travels through North and South Carolina, Georgia, East and West Florida, the Cherokee Country, the Extensive Territories of the Muscogulges, or Creek Confederacy, and the Country of the Choctaws* was published in 1791 and described the intricate interconnections he saw in the natural world, from the tiniest insects to 215 different species of native birds. His descriptions of the perfect organization of nature's design helped encourage the spread of the Romantic literary movement, which celebrated wilderness as an expression of rational beneficence. Accompanying his writings were his illustrations of flora and fauna, meticulous and highly accurate drawings that earned him recognition as the most influential natural history artist before John James Audubon. Overall, his work brought to light the rich flora of the North American continent, inspiring generations of naturalists, artists, and poets, including Samuel Coleridge and William Wordsworth. *Bibliography:* Terrie, Philip G. "William Bartram," in *American Nature Writers* Vol. 1, John Elder, ed. New York: Charles Scribner's Sons, 1996, pp. 63–74.

Berry, Wendell. Born August 5, 1934, Henry County, Kentucky. He grew up on land that had been in the family for over a hundred years. Making his home along the Kentucky River in a cabin on stilts built by his great-uncle, Berry nurtures a deep connection to the land through non-industrial farming, shunning the capitalist culture as much as possible, and chronicling his

observations, contemplations, and land-ethic in fiction, nonfiction, and poetry. His groundbreaking book *The Unsettling of America* (1977) explores
the loss of human potential that comes with the modern disconnection to the
land. The essays in the book argue that industrial agriculture as practiced today removes farming from its cultural context and is destructive to the entire
fabric of rural community life and, therefore, to American culture as a whole.
In advocating a more responsible approach to consumption and production,
Berry argues for a better understanding of ecology and a philosophical shift
away from the humans-against-nature paradigm toward a culturally and environmentally healthier humans-with-nature paradigm. Berry represents a
unique and successful model of rejecting unsustainable industrial technology:
He still writes longhand with a pencil and paper, and his works deliver an au-
thentic voice of integrity in late twentieth-century American literature. *Bibliography:* Nibellink, Herman. "Wendell Berry," in *American Nature Writers*
Vol. 1, John Elder, ed. New York: Charles Scribner's Sons, 1996, pp. 89–105.

Brown, Lester. Born March 28, 1934, Bridgeton, New Jersey. An active
member of 4-H as a child, Brown intended to go into farming, but eventually became very interested in world hunger. He completed a master's degree
in agricultural economics at the University of Maryland in 1958, and went
to work for the USDA, where he studied the link between food supply and
rapid population growth. In 1963, he received a master's degree in public administration from Harvard University. Three years later he was named administrator of the USDA's International Agricultural Development Service,
where he oversaw projects in over forty countries. In 1974, Brown founded
the Worldwatch Institute to raise public awareness of environmental threats
and to encourage effective public policy responses. The yearly report published by Worldwatch Institute, *The State of the World*, offers current up-
dates and analysis on agricultural, population, and economic trends. Brown
also has written many books addressing population growth, soil erosion,
rain forest depletion, and overfishing. These books include *World without
Borders* (1972); *In the Human Interest: A Strategy to Stabilize World Population* (1974); and *Building a Sustainable Society* (1981).

Burford, Anne Gorsuch. Born April 21, 1942, Casper, Wyoming, as Anne
McGill. She grew up in Denver and started taking college classes during
summers when she was 13. She graduated from the honors program in political science from the University of Colorado in 1961, and received a law
degree from the university's law school in 1964. That year she married
David Gorsuch. She held various legal positions until 1975, when she became
corporate counsel for Mountain Bell Telephone in Denver. When **Ronald
Reagan** became president in 1980, she sought a position within his administration and, with the backing of **Joseph Coors** and Interior Secretary **James**

Watt, she won the nomination to head the Environmental Protection Agency (EPA), though she had little experience with environmental legislation. Her anti-environmental ideology became clear once she took office: She weakened the EPA's power structure through reorganization and huge budget cuts, hired on her staff seven lawyers who had represented industry giants like Dow Chemical and Exxon, and relaxed regulations of the Clean Air Act. Public opinion of her near dismantling of the EPA, which Americans associate with the protection of public health, struck a highly disapproving note. A group of environmentalists and former EPA officials created a "Save the EPA" working group to try to balance the impact Gorsuch was having. In 1982 she remarried and changed her name to Anne Gorsuch Burford. Late that year, the House Energy Committee began pressuring the EPA to turn over documents regarding questionable decisions on hazardous waste dumps and the Superfund Program. Some of these documents were illegally destroyed, and the media began to focus on public perception of the EPA's incompetence and collusion with industry. Burford resigned amid controversy in March 1983. *Bibliography:* Helvarg, David. *The War against the Greens: The "Wise-Use" Movement, the New Right and Anti-Environmental Violence.* San Francisco: Sierra Club Books, 1994.

Cody, William Frederick (Buffalo Bill). Born February 26, 1846, LeClaire, Iowa; died January 10, 1917, Denver, Colorado. William Cody was raised on a farm and then moved with his family to the Kansas Territory in 1854. When he was eleven, his father died and he took on the role of breadwinner. He got work on a supply train, and a few years later gold fever drew him to Denver, though he returned penniless. He then rode for the Pony Express for a while before serving in the Civil War as a scout for the Union army in operations against Kiowas and Comanches. After the war he worked various odd jobs before becoming a buffalo hunter in 1867 for the Kansas Pacific Railroad. During the seventeen months of railroad construction he killed more than 4,000 buffalo to supply meat to the railroad workers. And, while he was earning a reputation for daring and skill in real life, he was also being promoted as a legend by E.Z.C. Judson (under the pen name Ned Buntline), who wrote dime novels about the exploits of "Buffalo Bill." In 1883, Cody began a career as an entertainer by organizing the highly successful "Buffalo Bill's Wild West Show," which featured Annie Oakley. Through a mix of incredible fact and overblown fiction, Buffalo Bill came to occupy a place in the popular imagination of America as a personification of the taming of the West. *Bibliography:* Walsh, Richard J. *The Making of Buffalo Bill: A Study in Heroics.* New York: A.L. Burt Company, 1928.

Commoner, Barry. Born May 28, 1917, New York City. He followed an interest in science through school, earning master's and doctor of philosophy degrees from Harvard University, both in biology. He joined the botany department at Washington University in St. Louis, Missouri, in 1953, and by 1965 was department chair. He became interested in the environmental consequences of some of the technological advances since World War II, such as nuclear fallout. In 1966, he decided to leave his academic studies and devote his career to solving environmental problems. He established the Center for Biology of Natural Systems (CBNS) at Washington University, which studies problems arising from society's dependence on electricity, chemicals, plastic, automobiles, and other unsustainable resources. Studies at the CBNS revealed to Commoner that environmental problems are best solved at their source rather than through regulatory mechanisms that merely mitigate damage. Because of his belief that the government should play a stronger role in controlling the environmental impact of industry, Commoner decided to run for president in 1980, advocating reductions in defense spending and public control of the energy industry. He lost the election to **Ronald Reagan**, but still won 250,000 votes. He still directs the CBNS, which has moved to Queens College at the City University in New York City. *Bibliography:* Becher, Anne, ed. *American Environmental Leaders: From Colonial Times to the Present,* Vol. 1. Santa Barbara, CA: ABC-Clio, 2000, pp. 195–197.

Cooke, Jay. Born August 10, 1821, Sandusky, Ohio; died February 16, 1905, Philadelphia, Pennsylvania. The son of a frontier lawyer, Cooke quit school at 14 and began working as a store clerk. In 1839, he took a job as a clerk on a canal packet line in Philadelphia, and from then on his name and activities were associated with this city. He was trained in banking at E.W. Clark and Company, where he worked until 1857. By 1861 he had enough resources to start his own banking house, Jay Cooke and Company, which was one of the most widely known banks in the country until 1873. During the Civil War he gained acclaim for selling $500 million's worth of Civil War Bonds for the U.S. Treasury in 1862, and then again in 1865. During the 1860s and 1870s, he got involved in financing the Northern Pacific Railroad, which was chartered to run from Duluth, Minnesota, to Tacoma, Washington, and became actively involved in the advancement of the railroad's development. For example, Cooke promoted the idea of establishing Yellowstone National Park, not because he wanted to protect its wilderness, but to create a demand for rail travel. In another attempt at drawing a tourist trade, he underwrote the art of Thomas Moran, whose work dramatized the western landscape. As part of the effort to unite the country from coast to coast with a transcontinental railroad, Cooke's enterprise was associated with enormous environmental disruption, including the extirpation of buffalo from most of the Great Plains. But Cooke's railroad empire crumbled in 1873, when the national economy turned downward and his bank could not meet the demands of their depositors. The office of Jay Cooke and Company went bankrupt, though he eventually recovered his wealth by investing in Utah mining interests. *Bibliography:* Larson, Henrietta M. *Jay Cooke: Private Banker.* Cambridge, MA: Harvard University Press, 1936.

Douglas, Marjorie Stoneman. Born April 7, 1890, Minneapolis, Minnesota; died May 14, 1998, Miami, Florida. As a high school student, she was encouraged to write, and she eventually made a career of it. After attending college at Wellesley, she moved to Miami, Florida, where her father had founded the *Miami Herald.* She held a reporting job for the *Herald* until the United States entered World War I. After the war, she turned to writing short stories, mostly set in southern Florida, an exotic region to most readers. In fifteen years, forty of her stories were published in various popular magazines. Her writer's curiosity led her to explore Florida's geography, ecology, and history, and she became particularly fascinated by the Everglades, a massive, shallow wetland on Florida's southern tip. Though widely unrecognized in the early 1900s, the Everglades serve several important ecological roles, such as flood control and water purification, in addition to providing extremely significant wildlife habitat. When developers began draining the Everglades, Douglas joined a citizen's committee that lobbied for protecting the area as a national park. Through the early 1940s, she explored this vast network of swamps by canoe and on foot, and worked on her book, *The Everglades: River of Grass* (1947), for which she would become famous. Though over a million acres of the Everglades did become a national park in 1947, the area was still threatened on all sides by development and agriculture. Douglas devoted the rest of her long life to protecting the Everglades—she founded Friends of the Everglades, gave numerous speeches, and organized protests against encroaching industry. She was awarded the Presidential Medal of Freedom in 1993.

Easterbrook, Gregg. Born March 2, 1953, Buffalo, New York, to George and Vimy Easterbrook, a dentist and a teacher, respectively. He received a bachelor's degree from Colorado College in 1976, and a master's degree in journalism from Northwestern University in 1977. He is a contributing editor for *Atlantic Monthly* and *Washington Monthly*, a senior editor at the *New Republic*, and a visiting fellow at the Brookings Institute. He has held prior positions as a columnist for ESPN, a contributing editor for *Newsweek* and *U.S. News and World Report*, a distinguished fellow of the Fulbright Foundation, a bartender, a bus driver, and a used-car salesman. In 1995, his *A Moment on the Earth: The Coming Age of Environmental Optimism* was published, presenting arguments against virtually every major environmental concern and claiming that environmentalists "are increasingly on the wrong side of the present, risking their credibility by proclaiming emergencies that do not exist." The book has been used by corporate public relations departments and conservative groups to argue against environmental protections and has sparked a burst of publicity as scientists and environmental activists offer ripostes and corrections to it. He also has written a novel, *This Magic Moment: A Love Story for People Who Want the World to Make Sense* (1987). He lives in Bethesda, Maryland, with his wife, who is a U.S. diplomat, and their three children.

Emerson, Ralph Waldo. Born May 25, 1803, Boston, Massachusetts; died April 27, 1882, Concord, Massachusetts. From childhood on, Emerson found meaning and satisfaction in the natural world. He attended Harvard and then became a minister at Boston's Second Unitarian Church at the age of 27. His interest in the natural world and his constant desire to learn led him away from the pulpit and toward natural history, which he felt could help him attain greater insights on spirituality and personal truth. Through lectures for the Natural History Society in Boston, he gained a reputation as a prophetic orator, and his addresses were often published and distributed by Boston literati. Emerson's essays—which covered a range of topics, such as the nature of literature, self-reliance, American scholarship, and language—inspired the transcendentalist movement, beginning in the mid-1830s. The guiding philosophy of transcendentalists lay in locating nature as the ultimate source of truth about the human mind and spirit. Emerson believed that the process of thinking about and interacting with nature informs the process of reading literature—and that not until the value of nature has been acknowledged can a scholar reflect accurately on the meaning of literature. Though he was more dedicated to his desk and his writing than to woodsmanship or scientific studies of nature, Emerson's influence on the American perception of the natural world has been substantial and transformative. His writings remain a prerequisite in the study of American literature, philosophy, and history. *Bibliography:* Brooks, Van Wyck. *The Life of Emerson.* New York: Dutton, 1932. Paul, Sherman. *Emerson's Angle of Vision: Man and Nature in the American Experience.* Cambridge, MA: Harvard University Press, 1952. Richardson, Robert D. *Emerson: The Mind on Fire.* Berkeley: The University of California Press, 1995.

Foreman, Dave. Born October 18, 1946, Albuquerque, New Mexico. His family moved often when he was young, and he took to seeking out natural areas in each place they lived. As a college student, Foreman joined the conservative Young Americans for Freedom and campaigned for Republican Barry Goldwater in his presidential bid. He joined the marines after college but was dishonorably discharged after two months. In 1972 he joined the staff of the Wilderness Society and became interested in environmentalism. By the late 1970s he had become disillusioned with mainstream environmental organizations and their tendency to compromise rather than demand changes. Foreman, along with four friends, decided to carve his own path. They created Earth First!—a loose organization of eco-activists dedicated to a "no compromises" ethic in defense of the environment. In 1981 they made their public debut—draping a 300-foot black plastic streamer off the Glen Canyon dam to mimic a crack. Through the 1980s, Earth First! used confrontational tactics, civil disobedience, and attention-grabbing strategies to fight many environmentally destructive projects. Their greatest successes were achieved through the media attention they attracted, which allowed them to get their message out. Foreman wrote a manual for Earth First! members called *Ecodefense: A Field Guide to Monkeywrenching*, which had the effect of putting the Federal Bureau of Investigation on his trail. He and four others were arrested in 1989 and accused of sabotaging nuclear installations in the Southwest. When the case went to trial in 1991, all but Foreman of the "Arizona Five" spent time in jail. He now works with more mainstream environmental groups, such as the Sierra Club, and he heads the Wildlands Project. *Bibliography:* Bookchin, Murray, Dave Foreman, Steve Chase, and David Levine. *Defending the Earth: A Dialogue between Murray Bookchin and Dave Foreman.* Cambridge, MA: South End Press, 1991. Foreman, Dave. *Confessions of an Eco-Warrior.* New York: Harmony Books, 1991.

Fossey, Dian. Born January 16, 1932, San Francisco, California; died December 24, 1985, Viruga Mountains, Rwanda. She received a bachelor's degree in occupational therapy from San Jose State College in 1954, and then worked as director of occupational therapy at Kosair Crippled Children's Hospital in Louisville. In 1963 she took out a loan to pay her way on a safari trip to Africa, where she first saw mountain gorillas and met anthropologists Louis and Mary Leakey. Three years later, Louis Leakey recruited Fossey to work on a long-term gorilla study. She learned basic wildlife-study techniques from Jane Goodall in Tanzania before beginning her own research on gorillas in the Republic of Congo. On July 10, 1967, she and several others were captured and held for two weeks, during which time Fossey was repeatedly raped. In September of that year, she established the Karisoke Research Center in the Parc National des Vulcans in Rwanda. Her research on the endangered gorillas banished their reputation as aggressive killers and brought to light a new understanding of their peaceful ways and strong family bonds. The gorillas may not have been fighters, but Fossey herself fought passionately for their protection from poaching, sometimes even facing violent confrontations with armed poachers. She once kidnapped the child of a poacher and would release the child only in exchange for a captured baby gorilla. During a three-year leave from the research center, Fossey taught at Cornell and wrote *Gorillas in the Mist* (1983). On December 27, 1985, her body was found in her camp in Rwanda. She had been hacked to death with a machete. Without her efforts, the mountain gorilla almost certainly would have become extinct. *Bibliography:* Montgomery, Sy. *Walking with the*

Great Apes: Jane Goodall, Dian Fossey, Birute Galdikas. Boston: Houghton Mifflin, 1991.

Fraser, Charles. Born June 13, 1929, Hinesville, Georgia; died December 15, 2002, Turks and Caicos Islands, Caribbean. He attended two years of college at Presbyterian College in Clinton, South Carolina; then transferring to the University of Georgia, where he received a bachelor's in business administration. In 1953, he received a law degree from Yale University and passed the Georgia bar. In 1957 he began developing Hilton Head Island in South Carolina—building roads and golf courses and erecting homes on 5,000 acres of tupelo, live oak, and palmetto swamp—with the dream of creating a resort community. The resulting Sea Pines Plantation became a major East Coast tourist destination. When he made plans for development on the ecologically rich Cumberland Island off the coast of Georgia, he met resistance from environmentalists like **David Brower.** The story of the opposition between Brower and Fraser was immortalized in John McPhee's *Encounters with the Archdruid* (1971), a book about the conservation passion of Brower. Eventually, due to immense pressure from environmentalists, Fraser sold Cumberland Island to the National Park Foundation.

Gibbs, Lois. Born June 25, 1951, Buffalo, New York. She lived a quiet, domestic life raising two children in the modest Love Canal subdivision of Niagara Falls until 1978, when she read a series of articles revealing problems with a local toxic-waste dump site at Love Canal. Concerned that her son's health problems were related, she began alerting neighbors and organizing a resistance movement that eventually led to President Jimmy Carter's declaration of Love Canal as a federal emergency area and to the relocation of over 200 families out of the immediate vicinity. But, as she chronicled in her memoir, *Love Canal: My Story* (1982), the problems still were not solved. Gibbs continued to fight for proper cleanup of the toxic waste and to advocate for fair compensation for families in the area. She overcame shyness to become a practiced speaker and outspoken activist, and eventually moved with her family to Washington, D.C., to found the Citizen's Clearinghouse for Hazardous Wastes (now the Center for Health, Environment and Justice), an organization dedicated to helping communities respond to issues of toxic waste and all other forms of industrial pollution. In response to the outcry she raised over Love Canal, the federal government established the Superfund Program in 1980 to deal with large-scale toxic pollution sites. For her courage and determination, Gibbs received the Goldman Environmental Prize in 1991 and the Heinz Award in the Environment in 1998.

Gottlieb, Alan Merril. Born May 2, 1947, Los Angeles, California. Gottlieb attended Georgetown University in 1970, but switched to the University of

Tennessee, where he received a bachelor of science degree in 1971. He had been a leader in the student conservative movement in college, and was active in political causes, serving as national director of Youth Against McGovern (1972 Democratic presidential candidate) and as a board member of Young Americans for Freedom. His experience with activism helped him start up several conservative organizations, including the Center for the Defense of Free Enterprise (CDFE) and the Second Amendment Foundation, both located in Bellevue, Wash. In 1984 he was working as a direct-mail fundraiser on **Ronald Reagan**'s re-election campaign when he met **Ron Arnold**. The two joined forces and organized the Wise Use movement to counteract the environmental movement. Gottlieb and Arnold became known for inflammatory anti-environmental rhetoric, which led to heightened media attention and greater visibility. Gottlieb has authored over fifteen books, including *The Wise Use Agenda: The Citizen's Policy Guide to Environmental Resource Issues* (1989), which was published by the CDFE's publishing division, the Free Enterprise Press. Most of his other books involve the protection of gun rights. He is the chair of the Citizens Committee for the Right to Keep and Bear Arms, which he founded. *Bibliography*: Helvarg, David. *The War against the Greens: The "Wise-Use" Movement, the New Right and Anti-Environmental Violence.* San Francisco: Sierra Club Books, 1994. Switzer, Jacqueline Vaughn. *Green Backlash: The History and Politics of Environmental Opposition in the U.S.* Boulder: Lynne Rienner Publishers, 1997.

Hickel, Walter J. Born August 18, 1919, Ellinwood, Kansas. Hickel dropped out of school at age 16 and left home three years later. Seeking adventure, he eventually found his way to Alaska, where he worked odd jobs and learned construction work. By 1946 he had become a successful builder and developer, and soon founded the Hickel Construction Company in Anchorage, which made him a millionaire owner of housing developments. Hickel entered political life, first as Alaska's Republican national committeeman from 1954 to 1964, and then in 1966, after a very narrow election, as governor of Alaska. His agenda pushed economic development that was heavily dependent on resource extraction industries. In 1968, President-elect Nixon tapped him for secretary of the Interior. In spite of his anti-conservation stance, he won the nomination. In 1990, Hickel was elected governor of Alaska as a candidate of the Alaskan Independence Party. He promoted opening the Arctic National Wildlife Refuge to oil development and proposed the building of major freeways into the wilderness. Under his leadership, the state of Alaska sued the United States in 1993, arguing that the establishment of national parks and wilderness areas in Alaska constitutes a breach of contract in that it denies the state revenue. In 1996, two years after Hickel's term ended, a federal judge ruled against the state.

Hill, Julia Butterfly. Born February 18, 1974, Mount Vernon, Missouri. Hill grew up traveling from town to town, following the career of her father, an itinerant preacher. In the summer of 1996, she was in a near-fatal car accident—an event that made her reevaluate her life and resolve to follow her beliefs. She moved to California and became involved in Earth First! logging protests, and eventually volunteered for a tree sit, a civil disobedience tactic designed to thwart logging. Hill's first tree sit lasted six days, and she soon came back for another one in December 1997. This time, Hill stayed in the tree, which she named Luna, for two years. During this time, despite scare tactics from the logging company that planned to cut the tree down, Hill never set foot on the ground. Support crews brought her food, and she adapted to the cold rainy winters and searing heat in the summer, living on a six-by-eight-foot tarp-covered platform. Her story made international news, and by the end of her remarkable tree sit, she had a cell phone, a pager, a video camera, and a radio in the tree with her to allow her to network with the press and get her message out to the public about destructive logging practices. She finally came down in December 1999, after making a deal with the lumber company to spare her tree. Her decision to compromise with the logging company was met with criticism by some activists. *Bibliography*: Hill, Julia Butterfly. *The Legacy of Luna*. San Francisco: Harper, 2000.

Jackson, Wes. Born June 15, 1936, on a farm near Topeka, Kansas. He received a doctor of philosophy degree in genetics from North Carolina State University. He taught at California State University in Sacramento, where he created the environmental studies program. In 1976 he left to pursue his interest in sustainable agriculture in Kansas. He eventually established the Land Institute south of Salinas, where he developed a revolutionary system of agriculture called "perennial polyculture," bucking the 10,000–year trend of using high-yielding annuals. His method avoids the problems that plague monocultures, like pests, diseases, and soil erosion. Through its Sunshine Farm Research Program, the Land Institute developed farming methods that do not rely on fossil fuels, irrigation, or chemicals. He has written books and initiated environmental education programs dedicated to his vision of integrating agriculture, ecology, and the rural economy into a coherent community.

Kahn, Herman. Born February 15, 1922, Bayonne, New Jersey; died July 7, 1983, Chappaqua, New York. An early interest in economics, public affairs, and science led to his eventual career as a physicist and consultant on military strategy. He studied at the University of California at Los Angeles (UCLA) but entered the U.S. Army before he graduated, serving from May 1943 to November 1945. In 1945 he received a bachelor of arts degree from UCLA, and in 1948 a master's degree from the California Institute of Technology. For his first professional position he worked as a mathematician for Douglas Aircraft Company, where he later worked as an analyst for the RAND Corporation, a non-profit research organization contracted by the U.S. Air Force. His association with the RAND Corporation qualified him as a military strategist, and he began briefing some of America's chief policymakers on weapons and tactics. He achieved notoriety with two controversial books, *On Thermonuclear War* (1960) and *Thinking about the Unthinkable* (1962), both dealing with the probability of nuclear war and insisting that an adequate defense program could alleviate its disastrous consequences. He also began to explore a combination of futures research and public policy analysis, focusing on issues such as environmental concerns. With economist **Julian Simon**, he edited *The Resourceful Earth: A Response to Global 2000* (1984), which refuted the environmental warnings of the 1980 *Global 2000 Report to the President*. Kahn and Simon argued that environmental constraints imposed on industry by political and institutional forces would "increasingly act as a brake upon progress," and that free-market economics should be the only guide for resource management. While president, **Ronald Reagan** adopted the views of Kahn and Simon and gave them increased exposure. *Bibliography*: Weinberg, Alvin M., and Herman E. Daly. "The Resourceful Earth Study by J. Simon and H. Kahn." *Environment* Vol. 26 (September 1984), pp. 25–28; Flattau, Edward. *Tracking the Charlatans: An Environmental Columnist's Refutational Handbook for the Propaganda Wars*. Washington, DC: Global Horizons Press, 1998.

Leopold, Aldo. Born Burlington, Iowa, January 11, 1886; died in Sand County, Wisconsin, April 21, 1948. The oldest of four children, he grew up hunting ducks and partridges in the Iowa woods. He entered the newly created School of Forestry at Yale, and graduated with a master's degree in forestry in 1909. Upon earning his degree, he began a nineteen-year-long career with the U.S. Forest Service. His first assignment was in New Mexico, where he eventually worked his way up to supervisor of Carson National Forest. In 1924 he was transferred to the Forest Products Lab in Madison, Wisconsin, but quit four years later to do private contract work, which mainly involved wildlife surveys and developing a system of wildlife management. He became the University of Wisconsin's first professor of wildlife management in 1933, and continued teaching there until his death. Following his constant interest in land conservation, Leopold and his family bought a run-down farm in Sand County, Wisconsin, in 1935 and began restoring it by planting trees and nurturing the soil. Leopold became best known as the author of *Sand County Almanac* (1949), a chronicle of life on the farm that included nature sketches, such as descriptions of the changing seasons, and philosophical arguments for a shift away from the typical human attitude that the land must be conquered. That slim volume has become one of the enduring expressions of ecological awareness and environmentalist ethos and, along with his reputation as a scientist and wilderness advocate, brought Leopold international recognition.

Limbaugh, Rush H., III. Born 1951, Cape Girardeau, Missouri. He began working in radio at age 16 as a disk jockey at a local radio station. After his freshman year at Southeast Missouri State College, Limbaugh dropped out and held a number of jobs at small radio stations around the country. In 1983, a Kansas City station hired him as a talk show host, and though he was eventually fired from the job, he had found his true passion. The following year he got his own talk show on KFBK in San Diego and found success with his outrageous and confrontational style. In 1988 he was unleashed to a national audience for the first time when he got a talk show on a radio syndicate with fifty member stations, based in New York City. His tirades against liberals (whom he characterized variously as "feminazis," "militant vegetarians," or "environmental wackos") were immediately and overwhelmingly popular with a largely white, conservative audience, and he soon developed both a following and a notorious reputation. His influence went beyond the sphere of radio, as well; in fact, he is widely credited with playing a role in the 1994 elections, when Republicans gained a majority in the House of Representatives. His first book, *The Way Things Ought to Be* (1992) is a collection of pronouncements on his various conservative beliefs, including bombastic criticisms of the environmental movement. It sold over four million copies in its first year.

Lindzen, Richard Siegmund. Born February 8, 1940, Webster, Massachusetts. Graduated from Harvard University with a bachelor's degree in 1960, a master's in 1961, and a Ph.D. in applied mathematics in 1964. He taught at the University of Chicago from 1968 to 1972, and then became a professor of meteorology at Harvard, where he taught from 1972 to 1983. He now teaches meteorology in the Department of Earth, Atmospheric and Planetary Sciences at the Massachusetts Institute of Technology. His studies and areas of expertise include climatology and upper atmosphere dynamics, and he has become known for his contrarian views on global climate change. He consistently refutes the findings of the Intergovernmental Panel on Climate Change (IPCC), the largest and most rigorously peer-reviewed scientific collaboration in existence. He has served on the advisory board of the George C. Marshall Institute, a think tank that receives support from conservative political foundations and has promoted President **Ronald Reagan**'s "star wars" program and issued reports dismissing climate change. Lindzen has been a paid consultant, sometimes charging $2,500 a day, for major oil and coal interests and has addressed meetings of OPEC delegates and industry lobby groups. Known for ideological extremism, he once said that the environmental movement holds the same criteria of group dynamics and behavior as the Nazi movement in Weimar Germany. He also has compared the environmental movement to the eugenics movement of the early 1920s, saying that both movements were born of flawed science that lead to destructive policies. *Bibliography*: Gelbspan, Ross. *The Heat Is On: The High Stakes Battle over the Earth's Threatened Climate*. Reading, MA: Addison-Wesley Publishing Group, 1997.

Lovins, Amory. Born November 13, 1947, Washington, D.C. At a young age he began participating in national and international science fairs. He attended Harvard University as a presidential scholar for two years before transferring to Magdalen College at Oxford as an advanced student in theoretical physics. He attempted to do his doctoral research on energy and resource policy, but was refused, as energy was not considered worthy of academic study at that time. He acted as a British representative of **David Brower**'s Friends of the Earth, and successfully campaigned to stop a copper mine in northern Wales. Amory and his wife, Hunter Lovins, served as policy advisers for Friends of the Earth until moving to Colorado to create the Rocky Mountain Institute (RMI) in 1982. RMI is a research institute that focuses on superefficient energy systems, profitable climate protection, community economic renewal, and global security. RMI has invented an ultralight hybrid-electric car that uses four to eight times less energy than average cars and emits only steam. By 1999, the automobile industry had invested five billion dollars in research and development on their hybrid car design. Other technological innovations include a solar-powered water purification system and "superwindows" that let in light without letting in unwanted heat.

Marsh, George Perkins. Born March 15, 1801, Woodstock, Vermont; died July 23, 1882, Vallambrosa, Italy. Exhibiting his remarkable intellect at an early age, Marsh had memorized an encyclopedia by the age of 5; he then began studying Greek and Latin. When he was 8, his eyesight grew weak, so he turned to the outside world for intellectual stimulation and immediately became fascinated with the natural world. He entered Dartmouth at age 15 and graduated at 19 in 1820. After becoming a lawyer, learning twenty languages, and collaborating on the writing of the *Oxford English Dictionary*, he was elected to the U.S. Congress in 1840. While there, he was instrumental in the founding of the Smithsonian Institution. In 1857 he began studying the decline of fish in Vermont's streams and rivers and discovered the cause to be deforestation. While serving as a minister to Italy in the 1860s, Marsh used his spare time to write a book called *Man and Nature; or, Physical Geography as Modified by Human Action* (1864), which summarized the environmental history of certain parts of the world and disparaged environmental destruction. He traced the cause of certain natural disasters to human activities, usually deforestation. His book was acclaimed widely in Europe, where foresters were agreeable to Marsh's suggestions. It was well-received in the United States, as well, though Americans were slow to be convinced of the need for conservation at that time. Only after several decades of further abuse to American forests did the full import of his book become clear, and it has since become recognized as an accurate management tool. *Bibliography*: Lowenthal, David. *George Perkins Marsh: Versatile Vermonter*. New York: Columbia University Press, 1958. Strong, Douglas Hillman. *Dreamers and Defenders: American Conservationists*. Lincoln: University of Nebraska Press, 1971.

Moon, Sun Myung. Born January 6, 1920, in the rural village of Kwangju Sangsa Ri, in what is now North Korea. Moon claims he has been clairvoyant since childhood—able to see into people's spirits. He went to high school in Seoul and received religious training at a Pentecostal church. On Easter day in 1936, he had a vision in which Jesus Christ appeared to him and told him he must relieve the burden of suffering of the human race. In 1954 he started the Unification Church in Seoul, and eventually began establishing international missions, including one in the United States. When the U.S. church established the right-wing Freedom Leadership Foundation in 1969, Moon began gaining more publicity. His proselytizing eventually succeeded in recruiting 30,000 American followers, though he was frequently criticized for brainwashing young adults. With more than a billion dollars in U.S. investments, Moon began backing a range of conservative and anti-environmental causes. In May 1982, he was convicted of income tax evasion and sentenced to eighteen months in prison. That year, he founded the *Washington Times*, a daily newspaper that provided comprehensive anti-environmental news coverage. During the 1980s, it provided highly favorable publicity for the **Ronald Reagan** administration. Moon also established the American Freedom Coalition, an organization that promotes Wise Use groups.

Norton, Gale. Born 1954, Wichita, Kansas. Her family moved to Colorado, and she grew up enjoying the Rocky Mountains. She earned her bachelor's degree from the University of Denver in 1975 and a law degree in 1978. From 1979 to 1983, she held the position of senior attorney for the conservative, pro-industry Mountain States Legal Foundation, where **James Watt** also worked at the time. Norton worked as associate solicitor of the U.S. Department of the Interior from 1985 to 1987, and from 1991 to 1999 she served as attorney general of Colorado. In 1998 she became co-chair of the Coalition of Republican Environmental Advocates, which included auto, coal mining, and developer lobbyists, and took a free-market approach to all environmental issues. In 2000, President George W. Bush nominated Norton to be U.S. Secretary of the Interior, prompting cheers from industry leaders and intense opposition from environmental groups. On January 30, 2001, she was sworn in as the first woman to head the Department of the Interior. In her first year of office, she argued for opening Alaska's Arctic National Wildlife Refuge to oil drilling, a move that angered conservationists.

She also has pursued energy developments, mountain-top removal for coal mining in Appalachia, captive breeding of endangered species instead of habitat protection, and restricting the amount of land set aside for wilderness protection, and she has reversed a ban on snowmobiles in Yellowstone and Grand Teton National Parks. Her overall approach to policy is based on her belief that government involvement in citizen affairs should be extremely limited, and her views on environmental issues reflect that. She made clear that her priority is to work with, not against, private landowners on environmental regulations. She lives with her husband, John Hughes, in Washington, D.C. *Bibliography*: Helvarg, David. "Unwise Use: Gale Norton's New Environmentalism." *Progressive* Vol. 76 (June 2003), p. 24–30.

Olmsted, Frederick Law. Born April 26, 1822, Hartford, Connecticut; died August 28, 1903, Waverly, Massachusetts. He attempted various careers, such as farming, business, and the merchant marine, but finally found his calling in 1850, when he toured England and Europe on foot to explore agriculture and landscape architecture. He developed a progressive landscape aesthetic based on his belief that nature and culture are intertwined and that humans are drawn to a balance between the wild and the civilized. In 1857 he was given a job as superintendent of Central Park in New York City, and he used the post as an opportunity to implement his goal of naturalizing human-constructed landscapes. Early in the 1860s he moved his family to California, where he got involved in turning the Yosemite Valley into a state park, arguing that the protection of the area would attract tourists and that the government should purchase the land before the wealthy entrepreneurs did so that the land would remain accessible to all citizens, not just the elite. Upon returning to the East, he designed many more urban parks, such as Brooklyn's Prospect Park and parks in Chicago, Boston, and Washington, D.C. Always his goal was to introduce more natural areas and greenery into cities that were becoming increasingly dirty and crowded thanks to the Industrial Revolution. His efforts helped to improve public health and overall quality of life for many city dwellers, particularly for the poor, who could not afford to escape into the cleaner countryside as the wealthier classes could. *Bibliography*: Fein, Albert. *Frederick Law Olmsted and the American Environmental Tradition*. New York: G. Braziller, 1972. Roper, Laura W. *FLO: A Biography of Frederick Law Olmsted*. Baltimore: Johns Hopkins University Press, 1973.

Orr, David. Born January 10, 1944, in Des Moines, Iowa. He was raised in the western Pennsylvania town of New Wilmington, spending summers in a cabin in the Allegheny Mountains. Since 1990, he has been on the faculty at Oberlin College and has become an influential figure in educational reform—specifically in the realm of environmental literacy. His belief that current environmental problems are partly due to shortcomings in the educational system and that colleges should be actual models of sustainability led to one of his most celebrated projects. He spearheaded the effort to design and build the Adam Joseph Lewis Center for Environmental Studies building on the Oberlin campus, a demonstration and education center that uses a photovoltaic system to produce some of its own energy (with the goal of becoming a net energy exporter as the system is upgraded) and treats its own wastewater. He wrote about the process of designing the building in *The Nature of Design: Ecology, Culture, and Human Intention* (2002). He is also the author of *Ecological Literacy* (1992); and *Earth in Mind* (1994). Dr. Orr is also the education editor of *Conservation Biology* and serves on the editorial advisory board of *Orion Magazine*. He received a Lyndhurst Prize in 1992, a National Conservation Achievement Award from the National Wildlife Federation in 1993, the Benson Box Award from Clemson University in 1995, and the Bioneers Award in 2002. He is currently professor and chair of the Environmental Studies Program at Oberlin College.

Powell, John Wesley. Born March 24, 1834, Mount Morris, New York; died September 23, 1902, Haven, Maine. Due to his family's frequent moves, Powell had to devise his own education, and thus became entranced by the marvels of the natural world. He taught at a country school for a few years and continued in his own studies of plants and animals. He fought in the Civil War and lost an arm during the Battle of Shiloh. On his return, he became a lecturer in geology at Illinois Normal University, and frequently led his students on long field trips through the Rocky Mountains. In 1875 he was named director of the U.S. Geographical and Geological Survey of the Rocky Mountain Region. From this post, he recommended that no land in the ecologically fragile, arid West be farmed. Powell went on to become director of the U.S. Geological Survey (USGS), which began printing its famous topographical maps under his directorship. He became known for his revolutionary land-use ideas, such as limiting ranch sizes and forming irrigation cooperatives to prevent land and water monopolies by large landowners. He became director of the Smithsonian's Bureau of Ethnology in 1894, and became a respected ethnologist.

Reagan, Ronald. Born February 6, 1911, Tampico, Illinois; died June 5, 2004, Los Angeles, California. He graduated from Eureka College in economics. Reagan entered the limelight as a sportscaster in Des Moines, Iowa, before being signed as a film actor by Warner Brothers in 1937. He starred in fifty films. During his Hollywood years he was a liberal Democrat, but moved increasingly toward conservative politics in the 1950s. He joined the Republican Party in 1962 and in 1966 was elected governor of California. After two unsuccessful bids for the Republican presidential nomination in 1968 and 1976, he was nominated in 1980 and defeated incumbent Jimmy Carter to become president. During his two terms, which spanned most of the 1980s, his administration attempted to undermine the legislative achievements of the environmental movement from the 1960s and 1970s. A proponent of reducing the size of government, of unrestricted free-market economy, and of eliminating environmental "roadblocks" to industry, Reagan's leadership sent the environmental movement scrambling. His nomination of **James Gaius Watt** to head the Interior Department and (soon-to-be) **Anne Gorsuch Burford** to head the EPA further infuriated the environmental community. The Reagan years transformed the environmental movement by greatly increasing membership in environmental organizations and prompting a new level of professionalism and media savvy.

Roosevelt, Theodore. Born October 27, 1858, New York City; died January 6, 1919, Sagamore Hill, New York. Like many conservationists, Roosevelt first became interested in the natural world at a young age. At 7 he began collecting specimens of birds and other small creatures and opened the "Roosevelt Museum of Natural History" in an upstairs closet of his family home. He attended Harvard, intent on making his boyhood hobby a career. Partway through college he became more involved in public affairs and decided to switch his course work to political economy. He was elected to the New York State Assembly in 1881. In 1882 he traveled to the Dakota Badlands on a buffalo hunt and became enchanted with the wide-open West. He bought a ranch in the Dakota Territory, where he lived during the 1880s, unhappily witnessing the rapid disappearance of the buffalo and other wild game in the West. Along with George Bird Grinnell, he founded the Boone and Crockett Club in 1887—a gentlemen's hunting club that promoted conservation. In 1898 he formed the Rough Rider Calvary squad and, in 1900, was elected vice president with William McKinley on the Republican ticket. Six months after inauguration, while hiking in the Adirondacks, he learned McKinley had been shot. President by accident, Roosevelt immediately made conservation the cornerstone of his domestic policy agenda. During his presidency he worked closely with forester and conservationist **Gifford Pinchot**, creating the U.S. Forest Service and adding over 150 million acres to its reserves. He also broke new ground by establishing the first national wildlife refuge—Pelican Island in Florida—in 1903, and went on to designate over fifty more. He also established eighteen national monuments and five national parks. *Bibliography*: Roosevelt, Theodore. *Theodore Roosevelt: An Autobiography*. New York: MacMillan, 1913. Cutright, Paul Russell. *Theodore Roosevelt: The Making of a Conservationist*. Urbana: University of Illinois Press, 1985.

Tall, Joann. Born 1953, Pine Ridge Reservation, South Dakota. Tall began working with the American Indian Movement (AIM) in 1973 when she participated in a protest movement involving the occupation of the historically significant town of Wounded Knee, which was the site of a massacre of over

200 unarmed Indian men, women, and children in 1890. During the 71-day sit-in at Wounded Knee that AIM organized in order to demand a hearing on the Fort Laramie Treaty which had been ignored by the United States, the protesters were surrounded by U.S. marshals, the FBI, and tribal police. Shots were fired, and two activists were killed. Tall went on to become involved in environmental activism, and in 1987 she organized a local protest movement against defense contractor Honeywell's plans to conduct weapons testing on the Pine Ridge Reservation, where she lives. More than 150 people camped out on the proposed testing site, and eventually Honeywell abandoned the project. Tall then founded the Native Resource Coalition (NRC). Its first action was to protest the proposed siting of a 5,000-acre landfill and waste incinerator on the Pine Ridge reservation. The NRC discovered that Indian reservations nationwide were frequently targeted for hazardous waste disposal sites. This is due to relaxed restrictions on reservations and the presence of a language barrier that often prevents Native American tribes from fully understanding what was being proposed for their land. In 1991, NRC and several other grassroots organizations convened a conference in the Black Hills to educate and inform tribal groups about this form of environmental racism. Thanks largely to Tall's leadership, the conference led to the rejection of toxic waste siting proposals on Pine Ridge and Rosebud Reservations, as well as several others. Another outcome of the conference was the establishment of the Indigenous Environmental Network, which now includes over fifty member organizations that educate native people about environmental threats.

Thoreau, Henry David. Born July 12, 1817, Concord, Massachusetts; died May 6, 1862, Concord, Massachusetts. He earned a bachelor's degree at Harvard University and returned to Concord, where he joined **Ralph Waldo Emerson**'s circle of transcendentalists. Emerson became a friend and encouraged Thoreau to keep a journal and to publish his writings. In 1839, after floundering through various jobs such as school teaching and farm labor, Thoreau took a trip in a dory with his brother, which he wrote about as *A Week on the Concord and Merrimack Rivers* (1839). On Independence Day 1845, he moved into a one-room cabin he had built on some of Emerson's remote land near Walden Pond. He continued writing in his journal, filling it with his detailed knowledge of the natural world, including flora, fauna, geology, and weather. He was a skilled and sensitive observer, and many children in Concord would remember his ability to persuade animals and birds to approach him. He spent two years on Walden Pond, rambling through the nearby woods and finding connections between the spheres of existence in nature and human wisdom. He was relatively unknown during his lifetime, and when *Walden* was published in 1854, sales were slow. An account of his stay on Walden Pond, *Walden* combines exquisite descriptions of nature with advice on living simply. It has become a classic of world literature and has provided a philosophical and aesthetic argument for the preservation of wilderness. In July 1846, he was arrested for failing to pay taxes and spent the night in jail, giving rise to a famous essay, *Civil Disobedience* (1849). Since his death, many of his other writings—including essays, journals, and poetry—have been published. *Bibliography*: Harding, Walter. *The Days of Henry Thoreau*. New York: Knopf, 1965. Krutch, Joseph Wood. *Henry David Thoreau*. New York: William Sloane, 1948. Richardson, Robert D. *Henry David Thoreau: A Life of the Mind*. Berkeley: University of California Press, 1986.

Wattenberg, Ben. Born August 26, 1933, New York City. After graduating from Hobart College in 1955 and spending two years in the air force, Wattenberg launched a career in journalism. His book, *This U.S.A.* (1965), co-written with Richard Scammon, director of the Census Bureau, examined the 1960 census and put an optimistic spin on issues such as environmental pollution and the nuclear arms race. Wattenberg's analyses gained the attention of the politically powerful, and he turned to public service. From 1966 to 1968 he served as a research assistant and speechwriter for President Lyndon Johnson. In 1972 he responded to the defeat of liberal Democrat George McGovern in that year's presidential election by co-founding and chairing the Coalition for a Democratic Majority, which rejected the politics of the New Left and attempted to draw the party to the political center. Meanwhile, he continued his demographic studies. In his book *The Real America* (1974) he maintained that although environmentalists, feminists, and anti-war activists were advocating broad social and political changes, there actually had been healthy improvements along these fronts. He also ventured into television, hosting on PBS several television series that promoted his views. He was appointed by President Carter to serve on his Advisory Board for Ambassadorial Appointments in 1977, and in the American delegation to the Madrid Conference on Human Rights in 1980. In 1984, his book, *The Good News Is the Bad News Is Wrong*, came out, once again presenting a comforting vision to those with concerns about the ecological health of the planet. It became a best seller. Since 1977, he has been a senior fellow at the American Enterprise Institute, a right-wing think tank in Washington, D.C.

Wolf, Hazel. Born March 10, 1898, Victoria, British Columbia; died January 19, 2000, Port Angeles, Washington. She grew up in poverty and developed an attitude of defiance toward rules and situations she considered unfair. She married young but soon divorced and immigrated to Seattle with her young daughter in 1923. During the Depression she relied on welfare and took whatever odd jobs she could find. Ever the reformer, she was fired from a job at the Works Progress Administration for trying to organize a union. In 1949, she took a job as a legal secretary for a well-known Seattle civil rights attorney and assisted him for twenty years on social reform cases.

At the age of 62, she reluctantly joined the National Audubon Society and found a new passion. She soon became secretary of the Seattle chapter of the Audubon Society, a position she held for thirty-seven years. During her years at Audubon, she helped organize more local chapters than anyone in the national organization's history. She also became a skilled coalition builder among other environmental and social reform organizations, and in 1993, she co-founded the first environmental justice group in the Seattle area: the Community Coalition for Environmental Justice, a multi-ethnic non-profit organization dealing with social, economic, and environmental issues. She became a much-loved public speaker and possessed a seemingly endless energy, which she constantly put toward testifying at hearings, lobbying officials, and participating in rallies and protests. For her 100th birthday, she was honored by having a 166-acre wetland on the Sammamish River named the Hazel Wolf Wetlands. *Bibliography*: Breton, Mary Joy. *Women Pioneers for the Environment*. Boston: Northeastern University Press, 1998.

SELECTED BIBLIOGRAPHY

There are many overviews and scholarly studies of the American environmental movement. Some of the most helpful are Philip Shabecoff, *A Fierce Green Fire: The American Environmental Movement* (New York: Farrar, Straus and Giroux, 1993); Robert Gottlieb, *Forcing the Spring: The Transformation of the American Environmental Movement* (Covelo, CA: Island Press, 1993); Kirkpatrick Sale, *The Green Revolution: The American Environmental Movement, 1962–1992* (New York: Hill and Wang, 1993); Charles T. Rubin, *The Green Crusade: Rethinking the Roots of Environmentalism* (New York: The Free Press, 1994); Mark Dowie, *Losing Ground: American Environmentalism at the Close of the Twentieth Century* (Cambridge, MA: The MIT Press, 1995); J. R. McNeill, *Something New under the Sun: An Environmental History of the Twentieth-Century World* (New York: W.W. Norton and Company, 2000); Philip Shabecoff, *Earth Rising: American Environmentalism in the 21st Century* (Covelo, CA: Island Press, 2000); Hal K. Rothman, *Saving the Planet: The American Response to the Environment in the Twentieth Century* (Chicago: Ivan R. Dee, 2000); and Roderick Frazier Nash, *Wilderness and the American Mind*, 4th ed. (New Haven: Yale University Press, 2001). For biographical collections, see Douglas Hillman Strong, *Dreamers and Defenders: American Conservationists* (Lincoln: University of Nebraska Press, 1971); Mary Joy Breton, *Women Pioneers for the Environment* (Boston: Northeastern University Press, 1998); and Anne Becher, ed., *American Environmental Leaders: From Colonial Times to the Present*, 2 vols. (Santa Barbara, CA: ABC-Clio, 2000). An excellent critique of the anti-environmental Wise Use movement is David Helvarg's *The War against the Greens: The "Wise-Use" Movement, the New Right and Anti-Environmental Violence* (San Francisco: Sierra Club Books, 1994). Jacqueline Vaughn Switzer also analyzes the anti-environmental movement in *Green Backlash: The History and Politics of Environmental Opposition in the U.S.* (Boulder: Lynne Rienner Publishers, 1997), while Sharon Beder examines the influence of large corporations in shaping public opinion on environmental issues in *Global Spin: The Corporate Assault on Environmentalism*, revised ed. (White River Junction, VT: Chelsea Green Publishing Company, 2002). Paul R. Ehrlich and Anne H. Ehrlich respond to the anti-environmental rhetoric generated by the "brownlash" movement in *Betrayal of Science and Reason: How Anti-Environmental Rhetoric Threatens Our Future* (Covelo, CA: Island Press, 1996), and Edward Flattau refutes the arguments of some of the most noted critics of the environmental movement in *Tracking the Charlatans: An Environmental Columnist's Refutational Handbook for the Propaganda Wars* (Washington, DC: Global Horizons Press, 1998). For a look at anti-environmental propaganda, see Ronald Bailey, ed., *Earth Report 2000: Revisiting the True State of the Planet* (New York: McGraw-Hill, 2000); and *Eco-Scam: The False Prophets of Ecological Apocalypse* (New York: St. Martin's Press, 1993); Julian Simon, *The Ultimate Resource* (Princeton, NJ: Princeton University Press, 1981); Gregg Easterbrook, *A Moment on the Earth: The Coming Age of Environmental Optimism* (New York: Viking, 1995); and Bjørn Lomborg, *The Skeptical Environmentalist: Measuring the Real State of the World* (New York: Cambridge University Press, 2001).

INDEX

About the Author

RACHEL WHITE SCHEUERING is a freelance writer and former field biologist. She was a contributing author on *American Environmental Leaders: From Colonial Times to the Present* and was a contributing author and editorial assistant on *Birds of Oregon: A General Reference*. She lives in Portland, Oregon.